AWS® For Admins

AWS For Admins

AWS For Admins

for **dummies**®

A Wiley Brand

AWS® For Admins

by John Paul Mueller

AWS® For Admins For Dummies®

Published by: **John Wiley & Sons, Inc.,** 111 River Street, Hoboken, NJ 07030-5774, www.wiley.com

Copyright © 2017 by John Wiley & Sons, Inc., Hoboken, New Jersey

Media and software compilation copyright © 2017 by John Wiley & Sons, Inc. All rights reserved.

Published simultaneously in Canada

For general information on our other products and services, please contact our Customer Care Department within the U.S. at 877-762-2974, outside the U.S. at 317-572-3993, or fax 317-572-4002. For technical support, please visit https://hub.wiley.com/community/support/dummies.

Wiley publishes in a variety of print and electronic formats and by print-on-demand. Some material included with standard print versions of this book may not be included in e-books or in print-on-demand. If this book refers to media such as a CD or DVD that is not included in the version you purchased, you may download this material at http://booksupport.wiley.com. For more information about Wiley products, visit www.wiley.com.

Library of Congress Control Number: 2016954413

ISBN 978-1-119-31248-2; ISBN 978-1-119-31250-5 (ebk); ISBN 978-1-119-31249-9 (ebk)

Manufactured in the United States of America

10 9 8 7 6 5 4 3 2 1

Contents at a Glance

Table of Contents

Introduction

Amazon Web Services (AWS) started out as a rather small undertaking that allowed a developer to create applications that queried all things Amazon. You could perform queries, obtain sales data, and even upload offerings for sale. However, the focus was on Amazon. That's not the case today! Now you can manage an entire company using AWS. The offerings are varied, more than any one organization is likely to need, and the focus is no longer on Amazon, but on your company and your company's needs.

Of course, you might wonder why Amazon deserves special attention given that there are many other cloud providers (such as Google, Microsoft, and IBM) available today. According to a recent *ComputerWorld* article (http://www.computerworld.com/article/3102904/cloud-computing/four-us-companies-rule-the-worlds-cloud-infrastructure.html), Amazon currently owns 31 percent of the cloud computing market, which means that your organization stands to benefit from Amazon's huge installed base of customer-tested services. According to *CIO* magazine, AWS is so popular that companies like Gartner that track statistics for it have had to change their charting methods just to keep AWS on the charts when compared to the competition. *AWS For Admins For Dummies* helps you understand not only why you need these services to remain competitive but also how to use them to gain the maximum effectiveness and efficiency for your organization.

Following the progress of AWS over the years gives me a unique perspective of the services it offers today, which is why you need *AWS For Admins For Dummies* if your job is to administer your organization's offerings and perform tasks like getting a cloud-based setup started. Just digging through the offerings and figuring out what you need is likely to prove daunting, which is why this book offers you clear-cut paths and helps you overcome the hype to do something useful in a short time.

About This Book

The purpose of *AWS For Admins For Dummies* is to help you figure out what you need and create a basic functional setup that enables you to become productive sooner than later. This book separates the programming aspects of AWS from the administrative aspects, so you don't have to read reams of developer-specific information to find the one item you really need as an administrator. Of course, this book isn't just for administrators, but for anyone who needs to get a basic AWS setup configured for any need. DevOps and developers can use this book as well, even though it does focus on administrative tasks.

AWS For Admins For Dummies is designed to make things simple. That's why it focuses on using the AWS consoles to perform tasks whenever possible and resorts to the command-line interface only when necessary. By following the procedures in this book, you can set up and configure a computing environment quickly and easily.

This book also helps you separate hype from reality. The Amazon documentation would often have you believe that everything works perfectly in AWS, which clearly can't happen. Every piece of software, even cloud software, has quirks and issues that you need to know about. Most important, this book helps you understand when moving to the cloud might be a bad idea because of a number of issues that even the media is less than thrilled to tell you about. Rather than be lured by the hype, you'll be best served by knowing when a cloud environment actually does meet your needs, rather than set you up for problems at some point or, worse yet, prove useless.

To help you absorb the concepts, this book uses the following conventions:

>> Text that you're meant to type just as it appears in the book is in **bold.** The exception is when you're working through a step list: Because each step is bold, the text to type is not bold.

>> Words for you to type in that are also in *italics* are meant as placeholders; you need to replace them with something that works for you. For example, if you see "Type **Your Name** and press Enter," you need to replace *Your Name* with your actual name.

>> I also use *italics* for terms I define. This means that you don't have to rely on other sources to provide the definitions you need.

>> Web addresses and programming code appear in `mono font`. If you're reading a digital version of this book on a device connected to the Internet, you can click the live link to visit a website, like this: `http://www.dummies.com`.

>> When you need to click command sequences, you see them separated by a special arrow, like this: File ⇨ New File, which tells you to click File and then click New File.

Foolish Assumptions

You might find it difficult to believe that I've assumed anything about you — after all, I haven't even met you yet! Although most assumptions are indeed foolish, I made certain assumptions to provide a starting point for the book.

The first assumption is that you're familiar with the platform you want to use, because the book doesn't provide any guidance in this regard. This book doesn't discuss any platform-specific issues. You really do need to know how to install applications, use applications, and generally work with your chosen platform before you begin working with this book.

You also need to be familiar with your browser and understand how to interact with browser-based applications. Sprinkled throughout are numerous references to online material that will enhance your learning experience. In addition, most of the tasks you perform with AWS require that you work in your browser.

This book is pretty much platform independent. However, none of the procedures are tested using small mobile devices, such as a smartphone (and some are almost guaranteed not to work on a small device). Differences in appearance will emerge when using a smaller device — that is, a control that appears as a button on a larger device could appear as a link or other control on a smaller device. You need access to the sort of setup that an administrator will use to create and configure online setups, which means a larger tablet, notebook, or, better yet, a full desktop system. The various individuals working on this book used desktop systems running the Windows, Linux, and Mac OS X platforms using a number of common browsers.

Icons Used in This Book

As you read this book, you encounter icons in the margins that indicate material of special interest (or not, as the case may be!). Here's what the icons mean:

TIP

Tips are nice because they help you save time or perform some task without a lot of extra work. The tips in this book are time-saving techniques or pointers to resources that you should try so that you can get the maximum benefit when performing AWS-related tasks.

WARNING

I don't want to sound like an angry parent or some kind of maniac, but you should avoid doing anything that's marked with a Warning icon. Otherwise, you might find that your configuration fails to work as expected, you get incorrect results from seemingly bulletproof processes, or (in the worst-case scenario) you lose data.

TECHNICAL STUFF

Whenever you see this icon, think advanced tip or technique. You might find these tidbits of useful information just too boring for words, or they could contain the solution you need to get an AWS service running. Skip these bits of information whenever you like.

REMEMBER

If you don't get anything else out of a particular chapter or section, remember the material marked by this icon. This text usually contains an essential process or a bit of information that you must know to work with AWS, or to perform cloud-based-setup tasks successfully.

Beyond the Book

This book isn't the end of your AWS learning experience — it's really just the beginning. I provide online content to make this book more flexible and better able to meet your needs. That way, as I receive email from you, I can address questions and tell you how updates to AWS or its associated add-ons affect book content. In fact, you gain access to these cool additions:

>> **Cheat sheet:** You remember using crib notes in school to make a better mark on a test, don't you? You do? Well, a cheat sheet is sort of like that. It provides you with some special notes about tasks that you can do with AWS that not every other person knows. You can find the cheat sheet for this book by going to www.dummies.com and searching **AWS For Admins For Dummies Cheat Sheet**. The cheat sheet contains really neat information such as figuring out which service you want to use.

>> Also, check out the blog posts with answers to reader questions and demonstrations of useful book-related techniques at http://blog.johnmueller books.com/.

Where to Go from Here

It's time to start your AWS adventure! If you're completely new to AWS, you should start with Chapter 1 and progress through the book at a pace that allows you to absorb as much of the material as possible. Chapter 2 is especially important because it helps you understand what Amazon means by free-tier services. You should also read Chapter 3, even if you have experience with AWS, because it provides information about the services discussed in the book.

Readers who have some exposure to AWS can move directly to Chapter 4. You can always go back to earlier chapters as necessary when you have questions. However, you do need to understand how each technique works before moving to the next one. Every technique and procedure has important lessons for you, and you could miss vital content if you start skipping too much information.

1

Getting Started with AWS

Chapter **1**

Starting Your AWS Adventure

mazon Web Services (AWS) started out as a tiny bit of software that enabled people to perform a limited number of tasks directly on Amazon, such as querying a product, placing a product request, or checking on an order status. The initial service didn't do much, but people loved it, so it grew and then kept growing. Today, AWS is a huge web service, so big that it's nearly impossible for anyone to explore it fully. It performs all sorts of tasks that don't even relate to buying and selling products. In fact, the buying and selling of products is more of a sideline today as people use AWS more for computing services of all types (things like data storage and running applications). The purpose of this chapter is to help you understand what makes AWS special — namely, those services that administrators are most likely to get excited about. The chapter doesn't cover many of the services because AWS is simply too large. For example, the chapter doesn't cover much about services that are specifically designed to meet developer needs.

Part of making AWS small enough to understand is to define the AWS environment. For such an understanding, you need to know a little about Infrastructure as a Service (IaaS), Software as a Service (SaaS), and Platform as a Service (PaaS). You don't delve too deeply into these topics in this chapter, but you do gain enough information to understand how the AWS environment meets specific administration needs.

After you gain an understanding of how AWS works, you need to consider how to actually use it to perform useful work. As organizations continue to downsize IT, administrators must become more efficient, and AWS has a lot to offer in that regard. In fact, even if you look only at the administrator-related services, you're likely to find the number of services nearly overwhelming. This chapter helps you make sense of how you might use various services to meet specific needs in your organization.

Even though you can use AWS quite well without a certification, obtaining an AWS certification will help you get a better job with the organization of your dreams. This chapter gives you a basic overview of what certification can do for you and helps you determine whether you really need certification to meet your needs today. Of course, those needs will change over time, so knowing what certification has to offer is helpful, even if you don't intend to get certified today.

Finally, you need to round out your AWS education to use AWS effectively. The last part of the chapter offers some ideas of the types of educational resources you might use. Of course, this book is your starting point, but to meet specific needs, you may need to do more.

Defining the AWS Cloud

Amazon Web Services (AWS) is actually a huge array of services that can affect consumers, Small to Medium-Sized Business (SMB), and enterprises. Using AWS, you can do everything from backing up your personal hard drive to creating a full-fledged IT department in the cloud. The installed base is immense. You can find case studies of companies like Adobe and Netflix that use AWS at `https://aws.amazon.com/solutions/case-studies/`. (The page also includes a link to create an account, a topic discussed in Chapter 2.) AWS use isn't just for private companies either — even the government makes use of its services.

The technologies that make all these services possible are actually simple in conception. Think of a pair of tin cans with a string attached between them. Amazon holds one tin can and you hold the other. By talking into one tin can, you can hear what is said at the other end. The implementation, however, relies on details that make communication harder than you might initially think. The following sections give you an overview on how the AWS cloud works.

Understanding service-driven application architectures

Service-driven application architectures, sometimes known as Service-Oriented Architectures (SOA), come in many forms. No matter how you view them, *service-driven application architectures* are extensions of the client-server technologies used in the early days of computing, in that a client makes a request that a server fulfills by performing an action or sending a response. However, the implementation details have changed significantly over the years, making modern applications far more reliable, flexible, and less reliant on a specific network configuration. The request and response process can involve multiple levels of granularity, with the term *microservice* applied to the smallest request and response pairs. Developers often refer to an application that relies on a service-driven application architecture as a *composite application* because it exists as multiple pieces glued together to form a whole. Service-driven application architectures follow many specific patterns, but in general, they use the following sequence to perform communication tasks.

1. Create a request on the client using whatever message technology the server requires.

2. Package the request, adding security or other information as needed.

3. Send the request using a protocol, such as Simple Object Access Protocol (SOAP), or an architecture, such as REpresentational State Transfer (REST). (You can discover how SOAP works at http://www.w3schools.com/xml/xml_soap.asp and how REST works at http://www.tutorialspoint.com/restful/ — a passing knowledge of both is helpful in working with AWS.)

4. Process the request on the server.

5. Perform an action or return data as required by the request.

6. When working with data, process the response on the client and present the results to the user (or other recipient).

REMEMBER

AWS provides a service-driven application architecture in which you choose a specific service, such as S3, to perform specific tasks, such as to back up files on a hard drive. In many cases, you must perform setup steps in addition to simply interacting with the service. For example, if you look at the ten-minute tutorial at http://aws.amazon.com/getting-started/tutorials/backup-files-to-amazon-s3/, you find that you must first create a bucket to store the files you want to upload to Amazon. This additional step makes sense because you have to establish a location from which to retrieve the files later, and you don't want your files mixed in with files from other people.

Even though many of the processes you perform with AWS require using an app (so that you have a user interface rather than code to work with), the underlying process is the same. The code provided in the app makes requests for you and then waits for a response. In some cases, the app must determine the success or failure of an action on the server. You need to realize, however, that these actions take place in code and that the code uses a sequence of steps to accomplish the task you've asked it to perform.

Understanding process- and function-driven workflows

In creating apps to help manage underlying services, AWS also defines workflows. A *workflow* is an organized method of accomplishing tasks. For example, when you want to save a file to AWS using S3, you must first create a bucket to hold the file. Only after you create a bucket can you save a file to AWS. In addition, you can't retrieve a file from the bucket until you first save a file there, which makes sense because you can't grab a file out of thin air. In short, a workflow defines a procedure for working with software, and the concept has been around for a long time. (The first workflows appeared in the mid-1970s with simple office automation prototypes at Xerox Parc and the University of Pennsylvania's Wharton School of Business.)

Workflows can consist of additional workflows. In addition, workflows manage the interaction between users and underlying services. A *process* is the aggregation of services managed by workflows into a cohesive whole. The workflows may perform generic tasks, but processes tend to be specific and help users accomplish particular goals. A process-driven workflow is proactive and attempts to circumvent potential problems by

>> Spotting failure patterns and acting on them

>> Looking for trends that tend to lead to failures

>> Locating and extinguishing potential threats

TIP

In looking through the tutorials at http://aws.amazon.com/getting-started/tutorials/, you find that they all involve using some type of user interface. The user interface provides the workflow used to manage the underlying services. Each major tutorial step is a workflow that performs a specific task, such as creating a bucket. When you combine these individual workflows into an aggregate whole, the process can help a user perform tasks such as moving files between the cloud and the user's system. Creating a cloud file system is an example of a process-driven workflow: The workflow exists to make the process viable. Workflows can become quite complex in large-scale operations, but viewing them helps you understand AWS better. You can find a more detailed discussion of workflows and processes at https://msdn.microsoft.com/library/bb833024.aspx.

A *function* is the reactive use of services managed by workflows to address specific problems in real time. Even though it would be nice if process-driven workflows worked all the time, the reality is that even with 99.999 percent reliability, the process will fail at some point, and a function-driven workflow must be in place to address that failure. Although process-driven workflows focus on flexible completion of tasks, function-driven workflows focus on procedurally attenuating the effect of a failure. In short, function-driven workflows address needs. The AWS services and workflows also deal with this issue through the user interface, such as by manually restoring a backup to mitigate a system failure.

Discovering IaaS

Even though this book frequently refers to virtual environments and services that you can't physically see, these elements all exist as part of a real computer environment that Amazon hosts on your behalf. You need to understand how these elements work to some extent because they have a physical presence and impact on your personal or business needs. Three technologies enable anyone to create a virtual computer center using AWS:

>> **IaaS:** A form of cloud computing that provides virtualized computing resources. You essentially use IaaS to replace physical resources, such as servers, with virtual resources hosted and managed by Amazon.

>> **SaaS:** A software distribution service that lets you use applications without actually having the applications installed locally. Another term used to describe this service is *software on demand*. The host, Amazon, maintains the software, provides the required licenses, and does all the other work needed to make the software available.

>> **PaaS:** A *platform* provides a complete solution for running software in an integrated manner on a particular piece of hardware. For example, Windows is a particular kind of platform. The virtual platform provided by PaaS allows a customer to develop, run, and manage applications of all sorts.

The following sections provide an extended discussion of these three technologies and help you understand how they interact with each other. The point of these sections is that each element performs a different task, yet you need all three to create a complete solution.

Defining IaaS

The simplest way to view *IaaS* is as a means of providing access to virtualized computer resources over an Internet connection. IaaS acts as one of three methods of sharing resources over the Internet, alongside SaaS and PaaS. AWS supports IaaS by providing access to virtualized hardware, software, servers, storage, and other infrastructure components. In short, you can use IaaS to replace every physical element in your computing setup except those required to establish and maintain Internet connectivity and those required to provide nonvirtualized services (such as printing). The advantages of IaaS are many, but here are the ones that most people consider essential:

>> The host handles tasks such as system maintenance, backup, and resiliency planning.

>> A client can gain immediate access to additional resources when needed and then doesn't need to worry about getting rid of them when the need has ended.

>> Detailed administrative tasks are handled by the host, but the client can manage overall administrative tasks, such as deciding how much capacity to use for a particular task.

>> Users have access to desktop virtualization, which means that their desktop appears on whatever device they happen to use at a given moment.

>> The use of policy-based services ensures that users must still adhere to company requirements when using computer resources.

>> All required updates (software and hardware) occur automatically and without any interaction required by the client.

WARNING

>> Keep in mind that there is no free lunch. AWS and other IaaS providers are interested in making a profit. They do so by investing in huge quantities of hardware, software, and management personnel to oversee it all. The benefits of scale help create profit, and many businesses simply can't create setups they require for less money.

However, you must consider the definite disadvantages of IaaS as well:

>> Billing can become complex because some services are billed at different rates and within different time frames. In addition, billing can include resource usage. The client must ensure that the amount on the bill actually matches real-world usage; paying too much for services that the client didn't actually use can easily happen.

>> Systems management monitoring becomes more difficult. The client loses control over the precise manner in which activities occur.

>> A lag often occurs between the time a change in service is needed and the host provides it, so the client can find that even though services are more flexible, they aren't as responsive.

>> Host downtime can affect a large group of people and prove difficult to fix, which means that a particular client may experience downtime at the worst possible time without any means to resolve it.

>> Building and testing custom applications can become more difficult. Many experts recommend using in-house equipment for application development needs to ensure that the environment is both protected and responsive.

REMEMBER

IaaS service contracts vary a great deal between vendors. Even though this book focuses on AWS, you need to consider other offerings, including Windows Azure, Google Compute Engine, Rackspace Open Cloud, and IBM SmartCloud Enterprise. In some cases, you might actually find it useful to obtain services from multiple hosts to obtain the best service for a particular need.

Comparing IaaS to SaaS

SaaS is all about cloud-based applications. Products like online email and office suites are examples of cloud-based applications. A client typically accesses the application using a local application, such as a browser. The browser runs on local hardware, but the application runs on the host hardware. What a client sees is the application running in the browser as if it is working locally. In most cases, the application runs within a browser without any alteration to the local system. However, some applications do require the addition of plug-ins.

The difference between IaaS and SaaS is the level of service. When working with IaaS, a client typically requires detailed support that spans entire solutions. A SaaS solution may include only the application. However, it can also include the following:

>> Application runtimes

>> Data access

>> Middleware

>> Operating system support

>> Virtualization

>> Server access

>> Data storage

>> Networking

SaaS typically keeps the host completely in control and doesn't offer any sort of monitoring. Even though the host keeps the application updated and ensures data security, the client company administrators typically can't access SaaS solutions in any meaningful way (SaaS offers application usage, but not necessarily application configuration, and is therefore not as flexible as other alternatives). In addition, the client company typically accepts the application as is, without any modifications or customizations. Using client-developed applications is out of the question in this scenario.

Comparing IaaS to PaaS

PaaS is more of a development solution than a production environment solution. A development team typically uses PaaS to create custom solutions or modify existing solutions. The development staff has full control over the application and can perform all development-related tasks, such as debugging and testing. As with the SaaS solution, the host normally maintains control over

>> Middleware

>> Operating system support

>> Virtualization

>> Server access

>> Data storage

>> Networking

In this case, however, the development staff can access the middleware to enhance application development without reinventing the wheel. Writing application code to make the application cloud-ready isn't necessary because the middleware already contains these features. The development team gains access to cloud-based application features that include the following:

>> Scalability

>> High availability

>> Multitenancy

>> SaaS enablement

Administrators can also perform monitoring and management tasks within limits when working with a PaaS (depending on the contract the client has with the host). However, realize that PaaS is oriented toward development needs, so the developer takes precedence when it comes to performing some tasks that an administrator might normally perform. In addition, PaaS relates to development, not production setups, so the host may take care of all administration tasks locally.

Determining Why You Should Use AWS

Even though AWS has a lot to offer, you still need to consider how it answers your specific needs. This consideration goes beyond simply determining whether you really want to move to cloud-based services, but also taking into account other offerings that might serve your needs just as well (if not better). Even though this book is about AWS, you should compare AWS with other cloud services. You may choose to use AWS as part of your solution rather than as the only solution. Of course, this means knowing the areas in which AWS excels. The following sections address both of these possibilities: using other cloud services instead of AWS, or in addition to it.

Comparing AWS to other cloud services

You have many ways to compare cloud services. One of the ways in which companies commonly look at services is by the market share they have. A large market share tends to ensure that the cloud service will be around for a long time and that many people find its services both useful and functional. A recent *InfoWorld* article (http://www.infoworld.com/article/3065842/cloud-computing/beyond-aws-the-clouds-next-stage.html) points out that AWS currently corners 70 to 80 percent of the cloud market. In addition, AWS revenues keep increasing, which lets Amazon continue adding new features while maintaining existing features at peak efficiency.

REMEMBER

Large market share and capital to invest don't necessarily add up to a cloud service that fulfills your needs. You also need to know that the host can provide the products you need in a form that you can use. The AWS product list appears at http://aws.amazon.com/products/. It includes all the major IaaS, SaaS, and PaaS categories. However, you should compare these products to the major AWS competitors:

>> Cisco Metapod (http://www.cisco.com/c/en/us/products/cloud-systems-management/metapod/index.html)

>> Google Cloud Platform (https://cloud.google.com/products/)

>> Joyent (https://www.joyent.com/)

>> Microsoft Azure (https://azure.microsoft.com/)

Of the competitors listed here, Google Cloud Platform comes closest to offering the same feature set found in AWS. However, in looking at the Google offerings, you should note the prominence of machine learning services that aren't found in AWS. On the other hand, AWS has more to offer in the way of the Internet of Things (IoT), applications, and mobile services.

Each of the vendors offering these services is different. For example, Joyent offers a simple setup that may appeal more strongly to an SMB that has only a few needs to address and no desire to become involved in a complex service. Microsoft, on the other hand, has strong SQL database-management support as well as the connection with the Windows platform that businesses may want to maintain. The point is that you must look at each of the vendors to determine who can best meet your needs (although, as previously stated, most people are voting with their dollars on AWS).

Defining target areas where AWS works best

In looking at the services that AWS provides, you can see that the emphasis is on enterprise productivity. For example, Google Cloud Platform offers four enhanced machine learning services that you could use for analysis purposes, but AWS offers only one. However, Google Cloud Platform can't match AWS when it comes to mobile service, which is an area that users most definitely want included for accessing applications. Unless your business is heavily involved in analysis tasks, the offerings that AWS provides are significantly better in many ways. Here are the service categories that AWS offers:

>> Compute

>> Storage and content delivery

>> Database

>> Networking

>> Analytics

>> Enterprise applications

>> Mobile services

>> IoT

>> Developer tools

>> Management tools

>> Security and identity

>> Application services

Understanding the AWS Certifications

A certification doesn't make you an expert. However, it does provide a quantified description of your minimum level of expertise — a textbook look of what you know, but not an assessment of real-world knowledge. In other words, you get a certification to prove that you have a given level of provable expertise and most employers will probably assume that you possess expertise in addition to what the certification tests.

The pursuit of a certification can also help you better understand areas in which your current education is weak. Going through the learning and testing process can help you become a better administrator. With the need to obtain the guidelines to achieve proficiency and later demonstrate proficiency in mind, the following sections discuss the various AWS certifications so that you can get a better idea of where to spend your time when getting one.

REMEMBER

Getting a certification is generally useful only when you want to apply for a new job or advance in your current job. After all, you likely know your own skills well enough to determine your level of proficiency to some degree without a certification. Filling out your education and then demonstrating what you know to others for specific personal gains are the reason to get a certification. Some people miss the point and discover later that they've spent a lot of money and time getting something they really didn't need in the first place.

Gaining an overview of the certifications

AWS currently provides a number of certifications, which you can see at https://aws.amazon.com/certification/. You can expect Amazon to add more as AWS continues to expand. The following list provides a quick overview of the levels of certifications:

» **AWS Certified Solutions Architect – Associate:** Tests the ability of a developer to perform basic AWS design and development tasks. Before you can even contemplate taking this exam, you need to know how to program and have experience designing applications on AWS. A number of sources also recommend this certification for administration because many of the administration tasks build on the knowledge you get here.

» **AWS Certified Solutions Architect – Professional:** Tests the ability of a developer to perform the next level of development tasks on AWS, such as migrating complex, multitier applications to AWS. The exam still focuses on development tasks but depends on the developer's having already passed the AWS Certified Solutions Architect – Associate exam and mastering new skills. (The resources specify a minimum of two years of hands-on AWS programming.)

>> **AWS Certified Developer – Associate:** Determines whether the developer can perform specific levels of application development using AWS. For example, you need to know which of the services to use to add specific features to an application. Rather than have you actually use AWS to host the application, this exam focuses more on using AWS in conjunction with existing applications.

>> **AWS Certified SysOps Administrator – Associate:** Determines whether an administrator has the skills required to deploy and manage applications on an AWS setup. In addition, the administrator must show proficiency in operating various AWS services and in determining which service to use to meet a specific need.

>> **AWS Certified DevOps Engineer – Professional:** Evaluates the ability of the test taker to perform *DevOps* (that is, create an interface between developers and other IT professionals). This means having some level of skill in both administration and development. In addition, the candidate must have knowledge of processes that enable smooth design, development, deployment, management, and operation of applications.

TIP

If you find that potential employers really do want you to obtain certifications to prove your skill level, you may find that obtaining just an AWS-specific certification may not be enough to get that six-figure income. Cloud administrators typically need to demonstrate proficiency with more than one service. Fortunately, you can often find online aids to help you decide which certifications are most popular at a given time. For example, the article at `https://anturis.com/blog/7-valuable-certifications-for-cloud-administrators/` provides a listing of the most popular certifications at the current time, one of which is the AWS Certified SysOps Administrator.

Locating certification resources

You can find all sorts of interesting aids online for getting your certification. However, the best place to start is directly on the Amazon website. Unfortunately, the information you find isn't the best organized at times. Start by ensuring that you meet the requirements in the Candidate Overview section. Until you meet those requirements, it isn't particularly useful to move forward (unless you want to end up with a *paper certification* — one that doesn't actually mean anything).

After you have fulfilled the minimum requirements, download the Exam Guide. The guide tells you that you need to be proficient in a number of areas in order to pass, which shouldn't surprise you. AWS wants to ensure that you actually know the material. Fortunately, you can also find online sources to help you make sense of the Exam Guide. For example, there is an excellent video on the requirements for the AWS Certified SysOps Administrator – Associate exam at `https://www.youtube.com/watch?v=JCkD81padj8`. Watching the video and going through the Exam Guide can help you get a better idea of what you need to do.

At some point, you want to download the example questions. However, given that AWS provides only one set of example questions and that those precise questions are unlikely to appear on the exam, memorizing them won't do you any good. What you need to do is study and when you feel you're ready, try the example questions, which can help you determine your weak areas. Unfortunately, there are only a few example questions — not enough to give you a good feel for the exam.

Every certification also comes with a Take a Practice Exam option. Be sure to save this feature for last. Again, you don't get many questions, the questions don't change, and they're not likely to appear on the exam in the precise form you see them. The purpose of the practice exam is to help you sense whether you're ready.

REMEMBER

Most people need information presented in more than one way and more than one time to remember it. By going through this book and participating in the various examples, you build skills and gain knowledge that you can couple with other sources to build your AWS knowledge. The essential thing is not to try to rush the process, because you're almost guaranteed not to pass if you do.

As you go through the book, make sure to also look at the Getting Started and FAQs for each of the services covered. These two sources of information contain a great deal of information that Amazon is likely to use for exam questions. You don't have to memorize the material, but being familiar with it gives you a definite advantage.

TIP

Everyone has different ways of learning material, and you may find that reading the exam materials simply doesn't work for you. Hands-on training can help, but sometimes you need a little more than that. If you're still confused, you may want to use Computer Based Training (CBT) courses, such as the ones found at `https://www.cbtnuggets.com/it-training/amazon-web-services-training` and `https://linuxacademy.com/amazon-web-services/training/course/name/aws-certified-sysops-administrator-associate-level`.

Getting a Well-Rounded Education

Obtaining a certification helps you prove your level of proficiency to someone else, which is one level of the education process. In many cases, you can skip this level unless you have specific needs that a certification can address. However, you must continue to build on your expertise. Simply learning the basics and then never cracking a book again will result in your eventual termination as an administrator because computer technology continues to change. In short, education is continuous when you're an administrator. Getting a well-rounded education is essential, as is continuing to learn more whenever you can and in whatever way that you can. Even dibs and dabs of time spent learning can make a big difference.

REMEMBER

The problem with computer technology is the vast amount of available information. Information overload is a serious problem because spending time learning the wrong information using an inappropriate approach costs you time without helping you to continue to develop your career at all. That's the point of this section: to list the approaches that other people use to improve their chances of getting the right information in the most efficient manner possible, enabling you to keep up with the current state of computer technology. Here are some techniques you can use to remain current when working with AWS and other cloud technologies:

>> Get a free AWS account (see Chapter 2 for details) and use it to practice new techniques that you don't dare try on your production system.

>> Keep track of the free tier offerings and try anything new, even if you don't have plans to use it in your business.

>> Read the trade press — let the people with the connections get the latest news for you.

>> Watch videos on sites such as YouTube (https://www.youtube.com/) that demonstrate techniques for working with AWS.

>> Ask questions on professional sites, such as Quora (https://www.quora.com/), to obtain additional insights into cloud strategies from other professionals.

Chapter **2**

Obtaining Free Amazon Services

O ne of the purposes of this book is to help you discover a lot more about Amazon Web Services (AWS) through experimentation. Of course, Amazon would just love to have you buy these services, but a free option, which is the focus of this chapter, is also available. The issue is one of figuring out just what Amazon means by free. This chapter's first section clears up the questions you might have about what free means, because some services are always free and others are free for a limited time. In addition, you must consider the limits of free. If you use some of these services too much, you end up paying for them. Therefore, you need to know the rules in order to get the services free.

The next two sections of the chapter consider hardware and network requirements. Note that Amazon likes you to have both Linux and Windows knowledge when you take your certification exams (see the "Understanding the AWS Certifications" section of Chapter 1), and such knowledge is helpful even if you don't want to obtain a certification. This chapter doesn't delve too deeply into platform specifics, but it does help you understand what you need to do to get a basic setup running.

Now that you have some idea of what you're getting and what you need in order to get it, it's time to get your free account. The rest of the book assumes that you have a free account to use. Going through the various procedures is the best way to build an understanding of AWS. Yes, some people can get a feeling for how things work just by reading, but doing things hands on really is better.

The chapter ends by having you perform a simple task using AWS, just to get a feel for how it works. Don't worry: You really can't mess up the account. If you do make an unfortunate choice, starting over is easy enough. Nothing will get damaged by the exercise in this chapter — it's totally safe. Make sure you have some fun doing it! After all, cloud computing should be an easier and more efficient way to perform administrative tasks, and you'll find that it truly is as the book progresses.

Discovering the Limits of Free Services

Amazon does provide the means for using many of its cloud services for free. In fact, you can see some of these services at `http://aws.amazon.com/free/`. However, as you look through the list of services, you see that the some expire, others don't. In addition, some have limits and others don't. Those that do have limits don't have the same limits, so you need to watch usage carefully. It's really quite confusing. The following sections help clarify what Amazon actually means by saying some services are free.

Expiring services versus nonexpiring services

Many of the AWS services you obtain through the free tier have expiration dates, and you need to consider this limitation when evaluating and possibly using the service to perform useful work. Figure 2-1 shows an example of a service with an expiration date. Notice that you must begin paying for the service 12 months after you begin using it.

In some cases, the product itself doesn't have an expiration date, but the service on which it runs does. For example, when viewing the terms for using the free software, the software itself is indeed free. However, in order to run the software, you must have the required service, which does come with an expiration date (see Figure 2-2).

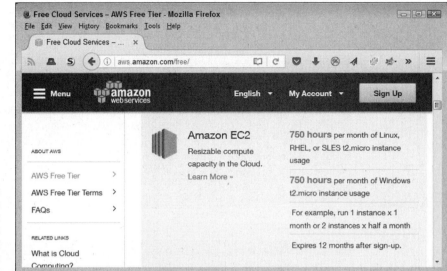

FIGURE 2-1:
Some services have an expiration date when you must begin paying for them.

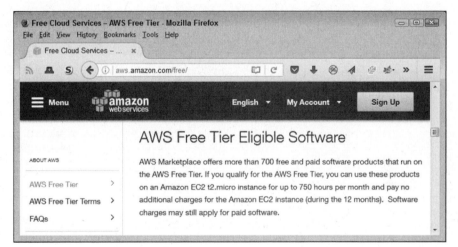

FIGURE 2-2:
Software may be free, but the service on which it runs might not be.

You also have access to some products that are both free and have no expiration date. These nonexpiring offers still have limitations, but you don't have to worry about using those products within the limits for however long you want (or until Amazon changes the terms). Figure 2-3 shows examples of these kinds of services.

REMEMBER

Knowing the terms under which you use a service is essential. The free period for services with an expiration date goes all too quickly, and you may suddenly find yourself paying for something that you thought remained free for a longer time frame. Given that Amazon can change the terms of usage at any time, you need to keep checking the terms of service for the services that you use. A service that lacks an expiration date today may have an expiration date tomorrow.

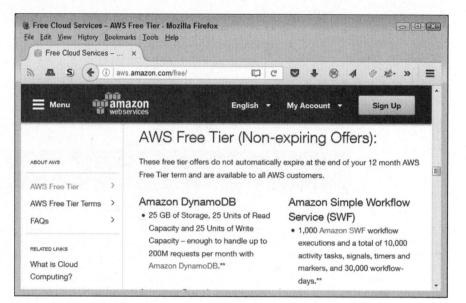

FIGURE 2-3:
A few services don't come with expiration dates.

Considering the usage limits

Look again at Figures 2-1 through 2-3. Note that all these products have some sort of usage limit attached to them — even the free software — because of the software's reliance on an underlying service. (Some software relies on more than one service, so you must also consider this need.) For example, you can use Amazon Elastic Compute Cloud (EC2) for 750 hours per month as either a Linux or Windows setup. A 31-day month contains 744 hours, so you really don't have much leeway if you want to use the EC2 service continuously.

WARNING

The description then provides you with an example of usage. Amazon bases the usage terms on instances. Consequently, you have access to a single Linux or single Windows setup. If you wanted to work with both Linux and Windows, you would need two instances and could use them for only 15 days and 15 hours each month. In short, you need to exercise care in how you set up and configure the services to ensure that you don't exceed the usage limits.

The free, nonexpiring services also have limits. For example, when working with Amazon DynamoDB, you have access to 25GB of storage, 25 units of read capacity, and 25 units of write capacity. Theoretically, this is enough capacity to handle 200 million requests each month. However, whether you can actually use all that capacity depends on the size of the requests and how you interact with the service. You could easily run out of storage capacity long before you run out of request capacity when working with larger files, such as graphics. Again, you need to watch all the limits carefully or you could find yourself paying for a service that you thought was free.

Considering the Hardware Requirements

No matter how many services AWS offers, you still require some amount of hardware to use the services. The amount of hardware you require when working with services in the cloud is minimal because the AWS hardware does all the heavy lifting. When working with services locally, you need additional hardware because AWS is no longer doing the heavy lifting for you. Therefore, you should consider different hardware requirements depending on where you host the AWS service. The following sections help you obtain additional information about working with both cloud and local services.

Hosting the services in the cloud

Hidden in the AWS documentation is all sorts of useful information about various services. For example, AWS Storage Gateway (http://aws.amazon.com/documentation/storage-gateway/) will connect an on-premises *software appliance* (an application combined with just enough operating system capability to run on hardware or on a virtual machine) with cloud-based storage. In other words, you use the gateway to connect your application to the data storage it requires. It might seem as if running the gateway in the cloud would be a good idea because you wouldn't need to invest in additional hardware. However, when you look at the requirements shown in Figure 2-4, you see that using an EC2 instance allows you to run only gateway-cached volumes and gateway-VTLs (you can't run gateway-stored volumes). You don't need to know what these terms mean, but you do need to understand that the cloud present limits that you must consider during any planning stage.

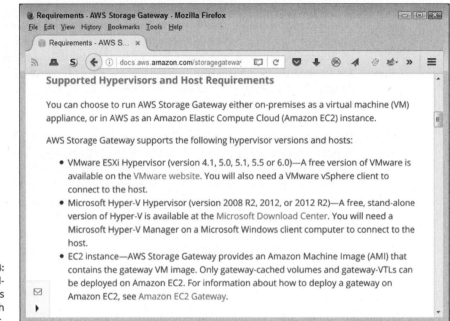

After you make certain that you can run your intended configuration, you can begin to consider the advantages and disadvantages of working in the cloud. For example, when hosting the service in the cloud, you get automatic scaling as needed, and Amazon performs many of the administrative tasks for you. Chapter 1 discusses many of the advantages of the cloud for you. However, for a realistic perspective, you must offset these advantages with disadvantages, such as:

» Potential for lower application speed

» Need to maintain a reliable Internet connection

» Loss of flexibility

» Vendors going out of business

Even though basic hardware needs become less expensive, you do need to consider additional expenses in the form of redundancies. Most organizations find that the hardware costs of moving to the cloud are substantially less than maintaining a full IT department, which is why they make the move. However, you must make the move with the understanding that you have other matters to consider when you do.

Hosting the services locally

When hosting services locally, you need to provide all the required infrastructure, which can get expensive. AWS does provide guidance on the minimum requirements for hosting a service locally. For example, Figure 2-5 shows the requirements for the AWS Storage Gateway.

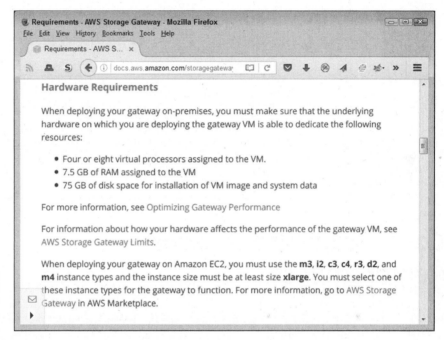

FIGURE 2-5:
Make sure that you can actually host the service locally.

TIP

A good rule of thumb when hosting services locally is to view any vendor-supplied requirements as minimums. If you don't plan to load the service heavily, these minimums usually work. However, when you click the Optimizing Gateway Performance link, the first suggestion you see is adding resources to your gateway, as shown in Figure 2-6. Planning for too much capacity is better than for not enough, but getting the configuration as close as possible to what you need will always help financially.

Not all the services will work locally, but you may be surprised to find that many do. The issue is one of defining precisely how you plan to use a given service and the trade-offs that you're willing to make. For example, when hosting a service locally, you may find it hard to provide the same level of connectivity that you could provide to third parties when hosting the same service in the cloud.

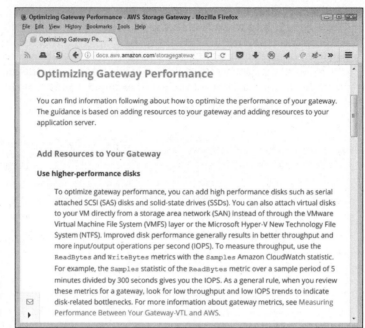

Optimizing Gateway Performance

You can find information following about how to optimize the performance of your gateway. The guidance is based on adding resources to your gateway and adding resources to your application server.

Add Resources to Your Gateway

Use higher-performance disks

To optimize gateway performance, you can add high performance disks such as serial attached SCSI (SAS) disks and solid-state drives (SSDs). You can also attach virtual disks to your VM directly from a storage area network (SAN) instead of through the VMware Virtual Machine File System (VMFS) layer or the Microsoft Hyper-V New Technology File System (NTFS). Improved disk performance generally results in better throughput and more input/output operations per second (IOPS). To measure throughput, use the ReadBytes and WriteBytes metrics with the Samples Amazon CloudWatch statistic. For example, the Samples statistic of the ReadBytes metric over a sample period of 5 minutes divided by 300 seconds gives you the IOPS. As a general rule, when you review these metrics for a gateway, look for low throughput and low IOPS trends to indicate disk-related bottlenecks. For more information about gateway metrics, see Measuring Performance Between Your Gateway-VTL and AWS.

FIGURE 2-6:
Plan ahead for sufficient resources.

Considering the Network Requirements

To use the AWS services, you need a network connection. In some cases, you need more than one. You not only need an Internet connection for the AWS user interface, but the services may require dedicated connections as well and these connections can become part of your business network. Because of this close relationship, creating the network configuration carefully is essential. Otherwise, you may find that the AWS network connection conflicts with the configuration used for your business (a problem that occurs more often than you might think).

TIP

Interestingly enough, when you host certain services, such as DynamoDB, locally, you may not need to spend much time considering the network requirements. The reason is that you're hosting the service locally, and the AWS hardware doesn't come into play. However, the local hosting scenario is for development purposes in most cases, so eventually you need to create a network connection to the online services.

The following sections discuss network requirements for AWS. The amount of configuration required depends on the services you use, how you use them, how you host them, and where your own business services come into play. The most important thing to consider is the need to plan carefully before you perform any setups.

Designing for connectivity

Many of the services that you use with AWS require some sort of connectivity solution when you host them in the cloud. A common way to create the required connectivity is to use Amazon Virtual Private Cloud (AmazonVPC) (https://aws.amazon.com/vpc/). For example, you can make AmazonVPC part of the EC2 setup. You use AmazonVPC to create the connection to your EC2 configuration. Chapter 4 discusses the configuration requirements in more detail, but be aware that you do need connectivity to access some of the services that Amazon offers.

Another method of creating the connection is to rely on Direct Connect (https://aws.amazon.com/directconnect/). In this case, you create a direct connection between AWS services and your network. This means that you can access the AWS services as just another resource on your network, and the services actually become invisible to end users. This implementation relies on the 802.1q VLAN standard to make the required connection. (You can find an 802.1a VLAN tutorial at http://www.microhowto.info/tutorials/802.1q.html.) When configured correctly, you can create a private IP interface for local network resources and a separate public IP interface for AWS services.

TIP

Amazon offerings are just the tip of the connectivity iceberg. For example, you could rely on a third-party vendor, such as AT&T, to help you make the connection. The AT&T NetBond service (https://www.business.att.com/enterprise/Family/cloud/network-cloud/) lets you connect your Virtual Private Network (VPN) to multiple cloud providers, so you can use a single connection to address all your connectivity needs. In this case, instead of just connecting to AWS using its service, you can connect with the following cloud services using a single connection, which makes managing the connections infinitely easier (assuming that you use more than one cloud provider).

>> Amazon Web Services

>> Blue Jeans Network

>> Box

>> Cisco WebEx

>> CSC Agility Platform

- » HP Helion
- » IBM Managed Cloud Service
- » IBM SoftLayer
- » Microsoft Azure and Office 365
- » Salesforce.com
- » Sungard Availability Services
- » VMware vCloud Air

The third-party options may seem complex and initially cost quite a bit more than the Amazon offerings, but they have distinct advantages as well. For example, according to *InformationWeek* (`http://www.informationweek.com/cloud/software-as-a-service/amazon-taps-atandt-for-private-line-cloud-connectivity/d/d-id/1316360`), the AT&T NetBond service lets larger organizations use Multi-Protocol Label Switching (MPLS), which the organization may have already installed. However, the big advantage is that this approach lets the organization skip the public Internet in favor of a private connection that can significantly improve network performance. For example, using a private connection can reduce *network latency* (the time it takes for a packet of data to get from one designated point to another) by 50 percent. After this kind of solution is in place, a larger organization can save as much as 60 percent on its monthly bill, so the savings eventually pay back the larger initial investment.

Balancing cloud and internal needs

The connectivity solution you choose must reflect a balance between cloud and internal needs. You don't necessarily want to move right into a Direct Connect solution when your only goal is to experiment with AWS to determine whether it can meet certain organizational goals. Likewise, a third-party solution, such as AT&T NetBond, is the better solution when you've already made a commitment to AWS but also plan to support a number of other cloud provider solutions. Choosing the right level of connectivity is essential to ensuring that you get the best performance at the right price, but with the least layout of initial capital.

To help you keep costs low and reduce the potential for serious problems with your own network, the exercises in the book assume that you're using the AmazonVPC solution. It presents the smallest investment and lowest risk. However, these features come at the cost of convenience, speed, and potentially cost.

Specifying a subnet

It's important to consider precisely how you plan to configure the service before you choose network settings. Using the default AWS subnet may cause conflicts with the local network when you host the service locally. However, choosing the wrong subnet can create conflicts as well. Make certain that you choose a subnet that actually works with your local networking setup.

The Amazon offerings usually provide more than one scenario for creating a subnet. For example, when using AmazonVPC, you have the options described at `http://docs.aws.amazon.com/AmazonVPC/latest/UserGuide/VPC_Scenarios.html` and shown in Figure 2-7. For example, Scenario 1: VPC with a Single Public Subnet works best for a single-tier, public-facing web application. You can also use it for development purposes.

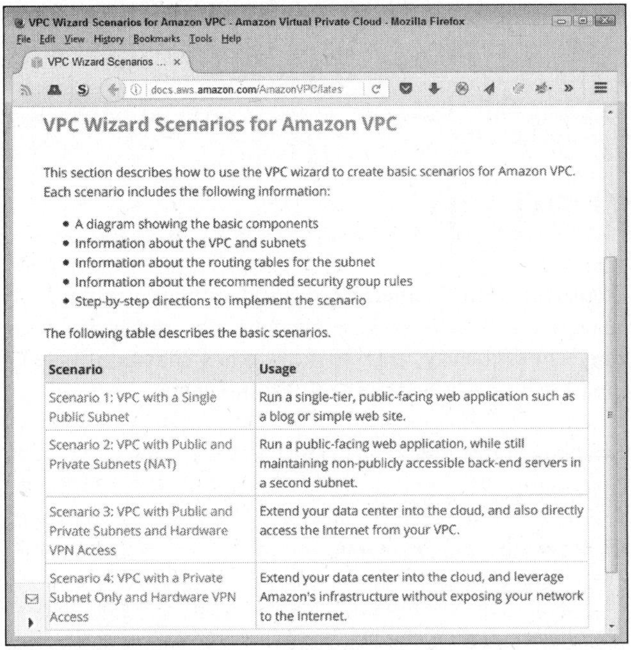

FIGURE 2-7: Use an appropriate subnet configuration for your network.

Each of the scenarios provides you with helpful information about the subnet configuration that includes a diagram similar to the one shown in Figure 2-8. Using the information found with each scenario helps you make a better decision about which configuration to use and decide how to configure it to meet your specific needs (potentially avoiding those conflicts that will cause problems later).

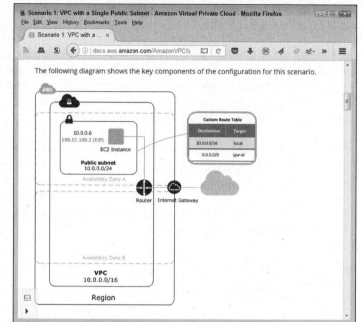

The following diagram shows the key components of the configuration for this scenario.

FIGURE 2-8:
Each scenario comes with diagrams and other aids to help you make good decisions.

Getting Signed Up

Before you can really do anything other than plan, you need an account. Discovering the wonders of AWS is a hands-on activity, so you really do want to work with it online. Consequently, this book assumes that you've gone through the free sign-up process described in the following steps:

1. **Navigate your browser to** http://aws.amazon.com/.

    The main Amazon Web Services page appears.

2. **Click Create a Free Account.**

    Unless you already signed into Amazon, you see a Sign In or Create an AWS Account dialog box like the one shown in Figure 2-9. If you already have an Amazon account and want that account associated with AWS, you can sign in using your Amazon account. Otherwise, you need to create a new account.

3. **Sign into an account or create a new one as required.**

    The Contact Information page appears, as shown in Figure 2-10. Notice that different pages exist for company and personal accounts.

4. **Supply the required company or personal contact information. Read and accept the customer agreement.**

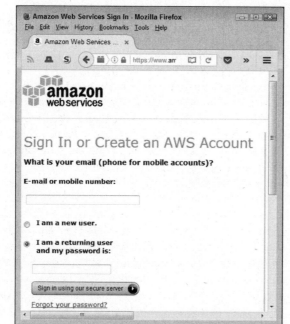

FIGURE 2-9:
Sign into or create an Amazon account.

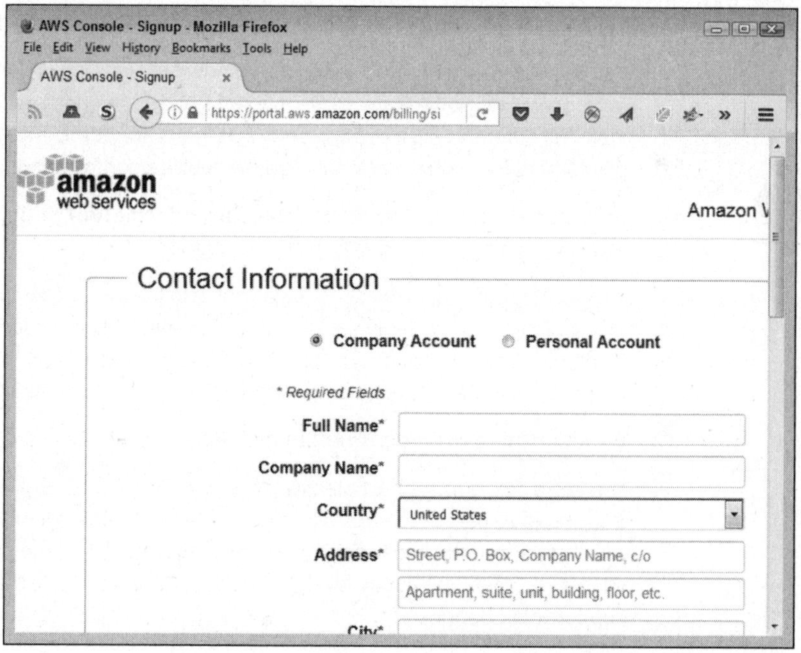

FIGURE 2-10:
Supply the required contact information for the kind of account you want.

BE SURE TO READ THE AWS CUSTOMER AGREEMENT!

Reading the customer agreement is essential because it contains items that you may not agree with. For example, Amazon states outright in section 3.2 that your data will remain private as long as law enforcement doesn't make a request to look at it. In addition, Amazon won't tell you about the disclosure of your information to the government should the government issue a gag order. These clauses are important because recent events have shed some interesting perspectives on these issues. For example, Apple refused to cooperate with the government in making iPhone data available by breaching iPhone security (see the article at https://www.washingtonpost.com/world/national-security/us-wants-apple-to-help-unlock-iphone-used-by-san-bernardino-shooter/2016/02/16/69b903ee-d4d9-11e5-9823-02b905009f99_story.html). Microsoft also has a pending lawsuit against the government with regard to electronic gag orders (see the article at http://www.nytimes.com/2016/04/15/technology/microsoft-sues-us-over-orders-barring-it-from-revealing-surveillance.html?_r=0). These issues are important and you need to know what you're signing before you sign it, so be sure to read the agreement.

5. **Click Create Account and Continue when you complete the form.**

   You see the Payment Information page shown in Figure 2-11. Be aware that Amazon will bill you for any usage in excess of the free tier level. You can click View Full Offer Details if you have any questions about the level of support provided before you enter your credit or debit card information.

6. **Provide the required credit or debit card information, supply the address information needed, and then click Continue.**

   You see the Identify Verification page shown in Figure 2-12. Amazon performs an automated call to verify your identity. You see a PIN provided onscreen. During the call, you say or type this PIN into your telephone keypad. The screen automatically changes as you perform each step of the identification process.

7. **Click Continue to Select Your Support Plan.**

   You see a listing of support plans as shown in Figure 2-13. Only the Basic plan is included as part of the free tier. If you want to obtain additional support, you must pay a monthly fee for it. This is an example of one of the potential charges that you might pay for the free tier service. You have the following support-plan options:

   - **Basic:** Free support that Amazon offers as part of the free tier support. Amazon doesn't offer any support through this option. You must instead rely on community support, which usually works fine for experimentation.

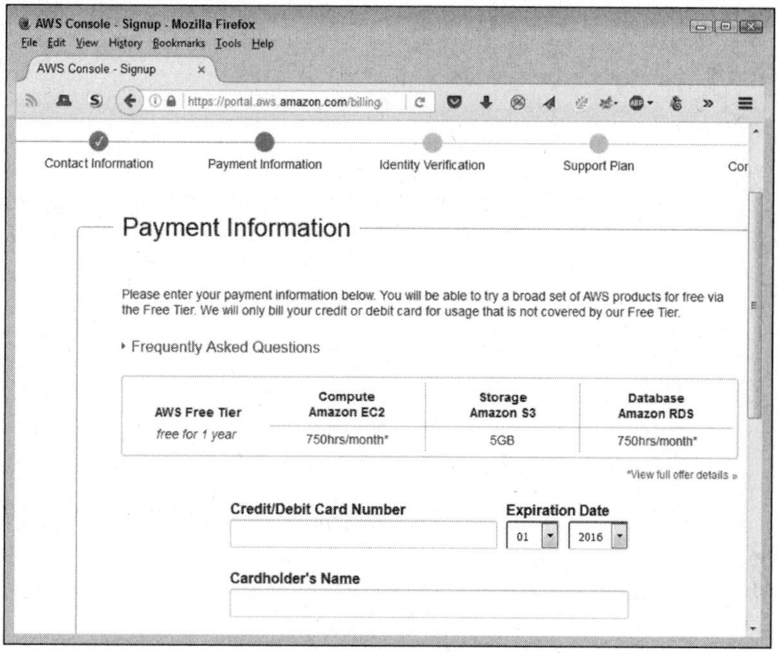

FIGURE 2-11:
Provide a credit or debit card to use as payment.

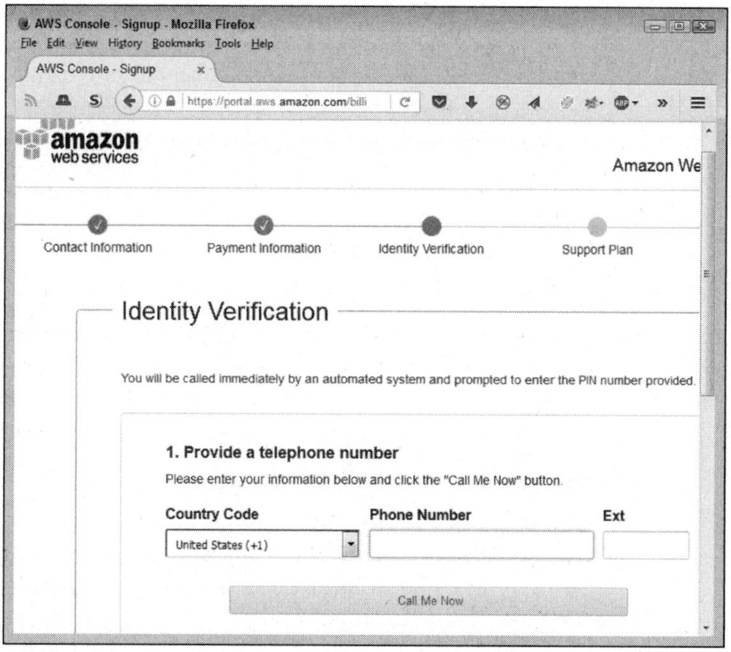

FIGURE 2-12:
Supply the information needed to verify your identity.

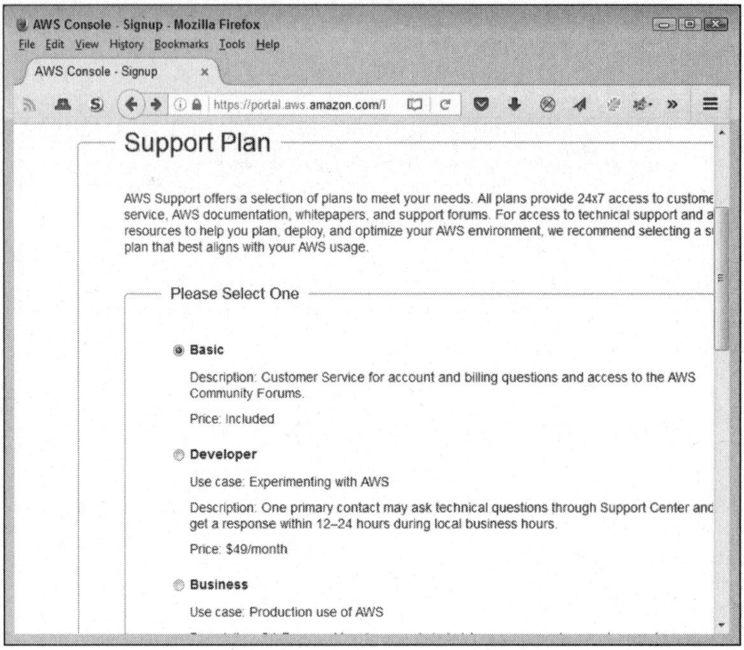

FIGURE 2-13:
Select the level of support needed for your AWS use.

- **Developer:** Support that comes at $49/month at the time of this writing. A single developer (or other organizational representative) can contact the Support Center and expect a response within 12 to 24 hours. However, if you're serious about developing an application and also anticipate using third-party products, you really need to consider the Business level.

- **Business:** Support that comes at $100/month at the time of this writing. A business user may contact the Support Center by phone and expect a one-hour response to urgent support problems as well as obtain help with third-party products.

- **Enterprise:** Support that comes at $15,000/month. This is the level of support provided for organizations that use AWS for mission-critical applications. The response time is only 15 minutes, and Amazon is willing to provide all sorts of technical help. Of course, the price is a tad on the steep side.

8. **Choose a support plan and click Continue.**

   Normally, you see a welcome page like the one shown in Figure 2-14. (However, you might also see a message saying that Amazon is setting up your account and will send you emails when your account is ready. Wait for the emails to arrive if you see these messages.) At this point, you can sign into the console and try a few tasks. The 10-minute tutorials are helpful in getting you started. The next section of the chapter gives you help getting started as well.

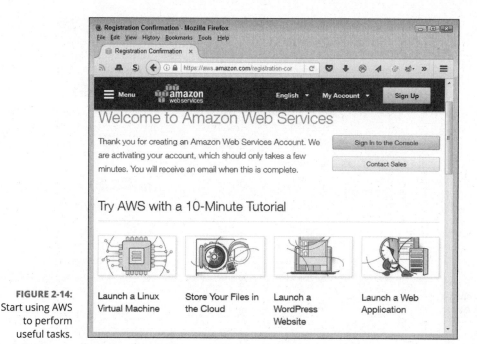

FIGURE 2-14:
Start using AWS
to perform
useful tasks.

Performing a Few Simple Tasks

Now that you have a free account to use, you can give something a try. In this case, you create an online storage area, move a file to it, copy the file back to your hard drive, and then delete the file in the online storage. Moving data between local drives and the AWS cloud is one of the most common activities you perform, so this exercise is important, even if it seems a bit simplistic. The following steps help you through the process of working with files in the cloud.

1. **Click Sign in to the Console or choose My Account ⇨ AWS Management Console.**

   You see a sign-in page similar to the one shown in Figure 2-9, even if you just completed the sign-up process.

2. **Sign in to your account.**

   You see a list of Amazon Web Services like the one shown in Figure 2-15. Remember that not all these services are free. Only the services in the free tier are free to use.

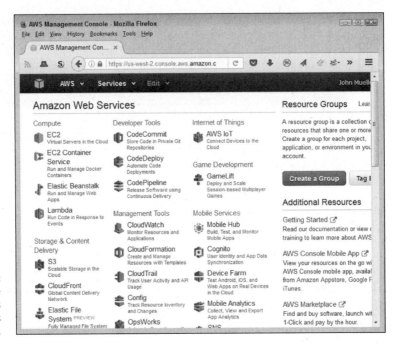

FIGURE 2-15:
The console
provides access
to all the services
you can use.

3. **Click S3 in the Storage & Content Delivery group (you may need to select S3 from the Services drop-down at the top of the page).**

You see an introduction to the Sample Storage Service (S3) page. This page explains a little about S3. Make sure to read the text before you proceed.

To use S3, you must first create a bucket. The bucket will hold the data that you transfer to AWS. In this case, you use the bucket to hold a file.

4. **Click Create Bucket.**

You see the Create a Bucket dialog box, shown in Figure 2-16. The Bucket Name field is simply the name that you want to give to your bucket. Choose a name that seems appropriate for the bucket's use. (See the restrictions for naming buckets at http://docs.aws.amazon.com/AmazonS3/latest/dev/ BucketRestrictions.html). The Region field tells where your bucket is physically stored. A local bucket will respond faster, but a bucket somewhere else in the world may provide additional resilience because it won't be as susceptible to local events, such as storms.

5. **Type a bucket name (the example uses johnm.test-bucket) and select a region (the example uses Oregon); then click Create.**

You see a new page with a list of all your buckets, as shown in Figure 2-17. You can configure each bucket differently using the properties shown on the right side of the screen. For now, use the default properties to work with a file.

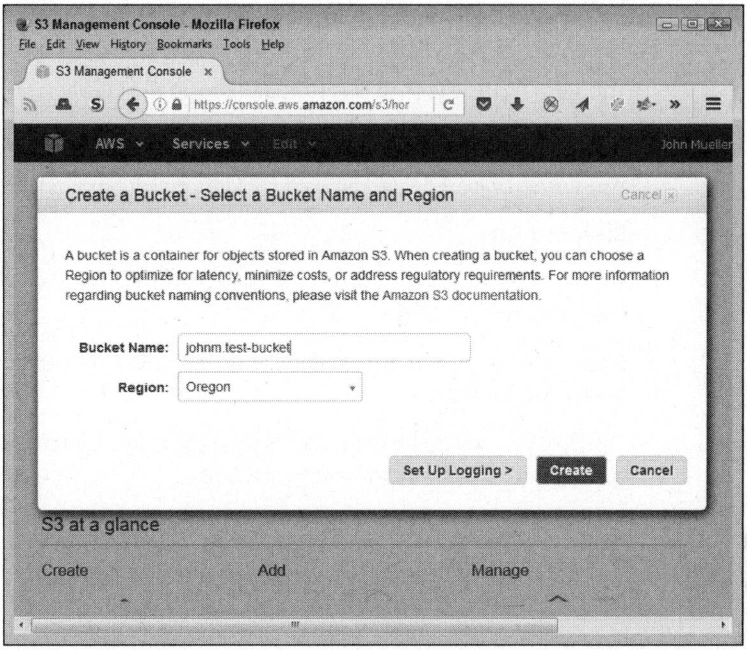

FIGURE 2-16:
Define a name
and region for
your bucket.

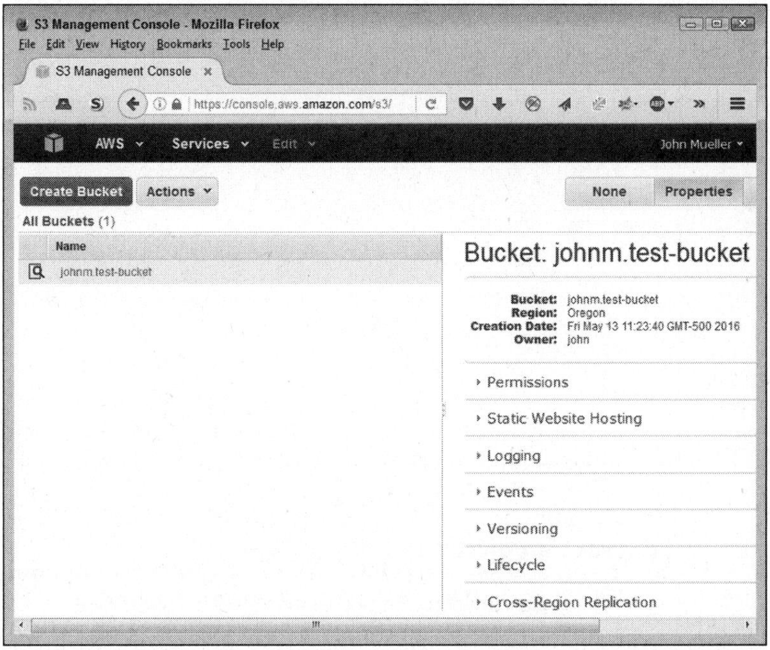

FIGURE 2-17:
S3 provides a
listing of the
buckets you
created.

6. **Click the bucket entry you just created.**

You see a console for that bucket that tells you the bucket is empty.

7. **Click Upload.**

You see an Upload – Select Files and Folders dialog box.

8. **Click Add Files.**

You see a File Upload dialog box that will conform to the standard used for your platform.

9. **Select the file you want to upload (the example uses the outline for this book) and click Open.**

The Upload – Select Files and Folders dialog box now contains a list of the files you plan to upload, as shown in Figure 2-18.

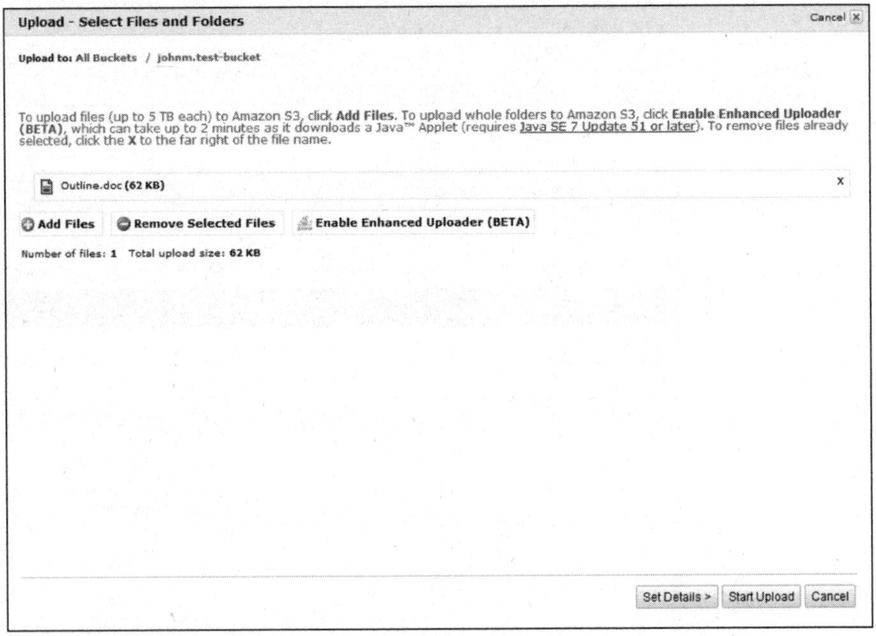

Upload - Select Files and Folders   Cancel ☒

Upload to: All Buckets / johnm.test-bucket

To upload files (up to 5 TB each) to Amazon S3, click **Add Files**. To upload whole folders to Amazon S3, click **Enable Enhanced Uploader (BETA)**, which can take up to 2 minutes as it downloads a Java™ Applet (requires Java SE 7 Update 51 or later). To remove files already selected, click the **X** to the far right of the file name.

📄 Outline.doc (62 KB)   X

⊕ Add Files   ⊖ Remove Selected Files   🔧 Enable Enhanced Uploader (BETA)

Number of files: **1**   Total upload size: **62 KB**

Set Details >   Start Upload   Cancel

FIGURE 2-18:
You can see a list of the files you plan to upload to S3.

10. **Click Start Upload.**

The file IS added to your bucket, as shown in Figure 2-19.

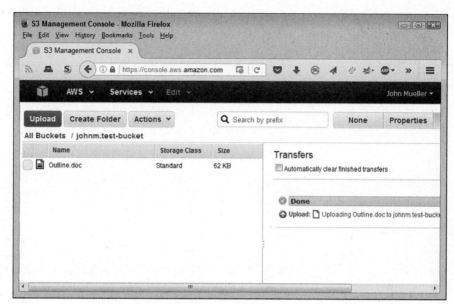

FIGURE 2-19:
The file now appears in your bucket.

11. **Check the box next to the file you uploaded.**

    Your browser displays a dialog box asking what to do with the file. Depending on the browser's capabilities, you can open the file for editing or simply download it to your system.

12. **Click Cancel to close the dialog box without doing anything with the file.**

13. **Choose Actions ⇨ Delete.**

    You see a dialog box asking whether you want to delete the file.

14. **Click OK.**

    S3 deletes the file. Your bucket is now empty again.

    Congratulations! You have now used S3 to perform the first set of tasks for the book.

15. **Choose <*Your Name*> ⇨ Sign Out.**

    AWS logs you out of the console. Logging out when you finish a session is always a good idea.

» Deciding on which services to use

» Overcoming potential security issues

Chapter **3**

Determining Which Services to Use

I n looking at some of the screenshots in Chapter 2, you might have felt instantly overwhelmed by the number of services within Amazon Web Services (AWS). You might also have a tough time deciding which services to use (or even try) because of the way Amazon categorizes them. You could quickly become mired in an exploration of a service that will never help you, wasting some of the 12 months that Amazon gives you as part of the free-tier services to explore. The first part of this chapter, "Getting a Quick Overview of Free-Tier Services," goes through the free-tier services one at a time and helps you better understand how you might employ each one in real-world situations.

Even after you get a better understanding of what task each service performs, you might still find choosing one difficult because some of the services seemingly overlap in functionality. The next section of the chapter, "Choosing the Services You Need," offers insights into how to choose a particular service. You may still have to experiment with more than one service to understand how each one works fully in your particular situation, but at least you'll have some sort of a plan in place to perform the exploration and make a determination in a modicum of time.

Using these services comes with security risks. Anytime you connect your computer to any other computer, the potential for security issues exists. Connecting with computers within your organization is bad enough, but when you start looking outside your organization for services and resources, you invite outsiders to try to break your security. That's why the third section of this chapter, "Considering AWS Security Issues," is so important. It gives you a view of security that no service provider will tell you about — that is, that your systems truly are vulnerable and you must be proactive in protecting them from harm. Keeping data, equipment, and people as safe as possible in a world in which hackers are all too happy to cause problems is a constant struggle, so it pays to be prepared.

Getting a Quick Overview of Free-Tier Services

Chapter 2 discusses specifics concerning the meaning of *free* when it comes to AWS. Some services are always free; some are free for a limited time frame. You must consider the limitations attached to all services, and some free items (such as software) are dependent on services that come with a price. With all these caveats in mind, the following sections discuss the various free services so that you know what tasks each free service performs. The goal is to understand how to potentially use each service to meet specific organizational needs. There isn't a best service for any particular need — just a service that meets your organization's needs best.

Understanding the free services

In looking at the AWS pages, you may have noticed that they don't supply a single list of all the free services. What you get instead are various mixes of services that tell you something about the services but don't really help you understand what services are actually available. Table 3-1 lists the various services and tells you the vital statistics about each one so that you now have a single list of what you can get free.

TABLE 3-1 **Free AWS Service Summary**

Service Name	Description	Non-expiring	Limitations	In Beta
Amazon API Gateway	Allows you to roll your own API for use in applications generated by your own organization or any third party to whom you give access. Developers can create, publish, maintain, monitor, and secure APIs at any scale. The APIs can interact with web applications hosted by your organization or with Amazon services such as Amazon EC2 and AWS Lambda.	No	1 million API calls/month	No

Service Name	Description	Non-expiring	Limitations	In Beta
Amazon AppStream	Delivers Windows applications to any device, including personal computers, tablets, and mobile phones. The application runs in the cloud, so the client platform need not run Windows to use the application. This service lets you integrate custom clients, subscriptions, identity, and storage solutions.	No	20 free hours/month	No
Amazon CloudFront	Defines a Content Delivery Network (CDN) used to send content from Amazon services to end users. This service supports dynamic, static, streaming, and interactive content.	No	50GB Data Transfer Out; 2,000,000 HTTP and HTTPS Requests	No
Amazon CloudWatch	Monitors the AWS cloud resources used by applications that you run on AWS. You can use this service to collect and track metrics, collect and monitor log files, set alarms, and automatically react to changes in your AWS resources. Essentially, this service enables you to track application activity through a variety of methods, such as log files.	Yes	10 Amazon Cloudwatch custom metrics; 10 alarms, 1,000,000 API requests; 5GB log data ingestion; 5GB log data archive; three dashboards with up to 50 metrics each/month	No
Amazon Cognito	Adds user sign-up and sign-in to web and mobile apps. It also allows user authentication using Facebook, Twitter, or Amazon, or a custom authentication solution. The resulting apps can make use of localized data storage when the device is offline, followed by data synchronization when the user reconnects.	Yes	50,000 Monthly Active Users (MAUs); 10GB cloud sync storage/month (12-month trial only) 1,000,000 sync operations/month (12-month trial only)	Yes
Amazon Data Pipeline	Transfers data between the various Amazon services as requested. For example, you can request to move data between services such as Amazon S3, Amazon RDS, Amazon DynamoDB, and Amazon Elastic MapReduce (EMR). This service also lets you transform the data so that the data appears in a form that the receiving service can accept. The focus of this service is on creating data transfer workloads.	No	Three low-frequency preconditions running on AWS/month; five low-frequency activities running on AWS/month	No

(continued)

TABLE 3-1 *(continued)*

Service Name	Description	Non-expiring	Limitations	In Beta
Amazon DynamoDB	Provides access to a NoSQL database service that supports both document and key-value store models. A NoSQL database is a high-speed nonrelational database model that specializes in ease of development, scalable performance, high availability, and resilience.	Yes	25GB storage; 25 units of read capacity; 25 units of write capacity	No
Amazon Elastic Transcoder	Converts (transcodes) media files from one format to another, normally to make the media play on devices such as mobile phones, tablets, and PCs.	Yes	20 minutes of Standard Definition (SD) transcoding or 10 minutes of High Definition (HD) transcoding	No
Amazon ElastiCache	Creates an in-memory data cache that improves application performance by transferring data from a long-term storage service, such as Amazon RDS, to memory. This service supports two open-source, in-memory caching engines: Memcached and Redis.	No	750 hours of Amazon ElastiCache cache/month	No
Amazon Elasticsearch Service	Deploys the open source Elastisearch service, now simply called Elastic (https://www.elastic.co/) to the AWS cloud, where you can use it to perform both search and analysis tasks. Analysis tasks can include checking logs, monitoring applications, and performing clickstream analysis.	No	750 hours/month of a single instance, 10GB/month of optional Elastic Block Store (EBS) storage (magnetic or general purpose)	No
Amazon Mobile Analytics	Measures app usage and revenue, which lets you make data-driven decisions about app monetization and engagement in real time.	Yes	100,000,000 events/month	No
Amazon Relational Database Service (RDS)	Allows storage of data objects as part of a relational database. Amazon RDS currently supports six database engines: Amazon Aurora Oracle Microsoft SQL Server PostgreSQL MySQL MariaDB You can also use any combination of RDS General Purpose (SSD) or Magnetic storage.	No	750 hours of Amazon RDS single instance/month; 20GB of database storage; 10 million I/Os; 20GB of backup storage for automated database backups and DB Snapshots	No

Service Name	Description	Non-expiring	Limitations	In Beta
Amazon Simple Email Service (SES)	Enables you to send transactional email, marketing messages, or other types of high-quality content as email messages. You can use this service to deliver messages to an Amazon S3 bucket, call custom code using an AWS Lambda function, or publish notifications to Amazon SNS.	Yes	62,000 Outbound Messages/month using Amazon SES from an Amazon EC2 instance directly or through AWS Elastic Beanstalk; 1,000 Inbound Messages/month	No
Amazon Simple Notification Service (SNS)	Creates a publication/subscription model for providing notifications to subscribers. You use this service to deliver messages. This service relies on the Amazon Simple Queue Service (SQS).	Yes	1,000,000 Requests; 100,000 HTTP notifications; 1,000 email notifications	No
Amazon Simple Queue Service (SQS)	Provides a fully managed queuing service. Queuing lets you decouple cloud application components so that components need not run at the same time. This service is often used with Amazon Simple Notification Service (SNS).	Yes	1,000,000 Requests	No
Amazon Simple Storage Service (S3)	Allows storage of data objects of any sort in the cloud. The three levels of storage enable you to perform short-term (Standard service), middle tier (Infrequent Access, IA), and long-term storage (Glacier). You can also configure data to the various storage levels based on policies and uses.	No	5GB of Amazon S3 standard storage; 20,000 Get Requests; 2,000 Put Requests	No
Amazon Simple Workflow Service (SWF)	Makes it possible for developers to build, scale, and run applications that have parallel processes and sequential steps in the background.	Yes	1,000 Amazon SWF workflow executions; 10,000 activity tasks, signals, timers, and markers; 30,000 workflow-days	No
AWS CodeCommit	Manages source using host secure and highly scalable private Git repositories. This storage technique works with any file type. You must supply the required Git tools.	Yes	5 active users/month; 50GB of storage/month; 10,000 Get Requests/month	No
AWS CodePipeline	Creates a continuous application update delivery pipeline. You use this service to build, test, and deploy your code based on the release process models you define.	Yes	One active pipeline/month	No

(continued)

TABLE 3-1 *(continued)*

Service Name	Description	Non-expiring	Limitations	In Beta
AWS Device Farm	Performs mobile app testing against real phones and tablets that appear within the cloud. Using this service lets you test your app against a wider assortment of devices to ensure that customers won't encounter problems.	Yes	One-time trial of 250 device minutes	No
AWS IoT	Allows connected devices to interact with cloud applications and other devices. Developers can also use this service to add AWS Lambda, Amazon Kinesis, Amazon S3, Amazon Machine Learning, Amazon DynamoDB, Amazon CloudWatch, AWS CloudTrail, and Amazon Elasticsearch Service support to applications.	No	250,000 messages (published or delivered)/month	Yes
AWS Key Management Service (KMS)	Manages keys used to encrypt data. The service lets you create and control keys using Hardware Security Modules (HSMs). You use this service with a number of other AWS services to provide a secure computing environment.	Yes	20,000 free requests/month	No
AWS Lambda	Runs custom application code without the need for provisioning or managing servers. You upload the code you want to run, and AWS Lambda does everything needed to run and scale your code with high availability.	Yes	1,000,000 free requests/month; 3.2 million seconds of compute time/month	No
Data Transfer	Transfers data between the various Amazon services automatically. For example, if you want to move data from EC2 to S3, you need to pay for the transfer.	No	15GB of bandwidth out aggregated across all AWS services	No
Elastic Compute Cloud (EC2)	Provides access to a web service that offers resizable cloud-based compute capacity. You use this service to access virtual server hosting.	No	750 hours of Windows or Linux platform support/month; 750 hours of an Elastic Load Balancer with 15GB data processing/month; 30GB of Amazon Elastic Block Storage; 500MB/month of Amazon EC2 Container Registry storage	No

REMEMBER

Consider some of the limitations within Table 3-1. For example, the AWS Device Farm service access doesn't expire. However, you get only a one-time free trial of 250 device minutes. This means that if you use five devices, you can test each of the devices for only 50 minutes before the free offer expires. You don't get a monthly allotment with this particular service, so carefully using the time you get is important.

When reviewing the terms of usage for various services, you need to read carefully and ask lots of questions. For example, the overview of Amazon AppStream tells you that you get 20 free hours per month, but that's where the description of what *free* means ends. The 20 free hours apply to the total of applications and devices you're using. For example, if you have four applications to run on five devices, you have only an hour of free usage per month, not 20 free hours as you might initially think.

WARNING

Some of the services will also seemingly appear out of the nowhere when you get an invoice for the services you used. For example, AWS Data Transfer entries will appear anytime you need to transfer data from one service to another. These transfers occur in the background, so you may not even realize that they're happening (see `https://forums.aws.amazon.com/thread.jspa?threadID=78446` for an explanation of one such instance). The blog post at `https://blog.cloudability.com/aws-data-transfer-costs-what-they-are-and-how-to-minimize-them/` tells you how you can minimize these costs. In addition, the blog post helps you understand how the costs are tiered based on where the move takes place, such as between regions.

Working with the online labs

People learn differently. For some people, structured, hands-on activities beat reading or experimenting when it comes to learning something new. Even if hands-on activities aren't a first choice, having multiple learning-activity types tends to reinforce new skills and make them easier to retain. That's why an online lab, such as quikLABS (`https://run.qwiklabs.com/`), in which you can obtain structured, hands-on activities , can be so important to getting up to speed quickly. Figure 3-1 shows the main page for this site.

quikLABS takes a gamelike approach to learning. You go on quests to obtain specific new skills. Each time you complete a quest, you get a badge. In this way, the site offers positive feedback to make the learning process easier. You use real Amazon services rather than mockups during the learning phase, so what you learn in quikLABS applies directly to what you need to use AWS.

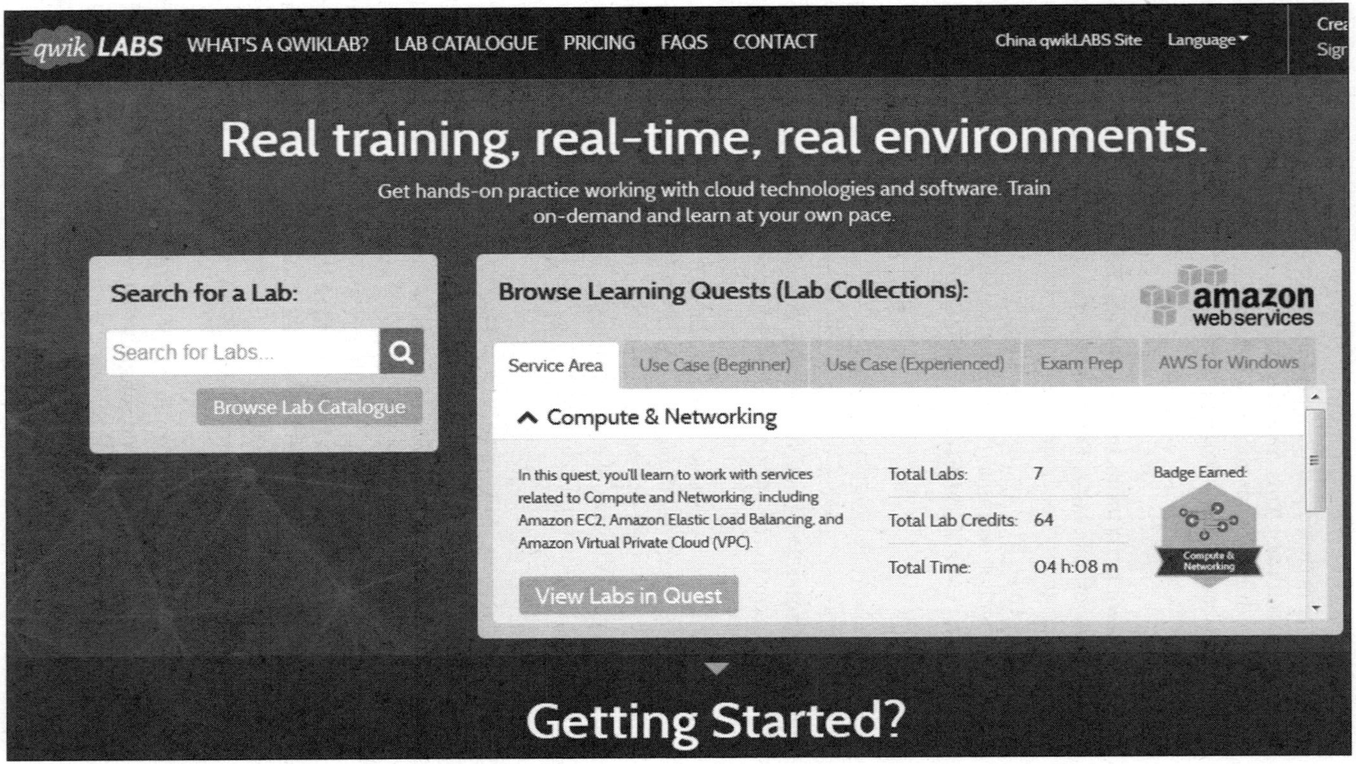

FIGURE 3-1: quikLABS provides you with hands-on activities that help you learn faster.

REMEMBER

As with most games, you need credits to buy services, and the credits cost money. As you can see in Figure 3-1, the Compute & Learning lab costs 64 credits. The pricing guide appears at `https://run.qwiklabs.com/payments/pricing`. The lab catalog (`https://run.qwiklabs.com/lab_catalogue`) gives you a list of each element for each of the quests and the number of credits required to complete that element. Fortunately, you can try before you buy. Check out the free labs at `https://run.qwiklabs.com/#section-5`. Just click View Free Labs to see a complete list of the free labs that you can try.

Choosing a free services path

The best way to start with AWS is to choose a service that you can use as a stand-alone service so that you have to deal with only a single service to start with. For example, the "Performing a Few Simple Tasks" section of Chapter 2 describes how to work with S3. Because of how S3 works, you can use it as a stand-alone product. Later, you can use S3 with other products, but during the initial learning stage, S3 makes an excellent service to try. Think about it this way: You really need to discover how to use the tools that go with the services, and learning about the tools is a lot easier when you don't have to juggle so many services.

The next step is to use a stand-alone service that can interact with a lot of other services and that you'll likely need to know about to perform tasks of any complexity level. For example, many AWS services rely on EC2, so it's a good idea to make EC2 the next step after you work with S3 for a while. S3 is relatively simple; EC2 is a step up in complexity and helps you see how AWS tools work in more detail. Chapter 4 gets you started with EC2 and helps you explore some of its more interesting features.

After you've spent enough time working with a single application and you understand how the AWS console works better, you can move on to another service, such as Lambda (see Chapter 6). When working with Lambda, you must associate the function you create with another service, such as S3. At this point, you begin seeing how services interact. Because you've already spent time obtaining the skills required to use the console, you won't find juggling multiple services quite as hard as if you had jumped right into Lambda use.

REMEMBER

Some simpler services, such as Elastic Beanstalk (see Chapter 5), are free, but they don't appear in Table 3-1 because they include hidden costs. In this case, you don't pay for the service, but you do pay for the resources that the service uses. Elastic Beanstalk is always free, but the resources you store will always cost you something, so you need to keep these kinds of issues in mind as you work through the discovery phase of your AWS planning. Interestingly enough, Elastic Beanstalk is actually one of the easier services to use because you upload your application directly from the Integrated Development Environment (IDE), such as Visual Studio or Eclipse, used to build the application. As an administrator, you need to be aware of when updates occur and how they affect your AWS setup.

Considering the eventual need for paid services

At some point, you need to consider the fact that you'll have to pay for services you need to use AWS effectively. Yes, you can perform a considerable amount of careful testing before payment becomes necessary, but eventually you'll have to pay for something. What this means is planning for the services that you must pay for in advance so that you don't suddenly find yourself buried in debt during the discovery phase of your AWS adventure. There are some of the ways in which you might find yourself paying for services without realizing it, such as when the free service time expires. Table 3-1 shows which services expire after 12 months.

WARNING

Amazon has a tendency not to tell you about any service costs — those costs just suddenly appear on your credit card statement. The following steps help prevent this scenario from happening:

1. **Choose My Account ⇨ Account Settings and log into the system if necessary.**

    You see the Billing Management Console shown in Figure 3-2 (my personal information is blocked out of the figure, but you'll see your personal information).

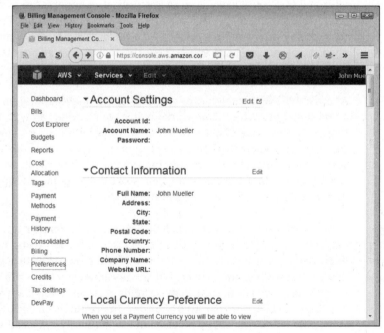

FIGURE 3-2:
The Billing Management Console lets you manage settings for your AWS account.

2. Click Preferences on the left side of the browser window.

You see a list of billing information preferences, as shown in Figure 3-3.

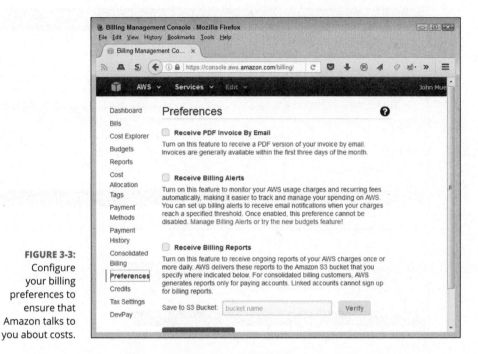

FIGURE 3-3:
Configure your billing preferences to ensure that Amazon talks to you about costs.

3. Select Receive Billing Alerts and then click Save Preferences.

4. Click Manage Billing Alerts.

Halfway down the page, you see the Alarm Summary section, shown in Figure 3-4.

5. Choose Metrics\Billing on the left side of the display.

You see the metrics shown in Figure 3-5. Notice that you can choose various metrics to monitor. For example, you could choose to monitor the charges with specific services instead of all the charges. This example assumes that you want to monitor all the charges.

6. Select USD under Billing > Total Estimated Charge (refer to Figure 3-5).

7. Click Create Alarm.

You see the Create Alarm dialog box, shown in Figure 3-6. Use the fields in this dialog box to determine the level at which you get informed about charges and the email address used to inform you.

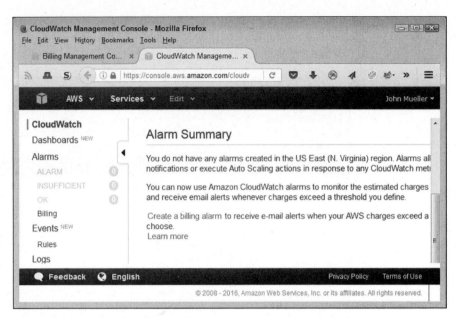

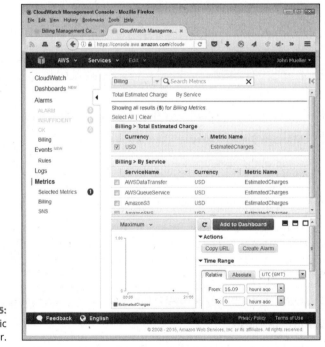

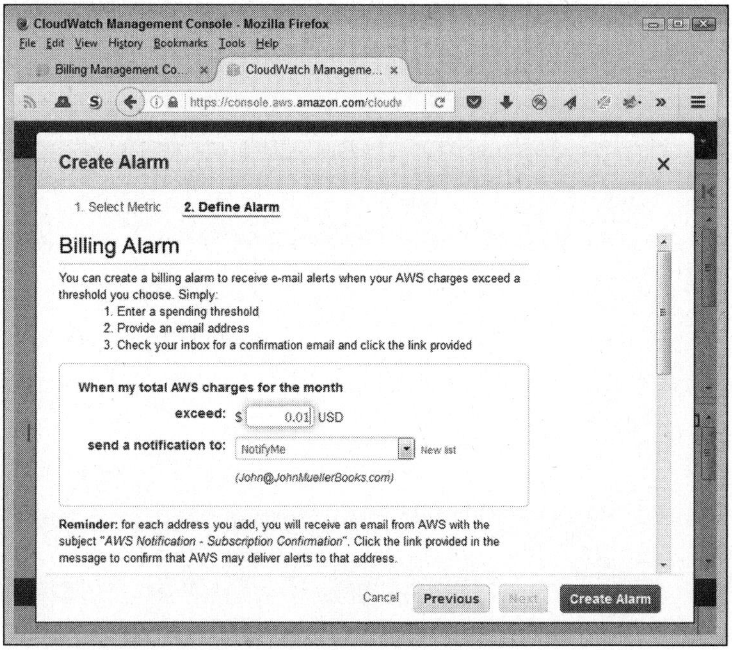

FIGURE 3-6:
Provide the
information
needed to create
the alarm.

8. Enter an amount in the Exceed field.

Entering a value of 0.01 ensures that you get alerts whenever Amazon adds a charge to your account. (You know about the charge after Amazon adds it, but knowing about the charge lets you make changes so that you don't keep accumulating additional charges.)

9. (Optional) Type an email address or select a group in the Send a Notification To field.

Using the default NotifyMe option sends the notification to the person who owns the account.

10. Click Create Alarm.

In most cases, you see the Confirm New Email Address dialog box shown in Figure 3-7. The alarm isn't active until you confirm the email address, but you don't have to do so immediately. If you don't confirm the email address in 72 hours, Amazon cancels the alarm. During the testing phase for this book, the notification didn't appear immediately, so you need to be patient.

11. Confirm the email.

Amazon begins notifying you whenever it charges your credit card for any amount exceeding the threshold you set. To verify that the alarm is set, choose Alarms\OK. You should see the alarm with a blank Config Status field (showing that you confirmed the alarm).

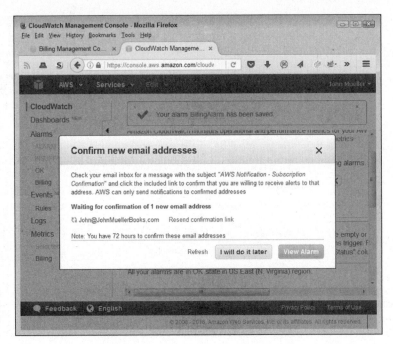

FIGURE 3-7:
Confirm the
email address
you want to use.

You must explicitly close your account when you finish using it. To close your account, choose My Account ⇨ Account Settings. Log in to the system, if necessary. At the bottom of the first page you see is a Close Account section. Click Close Account if you're certain that you're done using AWS. The same page has a Cancel Services section, in which you can cancel services you no longer need. This is a good option to use if you come to the end of the 12-month free usage period and decide you want to continue working with services that don't have an expiration date.

Choosing the Services You Need

Now that you understand what the services do, you need to start making choices about which services to try. Remember that you have only 12 months in which to make decisions about which services to use in your business. Twelve months may seem like a lot of time, but you'll find that it evaporates before your eyes as you try to juggle your day-to-day responsibilities, meetings, and other needs. In short, making a good decision on what to try during the limited time you have is essential. You may ultimately decide that AWS won't meet your needs at all (as unlikely as that might seem, given all that AWS has to offer).

TIP

Focusing on the important issues during the trial period is the key to making AWS work for you. When thinking about AWS, you must consider these issues:

>> **Cost:** Determine whether AWS will perform the task for less money.

>> **Speed:** Decide whether the speed penalty of using the cloud outweighs the benefits.

>> **Reliability:** Ascertain the risk of using the cloud versus keeping the task in-house (the cloud may actually prove more reliable).

>> **Security:** Define the security requirements for your application and then decide whether the risk of using the cloud is acceptable.

>> **Privacy:** Specify the application's privacy requirements (especially the legal ones). Enduring a privacy breach when the data is housed on someone else's system can prove hard to manage and cause permanent damage to a company's reputation.

>> **Flexibility:** Consider whether the use of a cloud service will reduce flexibility to the point at which the application becomes unmanageable. In most cases, relying on the cloud reduces flexibility because the host reserves some configuration opportunities for in-house use only.

After you determine that using AWS poses acceptable risks and provides benefits to offset any negatives, you need to determine precisely which services to use. You may find that you can't support some services because of legal or speed requirements, even if you have a cost incentive for using those services. Work through the services one at a time before you begin experimenting; doing so will save time that you can use to better test the services that will meet your needs.

Considering AWS Security Issues

The most secure computer in the world has no inputs whatsoever. Of course, this super-secure computer also has no real-world purpose because computers without inputs are useless. An individual-use computer, one without connections to any other computer, is the next most secure type. A computer whose connections exist only within a workgroup comes in next, and so on. The least secure computer is the one with outside connections. To use AWS, you must risk the security of your computer in a major way. Administrators and security professionals can quickly drive themselves crazy trying to keep these interconnected computers safe, but that's part of the job description. The following sections present some security issues that are specific to AWS.

A single section of a book can't present you with a complete security picture regarding the use of web services. In addition to the material presented in the following sections, you must also follow best practices in securing the computer systems, the data they contain, your local network, and any third-party products you use. In addition, you must consider user training and the fact that users undoubtedly forget everything you tell them the second they leave the classroom, so diligent oversight is required. In short, the following sections present a small part of a much larger security picture.

Understanding the Amazon view of security

Given that even the best efforts on the part of any vendor will likely provide only moderate security, the vendor should maintain a proactive stance on security. Amazon does spend a good deal of time trying to track and fix known security issues with its APIs, but it also realizes that some vulnerabilities are likely to escape notice, which is where you come into play. Amazon has a stated policy of encouraging your input on any vulnerabilities you find, as described at `https://aws.amazon.com/security/vulnerability-reporting/`.

Be sure to read Amazon's evaluation process. The process leaves room for Amazon to pass the blame for an issue onto a third party, or do nothing at all. Even though Amazon is proactive, you need to realize that you may still find vulnerabilities *that Amazon does nothing to fix*. As a result, security for AWS will always prove less than perfect, which means you also need to maintain a strong, proactive security stance and not depend on Amazon to do it all. The most important thing you can do when working with a cloud service vendor such as Amazon is to continue monitoring your own systems for any sign of unexpected activity.

Getting the expert view of security

As you work through your plan for using AWS to support your organization's IT needs, you need to read more than the Amazon view of issues such as security. Expecting Amazon to tell you about every potential security issue isn't unreasonable — it's just that Amazon deals with only those issues that it has proof are real. To get the full security story, you must rely on third-party experts, which means that you have to spend time locating this information online (a visit to my blog at `http://blog.johnmuellerbooks.com` will help in this regard, because I provide updates about issues, such as security, that affect my books).

A recent story serves to illustrate that Amazon is less than forthcoming about every security issue (see `http://www.bankinfosecurity.com/crypto-keys-stolen-from-amazon-cloud-a-8581/op-1`). In this case, white-hat hackers have managed to hack into a third party's EC2 instance from another instance. After gaining access to the third-party instance, the researchers were able to steal the security keys for that instance. Amazon is unlikely to tell you about this sort of research, so you need discover it yourself.

REMEMBER

The problem with many of these stories is that the trade press tends to sensationalize them — making them appear worse than they really are. You need to balance what you know about your organization's setup, what Amazon has actually reported about known security issues, and what the trade press has published about suspected security issues when determining the security risks of using AWS as your cloud solution. As part of your planning process, you also need to consider what other cloud vendors provide in the way of security. The bottom line is that using the cloud will never be as secure as keeping your IT in-house because more connections always spell more opportunities for someone to hack your setup.

Discovering the reality of Amazon security

The previous two sections discuss what Amazon is willing to admit when it comes to security and what researchers are trying to convince you is the actual state of security for AWS. These two opposing views are critical to your planning process, but you also need to consider real-world experiences as part of the mix. The security researchers at Worcester Polytechnic Institute created a condition under which AWS could fail. However, it hasn't actually failed in this way in the real world. The way in which AWS *has* actually failed is with its backup solutions.

The story at http://arstechnica.com/security/2014/06/aws-console-breach-leads-to-demise-of-service-with-proven-backup-plan/ tells of a company that is no longer operational. It failed when someone compromised its EC2 instance. This isn't a contrived experiment — it happened in the real world, and the hackers involved did real damage, so this is the sort of story to give greater credence to when you plan your use of AWS.

Another story (see http://gizmodo.com/security-hell-private-medical-data-of-over-1-5-million-1731548110) relates how unexpected data dumps on AWS made third-party information available. In this case, the data included personal information garnered from police injury reports, drug tests, detailed doctor visit notes, and social security numbers. Given the implications of this data breach, the organizations involved could be liable for both criminal and civil charges. When working with AWS, you must temper the need to save money now with the need to spend more money later defending yourself against a lawsuit.

Employing AWS security best practices

Amazon does provide you with a set of security best practices and it's a good idea for you to read the associated white paper as part of your security planning process. The white paper is at `https://aws.amazon.com/whitepapers/aws-security-best-practices/`. The information you get will help you understand how to configure your setup to maximize security from the Amazon perspective, but as the previous sections show, even a great configuration may not be enough to protect your data. Yes, you should ensure that your setup follows Amazon's best practices, but you also need to have plans in place for the inevitable data breach. This statement may seem negative, but when it comes to security, you must always assume the worst-case scenario and prepare strategies for handling it.

Configuring a Virtual Server

Chapter **4**

Creating a Virtual Server Using EC2

After looking through the various services that Amazon Web Services (AWS) has to offer, you might scratch your head in trying to figure out where to go first. Even though Chapter 2 starts with a Sample Storage Service (S3) example, the most commonly used service is actually Elastic Compute Cloud (EC2). That's because so many other AWS services use EC2 in so many ways. Yes, you also need storage, but the next step is EC2. Of course, before you can do anything, you need to know what EC2 will do for you, which is the purpose of the first section of this chapter.

Chapter 3 provides an overview of AWS security needs — the sort of general information that you need before you can do anything important with AWS. This chapter offers some security specifics for EC2 in the form of the Identity and Access Management (IAM) console. To keep your EC2 installation safe, you must use security best practices in providing access to your service setup. IAM also helps you manage security for all the other services discussed in the book, so this section is a must read.

The next section of this chapter looks at the Elastic Block Store (EBS) service, which is another kind of storage that you can use with EC2 in addition to S3. You need to know about the EBS alternative because you use it in place of S3 at times to gain significant speed or other benefits. This chapter helps you understand how to interact with EBS when using EC2. The information you gain in this chapter also helps you when working with other services.

Configuring EC2 means knowing about images and instances so that you can create these features as needed. Quite possibly, an entire book could be written about EC2 configuration, but this chapter keeps things simple and looks at the easiest method for getting an instance started. After you have your EC2 instance running, you want to connect to it so that you can start performing useful tasks. Fortunately, Amazon provides a number of methods for connecting with EC2, and here again, this chapter looks as the easiest method to use (along with descriptions of some of the other methods).

Getting to Know the Elastic Compute Cloud (EC2)

Consider the meaning of *elastic* in many of the AWS service names. When you see the word *elastic*, you should think of the ability to stretch and contract. All the AWS documentation alludes to this fact, but it often makes the whole process sound quite complicated when it really isn't. Just think about a computer that can stretch when you need more resources and contract when you don't. With AWS, you pay only for the services you actually use, so this capability to stretch and contract is important because it means that your organization can spend less money and still end up with just the right amount of services needed.

REMEMBER

Even though some members of your organization might fixate on the issue of money, the real value behind the term *elastic* is time. Keeping your own equipment right sized is time consuming, especially when you need to downsize. Using EC2 means that you can add or remove computing capacity in just a few minutes, rather than weeks or months. Because new requirements tend to change quickly today, the capability to right size your capacity in minutes is crucial, especially if you really do want that pay raise.

As important as being agile and keeping costs low are to an administrator, another issue is even more important: being able to make the changes without jumping through all sorts of hoops. EC2 provides two common methods for making configuration changes:

>> Manually using the AWS Console

>> Automatically using the AWS Application Programming Interface (API)

Just as you do with your local server, you have choices to make when building an EC2 *instance* (a single session used to perform one or more related tasks). The instance can rely on a specific operating system, such as Linux or Windows. You can also size the instance to provide a small number of services or to act as a cluster of computers for huge computing tasks (and everything in between). AWS bases the instance size on the amount of CPU type, memory, and storage required to perform the tasks you assign to the instance. In fact, you can create optimized instances for tasks that require more resources in the following areas:

» CPU

» Memory

» Storage

» GPU

As the tasks that you assign to an instance change, so can the instance configuration. You can adjust just the memory allocation for an instance or provide more storage when needed. You can also choose a pricing model that makes sense for the kind of instances you create:

» **On Demand:** You pay for what you use.

» **Reserved Instance:** Provides a significantly reduced price in return for a one-time payment based on what you think you might need in the way of service.

» **Spot Instance:** Lets you name the price you want to pay, with the price affecting the level of service you receive.

Autoscaling is an EC2 feature that you use to ensure that your instance automatically changes configuration as the load on it changes. Rather than require someone to manage EC2 constantly, you can allow the instance to make some changes as needed based on the requirements you specify. The metrics you define determine the number and type of instances that EC2 runs. The metrics include standards, such as CPU utilization level, but you can also define custom metrics as needed. A potential problem with autoscaling is that you're also charged for the services you use, which can mean an unexpectedly large bill. Every EC2 feature comes with pros and cons that you must balance when deciding on how to configure your setup.

AWS also provides distinct security features. The use of these security features will become more detailed as the book progresses. However, here is a summary of the security features used with EC2:

» **Virtual Private Cloud (VPC):** Separates every instance running on the physical server from every other instance. Theoretically, no one can access someone else's instance (even though it can happen in the real world (see `https://rhinosecuritylabs.com/2016/02/aws-security-vulnerabilities-and-the-attackers-perspective/` for details on how hackers have broken into EC2 instances in the past).

>> **Network Access Control Lists (ACLs) (Optional):** Acts as a firewall to control both incoming and outgoing requests at the subnet level.

>> **Identity and Access Management (IAM) Users and Permissions:** Controls the level of access granted to individual users and user groups. You can both allow and deny access to specific resources managed by EC2.

>> **Security Groups:** Acts as a firewall to control both incoming and outgoing requests at the instance level. Each instance can have up to five security groups, each of which can have different permissions. This security feature provides finer-grained control over access than Network ACLs, but you must also maintain it for each instance, rather than for the virtual machine as a whole.

>> **Hardware Security Device:** Relies on a hardware-based security device that you install to control security between your on-premises network and the AWS cloud.

WARNING

No amount of security will thwart a determined intruder. Anyone who wants to gain access to your server will find a way to do it no matter how high you build the walls. In addition to great security, you must monitor the system and, by assuming that someone will break in, deal with the intruder as quickly as possible. Providing security keeps the less skilled intruder at bay as well as helps keep essentially honest people honest, but skilled intruders will always find a way in. The severity of these breaches varies, but it can actually cause businesses to fail, as in the case of Code Spaces (see `http://arstechnica.com/security/2014/06/aws-console-breach-leads-to-demise-of-service-with-proven-backup-plan/` for details). A number of security researchers warn that AWS is prone to security lapses (see `http://www.crn.com/news/security/300073621/security-researcher-warns-amazon-web-services-security-prone-to-dangerous-lapses.htm` for details). However, don't assume that other cloud services provide better security. Any time you use external services, you take significant risks as well.

A final consideration is the use of storage. Each instance comes with a specific amount of storage based on the kind of instance you create. If the instance storage doesn't provide the functionality or capacity you need, you can also add Elastic Block Store (EBS) support. The main advantage of using EBS, besides capacity and flexibility, is the capability to define a specific level of storage performance to ensure that your application runs as expected.

PROBLEMS WITH AUTOSCALING

When you read the AWS documentation and get to the part about autoscaling, it sounds as if you won't ever need to worry about the load on your servers. In fact, the text in the documentation is correct, but it has some gaps. For example, the documentation doesn't really address issues like response time and latency. As you scale your AWS configuration up to meet additional demand, you may also find that response time and latency create a problem. The video at https://www.youtube.com/watch?v=Nswo-4ZIXkI is helpful in explaining this issue, but the essence of any scaling scenario is that more virtual machines means more communication between machines, which slows things down. Think about it this way: When a meeting takes place at work, having more people usually means that the meeting goes slower and that you accomplish less because you have more lines of communication to consider.

The problems of autoscaling are made worse in two ways. The first is that working in the cloud tends to be slower than using physical hardware because of the communication distances and the number of layers involved. The second is that autoscaling tends to increase the problem of having too many machines in the communication loop. If you manually scale your setup, you may decide to create a single instance with considerably greater capacity than the initial instance you created. Autoscaling would create a whole bunch of instances of that initial, smaller instance to do the same thing. Automation isn't always the correct way to handle scaling issues, so you need to consider this requirement as part of your EC2 configuration.

Working with the Identity and Access Management (IAM) Console

One of the more basic and prevalent security measures provided by Amazon is IAM. Even though this service appears in this chapter, it isn't solely associated with EC2. You also use this service for other needs:

>> Computing

>> Storage

>> Database

>> Application services

In short, you see a lot of IAM throughout the book because you need to know how to use it with a number of the services. The following sections provide a general overview of IAM, plus some EC2 specifics that you use when working through various procedures in this chapter. For example, the following sections tell you the general principles of working with IAM, which includes interacting with groups, users, and permissions in a manner similar to that used with physical servers that you may have used in the past. However, later chapters contain information about IAM specific to the services in those chapters.

Configuring root access

When you initially create your AWS account, Amazon assigns an identity to the account name and password that you provide as the *root user*. The root user has unrestricted access to all the AWS resources. As you might imagine, this makes the root user account dangerous, because anyone who gains access to it can also access everything your AWS account supports. Because root user access is so dangerous, Amazon recommends that you use it only to create your first administrative user and then lock the root user access so that no one can use it. The root user never goes away; you simply make it nonfunctional unless you really do need it at some point.

To begin this process, you must access the IAM Console at https://console.aws. amazon.com/iam/. You may see a sign-in page for your account when you aren't already signed into AWS. Provide your credentials as needed. After you sign in to your account, the page shown in Figure 4-1 appears.

USING YOUR EXISTING SECURITY

IAM enables you to use your existing security setup as input. For example, you can use the groups, users, permissions, and policies found in your Windows Active Directory setup. However, realize that your localized security setup, which works fine behind a firewall, may be lacking when you're working with systems that are exposed to the Internet in various ways. Anytime you create an outside connection, even if that connection is secured, you increase the risk to your applications and data.

Cloud-based solutions usually benefit from added security measures to ensure that outsiders don't gain inadvertent access to your applications or data. The trade-off of using enhanced security measures for your EC2 setup is increased time investment. Using your existing security setup will most definitely save time and effort for administrators. In addition, having to make security setups in two places, rather than one, can result in access errors that are time consuming and error prone to troubleshoot, so be sure to weigh the benefits against the costs of this solution. In most cases, even if you do choose to use your existing solution, you need to perform a security review to ensure that the existing security will actually protect your applications and data in the new environment.

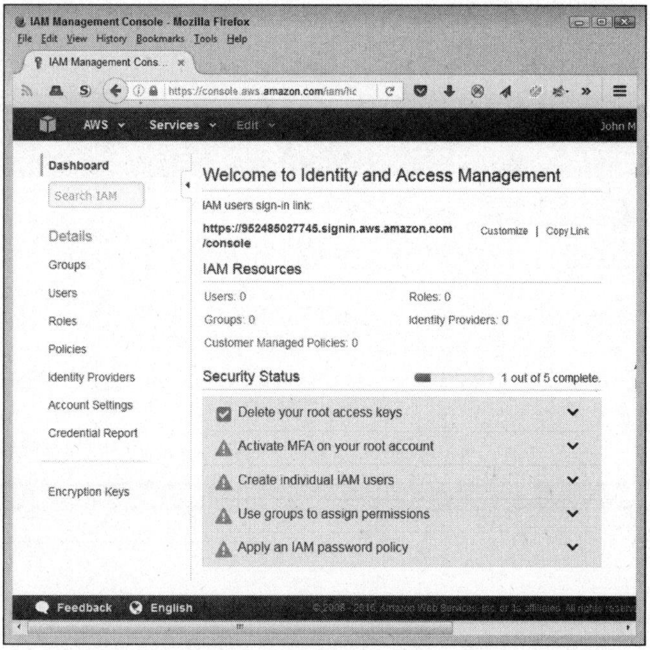

FIGURE 4-1:
Use the IAM Console to perform security-related tasks.

Now that you have access to the IAM Console, you can perform the tasks required to create an administrator account and assign it privileges. The following sections help you accomplish these goals.

You can close the left panel to see more of the selected page by clicking the left-pointing arrow in the tab near the top of the page. When the panel is closed, clicking the right-pointing arrow in the tab reopens it. By closing the panel until you need to use it, you can gain a better view of the task at hand.

TIP

Creating the Administrators group

Before you can create an Administrator user, you must provide a group for it. Every user who can perform administrative tasks is part of the Administrators group. The following steps describe how to perform this task.

1. **Click Groups on the left side (Navigation pane) of the IAM Console page.**

You see the Groups page, shown in Figure 4-2. The page currently lacks any groups because you haven't created any. As you create new groups, the page shows each of them, along with a list of users, the policy associated with the group, and when you created the group.

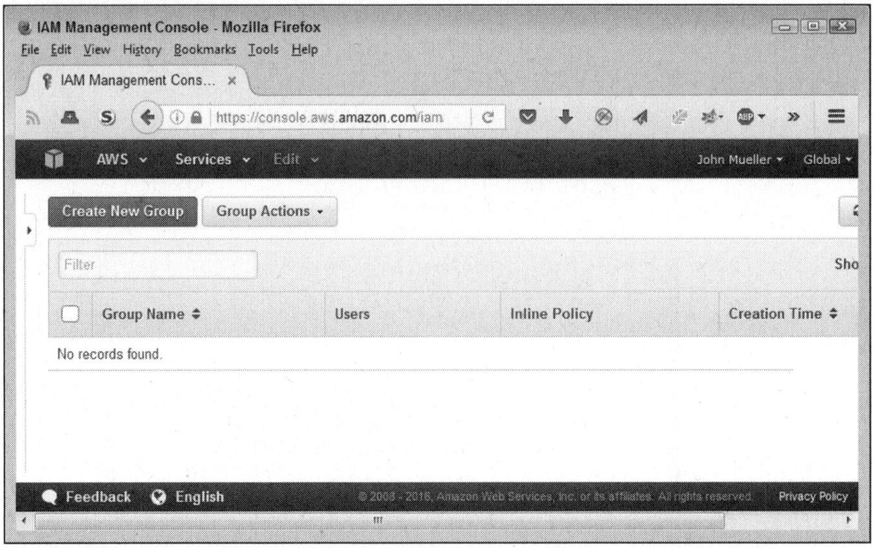

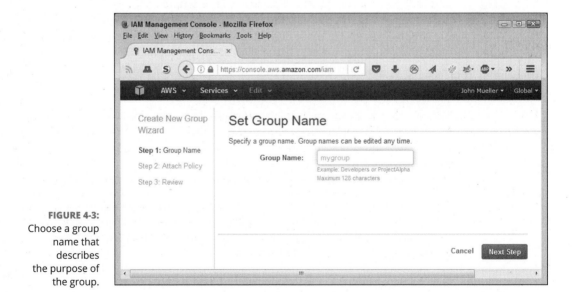

FIGURE 4-2:
The Groups
page shows a
listing of groups
you create.

2. **Click Create New Group.**

You see the Set Group Name page shown in Figure 4-3. You type the name of the group you want to create in the Group Name field. The group name field can support names up to 128 characters long, but you normally don't make them that long. Choose something simple, like Administrators, to describe your group.

FIGURE 4-3:
Choose a group
name that
describes
the purpose of
the group.

3. **Type** Administrators **(or the name of the group you want to create) and click Next Step.**

You see the Attach Policy page, shown in Figure 4-4. Each group can have one or more policies attached to it. In this case, the IAM Console automatically shows the only existing policy, which is AdministratorAccess.

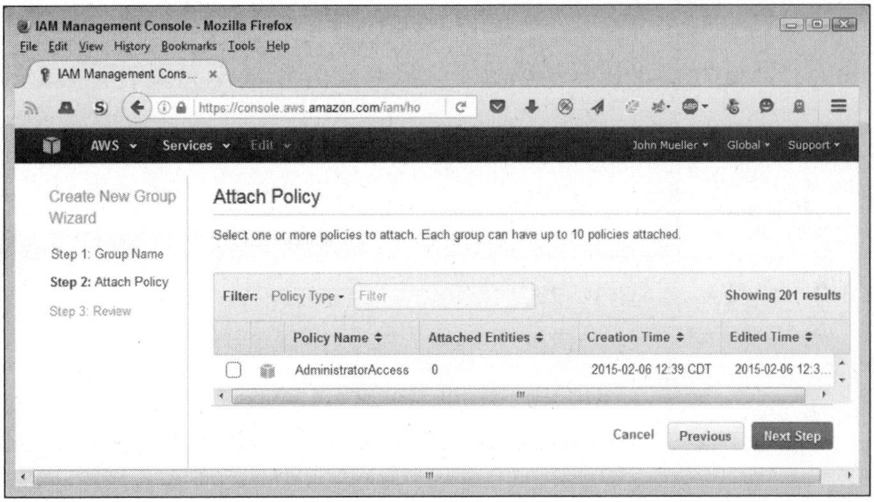

FIGURE 4-4:
Attach a policy that provides the access the group requires.

4. **Check AdministratorAccess and click Next Step.**

You see the Review page, shown in Figure 4-5. This page tells you the group name and shows the policies that are attached to it. If you find that the group name is wrong, click Edit Group Name. Likewise, if the policy is incorrect, click Edit Policies. The IAM Console helps you make required changes to the name or policy.

5. **Verify the group information and click Create Group.**

You see the group added to the Group page (refer to Figure 4-2).

Creating an Administrator user

Creating the Administrators group is the first step in ensuring that your AWS account remains safe. The next step is to create an account for yourself and assign it to the Administrators group so that you have full access to the administrative features of your AWS account. The following steps describe how to perform this task.

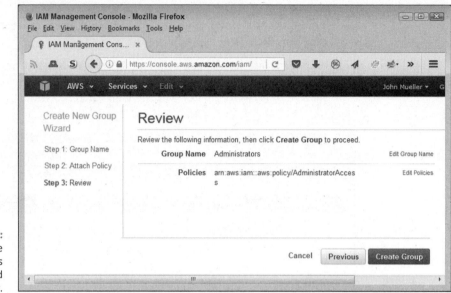

FIGURE 4-5:
Verify that the group is configured properly.

1. **Select Users in the Navigation pane.**

   You see the Users page, shown in Figure 4-6. This page shows all the users who can access the EC2 setup, what level of access they have, password details, access keys, and the time you created the account.

FIGURE 4-6:
The Users page shows a list of users that you create.

2. **Click Create New Users.**

   You see the Create User page, shown in Figure 4-7. You can create up to five new users at a time. Each username can contain up to 64 characters.

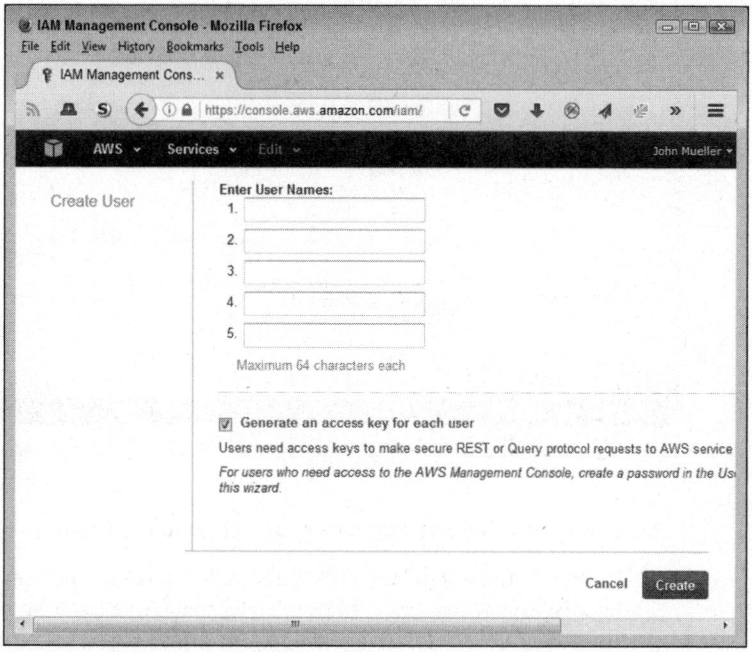

FIGURE 4-7:
The Users page
shows a list
of users that
you create.

3. **Type the username you want to use in field 1, deselect the Generate an Access Key for Each User check box, and click Create.**

   Amazon creates a new user with the name you specify and returns you to the Users page shown previously in Figure 4-6. Your new user account still doesn't belong to the Administrators group, however, so that's the next step in the process.

4. **Click the link associated with the username you specified for the administrator account.**

   You see the user specifics on the Summary page, as shown in Figure 4-8. Notice the tabs at the bottom of the page that you can use to configure the account.

5. **Click Add User to Groups.**

   You see a list of available groups.

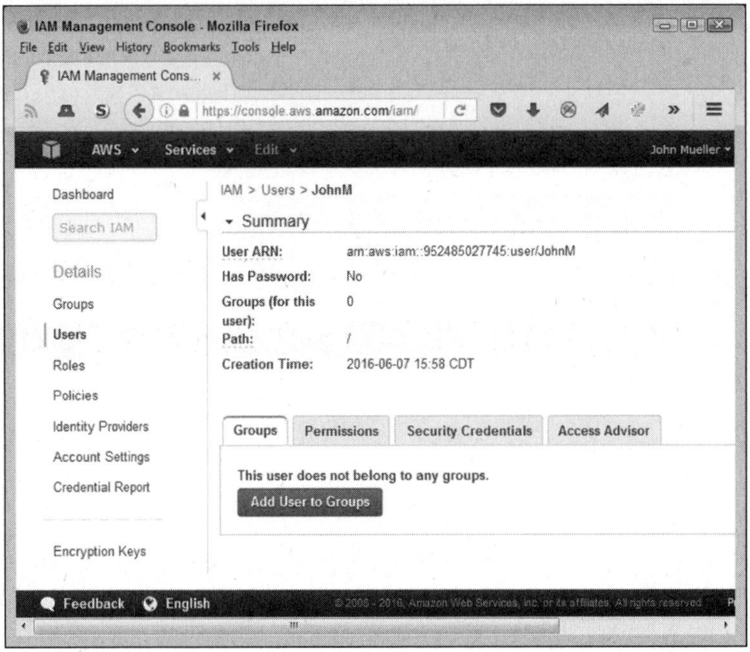

FIGURE 4-8:
Click a user's name entry to see the details for that user.

6. **Check the Administrators entry and click Add to Groups.**

The IAM Console returns you to the Summary page for the user shown in Figure 4-8. However, the Groups tab now shows that the user is part of the Administrators group. Note that you can remove access to a group by clicking the Remove from Group link next to the group entry.

7. **Select the Security Credentials tab of the Summary page.**

You see a number of security entries, including the Sign-In Credentials section, shown in Figure 4-9.

8. **Click Manage Password.**

You see the Manage Password page, shown in Figure 4-10. Note that you can assign an auto-generated password to the account or rely on a custom password. When creating accounts for other users, make sure to check the Require User to Create a New Password at Next Sign-in check box.

9. **Type the same password in the Password and Confirm Password fields and then click Apply.**

The IAM Console returns you to the Summary page, where you see that the user now has a password but hasn't ever used it.

10. **Sign out of your root user account.**

You need to sign back into AWS using the new administrator account that you just created.

FIGURE 4-9:
The Security
Credentials tab
displays the
user's security
information.

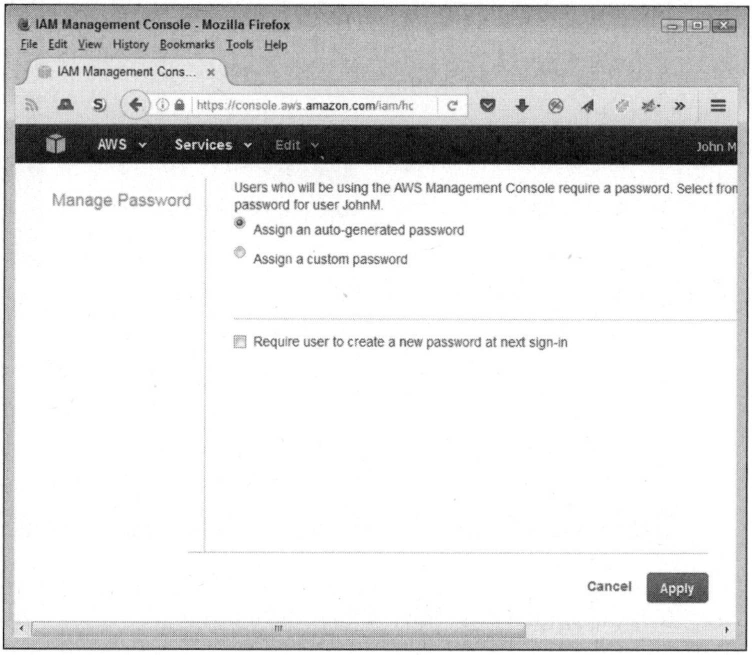

FIGURE 4-10:
Provide the user
with a new
password.

Accessing AWS using your new administrator account

Look again at the top of Figure 4-1, shown previously, to see a sign-in link. The figure shows `https://952485027745.signin.aws.amazon.com/console` as the sign-in link, but your link will be different. To use the new account you just created, you navigate to this URL using your browser. When there, you see a sign-in page like the one shown in Figure 4-11. Notice that the account name is already filled in for you.

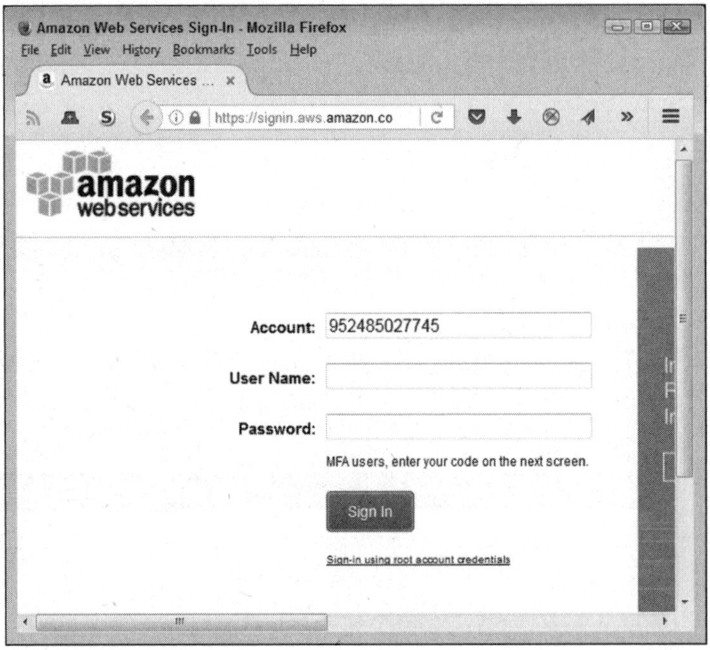

FIGURE 4-11: Your account has a custom sign-in page link associated with it.

Type your username and password into the appropriate fields; then click Sign In. You see the same AWS services as normal, but now you use your administrative account to access them.

Defining permissions and policies

Sometimes it's hard to figure out the whole idea behind permissions and policies. To begin with, a *permission* defines the following:

>> Who can access a resource

>> What actions individuals or groups can perform with the resource

REMEMBER

Every user starts with no permissions at all. In other words, a user can't do anything, not even view security settings or use access keys to interact with a resource. This is a good practice because it means that you can't inadvertently create a user with administrator rights simply because you forget to assign the user specific permissions.

Of course, assigning every user every permission required to perform what amounts to the same tasks is time consuming and error prone. A *policy* is a package of permissions that applies to a certain group of people. For example, in the "Creating the Administrators group" section, earlier in this chapter, you create a group named Administrators and assign the AdministratorAccess policy to it, which gives anyone in the Administrators group administrator-level permissions to perform tasks with AWS. AWS comes with only the AdministratorAccess policy configured, so if you want to use other policies, you must define them yourself.

Fortunately, policies come in several forms to make them easier to work with. The following list describes the policy types and describes how you use them:

>> **Managed:** Stand-alone policies that you can attach to users and groups, but not to resources. A managed policy affects identities only. When creating a managed policy, you use a centralized management page to create, edit, monitor, roll back, and delegate policies. You have access to two kinds of managed policies.

   • **AWS-Managed:** A policy that AWS creates and manages for you. These policies tend to support obvious needs that most organizations have. The reasons to use AWS managed policies are that they're simple to implement and they automatically change to compensate for changes to AWS functionality.

   • **Customer-Managed:** A policy that you create and manage. Use these policies to support any special organizational requirements. The main reason to use a policy of this type is to gain flexibility that the AWS-managed option doesn't provide.

>> **Inline:** Embedded policies that you create and attach to users, groups, or resources on an individual basis (without using a centralized manager). AWS views *identity policies* (those used for users and groups) differently from resource policies as described in the following list:

   • **Embedded User, Group, or Role:** An identity policy that you embed directly into a user, group, or role. You use an identity policy to define the actions that an entity can perform. For example, a user can have permission to run instances of EC2. In some cases, in addition to defining what action a user can take, the policy can also define the specific resource with which the user can work. This additional level of control is a *resource-level permission*, one that defines both the action and the specific resource.

- **Resource:** One or more permissions that determine who can access the resource and what actions they can perform with it. You can add resource-based permissions to Amazon S3 buckets, Amazon Glacier vaults, Amazon SNS topics, Amazon SQS queues, and AWS Key Management Service encryption keys. Unlike policies created for identities, resource-based permissions are unmanaged (inline only).

Creating customer-managed policies

When you initially create your AWS account, only one AWS-managed policy is in place: AdministratorAccess. However, after you create the first user and log in to AWS using your new administrator account, you can access a large number of AWS-managed policies. Whenever possible, you should use the AWS-managed policies to ensure that the policy receives automatic updates that reflect changes in AWS functionality. When using a customer-managed policy, you must perform any required updates manually. The following steps get you started using customer-managed policies.

1. **Sign in to AWS using your administrator account.**

2. **Navigate to the IAM Management Console at** https://console.aws. amazon.com/iam.

3. **Select Policies in the Navigation pane.**

   You see the Welcome to Managed Policies page, shown in Figure 4-12.

4. **Click Get Started.**

   You see a list of available AWS-managed policies, as shown in Figure 4-13. Each of the policy names starts with the word Amazon (to show that it's an AWS-managed policy), followed by the service name (EC2 in the figure), optionally followed by the target of the permission (such as ContainerRegistry), and ending with the kind of permission granted (such as FullAccess). When creating your own customer-managed policies, it's good to follow the same practice to make the names easier to use and consistent with their AWS-managed counterparts.

   Note that the policy list tells you the number of entities attached to a policy so that you know whether a policy is actually in use. You can also see the policy creation time and the time someone last edited it. The symbol on the left side of the policy shows the policy type, which is a stylized cube for AWS-managed policies.

REMEMBER

   Before you create a customer-managed policy, make certain no AWS-managed policy exists that serves the same purpose. Using the AWS-managed policy is simpler, less error prone, and provides automatic updates as needed.

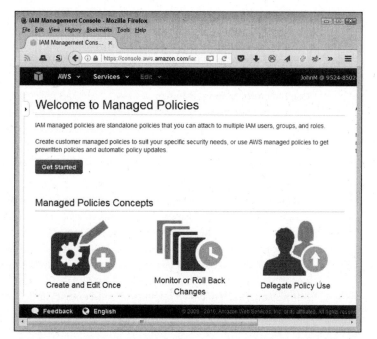

FIGURE 4-12:
The Welcome to Managed Policies page explains the policies' uses and gets you started.

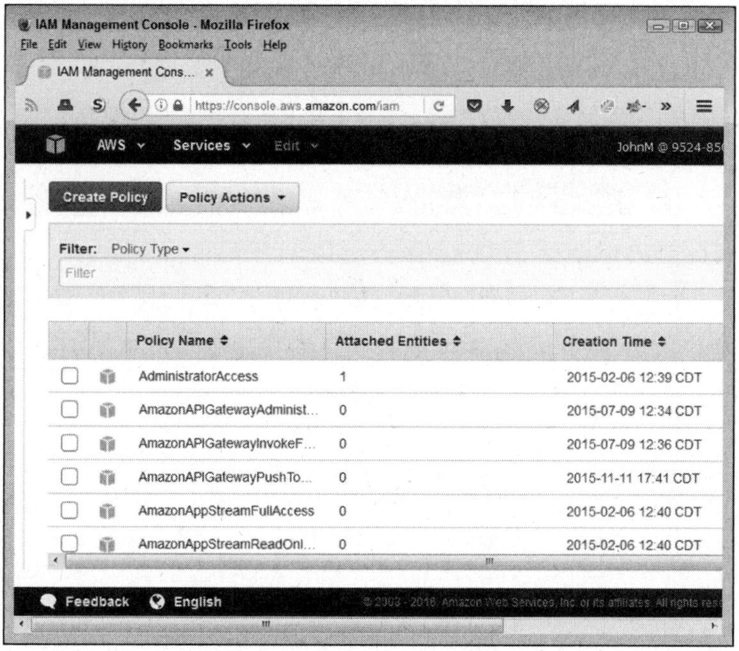

FIGURE 4-13:
The list of AWS-managed policies is relatively long.

5. Click Create Policy.

You see the Create Policy page, shown in Figure 4-14. AWS provides three options for creating a new policy (in order of complexity):

- **Copy an AWS Managed Policy:** An AWS-managed policy acts as a starting point. You then make changes required to customize the policy for your needs. Because this option helps ensure that you create a usable policy and requires the least work, you should use it whenever possible. This example assumes that you copy an existing AWS-managed policy because you follow this route most often.

- **Policy Generator:** Relies on a wizardlike interface to either allow or deny actions against an AWS service. You can assign the permission to specific resources (in some cases) using an Amazon Resource Name, ARN, or to all resources (using an *, asterisk). (The discussion at http://docs.aws. amazon.com/general/latest/gr/aws-arns-and-namespaces.html describes how to create and use ARNs.) A policy can contain multiple permissions, each of which appears as a statement within the policy. After you define policies, the wizard shows you the policy document, which you can edit manually if desired. The wizard uses the policy document to generate the policy. This is the best option to use when you need a single policy to cover multiple services.

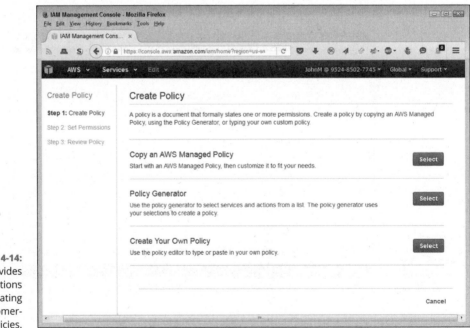

FIGURE 4-14: AWS provides three options for creating customer-managed policies.

- **Create Your Own Policy:** Defines a policy completely by hand. All you see is the policy document page, which you must fill in manually using appropriate syntax and grammar. The discussion at http://docs.aws.amazon.com/IAM/latest/UserGuide/access_policies.html tells you more about how to create a policy completely manually. You use this option only when necessary because the time involved in creating the document is substantial and the potential for error is high.

6. **Click Copy an AWS-Managed Policy.**

   You see a listing of AWS-managed policies, as shown in Figure 4-15.

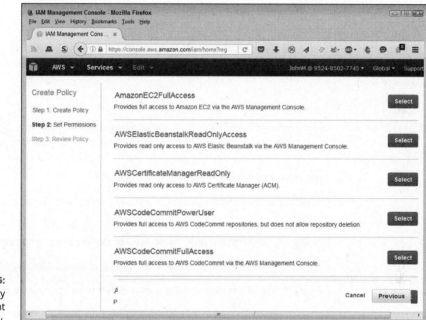

FIGURE 4-15: Choose the policy that you want to modify.

7. **Click Select next to the AWS-Managed policy that you want to use as the basis for your customer-managed policy.**

   The example uses the AmazonEC2FullAccess policy as a starting point, but the same steps apply to modifying other policies. You see the Review Policy page shown in Figure 4-16.

TIP

   Starting with a policy that has too many rights and removing the rights you don't want is significantly easier than starting with a policy that has too few rights and adding the rights you need. Adding rights entails typing new entries into the policy document, which requires a detailed knowledge of policies. Removing rights means highlighting the right statements you don't want and deleting them.

Review Policy

Customize permissions by editing the following policy document. For more information about the access policy language, see Overview of Policies in the *Using IAM* guide. To test the effects of this policy before applying your changes, use the IAM Policy Simulator.

Policy Name

AmazonEC2FullAccess-201606090954

Description

Provides full access to Amazon EC2 via the AWS Management Console.

Policy Document

```
12          "Resource": "*"
13      },
14  {
15          "Effect": "Allow",
16          "Action": "cloudwatch:*",
17          "Resource": "*"
18      },
19  {
20          "Effect": "Allow",
21          "Action": "autoscaling:*",
```

☑ Use autoformatting for policy editing   Cancel | Validate Policy | | Previous | | Create Policy |

FIGURE 4-16: The Review Policy page shows the details about the policy you're modifying.

8. **Type a new name in the Policy Name field.**

   The example uses MyCompanyEC2FullAccessNoCloudWatch as the policy name.

9. **Modify the Description field as needed to define the changes made.**

   The example adds that the policy doesn't allow access to CloudWatch.

10. **Modify the Policy Document field as needed to reflect policy changes.**

    The example removes the following policy section from the document:

    ```
    {
        "Effect": "Allow",
        "Action": "cloudwatch:*",
        "Resource": "*"
    },
    ```

WARNING

Make certain that you add and remove commas between policies as needed, or the policy won't work as expected.

11. **Click Validate Policy.**

    If the changes you made work as intended, you see a This Policy Is Valid success message at the top of the page. Always validate your policy before you create it.

12. **Click Create Policy.**

You see a success message on the Policies page, plus a new entry for your policy, as shown in Figure 4-17. Note that your policy doesn't include a policy type icon. The lack of an icon makes the policy easier to find in the list.

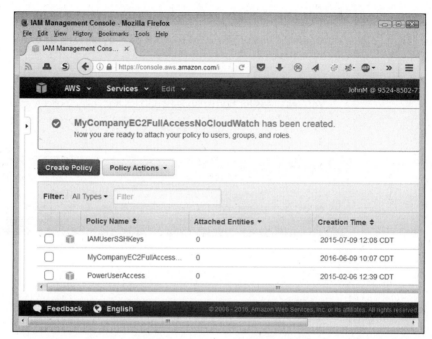

FIGURE 4-17:
AWS tells you when you've successfully added a new policy.

Creating groups

After you create all the policies needed to manage your EC2 setup, you need to create the groups you want to use. The technique for any group you want to create is the same as the one found in the "Creating the Administrators group" section, earlier in this chapter. However, you provide different names for each of your groups and assign the policies that are specific to that group.

Including inline policies

In general, you want to avoid using inline policies because they're hard to manage and you must go to the individual entities, such as groups, to make any required changes. In addition, the inline policies have a tendency to hide, making troubleshooting problems with your setup just that much harder. However, you may encounter situations in which an inline policy offers the only way to set security properly. The following steps help you create inline policies as needed. (This procedure uses an example group named EC2Users, but it works with any entity that supports inline policies.)

1. **Select the Groups, Users, or Roles entry in the Navigation pane.**

2. **Open the entity you want to work with by clicking its entry in the Object Type page.**

3. **Select the Permissions tab of the entity's Summary page.**

    You see areas for both managed policies and inline polices, as shown in Figure 4-18.

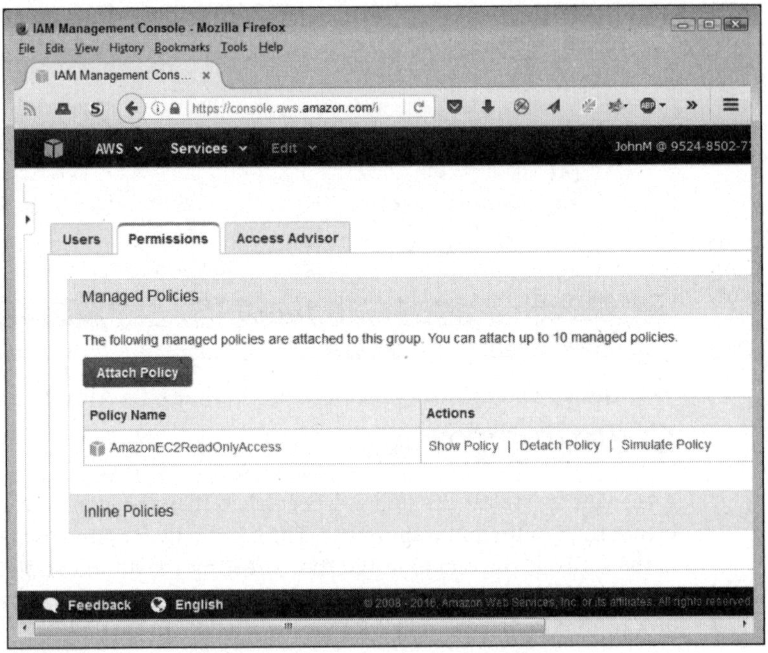

FIGURE 4-18:
The Permissions tab of the Summary page contains the entity's policies.

4. **Click Inline Policies.**

    If this is your first inline policy, you see a message saying "There are no inline policies to show. To create one, click here."

INTERFACES ON VARIOUS DEVICES

Web applications commonly use controls that work well with specific devices to ensure that users don't become frustrated trying to make a feature work. For example, a button that appears in a desktop browser might appear as a link on a tablet or a specialized icon on a smartphone. The procedures in this book (as stated in the Introduction) revolve around the needs of the desktop and notebook user because most administrators currently rely on such systems. Consequently, you see procedures where you're asked to click a button. However, if you choose to use another device, the same control could appear as a link. That's why the procedure also tells you what the button caption says, such as Click Here. When working with a smaller device, you might click the Click Here link or the Click Here icon instead of the Click Here button. Even though the interface differs slightly, the outcome of clicking the control doesn't. You still get to the next step of a wizard or perform some other task as described in the book.

5. **Click the Click Here button.**

   You see a Set Permissions page containing two options:

   - **Policy Generator:** Displays a wizard that lets you easily create a policy for use with your entity. Among the methods for creating an inline policy, this is the easiest.

   - **Custom Policy:** Displays an editor in which you manually type a policy using the appropriate syntax and grammar. This is the more flexible of the two options for creating an inline policy.

6. **Select a permission generation option and then click the Select button next to that entry.**

   The example assumes that you want to use the Policy Generator option. You see the Edit Permissions page, shown in Figure 4-19. This interface enables you to allow or deny actions against a specific AWS service and, optionally, a specific resource associated with that service.

7. **Configure the permission using the various permission entries and then click Add Statement to add the statement to the policy.**

8. **Click Next Step.**

   You see the Review Policy page (refer to Figure 4-16). Because you define the policy using a series of individual permissions, you probably don't need to edit the policy.

9. **Click Validate Policy.**

   If the changes you made work as intended, you see a This Policy Is Valid success message at the top of the page. Always validate your policy before you create it.

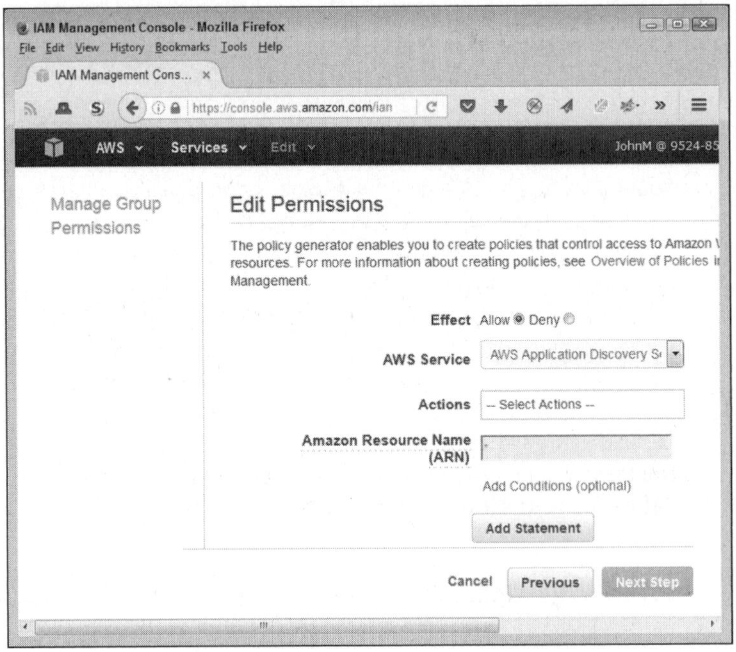

FIGURE 4-19:
The Edit Permissions page provides access to the permission options.

10. **Click Apply Policy.**

You see the policy added to the Inline Policies area of the Permissions tab of the entity's Summary page. In addition, the Inline Policies area now includes a button to create more policies, such as the Create Group Policy entry for groups.

TIP

To interact with an existing inline policy, use the links in the Actions column of the policy list. Here's an overview of the actions you can perform on an inline policy:

» **Show Policy:** Displays the code used to create the policy.

» **Edit Policy:** Lets you edit the code used to create a policy using the Review Policy page (refer to Figure 4-16).

» **Remove Policy:** Deletes the inline policy so that it no longer affects the entity. The deletion is final, so you must make that sure you actually want to delete the policy.

» **Simulate Policy:** Demonstrates the effect of the policy on the entity. You can set up various configurations and testing criteria so that you know that the inline policy works as expected.

Adding users

AWS provides numerous means for automatically generating users. However, the best policy is to ensure that you correctly configure each user from the outset. The procedure found in the "Creating an Administrator user" section, earlier in this chapter, works best for this purpose. Of course, you use a unique name for each user and assign the user to groups as needed. You can also attach managed or inline policies to the user by using the options found on the Permissions tab of the user's Summary page.

Attaching and detaching policies

Instead of attaching or detaching policies for individual entities, you can perform the task on a large scale. The Policies page contains a listing of all the policies you define for your setup, as shown in Figure 4-13.

When you want to attach a policy to one or more entities, select the box next to the policy you want to use and choose Policy Actions ⇨ Attach. You see an Attach Policy page like the one shown in Figure 4-20. Select the check box next to each of the entities that should receive the policy and then click Attach Policy to complete the action.

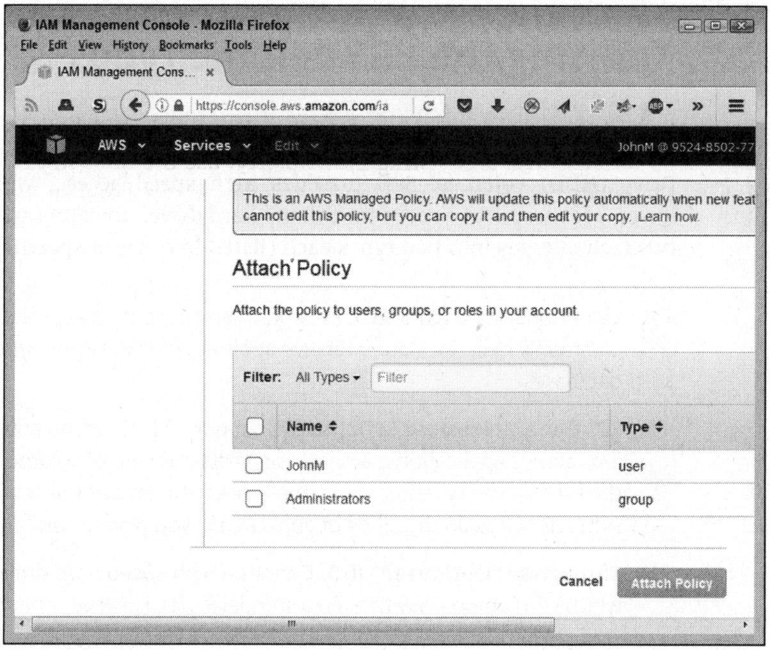

FIGURE 4-20: The Attach Policy page contains a listing of entities that can use the policy.

Likewise, when you want to detach a policy from an entity, select the check box next to the policy you want to use and choose Policy Actions ⇨ Detach. You see a Detach Policy page. Select the check box next to each of the entities that currently have the policy set but no longer need it; then click Detach Policy.

Working with Elastic Block Store (EBS) Volumes

The "Performing a Few Simple Tasks" section of Chapter 2 introduces you to S3, which is an object store. Chapter 7 spends more time with S3, but the most important piece of information to know about S3 now is that it isn't a file system and doesn't act like a hard drive. EBS is more like the hard drives you have in your physical file server. As the name states, EBS is block storage, just like any other hard drive, except that you access it in the cloud. You format the drive, just as you would with a drive in your physical server, and you can mount it to an EC2 instance. Chapter 8 provides more details on how the various Amazon storage options differ, but the main point is that EBS makes your EC2 instance work and act more like a physical server, so it provides the kind of storage that most administrators know. The following sections describe EBS in detail.

Knowing the EBS volume types

Just as there isn't one kind of hard drive, there isn't one kind of EBS volume. Amazon currently provides access to both Solid-State Drive (SSD) and Hard Disk Drive (HDD) volumes. SSD provides high-speed access, while HDD provides lower-cost access of a more traditional hard drive. Amazon further subdivides the two technologies into two types each (listed in order of speed):

>> **EBS Provisioned IOPS SSD:** Provides high-speed data access that you commonly need for data-intensive applications that rely on moderately-sized databases.

>> **EBS General Purpose SSD:** Creates a medium-high-speed environment for low-latency applications. Amazon suggests this kind of volume for your boot drive. However, whether you actually need this amount of speed for your setup depends on the kinds of applications you plan to run.

>> **Throughput Optimized HDD:** Defines a high-speed hard drive environment, which can't compete with even a standard SSD. However, this volume type will work with most common applications and Amazon suggests using it for big data or data warehouse applications. This is probably the best option to

choose when money is an issue and you don't really need the performance that SSD provides.

>> **Cold HDD:** Provides the lowest-speed option that Amazon supports. You use this volume type for data you access less often than data you place on the other volume types (think data you use once a week, rather than once every day). This isn't an archive option; it's more like a low-speed option for items you don't need constantly, such as a picture database.

REMEMBER

As you move toward higher-speed products, you also pay a higher price. For example, at the time of writing, a Cold HDD volume costs only $0.025/GB/month, but an EBS Provisioned SSD volume costs $0.125/GB/month. You can find price and speed comparison details at http://aws.amazon.com/ebs/details/#piops. The table provided contains some interesting statistics. For example, all the volume types top out at 16TB and support a maximum throughput per instance of 800MB/s.

Creating an EBS volume

Before you can use an EBS volume, you must create it. As discussed in previous sections, EBS volumes can take on many different characteristics. The following steps describe how to create a simple volume that you can use with EC2 for the procedures in this book. However, you can use these same steps for creating volumes with other characteristics later.

1. **Sign into AWS using your administrator account.**

2. **Navigate to the EC2 Console at** https://console.aws.amazon.com/ec2/.

    You see the page shown in Figure 4-21. Notice the Navigation pane on the left, which contains options for performing various EC2-related tasks. The Resources area of the main pane tells you the statistics for your EC2 setup, which currently includes just the one security group that you see how to create "Creating the Administrators group" section, earlier in this chapter.

3. **Choose a EC2 setup region from the Region drop-down list at the top of the page.**

    The example uses the Oregon region.

4. **Select Volumes in the Navigation pane.**

    The EC2 Console shows that you don't currently have any volumes defined.

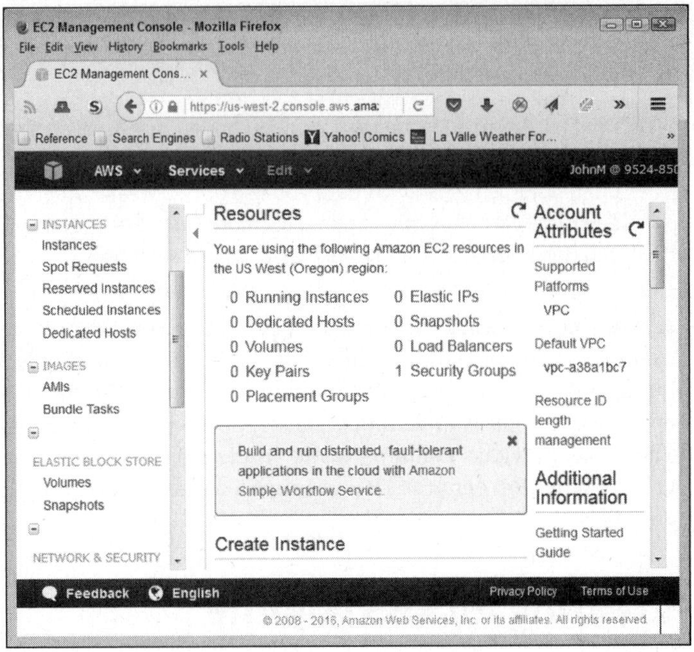

FIGURE 4-21:
The EC2 Console tells you all about your current EC2 configuration.

5. **Click Create Volume.**

   You see the Create Volume dialog box, shown in Figure 4-22. Notice that you can choose a volume type and size, but not the Input/output Operations Per Second (IOPS) or the throughput, which are available only with certain volume types. The Availability Zone field contains the location of the storage, which must match your EC2 setup. The Snapshot ID field contains the name of an S3 storage location to use for incremental backups of your EBS data. You can also choose to encrypt sensitive data, but doing so places some limits on how you can use EBS. For example, you can't use encryption with all EC2 instance types. The discussion at http://docs.aws.amazon.com/AWSEC2/latest/UserGuide/EBSEncryption.html provides additional information about encryption.

6. **Click Create.**

   AWS creates a new volume for you and displays statistics about it, as shown in Figure 4-22. The new volume lacks any sort of backup. The next step configures a snapshot that AWS uses to perform incremental backups of the EBS data, reducing the risk of lost data.

7. **Choose Actions ➪ Create Snapshot.**

   You see the Create Snapshot dialog box, shown in Figure 4-23. Notice that AWS fills in the Volume field for you and determines the need for encryption based on the volume settings.

FIGURE 4-22:
A new volume
displays all
pertinent
statistics, such as
the size and
speed.

8. **Type** EBS.Backup **in the Name field, type** Test Backup **in the Description field, and then click Create.**

You see a dialog box telling you that AWS has started the snapshot.

9. **Click Close.**

The volume is ready to use.

When you finish this example, you can delete the volume you created by selecting its entry in the list and choosing Actions ⇨ Delete Volume. You automatically create the required EBS volume required for your EC2 setup in the "Creating an instance" section, later in this chapter. However, in a real-world setup, you can attach this volume to any EC2 instance or detach it when it's no longer needed.

Discovering Images and Instances

An *Amazon Machine Image (AMI)* is a kind of blueprint. You tell AWS to use an AMI to build an instance. As with blueprints, AWS can use a single AMI to build as many instances as needed for a particular purpose. Every instance created with the AMI is precisely the same from the administrator's perspective. AMI is one of the EC2 features that enable you to autoscale. Amazon uses the AMI to create more instances as needed so that your application continues to run no matter how many people may want to access it.

REMEMBER

You don't have to create an AMI; Amazon provides several default AMIs that you can use. However, if you want to create a custom environment to use with EC2, you need to create your own AMI. This book assumes that you use one of the default AMIs. The following sections show the easiest method for creating an instance using one of Amazon's AMIs.

Before you can use an AMI, you must first create and configure it as described at http://docs.aws.amazon.com/AWSEC2/latest/UserGuide/AMIs.html. In addition, you must register the AMI with AWS. After you've registered it, you can tell AWS to create (launch) instances based on the AMI. A user or application connects to an instance in order to use it, and an administrator can configure an instance to meet particular requirements. You can copy your AMI between regions to help improve overall application speed if you want. To stop using an AMI, you deregister it. With these tasks in mind, the following sections describe how to use the Amazon Management Console to work with EC2 images and instances.

Generating security keys

To access your EC2 instance securely, you need to generate security keys. These keys enable you to be verified as the person logging on to the EC2 instance. The following steps help you create a key pair that you need when creating your instance in the next section:

1. **Select Key Pairs in the Navigation pane.**

   AWS tells you that you don't have any key pairs defined.

2. **Click Create Key Pair.**

   You see a Create Key Pair dialog box that asks for a key pair name.

3. **Type** MyKeyPair **in the Key Pair Name field and click Create.**

   You see a download dialog box for the browser that you use. Be sure to save a copy of the key pair as a Privacy-Enhanced Mail (.pem) file. The article at http://fileformats.archiveteam.org/wiki/PEM tells more about this particular file format.

4. **Save the** .pem **file to disk.**

   The Key Pairs page now shows a key pair named MyKeyPair with all the pertinent information.

Creating an instance

The process for creating an EC2 instance can become quite complex. You can manually create key pairs used to log in to the instance, for example, or create a special security group to help maintain EC2 security. In addition, you can use a custom AMI to configure your instance. The problem is that all these extra steps make what should be a relatively simple process for experimentation purposes quite difficult. With this in mind, the following steps show the easiest, fastest method for creating an EC2 instance. However, keep in mind that you can do a lot more with EC2 setups than described in this chapter. This procedure assumes that you have already logged in and selected the same region used for your EBS volume.

1. **Select Instances in the Navigation pane.**

AWS tells you that you don't have any EC2 instances running.

2. **Click Launch Instance.**

You see a series of AMI entries, as shown in Figure 4-23. Amazon owns all these AMIs. You can also choose to use your own AMI or obtain access to an AMI through the AWS Marketplace or Community.

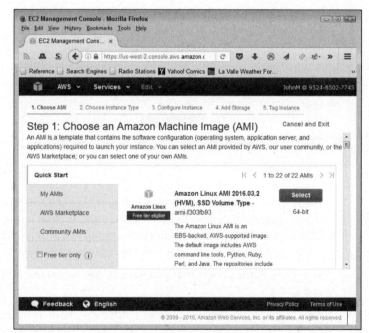

FIGURE 4-23:
To start an instance, you must select one of the available AMIs.

TIP

Note that the first AMI is marked as Free Tier Eligible. Unless you want to pay for using EC2, you must select one of the Free Tier Eligible entries, which include Amazon Linux, Red Hat Linux, SUSE Linux, Ubuntu Linux, and Windows Server (all in various versions). To ensure that you don't accidentally choose a paid option, select the Free Tier Only check box on the left side of the page.

3. **Click Select next to the Amazon Linux AMI 2016 entry.**

   You see a listing of instance types, as shown in Figure 4-24. One of the instance types is marked Free Tier Eligible. You must choose this option unless you want to pay for your EC2 instance.

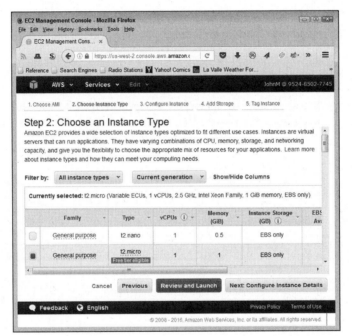

FIGURE 4-24:
Choose the kind of instance you want to create.

REMEMBER

Choosing to configure the instance details or change storage requirements will create a new instance type. The new instance type won't be free-tier eligible. You can view the various configuration options available, but click Cancel instead of creating the instance if you want to continue working with AWS free of charge.

4. **Select the instance type that you want to create and then click Review and Launch.**

   You see the Step 7: Review Instance Launch page, shown in Figure 4-25. The figure shows the Security Groups section. When you create your instance, Amazon warns you that anyone can access it. Given that you probably want to work with EC2 privately, you must modify the security group settings to reduce the risk of prying eyes.

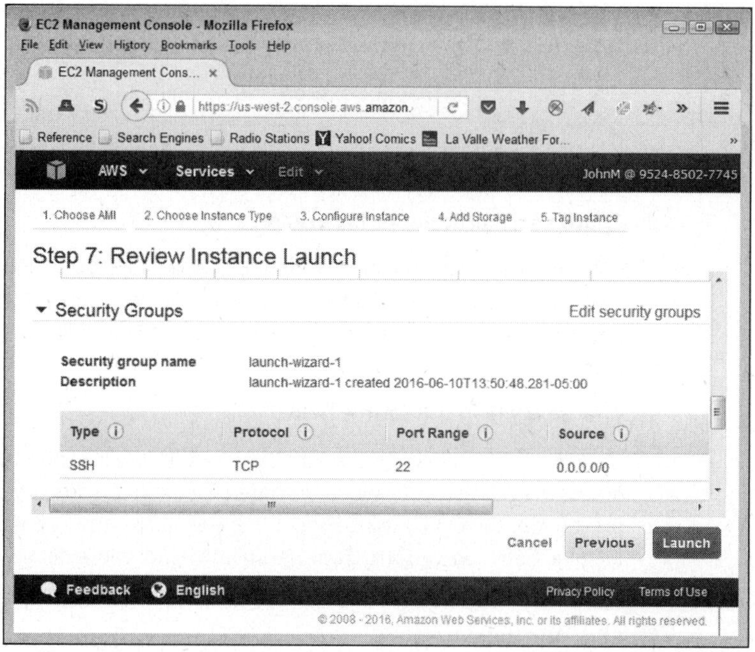

FIGURE 4-25:
Review the
instance
configuration
before you
launch it.

5. **Click Edit Security Groups.**

You see the Step 6: Configure Security Group page, shown in Figure 4-26.

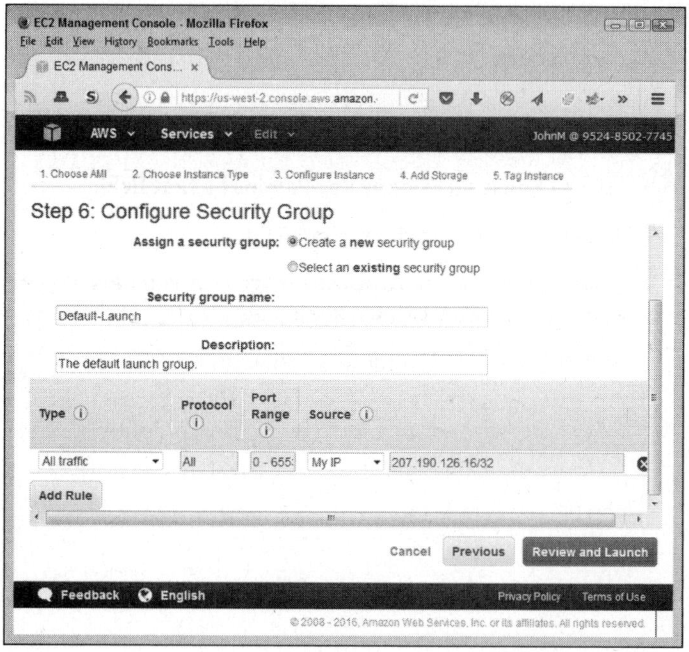

FIGURE 4-26:
Create a new,
more secure
security group for
your EC2 setup.

6. **Type** Default-Launch **in the Security Group Name field.**

   Use a group name that's both short and meaningful to avoid potential confusion later.

7. **(Optional) Type a group description in the Description field.**

8. **Choose All Traffic in the Type field.**

   Using this option gives you maximum EC2 access. However, in a real-world setup, you limit the Type field entries to just the protocols you actually plan to use. For example, if you don't plan to use Secure Shell (SSH) to interact with EC2, don't include it in the list of allowed protocols.

9. **Choose My IP in the Source field.**

   By limiting the access to just your IP, you reduce the likelihood that anyone will access the EC2 setup. However, intruders can find all sorts of ways around this precaution, such as by using IP spoofing (see `http://searchsecurity.techtarget.com/definition/IP-spoofing` for more details about this technique).

10. **Click Add Rule.**

    AWS adds the rule to the list. Click the X next to the new rule that AWS automatically generates in some cases to remove it — you don't need it.

11. **Click Review and Launch.**

    The EC2 Management console takes you back to the Step 7: Review Instance Launch page, shown in Figure 4-25.

12. **Click Launch.**

    You see a Select an Existing Key Pair or Create a New Key Pair dialog box, as shown in Figure 4-27.

13. **Select Choose an Existing Key Pair in the first field.**

14. **Select MyKeyPair in the second field.**

15. **Select the check box to acknowledge that you have access to the private key and then click Launch Instances.**

    AWS starts your EC2 instance, as shown in Figure 4-28.

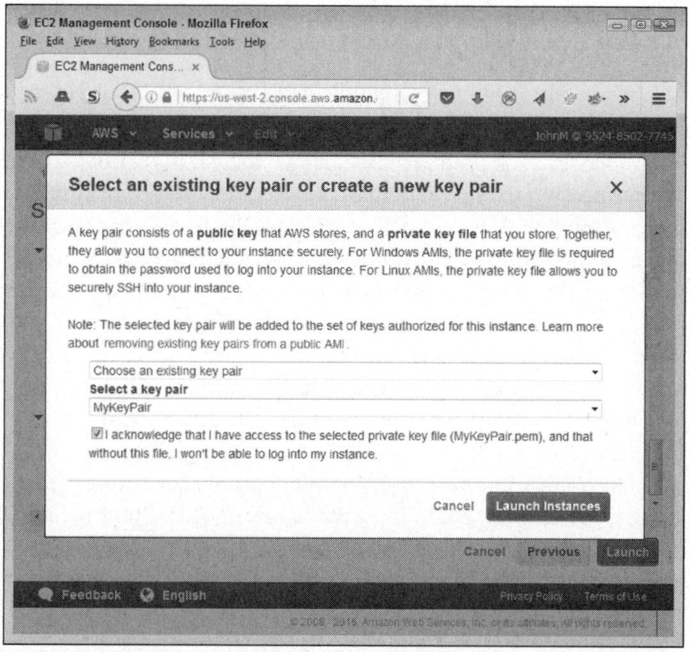

FIGURE 4-27:
Choose the key
pair that you
want to use.

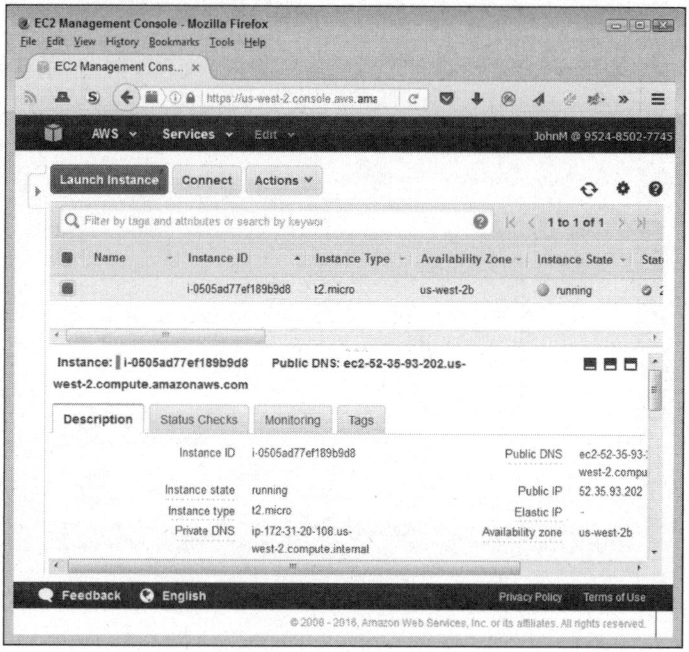

FIGURE 4-28:
Verify that your
instance is
running before
you attempt to
connect to it.

Connecting to the instance

You have all sorts of options for connecting to your instance. For example, Windows users have the option of using PuTTY (see `http://www.chiark. greenend.org.uk/~sgtatham/putty/` for details). However, the easiest method for connecting to your instance is to use the Connect button found on the Instances page, shown in Figure 4-28. Unfortunately, to use this option, your browser must support Java and you must have Java enabled. Because of security concerns, some browsers no longer support Java or create significant hurdles to using Java. If you have Java configured to start only with permission, you must provide the required permission when asked. If you truly don't want to work with Java, you can find additional, platform-specific options at `https://docs.aws.amazon. com/AWSEC2/latest/UserGuide/AccessingInstances.html`.

After you click Connect, you see two options for connecting to your instance, as shown in Figure 4-29. Using a Stand-alone SSH Client means installing a product such as PuTTY on your system. If you want the simple method, select the second option, A Java SSH Client Directly from My Browser (Java Required).

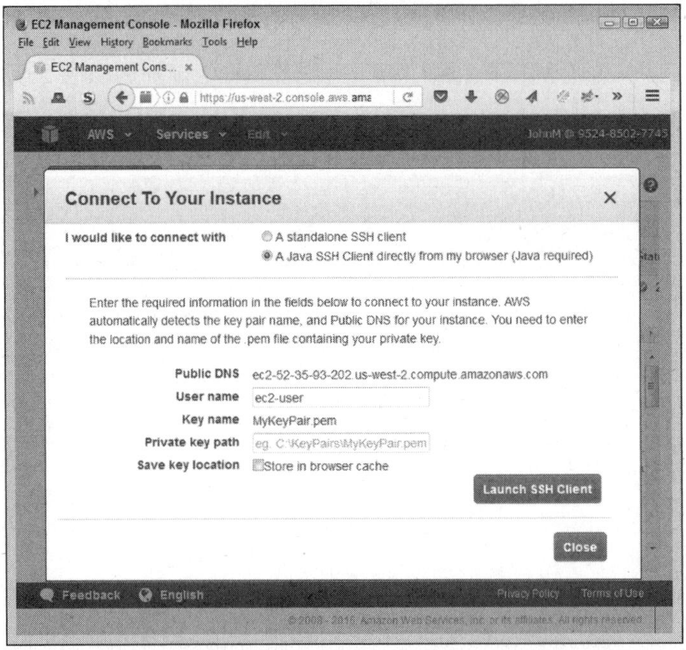

FIGURE 4-29:
Using a Java client is the easiest connection method.

You must supply the location of the key pair file on your hard drive in the Private Key Path field. After you supply this information, click Launch SSH Client. If this is the first time you use this feature, some warning messages appear and then the client installs on your system. After initialization, you see an SSH client similar to the one shown in Figure 4-30, and you can interact with your EC2 setup through this client.

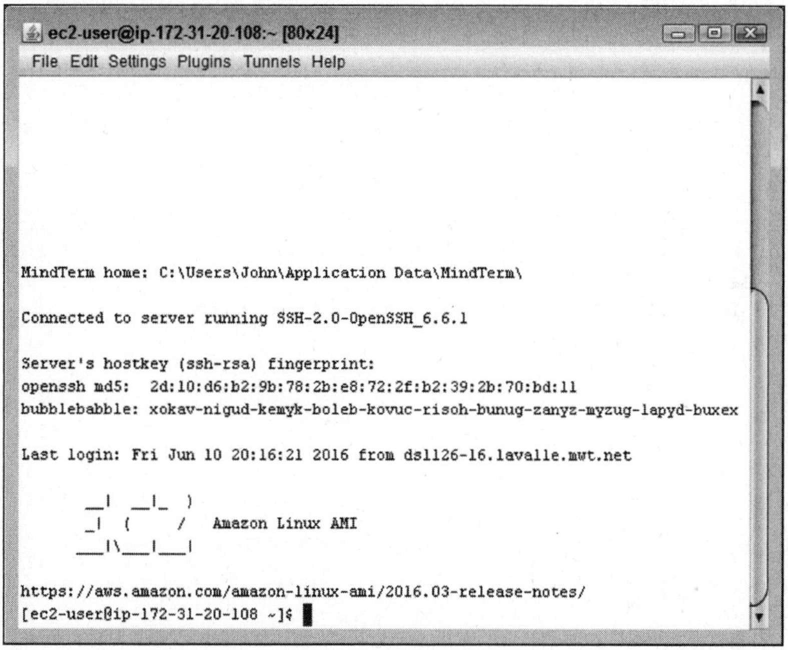

FIGURE 4-30: After you connect, you can begin working with your EC2 instance.

To prove to yourself that you really have connected to EC2, start a copy of Python by typing **Python** at the prompt and pressing Enter. A copy of Python starts and displays its version number. To exit Python, type **quit()** and press Enter. Type **exit** and press Enter to end the EC2 session. Choose File ⇨ Close to close the SSH client terminal.

Chapter **5**

Managing Web Apps Using Elastic Beanstalk

At one time, developers created desktop applications to harness the power and flexibility that desktop systems can provide. In many situations, developers still need this power and flexibility, but more and more application development occurs on the web. The reasons for this change are many, but they all come down to convenience. Users want to use applications that can run on any device, anywhere, and in the same way. To make this happen, developers use web applications that run in a browser or a browser-like environment, which is where Elastic Beanstalk (EB) comes into play. Using EB enables developers to create applications that run anywhere on any device, yet don't suffer from problems of reliability and scalability that can occur when using a company-owned host. Relying on the cloud makes things easier for administrators as well, because now it they can tweak an application configuration from anywhere. The first section of this chapter explores how EB makes moving applications to the cloud easier for everyone involved.

As administrators, you need to know how to install EB applications. This chapter doesn't show how to write any applications, but it does take you through the process of installing one. In addition, it discusses the requirements for making updates and getting rid of applications after you finish using them. These three tasks are an essential part of using EB, even if you plan to keep the application private to your organization.

Whether your application is public or private, you likely want to monitor it. This chapter shows how to use native EB functionality to perform the task. By using the EB monitoring features, you can integrate all your application activities using a single interface and ensure tight integration between the monitoring software and the application.

REMEMBER

There is no charge for EB. However, Amazon does charge for resources that your application uses (see the pricing information at `https://aws.amazon.com/elasticbeanstalk/pricing/`), so you need to exercise care when working through the examples in this chapter. In addition, some of the supplementary services discussed in this chapter, such as Amazon CloudWatch, also come with hidden costs. Make sure that you understand the pricing strategies for services, such as Amazon CloudWatch (`https://aws.amazon.com/cloudwatch/pricing/`) before you work through the examples. In addition, configuring your setup to provide email notifications of any charges is a good idea, as described in the "Considering the eventual need for paid services" section of Chapter 3.

Considering Elastic Beanstalk (EB) Features

A focus of EB is to easily be able to upload, configure, and manage applications of all sorts. An application isn't useful unless people can access it with ease and make it perform whatever tasks it's designed to perform in the most seamless manner possible. Achieving these goals requires that the hosting platform support various programming methodologies on a variety of platforms so that developers can use the tools most suited to a particular need. When working with AWS, you currently can create web applications (in the easiest-to-access form that's currently available) using these languages (with more to follow):

>> Java

>> .NET

>> PHP

>> Node.js

>> Python

>> Ruby

>> Go

>> Docker

The applications run in managed containers for the language you choose. A *managed container* is one in which the host manages application resources and ensures that the application can't easily crash the system. The container acts as a shield between the application you're working with and every other application that the system hosts.

Developers may create the applications, but administrators must manage them. To make administrators as efficient as possible, a host must support a number of platforms. Matching the language (to meet developer needs) with a platform (to meet administrator needs) on a host can prove difficult, but EB is up to the task because it provides support for these web application platforms:

>> Apache

>> Nginx

>> Passenger

>> IIS

In looking through the EB documentation, you may initially get the idea that this service is designed to meet developer needs — to simplify application deployment and management in a way that allows a developer more time to code. However, administrators need more time, too. The management features provided by EB address the needs of administrator and developer alike. This chapter focuses almost entirely on the administrator view of EB. The three cornerstones of EB application are the following:

>> **Deployment:** Getting the application onto the server so that someone can use it

>> **Management:** Configuring the application as people find problems using it

>> **Scaling:** Providing a good application experience for everyone by ensuring that the application runs fast, reliably, and without any security issues

As part of this whole picture, EB also relies on application health monitoring through Amazon CloudWatch. The Amazon CloudWatch service provides the means for determining when application health issues require the host to make changes in the application environment, such as by using autoscaling to make sure that the application has enough resources to run properly.

Deploying an EB Application

Before you can use your EB application, you must *deploy* it (make it accessible) on a server. Deployment means:

1. Creating an application entry.

2. Uploading the application to Amazon. You perform this step as part of creating the application entry.

3. Configuring the application so that it runs as anticipated, which is also part of creating the application entry on the first pass, but you can also change the configuration later.

4. Configuring the application environment so that it has access to required resources. You perform the initial setup while creating the application entry, but you make configuration changes later based on the results of monitoring that you perform.

5. Testing the application to determine whether it works as anticipated.

REMEMBER

EB comes with no additional charge; however, you must pay for any resources that your application uses. Be sure to keep this fact in mind as you work through the chapter. The examples don't require much in the way of resources, but you do need to pay for them, which means that you may need permission to install the applications before you proceed. The chapter structure is such that you can simply follow along with the text if desired. The following sections describe how to deploy an EB application.

Creating the application entry

Before you do anything else, you need to define an application entry in order to run an application using EB. The application entry acts as a sort of container for holding the application. The following steps describe how to create the application entry:

1. **Sign in to AWS using your administrator account.**

2. **Navigate to the Elastic Beanstalk Console at** `https://console.aws.amazon.com/elasticbeanstalk`.

   You see a Welcome page that contains interesting information about Elastic Beanstalk and provides links to additional information and sample applications.

3. **Click Create New Application.**

You see the Application Information page, shown in Figure 5-1. You need to provide an application name (identity) and, optionally, describe it.

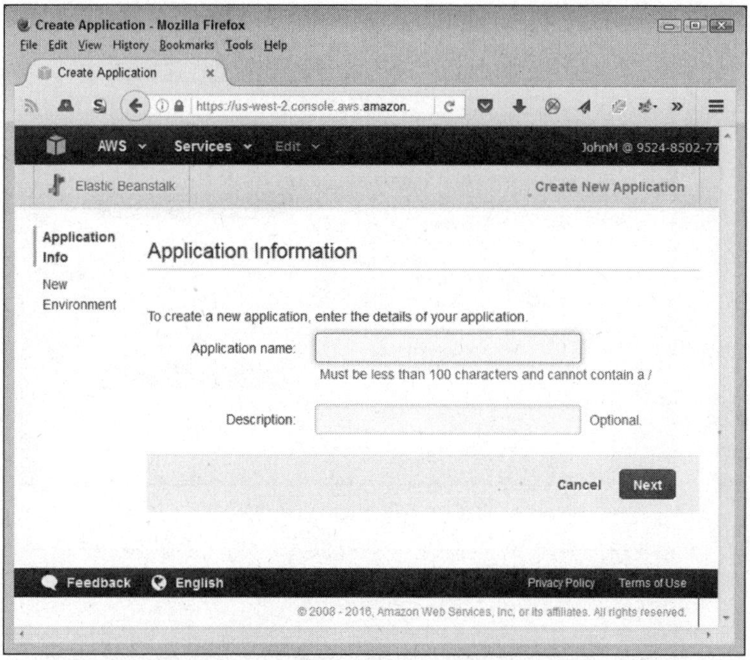

FIGURE 5-1:
Identify your application and describe it.

4. **Type** TestApp **in the Application Name field, type** A test application. **in the Description field, and then click Next.**

You see the New Environment page shown in Figure 5-2. EB provides two default environments:

- **Web Server Environment:** Lets you run web applications using any of the languages that support web development.

- **Worker Environment:** Creates a background application that you can call on in a variety of ways. Background applications don't provide user interfaces, so you normally use this option to create support for another application.

5. **Click Create Web Server.**

EB asks you to configure the environment type, as shown in Figure 5-3. The Preconfigured Configuration field contains a listing of languages that you can use. The Environment Type field defines how to run the application: single instance or using both load balancing and autoscaling.

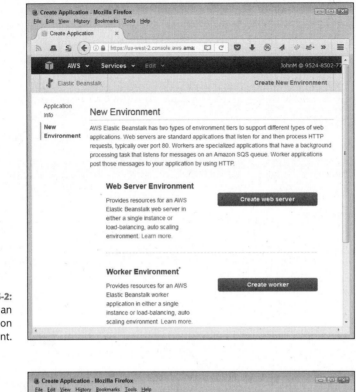

FIGURE 5-2:
Choose an
application
environment.

FIGURE 5-3:
Define the
application
environment
type.

6. **Choose PHP in the Preconfigured Configuration field, choose Single Instance in the Environment Type field, and then click Next.**

You see options for an application source, as shown in Figure 5-4. Normally you upload your own application or rely on an application defined as part of a Sample Storage Service (S3) setup. However, because this is an example, the next step will ask you to use a sample application. Working with sample applications makes experimenting easier because you know that nothing is wrong with the application code to cause a failure.

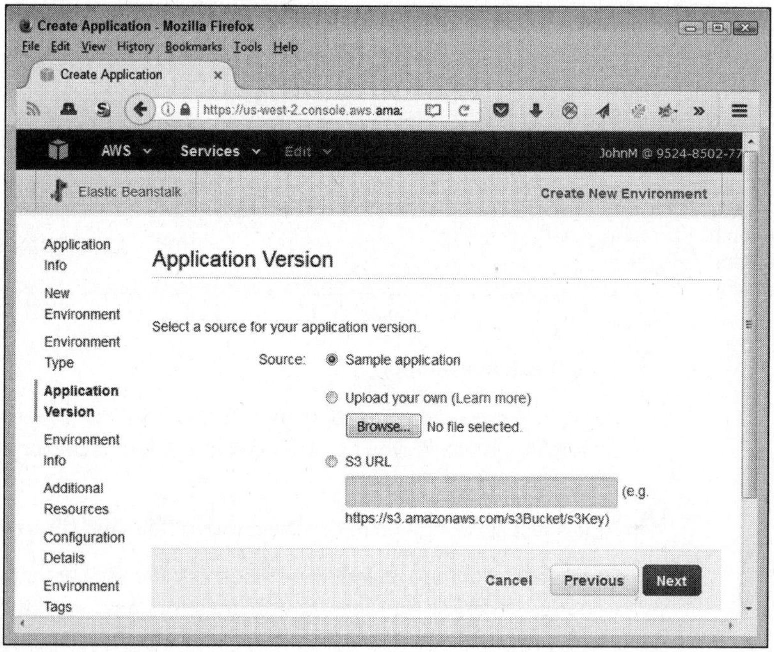

FIGURE 5-4: Specify the source of the application code.

7. **Select the Sample Application option and click Next.**

EB displays the Environment Information page, shown in Figure 5-5. You must create a unique environment name for your application.

8. **Type** MyCompany-TestEnv **in the Environment Name field.**

Note that EB automatically provides an Environment URL field value for you. In most cases, you want to keep that URL to ensure that the URL will work properly. The Environment URL field automatically provides the location of your EC2 instances to run the web application, so normally you won't need to change this value, either.

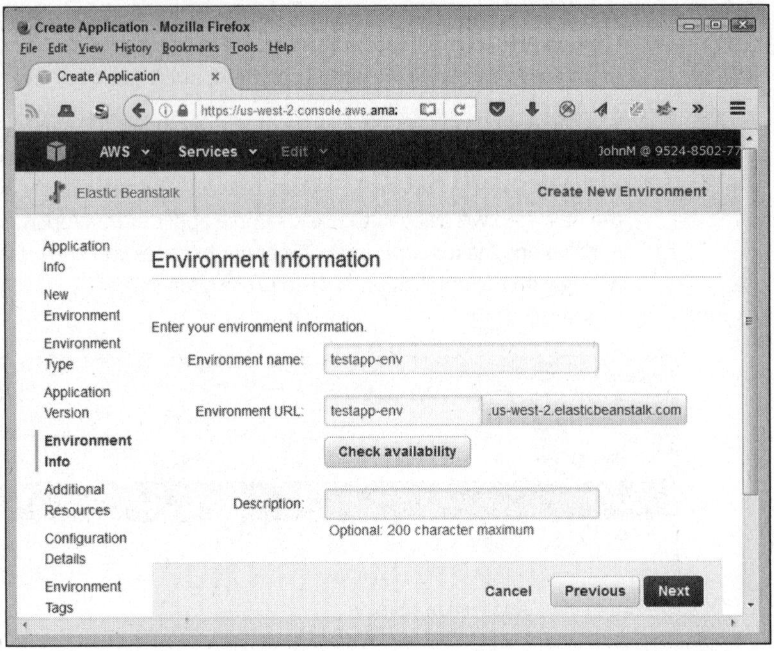

FIGURE 5-5:
Provide a name for the application environment.

9. **Click Check Availability.**

   The square around the Environment URL field changes to green if the check is successful. Otherwise, you need to provide a different Environment Name field entry.

10. **Type** A test environment. **in the Description field and then click Next.**

    EB asks about the use of additional resources. Remember that additional resources generally incur fees, so keep these options blank when working with a test application. The RDS DB option creates a link to a database to use with the application. The VPC option creates a Virtual Private Cloud (VPC) to run the application.

11. **Click Next.**

    At this point, you need to define the configuration details, shown in Figure 5-6. The options you use depend on how you want to run the application. However, the steps tell you how to maintain a free setup. Using other Instance Type field settings could incur costs.

12. **Choose t2.micro in the Instance Type field and the key pair (defined in the "Generating security keys" section of Chapter 4) that you want to use.**

13. **(Optional) Type your email address in the Email Address field.**

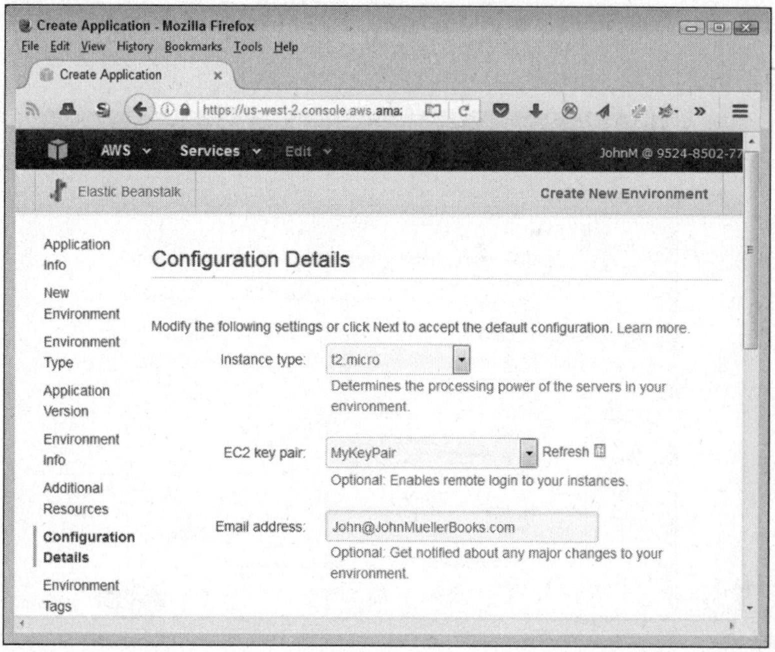

FIGURE 5-6:
Specify the instance environment for running the application.

14. **Choose Basic in the System Type field (Health Reporting section) and then click Next.**

EB asks whether you want to define Environment Tags. These are key value pairs used to help configure your application. The sample application doesn't require any tags.

15. **Click Next.**

The Permissions page contains options for creating or using permissions. The test setup doesn't contain any permissions, so you won't see any options in the Instance Profile or Service Role fields. If you had already defined another application, these fields would allow you to reuse those existing permissions. EB creates a set of default permissions for you, which you can later modify as needed.

16. **Click Next.**

You see a Review page that contains all the settings made so far in the procedure. Check the settings to ensure that you made the entries correctly.

17. **Click Launch.**

You see EB launching your application, as shown in Figure 5-7. Be patient: This process can require several minutes to complete.

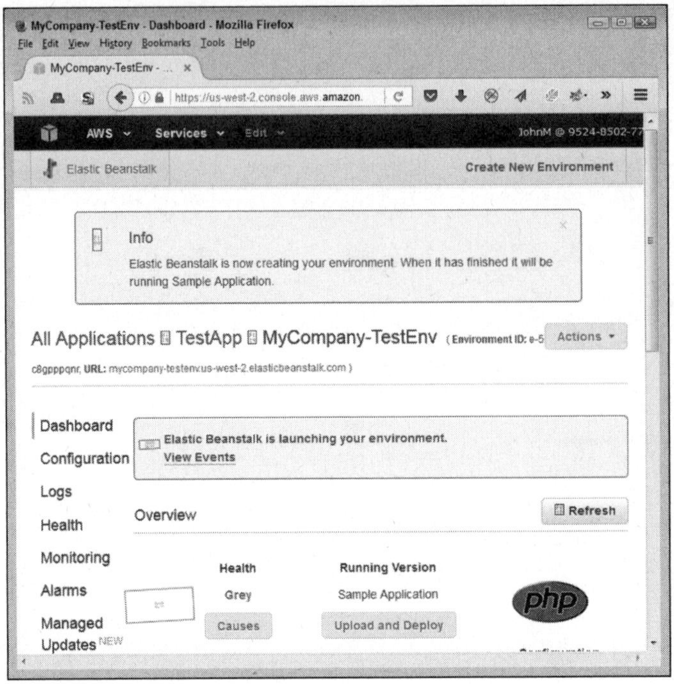

FIGURE 5-7:
Wait for the
application
to deploy.

You can find some sample applications at http://docs.aws.amazon.com/ elasticbeanstalk/latest/dg/RelatedResources.html. All you need to do is download the application and then use it as part of following the exercises in this section and the sections that follow. The sample applications cover a number of the languages and platforms, but not all of them. If you download an application and install it using the techniques found in this chapter, you must also pay for resources that the application requires to run.

TIP

Testing the application deployment

After you complete the steps in the previous section of the chapter, you have an application running. Look again at Figure 5-7, shown in the previous section, to see the URL field entry near the top of the page. (It's in really small print, so you might have to look hard to see it.) Click this link to see your application running. The sample PHP application displays the page shown in Figure 5-8.

Setting application security

Any code you deploy using EB becomes immediately public at the URL provided in the URL field unless you change the security rules. This means that you really do need to verify that the page is safe to display before you deploy it. However, you can also make the page private using the following steps.

1. **Choose Services ⇨ EC2 from the menu at the top of the page.**

   You see the EC2 Dashboard page.

2. **Choose Security Groups from the Navigation pane.**

   EC2 displays a list of security groups, as shown in Figure 5-9. The selected
   security group in the figure is the one used with EB. If you followed the
   procedure in the "Creating the application entry" section, earlier in this chapter,
   you should see a security group with a similar name.

3. **Select the security group entry for EB configuration and choose
   Actions ⇨ Edit Inbound Rules.**

   EC2 displays the Edit Inbound Rules dialog box, shown in Figure 5-10. You can
   change any configuration option for the security group that will modify the way
   in which incoming requests work. For example, you can change the HTTP type
   to HTTPS to create secure access to the page. However, in this case, you can
   use a simpler method to secure access to the page in a reasonable way: Simply
   disallow access from sources other than your system.

4. **Choose My IP in the Source field for both HTTP and SSH access of the
   security group.**

   EC2 modifies the rules as expected.

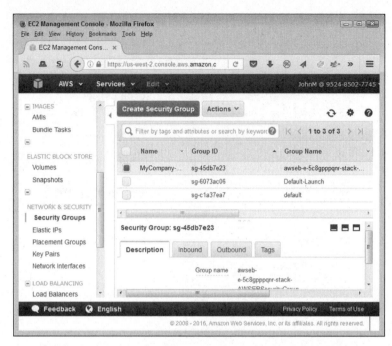

FIGURE 5-9:
The EC2 security groups contain the security group used to configure EB.

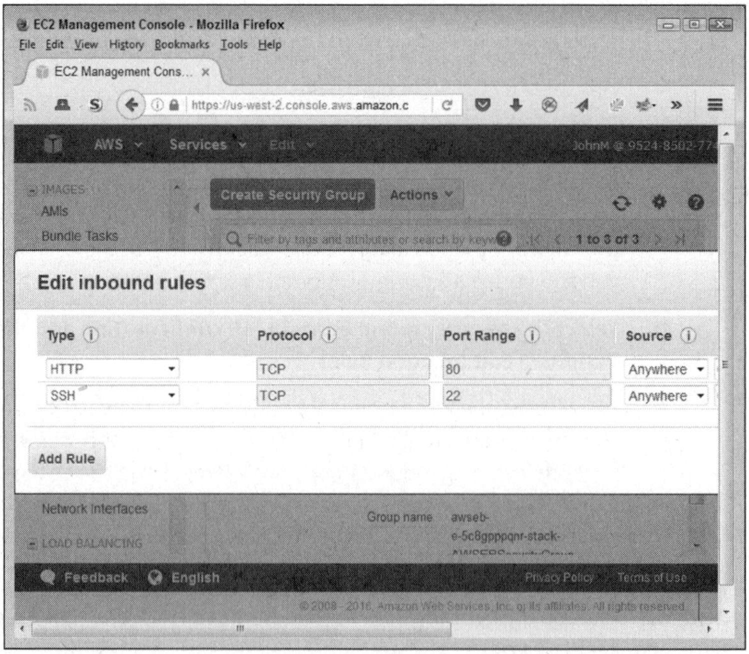

FIGURE 5-10:
Modify the rules to ensure that access remains restricted.

5. **Click Add Rule.**

   You see a new rule added to the list. To make this setup work, you must also provide access to the website to the instance security group. Otherwise, when you attempt to perform updates, the updates will fail.

6. **Choose All Traffic in the Type field and All in the Protocol field.**

   These two settings provide complete access to the security group.

7. **Choose Custom in the Source field and type sg in the text field after it.**

   You see a listing of security groups for your server. A source can consist of a Classless Inter-Domain Routing (CIDR) address, IP address, or security group ID. Typing sg tells EC2 that you want to use a security group.

8. **Click the security group for the website instance in the list.**

   The security group appears in the Source field.

9. **Click Save.**

   The inbound security rules now prevent access to the site by any entity other than the website instance or you.

REMEMBER

The IP address supplied when you choose My IP in the Source field uses the IP address of your current location. If other people use the same router (and therefore the same IP address), they also have access to the website. Consequently, setting the inbound rules does help provide security, but only a certain level of security. In addition, the IP address can change when you reset the router and then reconnect to the Internet provider. Consequently, you could find that you lose access to the test site you've created because of the change in IP address. If you suddenly find that you have lost access, verify that your IP address hasn't changed.

Configuring the application

You can modify the application configuration as needed. You initially set all these configuration options during the creation process, but getting the settings correct at the outset isn't always possible. Simply select the Configuration entry in the Navigation pane and you see the listing of application configuration entries shown in Figure 5-11.

To change a configuration option, click the button next to the heading, such as Scaling, that you want to modify. You see a new page that contains the configuration options. After you make the configuration changes, click Apply to make them active or click Cancel when you make a mistake.

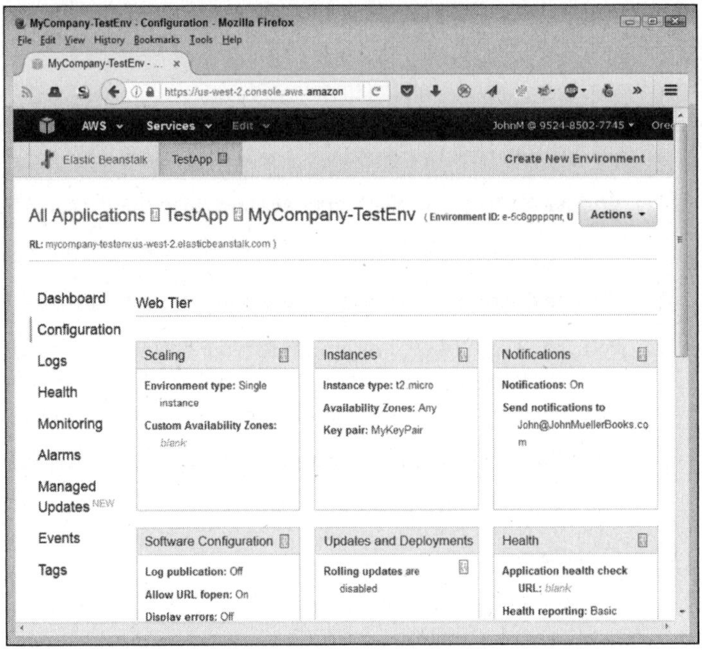

FIGURE 5-11:
Using the configuration entries to change how your application runs.

Monitoring the application environment

Monitoring lets you determine whether the application environment is sufficient for your application. For example, you may decide that you require a different instance type because of the amount of traffic. To monitor your application, choose the Monitoring option in the Navigation pane. EB displays the information shown in Figure 5-12.

As shown in Figure 5-12, the test application uses hardly any of the resource provided to it, so you don't need to make any changes. Of course, this is an expected outcome given that you're the only one with access to the application. The line graphs below the text output show graphically how many resources your application uses. You can also change the monitoring criteria for longer monitoring sessions (to show generalized trends over a 24-hour period, for example).

Each of the graphs in Figure 5-12 has a button associated with it. When you click the button, you see a page for creating an alarm, as shown in Figure 5-13. Each alarm entry must have a unique name. You then provide a monitoring period, metric-specific thresholds, and notification information. When you complete the form, click Add. You can see the alarms you set for your EB application by choosing Alarms in the Navigation pane. When an alarm occurs, you see a message about it using the notification method (such as an email message) that you selected.

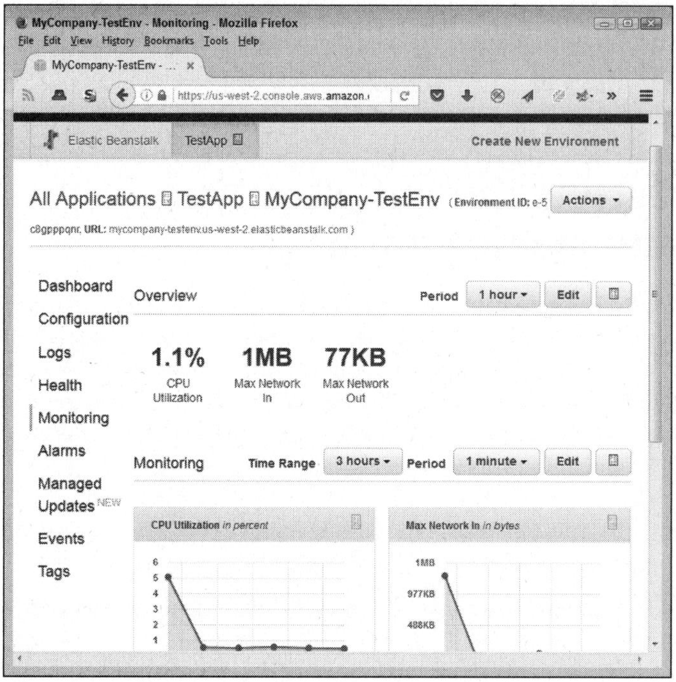

FIGURE 5-12: Monitor your application to determine when it requires environment changes.

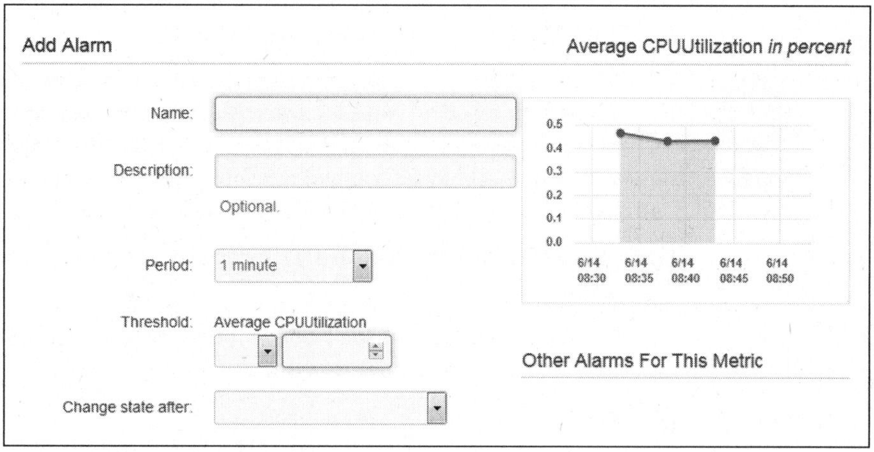

FIGURE 5-13: Set alarms as needed to prevent failures because of lack of resources.

Updating an EB Application

Applications don't exist in a vacuum: Organizational and other requirements change, environments evolve, user needs morph, and so on. As the application functionality and operation changes, so must the application configuration and setup. The environmental needs change as well. In other words, you must perform an EB update to keep the application current so that users can continue using it. The following sections describe the kinds of changes you need to consider during an update.

Getting the sample code and making a change

You're extremely unlikely to upload just one version of your application. An application actually has a life cycle, and change is simply part of the process. Making changes using the sample application means getting the current code and then doing something with it. The following steps help you get a copy of the current application and perform a small change on it. You most definitely don't need to be a developer to perform these steps.

1. **Download the** php-v1.zip **file found at** http://docs.aws.amazon.com/elasticbeanstalk/latest/dg/RelatedResources.html.

2. **Expand the archive into its own folder (directory) on your hard drive.**

   You see a number of application files, including index.php. The index.php file contains the code used to display the web page shown previously in Figure 5-8. Modifying the code changes how the web page appears.

3. **Open the** index.php **file using any text editor.**

   WARNING

   The text editor must output pure text files without any formatting. For example, Notepad on Windows systems, gedit on Linux systems, and TextEdit on Mac systems are all examples of pure text editors. On the other hand, Microsoft Word, LibreOffice, and FreeOffice are all examples of editors that you can't use to make modifications to PHP files.

4. **Locate the line that reads** <h1>Congratulations!</h1> **and replace it with** <h1>Hello There!</h1>.

   The change you've just made modifies the greeting you see. It's a small change, but it serves to demonstrate how modifications typically work.

5. **Save the file.**

   The modified file is now ready to upload to Amazon.

Uploading the modified application

To see any coding changes you make, you must upload the changes to AWS. It doesn't matter how complex the application becomes: At some point, you use the same process to upload changed files. The following steps describe how to perform this task:

1. **Place the files for your application into an archive.**

   The normal archive format is a `.zip` file.

2. **Open the application dashboard by clicking its entry in the initial EB page.**

   You see options for working with the application, as shown in Figure 5-14.

3. **Click Upload and Deploy.**

   You see an Upload and Deploy dialog box like the one shown in Figure 5-15.

4. **Click Browse.**

   You see a File Upload window consistent with your platform and browser.

5. **Select the file containing the modified application code and click Open.**

   EB displays the filename next to the Browse button.

6. **Type** Changed-Greeting **in the Version Label field and then click Deploy.**

   EB displays messages telling you that it's updating the environment. Be patient; this process can take a few minutes to complete. At some point, the application indictor turns green again (and you see the checkmark icon), which means that you can test the application using the same procedure found in the "Testing the application deployment" section, earlier in this chapter. What you should see is a change in greeting from "Congratulations!" to "Hello There!"

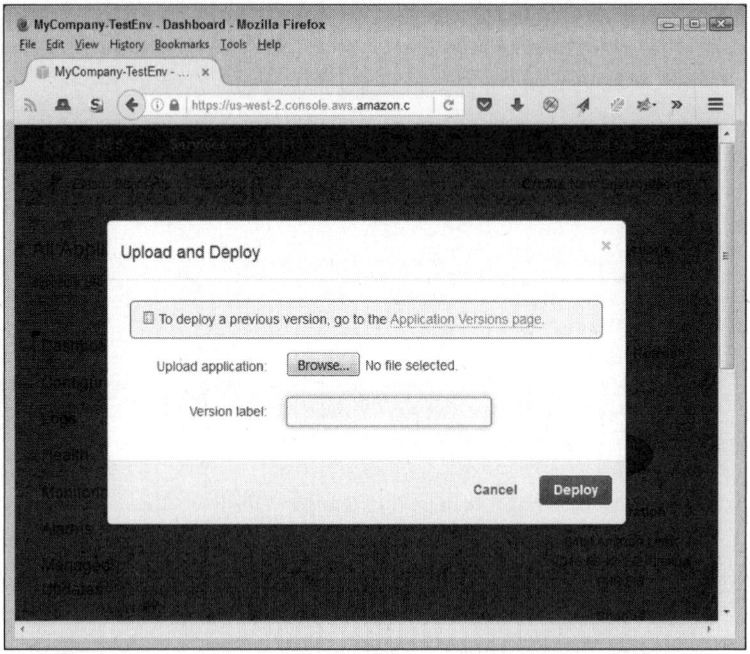

FIGURE 5-15:
Use the Upload
and Deploy dialog
box to upload
new application
versions.

Switching application versions

You now have two application versions uploaded to the EC2 instance. In some cases, you may have to switch between application versions. Perhaps a fix in a new version really didn't work out, so you need to go to an older, more stable version. The following steps describe how to switch between versions:

1. **Click Upload and Deploy.**

   Look again at Figure 5-15. Notice the Application Versions Page link. This page contains a listing of all the versions that are available for use.

2. **Click the Application Versions Page link.**

   You see the Application Versions page, shown in Figure 5-16. The last field of the table shows where each version is deployed. In this case, Changed-Greeting is deployed, but Sample Application isn't.

3. **Check the Sample Application version and click Deploy.**

   EB displays the deployment options, shown in Figure 5-17. The fields contain the same environment settings as before. You don't want to change these settings unless you want to create a new environment.

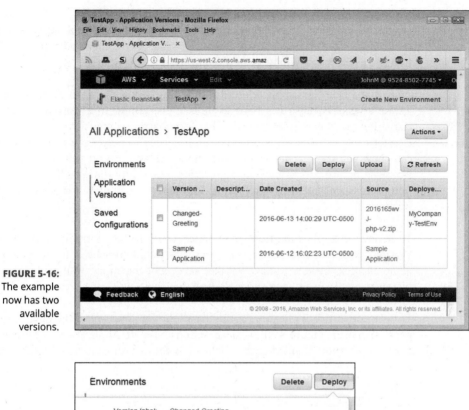

FIGURE 5-16:
The example
now has two
available
versions.

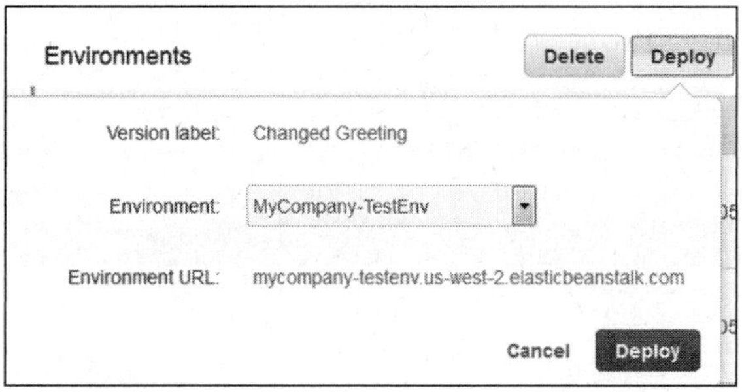

FIGURE 5-17:
You specify
deployment
options as part
of making an
update available.

4. **Click Deploy.**

   EB displays messages telling you that it's updating the environment. At some
   point, the application indictor turns green again, which means that you can test
   the application using the same procedure found in the "Testing the application
   deployment" section, earlier in this chapter.

Removing Unneeded Applications

EB applications get old just like any other application does. Software becomes
outdated to the point at which additional updates become counterproductive and

expensive; creating a new application becomes easier. When an application gets old enough, you need to shut it down in a graceful manner and remove it after training users to use whatever new application you have in place.

WARNING

Transitions from one application to another are one of the most difficult administrative tasks because it's hard to foresee everything that can go wrong, and transitions add layers of complexity that administrators may not understand. This chapter can't provide you with everything needed to perform a transition, but it can show you the mechanics of removing an EB application you no longer need. However, before you remove the application, make sure that you have the transition process well planned and have backup processes in place for when things go wrong.

To remove an application from an instance, you select its entry in the Application Versions page (refer to Figure 5-16) and click Delete. However, before you delete an application, be sure to have another version of the application deployed to the instance, or site users may suddenly find that they can't access your site.

To delete an entire application, including all the versions, select the Environments page, shown in Figure 5-18. Choose Actions ➪ Delete Application to remove the entire application. Removing the application doesn't remove the EC2 instance.

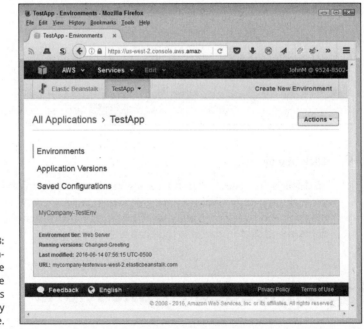

FIGURE 5-18: The Environments page shows the environments you currently have in place.

Chapter **6**

Responding to Events with Lambda

Administrators sometimes need to automate tasks, which can mean writing scripts (a kind of simple code) or providing specialized applications that someone else coded. This chapter isn't about coding, nor is it about development, but it is about running code in a serverless environment called Lambda that's tailor-made to administrator needs. You use Lambda to run the code, so what Lambda really provides is an execution environment. The Lambda environment can work with any application or back-end process, and Amazon automatically provides the scaling needed to ensure that the code you upload runs as expected (keeping in mind that the cloud environment can't run code as quickly as a dedicated host server can). Using and configuring Lambda is free, but you do pay for the computing time and other resources that the code uses, so keep costs in mind when you use this service. Typically, you use Lambda in one of two ways (the first of which the chapter covers):

» As a response to an event triggered by a service or application

» As part of a direct call from a mobile application or web page

REMEMBER

Lambda doesn't cost you anything. However, Amazon does charge you for each request that your code makes, the time that your code runs, and any nonfree services that your code depends on to perform useful work. In some cases, you may find that a given service doesn't actually cost anything. For example, you could use S3 with Lambda at the free-tier level to perform experimentation and pay only for the code requests and running time. The examples in this chapter don't require that you actually run any code — you simply set up the application to run should you desire to do so, but the setup itself doesn't incur any cost.

Considering the Lambda Features

Before you can actually work with Lambda, you need to know more about it. Saying that Lambda is a code-execution environment is a bit simplistic; Lambda provides more functionality because it helps you do things like respond to events. However, starting with the concept of a serverless code-execution environment, one that you don't have to manage, is a good beginning. The following sections fill in the details of the Lambda feature set. Even though this information appears as an overview, you really need to know it when working through the examples that follow in the this chapter.

Working with a server

Most applications today rely on a specific server environment. An administrator creates a server environment, either physical or virtual, configures it, and then provides any required resources a developer may need. The developer then places an application created and tested on a test server of (you hope) precisely the same characteristics on the server. After some testing, the administrator comes back and performs additional configuration, such as setting up accounts for users. Other people may get involved as well. For example, a DBA may set up a database environment for the application, and a web designer may create a mobile interface for it. The point is that a lot of people get involved in the process of getting this application ready for use, and they remain involved as the application evolves. The time and money spent to maintain the application is relatively large. However, the application environment you create provides a number of important features you must consider before moving to a serverless environment:

» The server is completely under the organization's control, so the organization chooses every feature about the server.

» The application environment tends to run faster than even the best cloud server can provide (much less a serverless environment, in which you have no control over the server configuration).

» Any data managed by the application remains with the organization, so the organization can reduce the potential for data breaches and can better adhere to any legal requirements for the data.

» Adding more features to the server tends to cost less after the organization pays for the initial outlay.

» A third party can't limit the organization's choice of support and other software to use with the application, nor can it suddenly choose to stop supporting certain software functionality (thereby forcing an unexpected application upgrade).

» Security tends to be less of a concern when using a localized server as long as the organization adheres to best practices.

Working in a serverless environment

Using a localized server does have some significant benefits, but building, developing, and maintaining servers is incredibly expensive because of the staffing requirements and the need to buy licenses for the various pieces of software. (You can mitigate software costs by using lower-cost open source products, but the open source products may not do everything you need or may provide the same services in a less efficient environment.) However, organizations have more than just cost concerns to consider when it comes to servers. Users want applications that are flexible and work anywhere today. With this in mind, here are some reasons that you may want to consider a serverless environment for your application:

» **Lower hardware and administration cost:** You don't have hardware costs because Amazon provides the hardware, and the administration costs are theoretically zero as well. However, you do pay for the service and need to consider the trade-off between the cost of the hardware, administration, and services.

» **Automatic scaling:** You can bring on additional hardware immediately without any startup time or costs.

» **Improved development team efficiency:** Reducing the number of people in a process generally increases efficiency because you have fewer lines of communication and fewer human failure points as well. In addition, the developer needs to worry only about writing great code — not whether the server will function as expected.

» **Low learning curve:** Working with Lambda doesn't require that you learn any new programming languages. In fact, you can continue to use the third-party libraries that you like, even if those libraries rely on native code. Lambda provides an execution environment, not an actual coding environment. You use a Lambda function (explained in the "Creating a Basic Lambda Application" section, later in this chapter) to define the specifics of how your application runs.

TIP

Lambda does provide a number of prebuilt function templates for common tasks, and you may find that you can use one of these templates instead of building your own. It pays to become familiar with the prebuilt templates because using them can save you considerable time and effort. You just need to tell Lambda to use a particular template with your service resources.

>> **Increased reliability:** In general, because Amazon can provide additional systems immediately, a failure at Amazon doesn't spell a failure for your application. What you get is akin to having multiple sets of redundant failover systems.

WARNING

Many of Amazon's services come with hidden assumptions that could cause problems. For example, with Lambda, Amazon fully expects that you use other Amazon services as well. A Lambda app can react to an event such as a file being dropped into an S3 bucket by a user, but it can't react to an event on your own system. The user may drop a file onto a folder on your server, but that event doesn't create an event that Lambda can see. What you really get with Lambda is an incredible level of flexibility with significantly reduced costs as long as you want to use the services that Amazon provides with it. In the long run, you may actually find that Lambda locks you into using Amazon services that don't really meet your needs, so be sure to think about the ramifications of the choices you make during the experimentation stage.

Starting the Lambda Console

The Lambda console is where you interact with Lambda and gives you a method for telling Lambda what to do with the code you upload. Using the Lambda Console takes what could be a complex task and makes it considerably easier so that you can focus on what you need to do, rather than on the code-execution details. Lambda automatically addresses many of the mundane server setup and configuration tasks for you. With this time savings in mind, use these steps to open a copy of the Lambda console:

1. **Sign into AWS using your administrator account.**

2. **Navigate to the Lambda Console at** https://console.aws.amazon.com/lambda.

   You see a Welcome page that contains interesting information about Lambda and what it can do for you. However, you don't see the actual console at this point.

3. **Click Get Started Now.**

You see the Select Blueprint page, shown in Figure 6-1. This book assumes that you use blueprints to perform most tasks as an administrator (in contrast to a developer, who would commonly rely on the associated Application Programming Interface, or API).

TECHNICAL STUFF

If you'd like to use the API instead, you want to start by reviewing the developer-oriented documentation at https://docs.aws.amazon.com/lambda/latest/dg/lambda-introduction.html and then proceed to the API documentation at https://docs.aws.amazon.com/lambda/latest/dg/API_Reference.html. However, using the approach in this chapter works as a good starting point for everyone, even developers. You can access the AWS documentation pages at https://aws.amazon.com/documentation/ at any time, even if you aren't logged into an account, so you can review this material at any time.

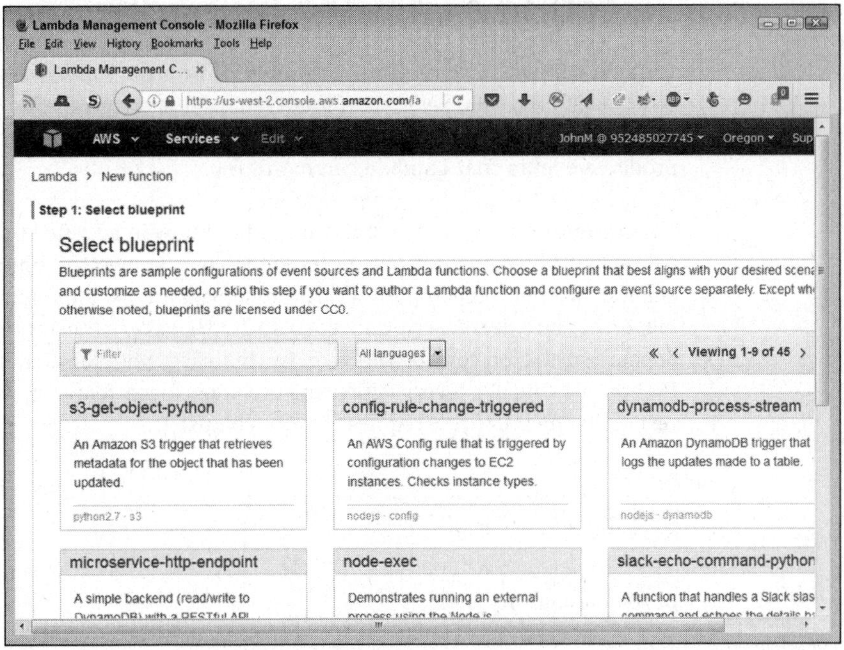

FIGURE 6-1: Access the Lambda functionality through blueprints to make tasks easy.

Creating a Basic Lambda Application

The previous section discusses the Lambda console and shows how to start it. Of course, just starting the console doesn't accomplish much. In order to make Lambda useful, you need to upload code and then tell Lambda how to interact with it. To make things easier, Lambda relies on the concept of a blueprint, which works much like the name implies. It provides a basic structure for creating the function that houses the code you want to execute. The following sections describe how to create a Lambda application and interact with the application in various ways (including deleting the function when you finish with it).

REMEMBER

Creating, configuring, and deleting a function won't cost you anything. However, if you actually test your function and view metrics that it produces, you may end up with a charge on your credit card. Be sure to keep the requirement to pay for code-execution resources in mind when going through the following sections. If you configured your AWS account as described in the "Considering the eventual need for paid services" section of Chapter 3, you should receive an email telling you about any charges accrued as the result of performing the procedures in the following section.

Selecting a Lambda blueprint

Lambda supports events from a number of Amazon-specific sources such as S3, DynamoDB, Kinesis, SNS, and CloudWatch. This chapter relies on S3 as an event source, but the techniques it demonstrates work with any Amazon service that produces events that Lambda can monitor.

When working with blueprints, you need to know in advance the requirements for using that blueprint. For example, Figure 6-2 shows the blueprint used in this chapter, s3-get-object-python. The blueprint name tells you a little about the blueprint, but the description adds to it. However, the important information appears at the bottom of the box. In this case, you see that the blueprint uses Python 2.7 and S3. Every blueprint includes these features, so you know what resources the blueprint requires before you use it.

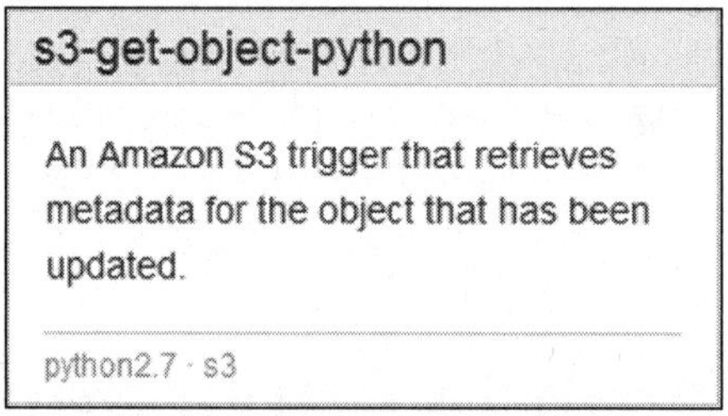

> ### s3-get-object-python
>
> An Amazon S3 trigger that retrieves metadata for the object that has been updated.
>
> ---
> python2.7 · s3

FIGURE 6-2:
Determine the requirements for using a blueprint at the outset.

TIP

Amazon provides a number of blueprints, and finding the one you need can be time consuming. Adding a condition to the Filter field or choosing a programming language from the Language field reduces the search time. For example, to locate all the S3-specific blueprints, type **S3** in the Filter field. Likewise, to locate all the Python 2.7 blueprints, choose Python 2.7 in the Languages field.

A WORD ABOUT PRODUCT VERSIONS

An interesting detail about the use of Python 2.7 is that it isn't the most current version of Python available. Many people have moved to Python 3.4.4 (see the downloads page at https://www.python.org/downloads/ for details). In fact, you can find versions as high as 3.5.1 used for applications now, so you may question the wisdom of using an older version of Python for your lambda code.

Python is unique in that some groups use the 2.7.*x* version and other groups use the 3.4.*x* and above version. Because developers, data scientists, and others who perform data-analysis tasks mainly use the 2.7.*x* version of Python, Amazon has wisely chosen to concentrate on that version. (Eventually, all development tasks will move to the 3.*x* version of the product.) Using the 2.7.*x* version means that you're better able to work with other people who perform data-analysis tasks. In addition, if Amazon used the 3.*x* version instead, you might find locating real-world application examples difficult. The Python 2.7.*x* code does have compatibility issues with Python 3.*x*, so if you choose to use Python 3.*x* anyway, you also need to update the Amazon code.

You may find that Amazon uses odd versions of other languages and products as well. In some cases, the choice of language or product version has to do with updating the Amazon code, but in other cases, you may find that the older version has advantages, such as library support (as is the case with Python). Be sure to look at the versions of products when supplied because you need to use the right version to get good results when working with Lambda.

REMEMBER

Amazon licenses most of the blueprints under the Creative Commons Zero (CC0) rules (see https://creativecommons.org/publicdomain/zero/1.0/ for details). This means that Amazon has given up all copyright to the work, and you don't need to worry about getting permission to use the blueprint as part of anything you do. However, the operative word in the Amazon wording on the blueprint page is "most," which means that you need to verify the copyright for every blueprint you use to ensure that no hidden requirements exist that oblige you to get a license.

Configuring a function

Using the Lambda console and a blueprint means that the function-creation process is less about coding and more about configuration. You need to tell Lambda which blueprint to use, but the blueprint contains the code needed to perform the task. In addition, you tell Lambda which resources to use, but again, it's a matter of configuration and not actual coding. The only time that you might need to perform any significant coding is when a blueprint comes close to doing what you want to do but doesn't quite meet expectations.

The example that follows uses the S3 bucket that you see how to create in the "Performing a Few Simple Tasks" section of Chapter 2. However, you can use any bucket desired. The bucket simply holds objects that you want to process, so it's a matter of choosing the right bucket to perform the required work. The blueprint used in this section, s3-get-object-python, simply reports the metadata from the objects dropped into the bucket.

1. **Click s3-get-object-python.**

   You see the Configure Event Sources page, shown in Figure 6-3.

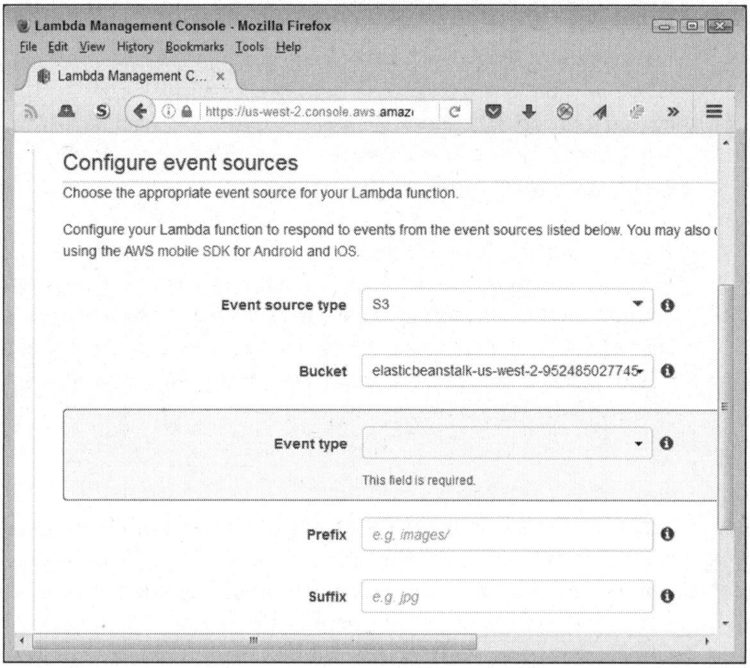

Lambda Management Console - Mozilla Firefox
File Edit View History Bookmarks Tools Help
Lambda Management C...
https://us-west-2.console.aws.amaz
Configure event sources
Choose the appropriate event source for your Lambda function.
Configure your Lambda function to respond to events from the event sources listed below. You may also
using the AWS mobile SDK for Android and iOS.
Event source type
S3
Bucket
elasticbeanstalk-us-west-2-952485027745
Event type
This field is required.
Prefix
e.g. images/
Suffix
e.g. jpg

FIGURE 6-3: Define the event source you want to use.

TIP

Even though the blueprint automatically chooses event-source information for you, you can still control the event source in detail. For example, you can change the Event Source Type field to choose a service other than S3, such as Kinesis, S3, CloudWatch, or DynamoDB.

2. **Select an object source in the Bucket field.**

   The example assumes that you want to use the bucket that Chapter 2 tells you how to create. However, any bucket you can access that receives objects regularly will work fine for this example. AWS simply chooses the first S3 bucket, so configuring this field is essential.

3. **Choose the Object Created (All) option in the Event Type field.**

S3 supports three event types: Object Created (All); Object Removed (All); and Reduced Redundancy Lost Object. Even though Lambda receives all the events, you use the entries in the Prefix and Suffix fields to filter the events so that you react only to the important events. For example, you can choose to include a folder path or part of a filename as a prefix to control events based on location or name. Adding a file extension as the suffix means that Lambda will process only files of a specific type. The example provides simple processing in that it reacts to any item created in the bucket, so it doesn't use either the Prefix or Suffix fields.

4. **Click Next.**

You see the Configure Function page, shown in Figure 6-4. As with the Configure Event Sources page, it pays to check out the Runtime field. In this case, you can choose between Python 2.7 and Java 8. Even when the blueprint description tells you that it supports a specific language, you often have a choice of other languages you can use as well.

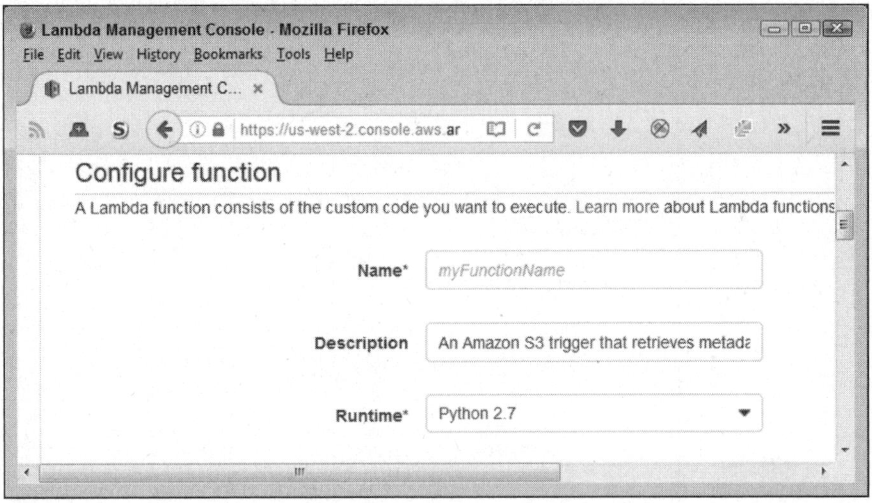

FIGURE 6-4: Name and describe your function.

5. **Type** MyFunction **in the Name field.**

Normally, you provide a more descriptive function name, but this name will do for the example and make it easier to locate the function later when you want to remove it.

6. **Scroll down to the next section of the page.**

You see the function code. At this point, you can use the online editor to make small coding changes as needed. However, you can also upload a .zip file containing the source code you want to use, or you can upload existing source code from S3. This example relies on the example code that Amazon provides, so you don't need to make any changes.

REMEMBER

Notice that the Python code contains a function (specified by the def keyword) named lambda_handler. This function handles (processes) the information that S3 passes to it. Every language you use has a particular method for defining functions; Python uses this method. As part of configuring the Lambda function, you need to know the name of the handler function.

7. **Scroll down to the next section of the page.**

You see two sections: the Lambda Function Handler and Role section and the Advanced Settings section, as shown in Figure 6-5. The blueprint automatically defines the Handler field for you. Note that it contains the name lambda_handler as the handler name. When you use custom code, you must provide the name of the function that handles the code in this section.

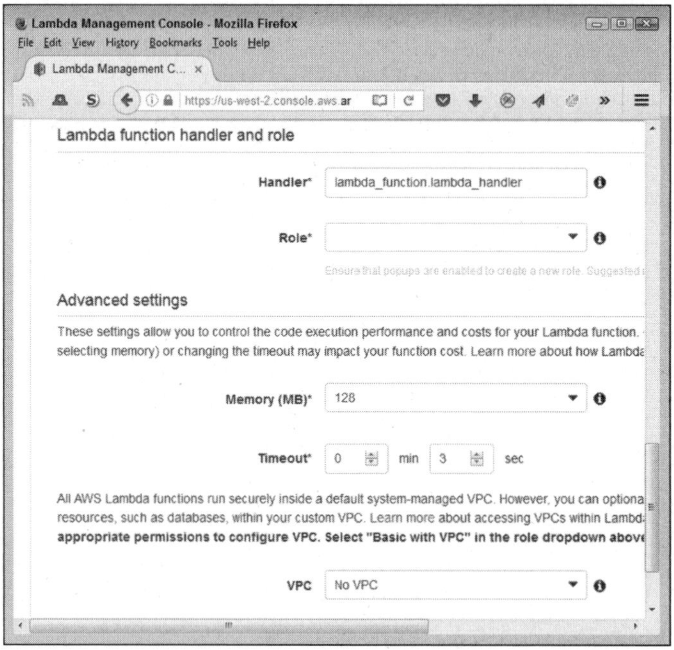

FIGURE 6-5:
Define the execution specifics of the Lambda function.

The first part of the entry, lambda_function, is the name of the file that contains the handler function. As with the function name, the blueprint automatically provides the appropriate name for you. However, if you upload a file containing the code, you must provide the filename (without extension) as the first entry. Consequently, lambda_function.lambda_handler provides the name of the file and associated handler function. The filename is separated from the handler function name by a period.

8. **Choose S3 Execution Role in the Role field.**

   You must tell AWS what rights to use when executing the lambda code. The environment provides several default roles, or you can create a custom role to use instead. AWS opens a new page containing the role definition, as shown in Figure 6-6. AWS fills in the details for you. However, you can click View Policy Document to see precisely what rights you're granting to the Lambda function.

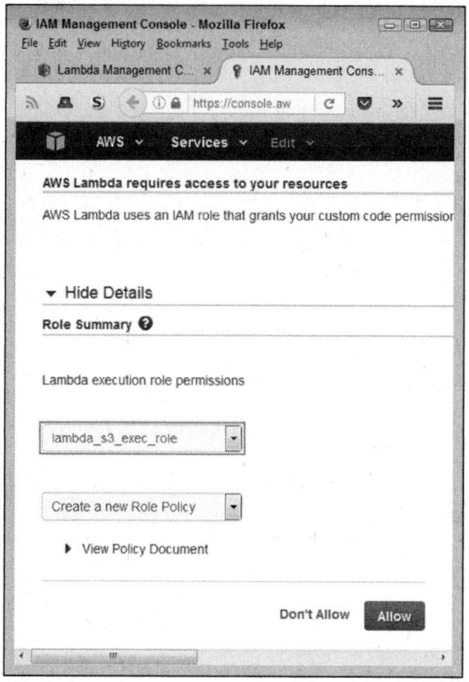

FIGURE 6-6: Define the execution specifics of the Lambda function.

9. **Click Allow.**

   AWS returns you to the Lambda Function Handler and Role section of the page shown previously in Figure 6-5.

   The Advanced Settings section contains the settings you need to use for this example. The Memory field contains the amount of memory you want to set aside for the Lambda function (with 128MB being the smallest amount you can provide).

   The Timeout field determines how long the Lambda function can run before AWS stops it. Setting the value too high can make your application pause when it encounters an error (resulting in frustrated users); setting it too low may unnecessarily terminate a function that could complete given more time. In most cases, you must experiment to find the best setting to use for your particular function, but the default setting provided by the blueprint gives you a good starting point.

You use the VPC field to define which VPC to use to access specific resources. This particular example doesn't require the use of a VPC.

10. **Click Next.**

The Review page, shown in Figure 6-7, shows the settings for this function.

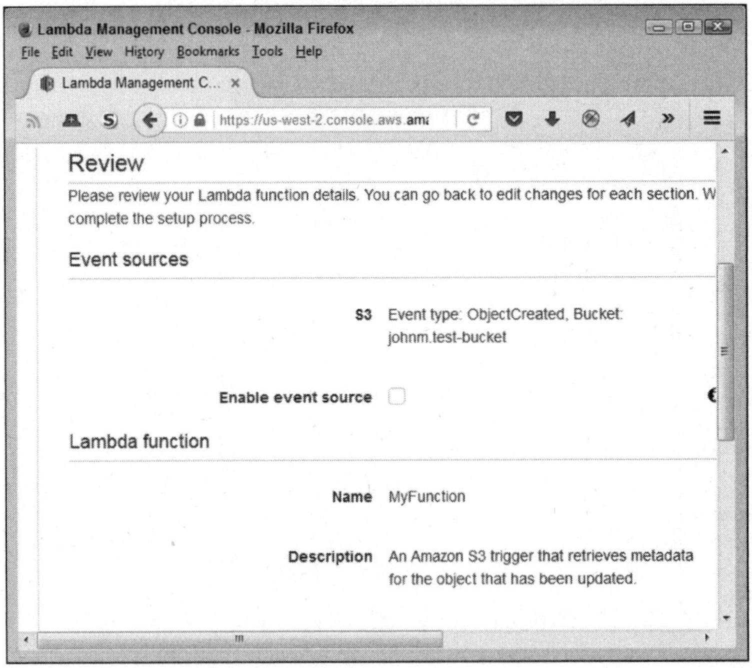

FIGURE 6-7:
Verify that the function settings are correct.

Pay particular attention to the Enable Event Source check box. If you select this option and create the function, the function becomes active immediately. Amazon recommends that you leave this check box blank so that you can test the function before you enable it.

REMEMBER

11. **Click Create Function.**

If you chose not to enable the function, the function exists, but it doesn't do anything. You aren't incurring any costs at this point. AWS displays the page shown in Figure 6-8. Note the Test button in the upper-left corner.

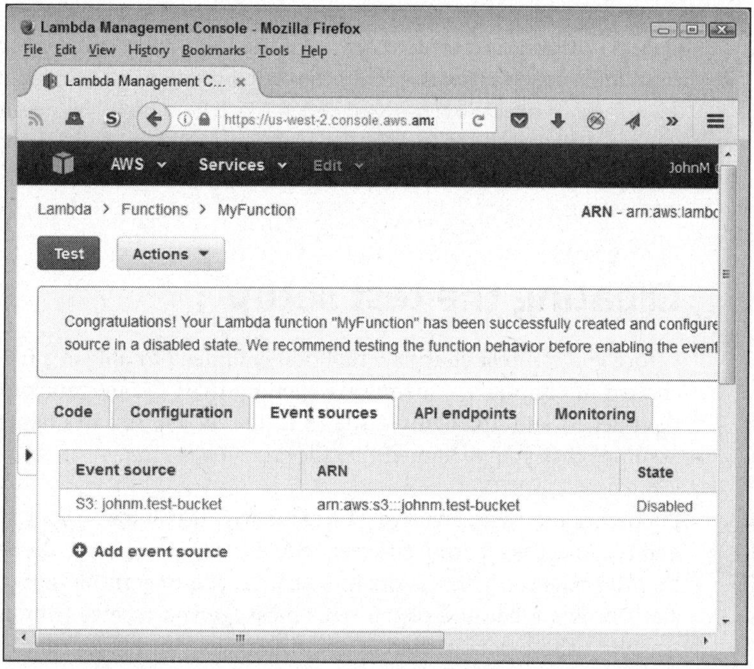

FIGURE 6-8:
The function is ready to use.

Using ensembles of functions

Sometimes you can accomplish some incredibly interesting tasks without performing any coding at all by creating ensembles of functions available as blueprints. For example, you can use the s3-get-object blueprint to retrieve objects from an S3 bucket of specific types and then pass the object onto DynamoDB, where another Lambda function, such as `microservice-http-endpoint`, passes it onto a microservice that your company owns for further processing.

You can even double up on blueprints. The same DynamoDB content can trigger another Lambda function, such as `simple-mobile-backend`, to send alerts to mobile users about new content. You can achieve all these tasks without any significant coding. All you really need to do is think a little outside the box as to how you can employ the blueprints that Amazon provides and combine them in interesting ways.

Most of the Amazon blueprints are used for other purposes online. For example, you can see how to modify the s3-get-object-python blueprint to accommodate a product named Logentries (`https://logentries.com/`) at `https://logentries.com/doc/s3-ingestion-with-lambda/`. Another product, Logsene (`https://sematext.com/logsene/`) also uses the blueprint as a starting point (see details at https://github.com/sematext/logsene-aws-lambda-s3). For an example of a combined-service use, check out the article at https://micropyramid.com/blog/using-aws-lambda-with-s3-and-dynamodb/, which is about using S3 with DynamoDB. These blueprints get real-world use by third-party companies that use the blueprint as a starting point to do something a lot more detailed and interesting.

Creating the test setup

Before you can test your new function, you need to upload a file to the bucket you created in Chapter 2. This means opening the S3 Management Console, selecting the bucket, and uploading a file to it just as you did in Chapter 2. The example assumes that you've named this file HappyFace.jpg.

Filenames are case sensitive. Consequently, if you name your file happyface.jpg and try to access it from the test code as HappyFace.jpg, the output will tell you that the code can't access the file. At first, you may think that you have a permissions problem because of the error message you receive from Amazon. However, verifying the capitalization of the filenames you use during the testing process can save you a lot of time and frustration.

Testing the function

Every Lambda handler function receives two pieces of information: an event and its context. The event and context can include any sort of data, but to make things simple during testing, the test functionality relies on *strings*, that is, text that appears within double quotation marks ("). The text is bundled within a pair of curly brackets ({})so that the test function receives information just as it normally would. The following steps show how to test your new Lambda function:

1. **Click Test.**

   AWS displays the default testing template, which is Hello World. You need to select the testing template for S3 or the test will fail.

2. **Choose S3 Put in the Sample Event Template field.**

   You see the Input Test Event page, shown in Figure 6-9. To make this template function correctly, you make three small code changes, as the next steps explain.

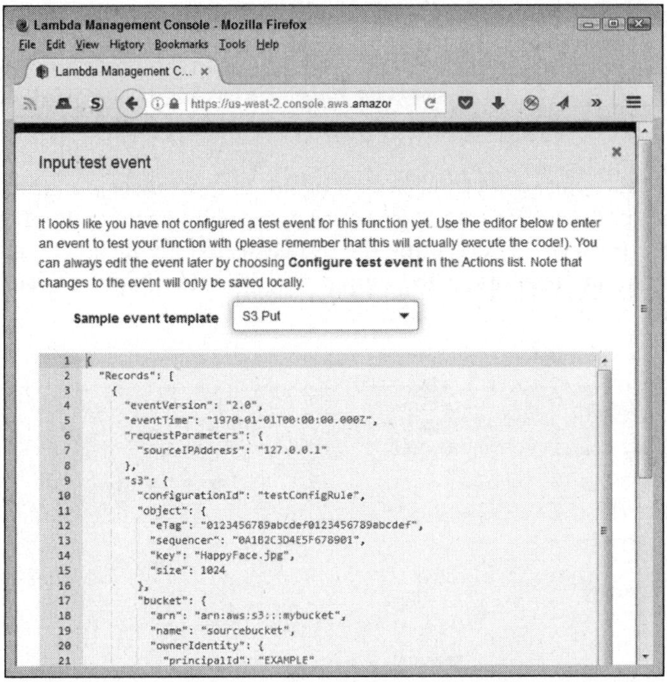

FIGURE 6-9:
The test code data to the function.

The screenshot shows a Lambda Management Console browser window with the following content:

Input test event

It looks like you have not configured a test event for this function yet. Use the editor below to enter an event to test your function with (please remember that this will actually execute the code!). You can always edit the event later by choosing **Configure test event** in the Actions list. Note that changes to the event will only be saved locally.

Sample event template: S3 Put

```
1  {
2    "Records": [
3      {
4        "eventVersion": "2.0",
5        "eventTime": "1970-01-01T00:00:00.000Z",
6        "requestParameters": {
7          "sourceIPAddress": "127.0.0.1"
8        },
9        "s3": {
10         "configurationId": "testConfigRule",
11         "object": {
12           "eTag": "0123456789abcdef0123456789abcdef",
13           "sequencer": "0A1B2C3D4E5F678901",
14           "key": "HappyFace.jpg",
15           "size": 1024
16         },
17         "bucket": {
18           "arn": "arn:aws:s3:::mybucket",
19           "name": "sourcebucket",
20           "ownerIdentity": {
21             "principalId": "EXAMPLE"
```

3. **Change the** "key" **entry as shown here:**

```
"key": "HappyFace.jpg"
```

4. **Change the** "arn" **entry to match the arn for your bucket.**

The Amazon Resource Name (ARN) tells AWS where to find the bucket. The ARN for your S3 bucket will differ from the ARN I use here. However, your ARN entry will look something like this:

```
"arn": "arn:aws:s3:::johnm.test-bucket",
```

⚠️ **WARNING**

Make sure to create the ARN correctly. The number of colons between various elements is essential. The best way to avoid problems is to copy the ARN from a screen location that you know is correct and paste it into your code. Otherwise, you can spend hours trying to find the one missing or extra colon in your code.

5. **Change the** "name" **field to match the name of your bucket.**

In this case, you provide only the bucket name. It should look something like this:

```
"name": "johnm.test-bucket",
```

6. Click Save.

AWS saves the test code for you and returns you to the test page shown in Figure 6-8.

At this point, you can click Test again. In most cases, Amazon won't charge you anything because your S3 resource usage will remain within the limits of the free tier. However, by executing the test code, you can incur a small cost. Figure 6-10 shows an example of the output you see. The output correctly shows that the content type for HappyFace.jpg is "image/jpeg".

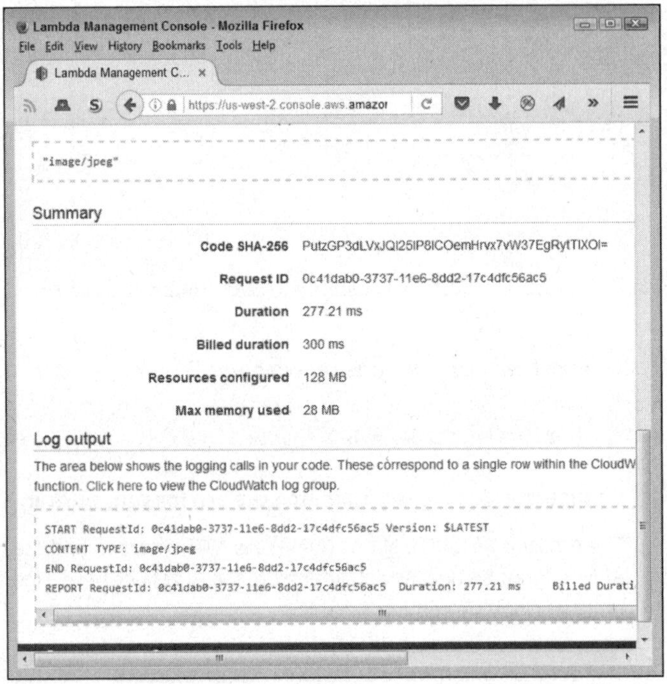

FIGURE 6-10: The test output correctly identifies the content type.

Checking the function metrics

In addition to various levels of testing, you can also view the metrics for your function by clicking the Monitoring tab. Figure 6-11 shows typical metrics for Lambda functions. In this case, you see how many times events have triggered the function, the duration of each call, and the number of errors that the functions have experienced.

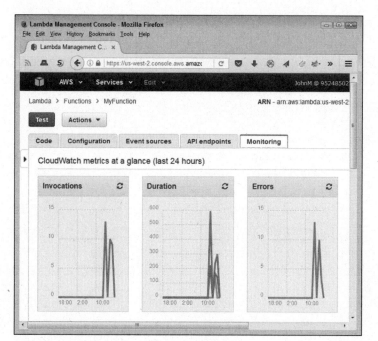

FIGURE 6-11:
Metrics can help you determine how well the function works.

Deleting the function

You don't want to keep a function around any longer than necessary because each function invocation costs money. One way to keep costs down is to disable the function by clicking the Enabled link for the function in the Event Sources tab and choosing Disable when you see the configuration dialog box. The function will continue to perform its task as long as just one of the event sources remains enabled, so you must disable all event sources to stop the function from responding to events.

At some point, you simply won't need the function, and keeping it around is a recipe for unexpected costs. To delete a function, choose Actions ⇨ Delete Function. AWS will ask whether you're sure that you want to delete the function. Click Delete to remove the function and all its configuration information.

3

Working with Storage

IN THIS PART . . .

Store objects using S3.

Use EFS as a cloud-based file system.

Discover the best storage system for your needs.

Create an archive using Glacier.

Chapter **7**

Working with Cloud Storage Using S3

An essential part of any cloud computing solution is storage. In fact, long before anyone considered creating Infrastructure as a Service (IaaS), Software as a Service (SaaS), or Platform as a Service (PaaS), vendors offered various types of online storage solutions. In some respects, storage is the simplest kind of service a vendor can offer. At least, storage starts out simply. As you find in this chapter, however, the S3 feature set is anything but simplistic because the moment you start adding complex applications, robust user needs, and interacting enterprise policies, storage becomes quite complex indeed. The heart of every enterprise — the most important asset it owns — is data. Everything else is replaceable, but getting data back can be difficult, if not impossible.

Early online storage configurations also focused on files. However, computing environments support more than just files. To make online storage useful, AWS has to provide support for objects, which does include files but also includes a lot of other object types that include sounds, graphics, security settings, application settings, and on and on. This chapter helps you focus on the kinds of objects that S3 supports. By supporting a large number of objects, S3 enables you to perform the most important task of all: reliable backups.

Also, S3 is more than storage, despite the name that Amazon attached to it, because of how you can use it to interact with other services and store objects other than files. The next two sections of the chapter discuss nontraditional storage tasks that you can perform with S3. In the first case, you create a website using the functionality that S3 provides. In the second case, you use S3 with Lambda to perform certain tasks using code. The capability to perform these tasks makes S3 a powerful service that helps you accomplish common tasks with a minimum of effort in many cases.

The final section of the chapter discusses long-term storage, or archiving. Everyone needs to archive data, both individuals and organizations. Data often becomes outdated and, some might feel, not useful. However, data often has a habit of becoming useful when you least expect it, so saving it in long-term storage is important. If for no other reason than historical research, you need to save your outdated information in a way that you can retrieve it, even if the retrieval is somewhat slowed by the storage technology. Of course, archived data can go bad if not stored properly, so finding a reliable archive is important. In addition, you always need to know where the data is stored (so that it doesn't end up in never-never-land), so an important aspect of archival storage is knowing precisely where you can find the data later.

Considering the Simple Storage Service (S3) Features

S3 does so much more than just store information. The procedure you see in the "Performing a Few Simple Tasks" section of Chapter 2 is a teaser of a sort — but it doesn't even begin to scratch the surface of what S3 can do for you. The following sections help you understand S3 more fully so that you can grasp what it can do for you in performing everyday tasks. These sections are a kind of overview of common features; S3 actually does more than described.

Introducing S3

The idea behind S3 is straightforward. You use it to store objects of any sort in a directory structure you choose, without actually worrying about how the objects are stored. The goal is to store objects without considering the underlying infrastructure so that you can focus on application needs with a seemingly infinite hard drive. S3 focuses on objects, which can be of any type, rather than on a directory structure consisting of folders that hold files. Of course, you can still organize your data into folders, and S3 can hold files. It's just that S3 doesn't care what sort of object you put into the buckets you create. As can a real-world bucket, an S3 bucket can hold any sort of object you choose to place in it. The bucket automatically grows and shrinks to accommodate the objects you place in it, so most of the normal limits placed on storage don't exist with S3.

REMEMBER

Even though you see a single bucket in a single region when you work with S3, Amazon actually stores the data in multiple locations at multiple sites within the region. The automatic replication of your data reduces the risk of losing it as a result of any of a number of natural or other kinds of disasters. No storage technology is foolproof, however, and your own applications can just as easily destroy your data store as a natural disaster can. Consequently, you need to follow all the usual best practices to protect your data. The Amazon additions act as a second tier of protection. Also, versioning (see the "Employing versioning" section, later in this chapter, for details) provides you with a safety net in that you can recover a previous version of an object when a user deletes it or an application damages it in some way.

Amazon provides a number of storage-solution types, which are mentioned as the book progresses. Some of these storage solutions, such as the Elastic File System described in Chapter 8, are more like the standard hard drives you have used in the past. S3 is a new approach that you can use in the following ways:

» **Data storage:** The most common reason to use S3 is to store data. The data might originally appear on your local systems or you might create new applications that generate and use data in the cloud. A big reason to use S3 is to make data available anywhere to any device using any application you deem fit to interact with it. However, you still want to maintain local storage when security or privacy is the primary concern, or when your own infrastructure provides everything needed to store, manage, and access the data. When you think about S3 as a storage method, think about data with these characteristics:

- It's in constant flux.

- Applications require high accessibility to it.

- The cost of a data breach (where hackers steal the data and you must compensate the subjects of the data in some way) is relatively low.

» **Backup:** Localized backups have all sorts of problems, including the fact that a natural disaster can wipe them out. Using S3 as part of your data backup strategy makes sense when the need to keep the data available for quick access is high, the storage costs are acceptable, and the risk from a data breach is low. Of course, backups imply disaster recovery. You make a backup on the assumption that at some point, you need the backup to recover from a major incident. As with health or car insurance, you hope that the reason you're keeping it never occurs, but you don't want to take the risk of not having it, either.

TIP

Amazon provides all the best-practice storage techniques that your organization would normally employ, such as periodic data integrity checks to ensure that the data is still readable. In addition, Amazon performs some steps that most organizations don't, such as performing checksums on all network data to catch data corruption problems before the data is stored (making it less likely that you see any data corruption later).

>> **Data analysis:** The use of an object-storage technique makes S3 an excellent way to store data for many types of data analysis. Organizations use data analysis today to study trends of all sorts, such as people's buying habits or the effects of various strategies on organizational processes. The point is that data analysis has become an essential tool for business.

>> **Static website hosting:** Static websites may seem quaint because they rely on pages that don't change often. Most people are used to seeing dynamic sites whose content changes on an almost daily basis (or right before their eyes, in the case of ads). However, static sites still have a place for data that doesn't change much, such as providing access to organizational forms or policies. Such a site can also be useful for product manuals or other kinds of consumer data that doesn't change much after a product comes on the market.

Working with buckets

The bucket is the cornerstone of S3 storage. You use buckets to hold objects. A bucket can include organizational features, such as folders, but you should view a bucket as the means for holding related objects. For example, you might use a single bucket to hold all the data, no matter what its source might be, for a particular application. Amazon provides a number of ways to move objects into a bucket, include the following:

>> **Direct Connect:** The method employed in Chapter 2 to transfer data and that you encounter again (see "Working with Objects," later in this chapter) when you find out how to create a direct connection between your local system and S3.

>> **Amazon Kinesis:** A method of streaming data continuously to your S3 storage. You use Kinesis to address real-time storage needs, such as data capture from a device like a data logger. Because the majority of the Kinesis features require programming, this book doesn't cover Kinesis extensively.

>> **Physical media:** You can send physical media to Amazon to put into your S3 bucket if your data is so huge that moving it across the Internet proves too time consuming.

When working with Direct Connect, you can speed data transfers using Transfer Acceleration. Chapter 9 offers some information about using Transfer Acceleration to speed data transfers to Glacier. You can also read more about Transfer Acceleration at http://docs.aws.amazon.com/AmazonS3/latest/dev/ transfer-acceleration.html. Essentially, Transfer Acceleration doesn't change *how* a transfer occurs, but rather how *fast* it occurs. In some cases, using Transfer Acceleration can make data transfers up to six times faster, so it can have a huge impact on how fast S3 is ready to use with your application or how fast it can restore a backup onto a local system. To use Transfer Acceleration, you simply select a box in the S3 Management Console when configuring your bucket.

TIP

The best way to reduce costs when working with S3 is to ensure that you create a good archiving strategy so that AWS automatically moves objects you don't use very often to Glacier. Chapter 9 tells you about archiving data using Glacier. The important thing to remember is that S3 works best as storage for objects that you're currently using, rather than as long-term storage for objects you may use in the future.

Managing objects using buckets

You can manage objects in various ways and at various levels in S3. The management strategy you use determines how much time you spend administering, rather than using, the data. The following list describes the management levels:

>> **Bucket:** The settings you provide for the bucket affect every object placed in the bucket. Consequently, this course management option creates the general environment for all objects stored in a particular S3 bucket. However, it also points to the need for creating buckets as needed, rather than using a single catchall bucket for every need. Use buckets to define an environment for a group of related objects so that you can reduce the need for microman-agement later.

>> **Folder:** It's possible to add folders to buckets. As with folders (directories) on your local hard drive, you use folders to better categorize objects. In addition, you can use folder hierarchies to organize objects in specific ways, just as you do on your local hard drive. Configuring higher-level folders to provide the best possible environment for all objects that the folder contains is the best way to reduce the time spent managing objects.

>> **Object:** Configuring individual objects is an option of last choice because individual object settings tend to create error scenarios when the administra-tor who performed the configuration changes jobs or simply forgets about the settings. The object tends to behave differently from the other objects in the folder, creating confusion. Even so, individual object settings are sometimes necessary, and S3 provides the support needed to use them.

Setting bucket security

AWS gives you several levels of security for the data you store in S3. However, the main security features are similar to those that you use with your local operating system (even though Amazon uses different terms to identify these features). The basic security is user-based through Identity and Access Management (IAM). You can also create Access Control Lists (ACLs) similar to those used with other operating systems.

In addition to standard security, you can configure bucket policies that determine actions that requestors can perform against the objects in a bucket. You can also require that requestors provide authentication as part of query strings (so that every action passes through security before S3 performs it).

WARNING

Even though the Amazon documentation mentions security support for Payment Card Industry (PCI) and Health Insurance Portability and Accountability Act (HIPAA) support, you need to exercise extreme care when using S3 for this purpose. Your organization, not Amazon, is still responsible for any breaches or other problems associated with cloud storage. (At least some security experts argue that cloud storage may actually provide better security, such as in the article at http://searchhealthit.techtarget.com/tip/Cloud-storage-security-considerations-for-health-care-providers.) Be sure to create a compliant configuration by employing all the AWS security measures correctly, before you store any data. In fact, you may want to work with a third-party vendor, such as Connectria (http://www.connectria.com/cloud/hipaa_aws.php), to ensure that you have a compliant setup.

Employing encryption

Making data unreadable to a third party while continuing to be able to read it yourself is what *encryption* is all about. Encryption employs cryptography as a basis for making the message unreadable, and cryptography is actually a relatively old science (see the articles at https://access.redhat.com/blogs/766093/posts/1976023 and http://www.inquiriesjournal.com/articles/41/a-brief-history-of-cryptography for details). Encryption occurs at two levels when working with AWS:

>> **Data transfer:** As with any Internet access, you can encrypt your data using Secure Sockets Layer (SSL) encryption to ensure that no one can read the data as it moves between S3 and your local system.

>> **Storage:** Keeping data encrypted while stored is the only way to maintain protection provided during the data transfer. Otherwise, someone can simply wait until you store the data and then read it from the storage device.

REMEMBER

Theoretically, encryption can work on other levels as well. For example, certain *exploits* (hacker techniques used to access your system surreptitiously) can attack machine memory (see the article at `http://arstechnica.com/security/2016/04/dram-bitflipping-exploits-that-hijack-computers-just-got-easier/` for just one of the more interesting examples) and read the data while you have it loaded in an application. Because your data is stored and processed on Amazon's servers, the potential for using these other exploits is limited and therefore not discussed in this book. However, you do need to consider these exploits for any systems on your own network. Modern operating systems assist you in protecting your systems. For example, Windows includes built-in memory protection that's effective against many exploits (see the articles at `https://msdn.microsoft.com/library/windows/desktop/aa366553.aspx` and `https://msdn.microsoft.com/library/windows/desktop/aa366785.aspx` as examples).

Storage is one of the main encryption concerns because data spends more time in storage than in being moved from one place to another. AWS provides the following methods for encrypting data for storage purposes:

» **Server-side encryption:** You can request that S3 encrypt data before storing it on Amazon's servers and then decrypt it before sending it to you. The advantage of this approach is that you can often obtain higher transfer speeds, encryption occurs automatically, and the amount of work you need to perform is less. However, a third party could gain access to the data during the short time it remains unencrypted between decryption and transfer to your system, so this option isn't as safe as the other options in this list.

» **Client-side encryption:** You encrypt the data before sending it to S3. Because you encrypt the data prior to transfer, the chance that someone will read it is reduced. Remember that you also encrypt the data as part of the transfer process. The potential problems with this approach include a requirement that the client actually performs the encryption (it's less safe than relying on the automation that a server can provide) and the application will likely see a speed penalty as well.

» **Both:** The Amazon documentation doesn't mention that you can doubly encrypt the data, both on the client and on the server, but this option adds a level of safety because a hacker would have to undo two levels of encryptions (probably relying on different algorithms). This option is the slowest because you must pay for two levels of encryption, so the application suffers a definite speed loss. However, when working with sensitive data, this method presents the safest choice.

Using S3 events and notifications

In looking at some of the S3 screens and reviewing the documentation, you might initially get the idea that S3 provides event notifications — treating events and notifications as a single entity. Events and notifications are separate entities, however. An *event* occurs when something happens with S3. For example, adding a new object to a bucket generates an event because something has happened to the bucket. The event always occurs. A *notification* is a response to the event. When you tell S3 that you want to know about an event, S3 tells you every time that the event happens (or you can provide automation to do something about the event in your absence). It pays to keep the concepts of event and notification separate because combining the two leads to confusion.

You don't have to subscribe to every notification that S3 provides. In fact, you can create subscriptions to events in a detailed way. S3 supports the following events, each of which you can subscribe to separately:

>> **Object created:** Occurs whenever the bucket receives a new object. You use the * (asterisk) wildcard or All option to select all object-creation methods. A bucket can receive objects in the following ways:

- **Put:** Writes an object directly to the bucket using direct means.

- **Post:** Writes an object to the bucket using HTML forms, which means obtaining information needed to upload the object from the HTTP headers.

- **Copy:** Writes an object to the bucket using an existing object as a data source.

- **Complete multipart upload:** Writes multiple objects to the bucket as individual pieces (parts) and then reassembles those parts into a cohesive unit. This notification signifies the completion of the process.

>> **Object deleted:** Occurs whenever a bucket has an object removed or marked for removal. You use the * (asterisk) wildcard or All option to select all object-deletion methods. A bucket can have objects removed in the following ways:

- **Delete:** The object is actually removed from the bucket (making it inaccessible). This form of deletion applies to nonversioned object or complete versioned-object removal.

- **Delete marker created:** The object is only marked for removal from the bucket and becomes inaccessible as a result. This form of deletion normally applies to objects with multiple versions.

>> **Object lost:** Occurs whenever S3 loses a Reduced Redundancy Storage (RRS) object. An RRS object is one that you mark as being noncritical. By marking an object as RRS, you save money storing it with the potential problem of losing the object at some point. You can read more about RRS objects at `https://aws.amazon.com/about-aws/whats-new/2010/05/19/announcing-amazon-s3-reduced-redundancy-storage/`.

Notifications are useless unless you provide a destination for them. AWS supports the following notification destinations (you can use any or all of them as needed):

>> **Amazon Simple Notification Service (Amazon SNS) topic:** When working with SNS, AWS publishes notifications as a topic that anyone with the proper credentials can subscribe to in order to receive information about that topic. Using this approach lets multiple parties easily gain access to the information at the same time. This approach represents a push strategy through which AWS pushes the content to the subscribers.

>> **Amazon Simple Queue Service (Amazon SQS) queue:** When working with SQS, AWS places event notifications in a queue. One or more parties can query the queue to obtain the necessary information. Each party must separately query the queue, and a single party can remove the notification from the queue. This pull strategy works much like email and often is used by single parties or groups.

>> **AWS Lambda function:** Defines a method of providing an automated response to any given event. Chapter 6 describes the inner workings of Lambda in more detail.

Employing versioning

During the early days of computing, the undo feature for applications was a major innovation that saved people countless hours of fixing errors. Everyone makes mistakes, so being able to undo a mistake, rather than fix it, is nice. It makes everyone happier. *Versioning* is a kind of undo for objects. Amazon can automatically store every version of every object you place in a bucket, which makes it possible to

>> Return to a previous version of an object when you make a mistake in modifying the current version

>> Recover an object that you deleted accidentally

>> Compare different iterations of an object to see patterns in changes or to detect trends

>> Provide historical information when needed

Seemingly, you should make all your buckets versioned. After all, who wouldn't want all the wonderful benefits that versioning can provide? However, versioning also comes with some costs that you need to consider:

>> Every version of an object consumes all the space required for that object, rather than just the changes, so the storage requirements for that object increase quickly.

>> After you configure a bucket to provide versioning, you can never stop using versioning. However, you can suspend versioning as needed.

>> Deleting an object doesn't remove it. The object is marked as deleted, but it remains in place, which means that it continues to occupy storage space.

>> Overwriting an object results in a new object version rather than a deletion of the old object.

>> Adding versioning to a bucket doesn't affect existing objects until you interact with those objects. Consequently, the existing objects don't have a version number.

Working with Objects

The term *object* provides a generic reference to any sort of data, no matter what form the data may take. As you discover in Chapter 2, S3 stores the objects you upload in buckets. These buckets provide the means to interact with the data. After you create a bucket, you can use any of a number of organizational methods to interact with the objects you upload to the bucket. Therefore, Chapter 2 is just a starting point. If you haven't already created the bucket as Chapter 2 explains, you need to do that before working with the sections that follow. Next, use these steps to access the S3 Management Console:

1. **Sign into AWS using your administrator account.**

2. **Navigate to the S3 Management Console at** `https://console.aws.amazon.com/s3`.

   You see a listing of any buckets you have created, along with any buckets that Amazon created automatically on your behalf (such as one for Elastic Beanstalk, covered in Chapter 5). The bucket used for the examples that follow is the one you created in Chapter 2.

S3 bucket names are unique, which means that the bucket names you see in this chapter won't match the name of the bucket you see on your system. All screenshots will show the johnm.test-bucket created in Chapter 2, but the procedures apply to any bucket you create.

3. **Click the link for the bucket you created from the instructions in Chapter 2.**

   You see any objects you created as part of working through the Chapter 2 example.

After you sign in, you can begin interacting with the S3 bucket you created. The following sections help you understand the details of working with objects in S3.

Creating folders

As with your local hard drive, you use folders to help organize data within buckets. And just as with local folders, you can create hierarchies of folders to store related objects more efficiently. Use the following steps to create new folders.

1. **Navigate to the location that will hold the folder.**

   When creating folders for the first time, you always start in the bucket.

2. **Click Create Folder.**

   A textbox appears with a blank area that you can use to type the folder name, as shown in Figure 7-1.

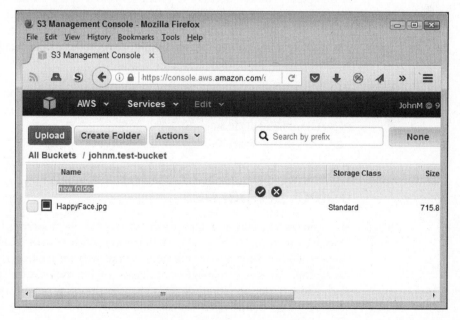

FIGURE 7-1:
A new folder appears as a textbox, in which you can type the folder name.

3. **Type the folder name and press Enter.**

The example uses a folder name of My Folder 1. You see the folder added to the list of objects in the bucket, as shown in Figure 7-2.

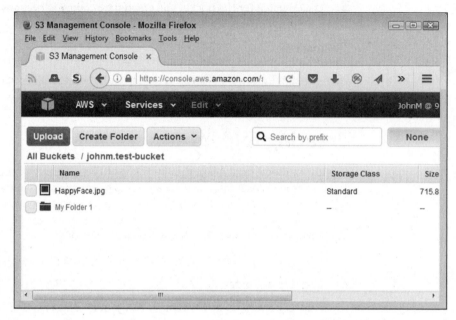

FIGURE 7-2:
Amazon
automatically
sorts new folder
entries for you.

At this point, you can access the folder if desired. Simply click the folder's link. When you open the folder, Amazon tells you that the folder is empty, as shown in Figure 7-3. Folders can hold the same objects that a bucket can. For example, if you want to add another folder, simply click Create Folder again to repeat the process you just performed.

TIP

When you open a folder, the navigation path shows the entire path to the folder. To move to another area of your S3 setup, simply click that entry (such as All Buckets) in the navigation path.

Setting bucket, folder, and object properties

After you create a bucket, folder, or object, you can set properties for it. The properties vary by type. For example, when working with a bucket, you can determine how the bucket supports permissions, static website hosting, logging, events, versioning, life-cycle management, cross-region replication, tags, requestor pays, and transfer acceleration. This chapter discusses most of these properties because you set them to perform specific tasks.

FIGURE 7-3:
Folders start in an
empty state.

Likewise, folders let you set details about how the folder reacts. For example, you can set the storage class, which consists of Standard, Standard – Infrequent Access, or Reduced Redundancy. The storage class determines how the folder stores data. Using the Standard – Infrequent Access option places the folder content in a semi-archived state. With the content in that state, you pay less money to store the data but also have longer retrieval times. (The article at https://aws. amazon.com/s3/storage-classes/ describes the storage classes in more detail.) You can also set the kind of encryption used to protect folder content.

Objects offer the same configuration options as folders and add the capability to set permissions and change the object metadata. The metadata describes the object type and provides information that an application might use to find out more about it. The standard metadata entry defines a content type, but you can add any metadata needed to identify the object fully.

To set properties for an individual item, check that item's entry in the management console and choose Actions ⇨ Properties. A Properties pane opens that's similar to the one shown in Figure 7-4 for My Folder 1. Make any changes you want and click Save to save the changes.

If you select multiple items, the Properties pane shows the properties that are common to all the items you selected. Any changes you make affect all the items. When you finish setting properties, you can close the Properties pane by clicking the X in the corner of the pane.

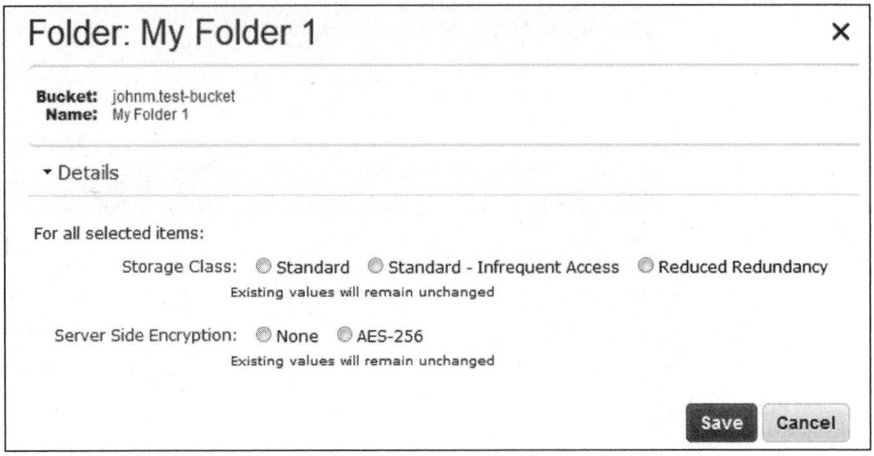

FIGURE 7-4: Use the Properties pane to adjust item properties.

Deleting folders and objects

At some point, you may find that you need to delete a folder or object because it no longer contains pertinent information. (Remember, when you delete folders or objects in buckets with versioning enabled, you don't actually remove the folder or object. The item is simply marked for deletion.) Use the following steps to delete folders and objects:

1. **Click the box next to each folder or object you want to delete.**

   The box changes color and becomes solid to show that you have selected it. (Clicking the box a second time deselects the folder or object.)

2. **Choose Actions ⇨ Delete.**

   You see a dialog box asking whether you want to delete the selected items, as shown in Figure 7-5.

3. **Click OK.**

   The Transfers pane, shown in Figure 7-6, opens to display the status of the operation. When the task is complete, you see Done as the status. Selecting the Automatically Clear Finished Transfers option automatically clears messages for tasks that complete successfully. Any tasks that end with an error will remain. You can also manually clear a transfer by right-clicking its entry and choosing Clear from the context menu.

4. **Click the X in the upper-right corner of the Transfers pane to close it.**

   You see the full entry information as you normally do.

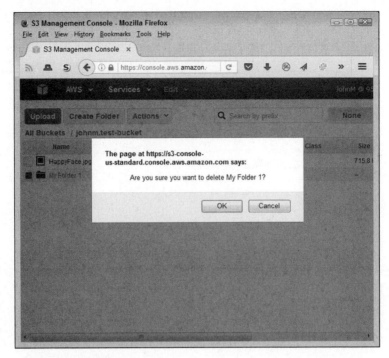

FIGURE 7-5:
Amazon asks
whether you're
sure you want to
delete the folder
or object.

Transfers   ✕

☐ Automatically clear finished transfers

FIGURE 7-6:
The Transfers
pane shows the
status of
deletions you
perform.

⊘ **Done**

⊖ Delete: 🗋 Deleting My Folder 1 from johnm.test-bucket

Uploading objects

The only method that you can use to upload an object from the console is to employ the same technique shown in Chapter 2. This means clicking Upload, selecting the files that you want to send to S3, and then starting the upload process.

Chapter 2, however, leaves out some useful additional settings changes you can make. After you select one or more objects to upload, click Set Details to display the Set Details dialog box, which lets you choose a storage class and determine whether you want to rely on server-side encryption, as shown in Figure 7-7.

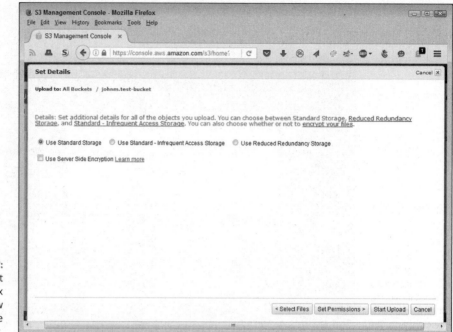

FIGURE 7-7:
Use the Set
Details dialog box
to configure how
S3 stores the
object.

The next step is to click Set Permissions. You use the Set Permissions dialog box, shown in Figure 7-8, to define the permissions for the objects you want to upload. Amazon automatically assumes that you want full control over the objects that you upload. The Make Everything Public check box lets everyone have access to the objects you upload. You can also create custom permissions that affect access to all the objects you upload at a given time.

Finally, you can click Set Metadata to display the Set Metadata dialog box, shown in Figure 7-9. In general, you want Amazon to determine the content types automatically. However, you can choose to set the content type manually. This dialog box also enables you to add custom metadata that affects all the objects that you upload at a given time.

TECHNICAL
STUFF

To perform other kinds of uploads to S3, you must either resort to writing application code using one of the AWS Application Programming Interfaces (APIs) or rely on another service. For example, you can use Amazon Kinesis Firehose (https://aws.amazon.com/kinesis/firehose/) to stream data to S3. The techniques used to perform these advanced sorts of data transfers are outside the scope of this book, but you need to know that they exist.

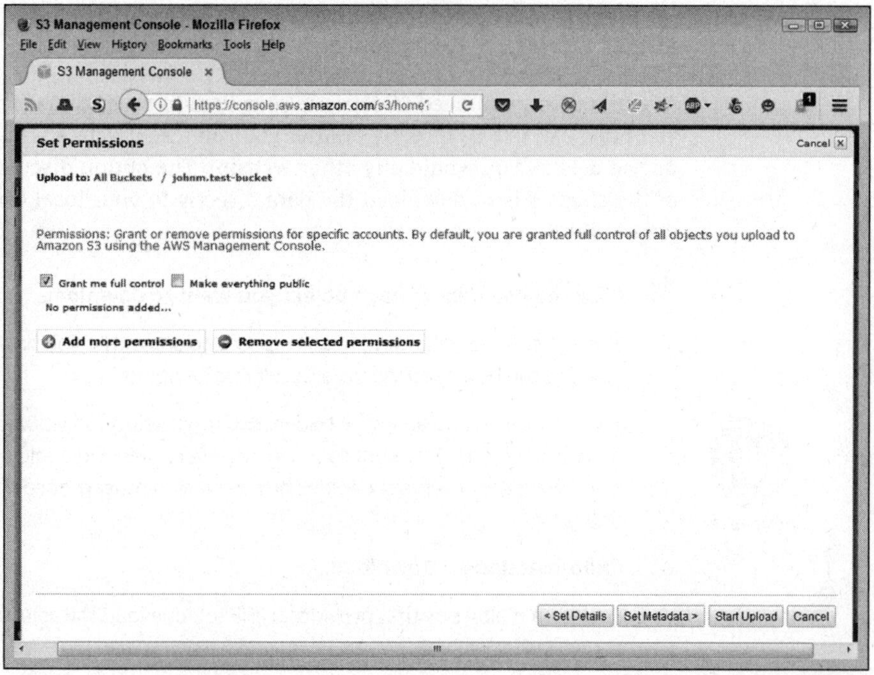

FIGURE 7-8:
Use the Set
Permission dialog
box to define
object access.

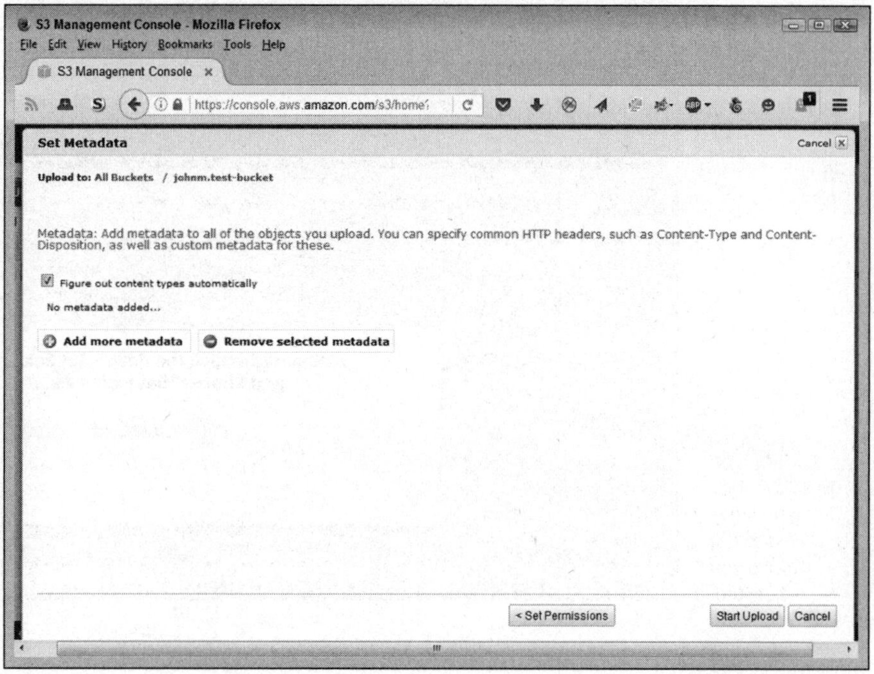

FIGURE 7-9:
Use the Set
Metadata dialog
box to provide
object labeling.

Retrieving objects

At some point, you need to retrieve your data in order to use it. Any applications you build can use S3 directly online. You can also create a static website to serve up the data as you would any other website. The option discussed in this section of the chapter is to download the data directly to your local drive. The following steps tell how to perform this task.

1. **Click the box next to each object you want to download.**

   The box changes color and becomes solid to show that you have selected it. (Clicking the box a second time deselects the object.)

   REMEMBER

   You can't download an entire folder. You must select individual objects to download (even if you want to download every object in a folder). In addition, if you want to preserve the folder hierarchy, you must rebuild it on your local drive.

2. **Choose Actions ▷ Download.**

   You see a dialog box that provides a link to download the selected objects, as shown in Figure 7-10.

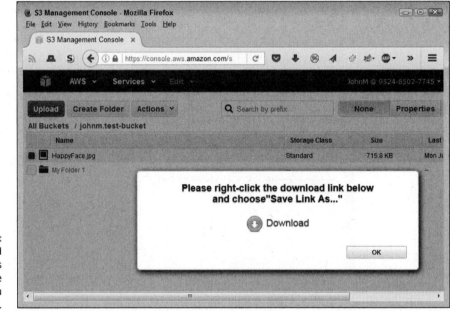

FIGURE 7-10:
The Download link provides access to the objects you selected.

Clicking the Download link performs the default action for your browser with the objects. For example, if you select a .jpg file and click Download, your browser will likely display it in a new tab of the current windows. Right-click the Download link to see all the actions that your browser provides for interacting with the selected objects. Of course, this list varies by browser and the kinds of extensions you add to it.

3. **Right-click the Download link and choose an action to perform with the selected objects.**

   Your browser accomplishes the action as it normally would when right-clicking a link and choosing an option. Some third-party products may experience permissions problems when you attempt the download.

4. **Click OK.**

   You see the full entry information as it normally appears.

Performing Backups

Data is subject to all sorts of calamities — some localized, some not. In days gone by, individuals and organizations alike made localized backups of their data. They figured out before long that multiple backups worked better, and storing them in a data safe worked better still. However, major tragedies, such as flooding, proved that localized backups didn't work well, either. Unfortunately, storing a backup in a single outside location was just as prone to trouble. That's where using cloud backups comes into play. Using S3 to create a backup means that the backups appear in more than one location and that Amazon creates more than one copy for you, reducing the risk that a single catastrophic event could result in a loss of data. The following sections explore using S3 as a backup solution.

Performing a manual backup

Amazon's backup suggestions don't actually perform a backup in the traditional sense. You don't see an interface where you select files to add to the backup. You don't use any configuration methods for whole drive, image, incremental, or differential backups. After you get through all the hoopla, what it comes down to is that you create an archive (such as a .zip file) of whatever you want in the backup and upload it to an S3 bucket. Yes, it's a backup, but it's not what most people would term a full-backup solution. Certainly, it isn't an enterprise solution. However, it can still work for an individual, home office, or small business. The "Working with Objects" section, earlier in this chapter, tells you how to perform all the required tasks using the console.

Automating backups

You can provide some level of backup automation when working with S3. However, you need to use the initial Command Line Interface (CLI) instructions found at https://aws.amazon.com/getting-started/tutorials/backup-to-s3-cli/ to make this task possible. After you have CLI installed on your system, you can use your platform's batch-processing capability to perform backups. For example, a Windows system comes with Task Scheduler to automate the use of batch files at specific times. Of course, now you're talking about performing a lot of programming, rather than using a nice, off-the-shelf package. Unless your organization just happens to have the right person in place, the Amazon solution to automation is woefully inadequate.

You do have other alternatives. For example, if you have a Python developer in-house, you can use the pip install awscli command to install AWS CLI support on your system. The process is straightforward and incredibly easy compared to the Amazon alternative (see Figure 7-11). You likely need administrator privileges to get the installation to work as intended. After you have the required Python support in place, you can rely on S3-specific Python backup packages, such as the one at https://pypi.python.org/pypi/s3-backups, to make your job easier. However, you still need programming knowledge to make this solution work. (You can obtain this information from *Beginning Programming with Python For Dummies*, by John Paul Mueller.)

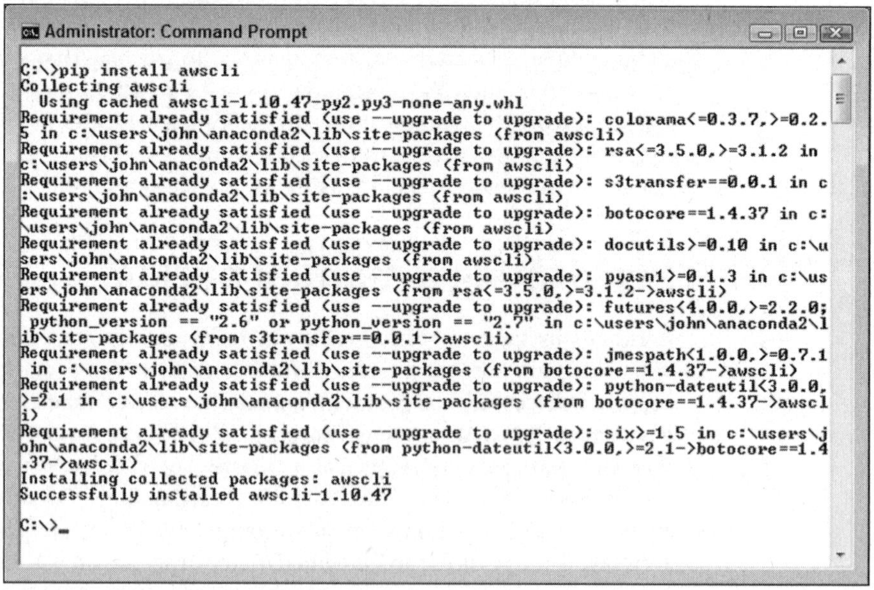

FIGURE 7-11: Use the built-in features of a language like Python to make performing S3 backups easier.

There are currently no optimal solutions for the administrator who has no programming experience whatsoever, but some off-the-shelf packages do look promising. For example, S3cmd (http://s3tools.org/s3cmd) and S3Express (on the same page) offer a packaged solution for handling backups from the Linux, Mac, and Windows command line. Look for more solutions to arrive as S3 continues to gain in popularity as a backup option.

Developing a virtual tape library

Most businesses likely have a backup application that works well. The problem is making the backup application see online storage, such as that provided by S3, as a destination. The AWS Storage Gateway (https://aws.amazon.com/storage gateway/) provides a solution in the form of the Gateway Virtual Tape Library (Gateway-VTL) (https://aws.amazon.com/about-aws/whats-new/2013/11/05/aws-storage-gateway-announces-gateway-virtual-tape-library/). This solution lets you create the appearance of virtual tapes that your backup application uses in place of real tapes. Consequently, you get to use your existing backup product, but you send the output to the cloud instead of having to maintain backups in-house.

Amazon does provide you with a trial period to test how well a Gateway-VTL solution works for you. Just how well it works depends on a number of factors, including the speed of your Internet connection. The most important consideration is that a cloud-based solution is unlikely to work as fast as dedicated high-speed local connectivity to a dedicated storage device. However, the cost of using Gateway-VTL may be considerably lower than working with local devices. You can check out the pricing data for this solution at https://aws.amazon.com/storagegateway/pricing/.

Using S3 to Host a Static Website

Another way to use S3 is to host a static website. A *static website* is one in which you deliver the content to the viewer precisely as stored. Most modern websites, especially those used by business, rely on dynamic techniques that create custom content from various sources. (You can read about the differences between static and dynamic websites at http://edinteractive.co.uk/static-vs-dynamic-websites-difference/.) However, a static website can still serve useful purposes for content that doesn't change often. For example, you can potentially use it for service manuals, corporate forms, or simply as a welcome page for a much larger site. The point is to be aware at the outset that static sites can contain all sorts of content, but the content always appears precisely as you put it together.

Creating a static website from your S3 bucket requires a few small changes. The following steps show how to make these changes and then help you view the static site on a browser.

1. **Select the file in the bucket that you want to use for the index page and click Properties.**

   You can use any file for this example. In fact, the example uses a .jpg file just for demonstration purposes. S3 shows a list of properties for the file.

2. **Open the Permissions section.**

   S3 shows the permissions associated with this file.

3. **Click Add More Permissions.**

   S3 adds a new permissions entry to the list.

4. **Configure the property to allow Everyone the Open/Download permission.**

   Your display should look similar to the one shown in Figure 7-12.

Object: HappyFace.jpg ✕

Bucket:	johnm.test-bucket
Name:	HappyFace.jpg
Link:	https://s3-us-west-2.amazonaws.com/johnm.test-bucket/HappyFace.jpg
Size:	733067
Last Modified:	Mon Jun 20 17:21:12 GMT-500 2016
Owner:	john
ETag:	63503d33d8f2b61f91c6db327eb3afe0
Expiry Date:	None
Expiration Rule:	N/A

▸ Details

▾ Permissions

You can control access to the bucket and its contents using access policies. Learn more.

Grantee: john ☑ Open/Download ☑ View Permissions ✕
☑ Edit Permissions

Grantee: Everyone ☑ Open/Download ☐ View Permissions ✕
☐ Edit Permissions

⊕ **Add more permissions**

5. Click Save.

S3 makes the change to the file permissions.

6. Select the bucket that you want to use for the static website; then click Properties.

The Properties pane opens on the right side of the page.

7. Open the Static Website Hosting entry.

S3 shows the static website configuration options (see Figure 7-13).

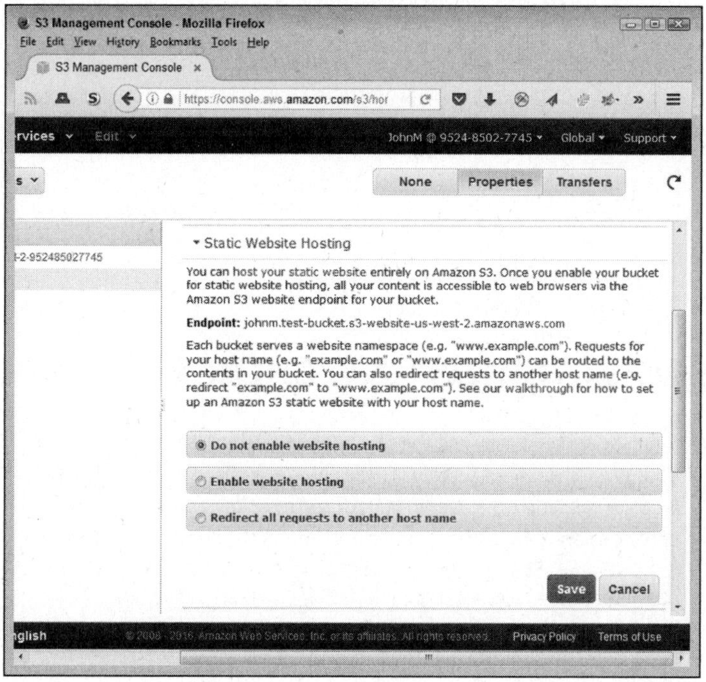

FIGURE 7-13:
Use these options to enable static website functionality for your S3 bucket.

8. Choose Enable Website Hosting.

S3 asks you to provide the name of a file to use for an index page and another file to use for an error page, as shown in Figure 7-14. You need to provide only an index page entry; the error page entry is optional. Normally, you use HTML coded pages for this task, but any file will do. The file shown in the figure is the same one that appears in Figure 7-12, shown previously, with the required permissions in place.

9. Click the Endpoint link.

The test page opens in your default browser.

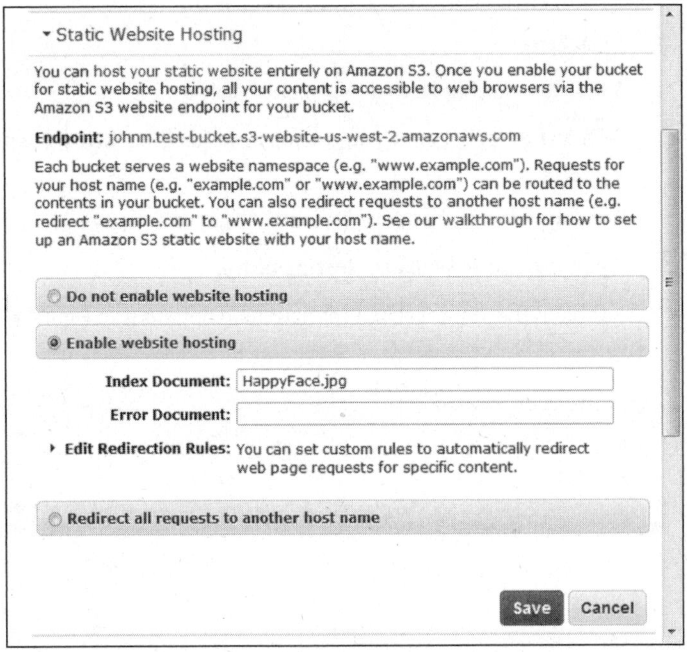

FIGURE 7-14:
Provide the name of a file to use for the index page.

MAKING HOSTING CHOICES CAREFULLY

Even though you may see the S3 capability to host a static website as a benefit to your organization (or yourself) today, you need to consider whether the same static website will hold up as beneficial tomorrow. Moving an application from one cloud service to another, or from one cloud vendor to another, can prove problematic (see http://www.cio.com/article/2922771/cloud-computing/switching-cloud-providers-is-no-cakewalk-but-do-your-users-know-that.html to discover some of the issues in moving from one cloud vendor to another). In fact, according to a recent Forester white paper (see http://www.forrester.com/pimages/rws/reprints/document/122895/oid/1-X0BOKB), the problem is less one of compatibility and more one of losing access to valuable service features. The higher the value of the service you choose to host an application, the greater the loss when you choose to move to another service, especially a service hosted by another vendor. Consequently, researching the hosting choices carefully is essential (especially because AWS offers so many options) before you begin developing an application in earnest.

Have no doubt about it: Amazon provides high-value services in order to lock you into the particular services you use or into using AWS in general at the least (for example, to move the data back to your local drive later). Even though this book touts the free services that AWS provides and helps you understand the limits of those services, ultimately, Amazon survives by selling you products. It doesn't actually give you anything free. If you continue to use AWS, eventually you pay for the free services you played with at the outset, which means that you need to make good choices during the free period that AWS provides.

Because enterprises naturally hate lock-in, you can find a number of open source alternatives online such as OpenStack (`https://www.openstack.org/`), Cloud Foundry (`https://www.cloudfoundry.org/`), and Docker (`https://www.docker.com/`). These offerings come with a price as well. They aren't interoperable or portable for the most part (thereby providing a kind of lock-in) and they don't offer the same kinds of high-value services that AWS provides. The video at `https://www.openstack.org/summit/vancouver-2015/summit-videos/presentation/openstack-docker-and-cloud-foundry-how-does-the-leading-open-source-triumvirate-come-together` is eye opening because the product does present a certain level of interoperability, but watch carefully so that you understand the caveats that come with using an open source solution.

The most important reason to experiment fully and carefully, though, is that the service you select may not provide all the features you need (which is why this book spends so much time discussing feature sets in an unbiased manner). For example, Land O'Lakes, an agricultural firm that services farmers' needs, recently decided to use Google's public cloud so that a Land O'Lakes application could gain access to Google Maps (read the article at `http://www.computerworld.com/article/3078181/cloud-computing/land-olakes-maps-out-farmings-future-with-google-cloud.html` for details). The fact that AWS doesn't provide this functionality means that even though AWS provides many superior services to Google, it doesn't provide the one essential service required to make this application work.

As an alternative to using the endpoint that Amazon provides, you can also choose to redirect the S3 bucket to another host. However, for this option to work, you must make the redirection to another S3 bucket. For example, you can link it to an existing Elastic Beanstalk setup. To make this option work, you use the Redirect All Requests to Another Host Name option.

Combining S3 with Lambda

Lambda enables you to run code on AWS without provisioning or managing a server. Chapter 6 introduces you to Lambda and demonstrates how it works. The purpose of the current chapter is to show that you can combine Lambda with other services —S3, in this case. Combining Lambda with S3 creates a more powerful use of both services by allowing you to do more. AWS provides many other solutions for running code, but this particular solution will appeal to administrators who need to perform a task quickly and without a lot of fuss.

REMEMBER

The Lambda function that you want to use must exist before you try to create a connection between it and S3. You use the following steps to connect S3 with Lambda:

1. **Select the bucket that you want to use for the static website and then click Properties.**

   The Properties pane opens on the right side of the page.

2. **Open the Events entry.**

   S3 shows the static website configuration options (see Figure 7-15). Even though this section discusses Lambda, note that you can create other sorts of actions based on S3 events that include an SNS topic and an SQS queue, as described in the "Using S3 events and notifications" section, earlier in this chapter.

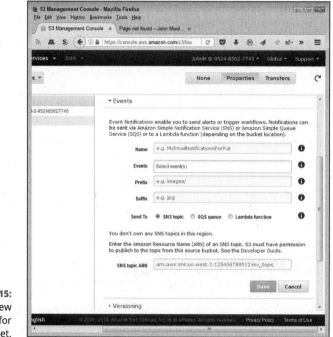

FIGURE 7-15:
Create a new event entry for your bucket.

3. **Type a name for the event.**

   The example uses MyEvent.

4. **Click the Events field.**

   You see a list of the potential events that you can use to initiate an action, as shown in Figure 7-16. The "Using S3 events and notifications" section, earlier in this chapter, describes the various events.

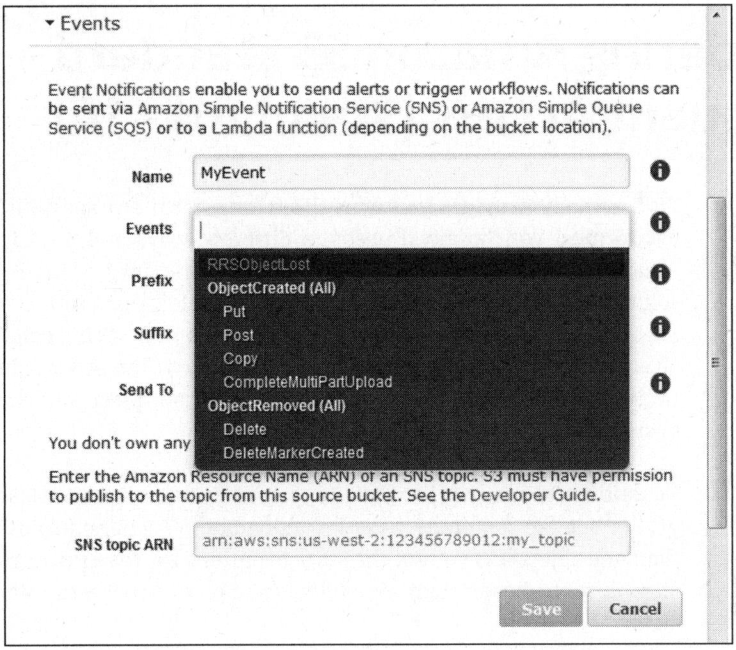

FIGURE 7-16:
Choose one of
the events to use
for your Lambda
function.

5. **Choose one or more of the events.**

   You can choose as many events as desired. Every time one of these events occurs, S3 will call your Lambda function.

6. **Optionally type a value in the Prefix field to limit events to objects that start with a particular set of characters.**

   The prefix can include path information so that events occur only when something changes in a particular folder or folder hierarchy.

7. **Optionally, type a value in the Suffix field to limit events to objects that start with a particular set of characters.**

8. **Select Lambda Function in the Send To field.**

9. **Select a Lambda function to execute when the events occur.**

   You may choose an existing event or choose the Add Lambda Function ARN option to access a Lambda function by its Amazon Resource Name (ARN).

10. **Click Save.**

   The events you selected for the S3 bucket will now invoke the Lambda function.

Considering Amazon S3 Standard – Infrequent Access (Standard – IA)

AWS actually provides you with three long-term storage solutions that you can use to meet your archival needs in different ways and at different price points. Amazon S3 Standard – Infrequent Access (Standard – IA) is just one of those solutions. You find a comparison of the three solutions in the "Comparing EFS to S3, Standard – IA, and Glacier" section of Chapter 8. This chapter focuses exclusively on Standard – IA and doesn't cover any of the other solutions. Standard – IA is covered first because it provides the simplest solution and appeals to businesses with basic needs.

In contrast to many other options, you can't set a storage class for a bucket as a whole. You set a storage class for individual objects and folders. Selecting more than one object lets you set the storage options for the entire group. The following steps describe how to configure folders and objects to use the Standard – IA storage class:

1. **Select the folders and objects that you want to use for the static website and then click Properties.**

   The Properties pane opens on the right side of the page. This particular example uses one object and one folder so that you can see how multiple selections appear. However, you can set the storage class for single objects and folders as well.

2. **Open the Details entry.**

   S3 shows the details for the folder, object, or combination of selections, as shown in Figure 7-17. The default is to use the Standard storage class, even when you haven't selected any of the storage classes.

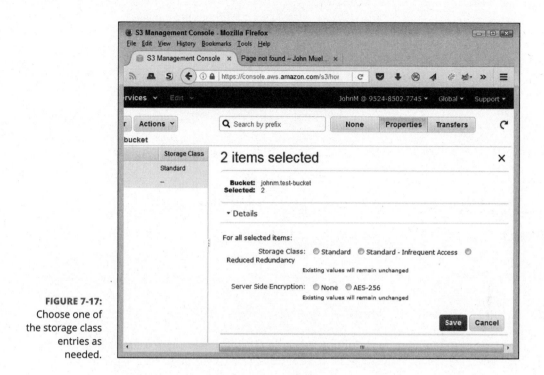

FIGURE 7-17:
Choose one of
the storage class
entries as
needed.

3. **Select the Standard – Infrequent Access option and click Save.**

The selected folders and objects now use the Standard – Infrequent Access storage class as described at https://aws.amazon.com/s3/storage-classes/.

Chapter **8**

Managing Files Using the Elastic File System

The Elastic File System (EFS) provides a third option for storing information on Amazon Web Services (AWS). This is the most feature rich of the three options discussed so far in the book. However, features don't always translate into additional usability. Choosing the right storage method will save you time, effort, and money. The more you ask AWS to do, the more Amazon charges for the service. That's why the first section of this chapter spends time comparing the three options so that you have a better idea of what you actually get with each option.

After you know how EFS works and how it compares to the other storage options, you can start working with it. This chapter helps you with all the standard tasks that you might perform with EFS. The goal is to configure EFS so that you can actually interact with it on your EC2 setup.

One of the services that EFS supports is Elasticsearch. The Elasticsearch is an open source search and analytics engine. You use it to perform various sorts of analysis, such as checking out your log files or performing real-time application monitoring. When you combine EFS with Elasticsearch, you gain considerable functionality in turning your EC2 server into something that can help your organization control precisely how people use and interact with your server. You can also begin avoiding those embarrassing slowdowns or complete application failures that cause people to go to any other site they can find.

Considering the Elastic File System (EFS) Features

You use EFS to perform tasks at the file-system level. Most business users are quite familiar with the file-system level because they use it to retrieve files when working with applications such as word processors. A file system uses the filing cabinet metaphor, which means that individual files appear in folders, and folders appear in drawers (individual hard-drive partitions). This particular metaphor has appeared as part of computer systems almost since the start of computing. The only difference with EFS, as the following sections detail, is that the filing cabinet now appears in the cloud rather than on a local or network hard drive.

Introducing EFS

Most operating systems today provide about the same paradigm for managing files. A drive contains a root directory. This root directory can contain as many folders as needed to organize the data that the drive contains. Subfolders contain content that becomes more specific as the hierarchy depth increases. Each folder or subfolder can contain files that contain data. Depending on the characteristics of the file system, the files can contain simple, complex, fully populated, or sparse data. Some files can even contain multiple data streams (as explained at `http://ntfs.com/ntfs-multiple.htm`). EFS replicates the most common features of file systems found on operating systems today. It doesn't replicate every feature, but it replicates enough features to make using the file system easy. An EFS drive looks like any other drive you use on any other operating system.

You can use EFS independently, in conjunction with other AWS services, or through a gateway (to make it appear as part of your local network). The most common service to connect to EFS is Elastic Compute Cloud (EC2), covered in Chapter 4. In fact, a major attraction of using EFS is that you can connect multiple EC2 instances to a single EFS drive. This means that all the EC2 instances share data and enable all of them to interact with it in meaningful ways. The common storage uses for EFS are

>> Application data

>> Big data

>> Analytics

>> Media processing workflows

>> Content management

>> Web application data and content

>> User home directories

REMEMBER

EFS emphasizes shared file storage, which implies access from multiple services or applications from multiple locations. You need to consider the construction of a service before you put it into use — that is, you should develop an understanding of the goals that engineers had in designing it. Because EFS emphasizes shared access, it doesn't necessarily provide speed or some types of flexibility. The goal is to ensure that services, applications, and devices of all sorts can gain access to specific kinds of data, rather than provide flexible configuration options.

As with other Amazon storage options, EFS scales to meet your current storage demands. Amazon provides the same levels of redundancy and automatic backup for EFS that it does for the other storage options. In addition, Amazon stresses that you pay only for the resources that you actually use to perform tasks. You don't pay a minimal fee for storage or for setup costs. EFS also provides the same sort of permission system used by the other storage systems. Chapter 7 provides some insights into how permissions work. Essentially, you assign specific rights to groups or individual users based on access requirements.

Understanding the connection to Network File System version 4 (NFSv4)

EFS relies on a standardized Internet Engineering Task Force (IETF) file system, NFSv4 (see the standards documentation at `https://www.ietf.org/rfc/rfc3530.txt`). Compliance with a standard is important because most Network Attached Storage (NAS) and many operating system vendors also comply with NFSv4, enabling these data sources to interoperate seamlessly and appear to have all the data sources residing on the local machine (even when they're miles apart). NFS is a mature file system that has seen use for at least the last 20 years in its various incarnations, so you can also be sure that the developers have worked the bugs out. The Storage Networking Industry Association (SNIA) provides a white paper outlining the details of NSFv4 at `http://www.snia.org/sites/default/files/ESF/FINAL_SNIA_An_Overview_of_NFSv4-4_20Oct2015.pdf`.

WARNING

Amazon doesn't provide full NFSv4 support. The page at `http://docs.aws.amazon.com/efs/latest/ug/nfs4-unsupported-features.html` describes the NFSv4 features that EFS doesn't support, and some of the omissions are extremely important. For example, EFS doesn't support NFSv4 Access Control Lists (ACLs), Kerberos-based security, lock upgrades or downgrades, or deny share (which means that every time you share a file, you must share it with everyone). These omissions will affect your security planning if you aren't aware of them and take measures to overcome the potential security problems they present. How much these omissions affect security depends on the kinds of information you attempt to store on EFS, so you must look at your data needs carefully.

EFS doesn't support certain file attributes. It shouldn't surprise you that EFS lacks support for block devices because Elastic Block Storage (EBS) meets this need. Many of the attribute omissions are for optional features, however, so they may not present much of a problem unless you have specific needs. Be sure to check the Amazon documentation carefully to ensure that omissions, such as namespace support, won't cause problems for your particular applications.

Comparing EFS to S3, Standard – IA, and Glacier

When comparing EFS to S3, S3 Standard – Infrequent Access (Standard – IA), and Glacier, the first thing that comes to mind is money. EFS is the most expensive of the Amazon storage options, and S3 is the least expensive. The difference that you pay between the various storage options is substantial, so you need to consider how you use storage in connection with your business carefully. Using all these services together often obtains the best value for your storage needs. For example, if you really don't plan to use some of your data for an extended time (with *extended* being defined by your business model), storing it on EFS will waste money. Using Glacier to store data that you use relatively often, however, will most definitely waste time. Considering the trade-offs between the various storage options is the smart way to do things.

The additional money you spend on EFS does purchase considerable added functionality. The most important feature that comes with EFS when compared to the other options in this section is the capability to secure files individually. EFS provides full locking support, so you can use it for database management applications or other needs for which locking all or part of a file is essential. Even though S3 and its associated storage options provide support for group and individual user permissions, you also find that EFS provides better security support (see the "Configuring EFS security" section, later in this chapter, for details).

Speed is also a consideration. S3 comes with HTTP overhead that robs it of some speed. However, the main speed difference comes from EFS's use of Solid-State Drives (SSDs) that make access considerably faster. From a visualization perspective, think of EFS as a kind of NAS, while S3 is most definitely a kind of Binary Large Object (BLOB) Internet storage. Amazon has also optimized S3 for write-once, read-many access, which means that writing incurs a speed penalty that you don't see when working with EFS.

S3 does offer some functionality that's not possible with EFS. For example, you can use S3 to offer files as a static website — something that you'd need to configure on EFS by hosting it on a web server. The point is that EFS is more like the file system you're used to using, and S3 is more akin to a special-purpose, blog-based database that provides direct web access at the cost of speed.

TIP

You can get past some of the S3 limitations by using an S3 File System (S3FS) solution such as s3fs-fuse (`https://github.com/s3fs-fuse`) or S3FS Node Packager Manager, S3FS NPM (`https://www.npmjs.com/package/s3fs`). However, even though these alternatives overcome some of the interface issues with S3, they still can't overcome the security and individual object size issues. (A single object can contain 5GB of data.) You can read a fuller comparison of these issues at `https://www.turnkeylinux.org/blog/exploring-s3-based-filesystems-s3fs-and-s3backer`.

Comparing EFS to EBS

The first thing you notice when working with EBS is that it's the only storage option without a console. You must configure EBS through an EC2 setup. That's because EBS provides services to only a single EC2 instance. If you need multiple-instance support, EBS won't work for you.

EFS is also designed to support organizations that require large distributed file systems of the type provided by Isilon (`https://www.emc.com/en-us/storage/isilon/index.htm`) and Gluster (`https://www.gluster.org/`). However, in addition to getting a large distributed file system, you can make this installation available across regions using EFS, which is something you can't do with these off-the-shelf solutions. What you get is a large distributed file system that provides region-specific support without your having to build this support yourself. Because EFS scales automatically, you don't need to worry about the amount of resources that each region requires to satisfy its needs. EBS is restricted to a single region because of its single EC2 instance focus and the fact that it acts like a Storage Area Network (SAN), which provides dedicated network support.

REMEMBER

Some applications require block storage devices, such as that provided by EBS, to avoid the rules that a file system imposes and gain a speed benefit. For example, Oracle Automatic Storage Management, or ASM (`https://docs.oracle.com/cd/B16276_01/doc/server.102/b14196/asm001.htm` and `https://docs.oracle.com/cd/B28359_01/server.111/b31107/asmcon.htm`), falls into this category. EFS doesn't answer the needs of a block storage device application; you need a product such as EBS in this case. Oracle ASM still has a file system, but the file system is built into the product, so having another file system would prove redundant and counterproductive because the two file systems would fight each other.

Working with EFS

As with the other services, EFS comes with its own management console that helps you create, delete, configure, and monitor the storage that you need. The process for creating and using an EFS drive is similar to the process used for a local hard drive, but some of the automation found on your local system isn't present with EFS. For example, you must mount the file system (a task that a local setup normally performs automatically for you). As with most local drives, security on an EFS drive relies on both group and individual use access rights. Unlike your local drive, however, an EFS drive can automatically scale to accommodate the needs of your applications (so that you don't run out of storage space). The following sections describe how to work with EFS drives and ensure that the data they contain remains safe.

Starting the Elastic File System Management Console

Before you can perform any tasks with EFS, you need to access the Elastic File System Management Console. The following steps assume that you haven't used EFS before and need to start a new setup from scratch. If you have already worked with EFS, you can skip to the next subsection, "Mounting the file system."

1. **Sign into AWS using your administrator account.**

2. **Navigate to the Elastic File System Management Console at** `https://console.aws.amazon.com/efs`.

   You see a Welcome page that contains interesting information about EFS and what it can do for you. However, you don't see the actual console at this point.

3. **Click Create File System.**

   You see the Create File System page, shown in Figure 8-1. As shown in the figure, the first step to create a file system is to decide how to access it. You can assign your EFS to one or more Virtual Private Clouds (VPCs).

4. **Choose one or more VPCs with which to interact.**

   If you have only one VPC, Amazon selects it for you automatically.

5. **Scroll down to the next section of the page.**

   Amazon asks you to choose mount targets for your EFS setup, as shown in Figure 8-2. A mount target determines the locations that can mount (make accessible) the drive.

WHAT DOES SCALING MEAN?

You often hear terms used in the computer industry without definition or context, so you can easily misuse the term and create an environment in which one person has a misconceived idea of what another person means by a particular term. *Scaling* is one of those terms. You hear it used in many different ways, and the different uses lead to all sorts of questions (such as the one found at https://www.quora.com/What-does-scaling-a-website-mean). Amazon uses the term *scaling* profusely, yet never really defines what it means by the term, so the term becomes meaningless at some point. This book, out of necessity, also uses scaling quite a bit, but unlike other information sources, it also provides a specific definition that appears throughout to identify *scaling* as a specific kind of performance measure. In this case, an application or service that *scales well* offers the appearance of constant speed, even when the number of people or other services using the application or service is large.

Scaling implies a range. A single server can scale to meet the demands of a specific number of users. When the number of users exceeds that range, application speed suffers unless other servers come online to address the overflow. In using scaling as a measure, an application or service scales well when it uses resources in a manner that requires fewer added resources when the load exceeds a specific threshold. In other words, an application that scales well has a larger range of acceptable loads than one that doesn't. Amazon automatically adds resources, such as servers, when needed to address an overflow while maintaining the appearance of constant application speed. The end user purportedly never sees the addition of resources, just the result of the addition, which means that the user doesn't notice the increase in load at all.

When working with AWS, scaling also implies automation. Even though the documentation never actually refers to scaling in this regard, it does constantly mention the fact that the services add resources as needed to ensure constant application speed. The only way to accomplish this task seamlessly is by using monitors and events to alert the service to the need to add resources automatically. Waiting for a human to manually add the resources would necessarily mean a drop in application speed at some point and defeat goals behind the kind of scaling that AWS provides. (The "Problems with autoscaling" sidebar in Chapter 4 provides additional details about how automation and scaling work hand in hand with AWS.)

TIP

Using all the availability zones in a particular region won't cost you additional money when you're working with the free tier. However, using multiple regions will add a charge. Remember that you get to use only one region when working at the free tier.

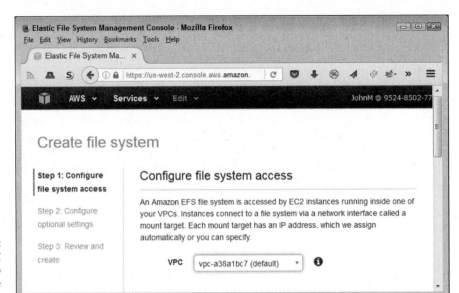

FIGURE 8-1:
Choose the VPC
you want to
use with the
EFS setup.

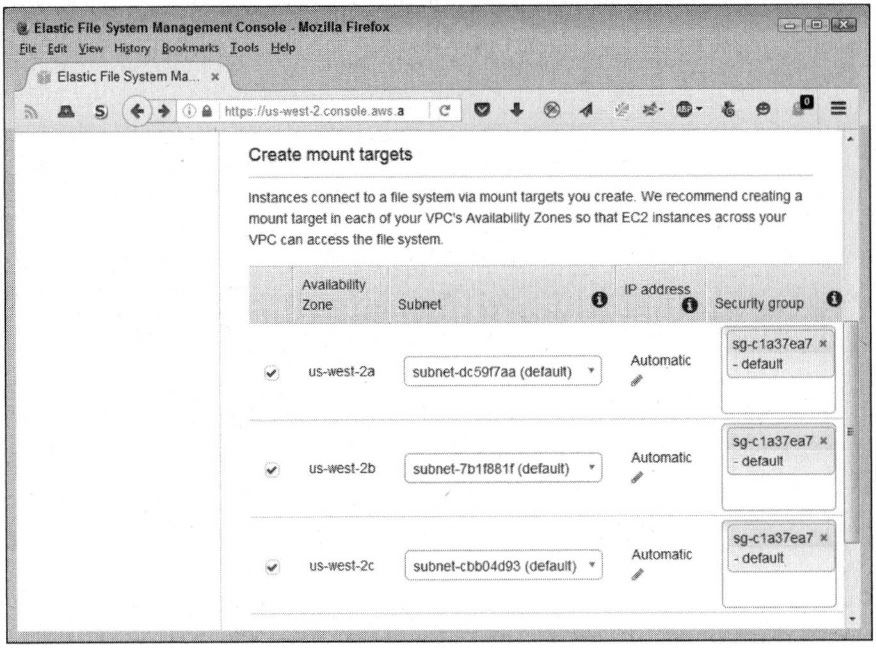

FIGURE 8-2:
Configure the
availability zones
you want to use.

6. **Select the availability zones that you want to use and then click Next Step.**

You see the Configure Optional Settings page, shown in Figure 8-3. These settings help you configure your EFS setup to provide special support, but you don't have to change the settings unless you want to. This page contains two optional settings:

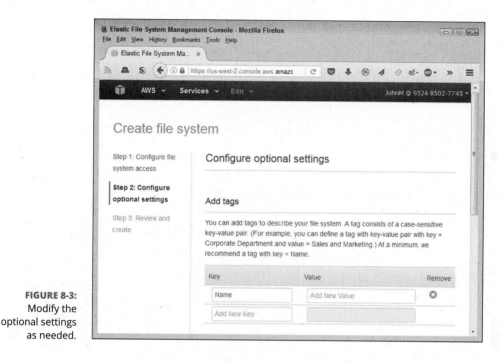

FIGURE 8-3:
Modify the optional settings as needed.

- **Add Tags:** Using tags allows you to add descriptive information to your setup. The descriptive information is useful when you plan to use more than one EFS setup with your network. Developers can also find the use of tags helpful when locating a particular setup to manipulate programmatically.

- **Choose Performance Mode:** Changing the performance mode enables EFS to read files faster, but at the cost of higher latency (time to find the file) when using the Max I/O setting. Amazon chooses the General Purpose setting by default, which means that transfer rates and file latency receive equal treatment when determining overall speed.

7. **Perform any required optional setup and then click Next Step.**

The example doesn't change any of the optional settings. You see the Review and Create page, shown in Figure 8-4.

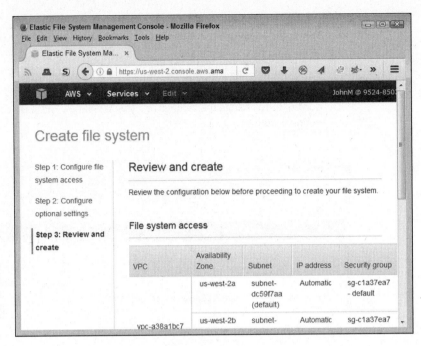

FIGURE 8-4:
Make sure that the settings reflect the requirements for your application.

8. **Verify the settings and then click Create File System.**

   The File Systems page appears with the new file system that you created, as shown in Figure 8-5. Even though the file system is accessible at this point, the drive may not be available immediately. The Creating status indication in the Life Cycle Status column of the Mount Targets table on this page tells you that the process of configuring EFS is ongoing.

Creating additional file systems

You can create as many EFS setups as needed to interact with your EC2 instances and associated applications. To create another EFS setup, click Create File System (refer to Figure 8-5) and you see the initial configuration page (shown previously in Figure 8-1). Follow the steps in the preceding section, "Starting the Elastic File System Management Console," to complete the new EFS configuration.

After you create a new EFS, you see multiple entries in the Elastic File System Management Console. Select the individual EFS setup that you want to work with when making changes.

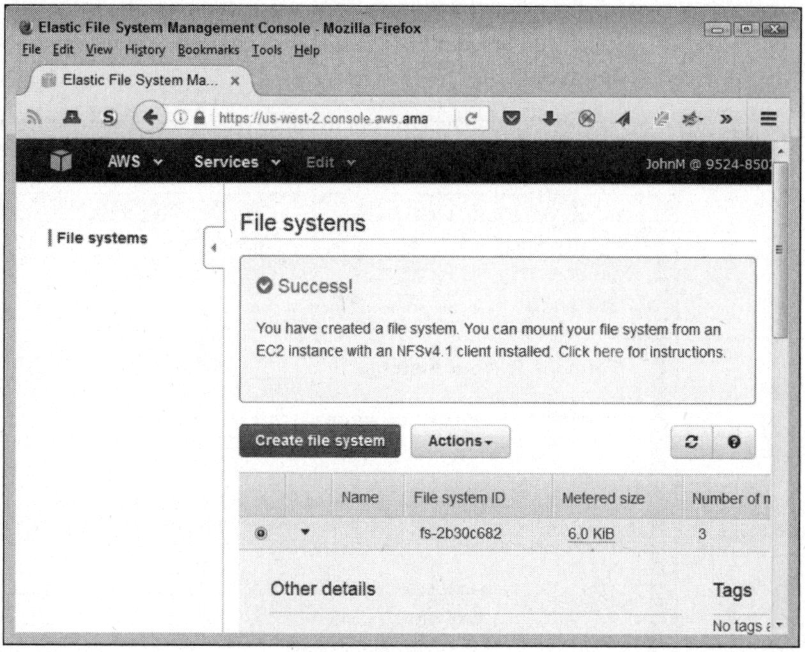

FIGURE 8-5:
The EFS
configuration is
available to
access.

Mounting the file system

Unlike many of the activities you perform in this book, mounting an EFS file system onto the EC2 instance that you create in Chapter 4 requires that you use the Secure Shell (SSH) client. You have many options for gaining access through SSH. This chapter (and all others that require you to use SSH) depends on the easiest and safest method possible — using the EC2 Management Console. After you have a connection to the instance, you can type commands to mount the EFS file system. The following sections describe how to perform both tasks.

Connect to an EC2 instance using a browser

To use SSH, you must create a connection to your EC2 instance. This means ensuring that you have access to the key file that you create in the "Generating security keys" section of Chapter 4. The following steps help you connect to your EC2 instance:

1. **Select Services ⇨ Compute ⇨ EC2.**

You see the EC2 Management Console.

2. **Choose Instances in the Navigation pane.**

The EC2 Management Console displays all the instances that you have configured for your setup. The book relies on just one instance, so you use that instance to perform the tasks in the procedures for this chapter.

3. **Select the box next to the instance that you want to use and click Connect.**

   You see the Connect to Your Instance dialog box, shown in Figure 8-6.

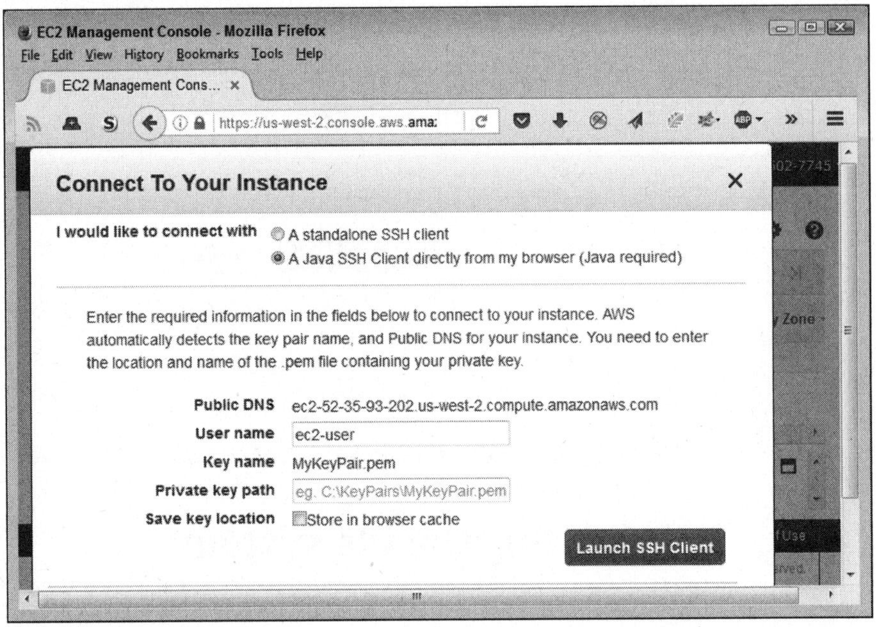

FIGURE 8-6:
Connect to your
instance using
the browser
method.

4. **Select the A Java SSH Client Directly from My Browser option.**

5. **Type the location of the key file in the Private Key Path field and then click Launch SSH Client.**

   Amazon starts the MindTerm SSH terminal for you, as shown in Figure 8-7, and logs you into your EC2 instance. If you find that you don't connect to your instance, you may lack the proper Java support or access to your security key file.

Update the EC2 instance

Before making any major change to your EC2 instance, it pays to perform an update to ensure that you have the latest versions of any required products. Performing this step each time you perform a major task may seem like too much work, but doing so will save time, effort, and troubleshooting in the long run. The following steps describe how to update your EC2 instance:

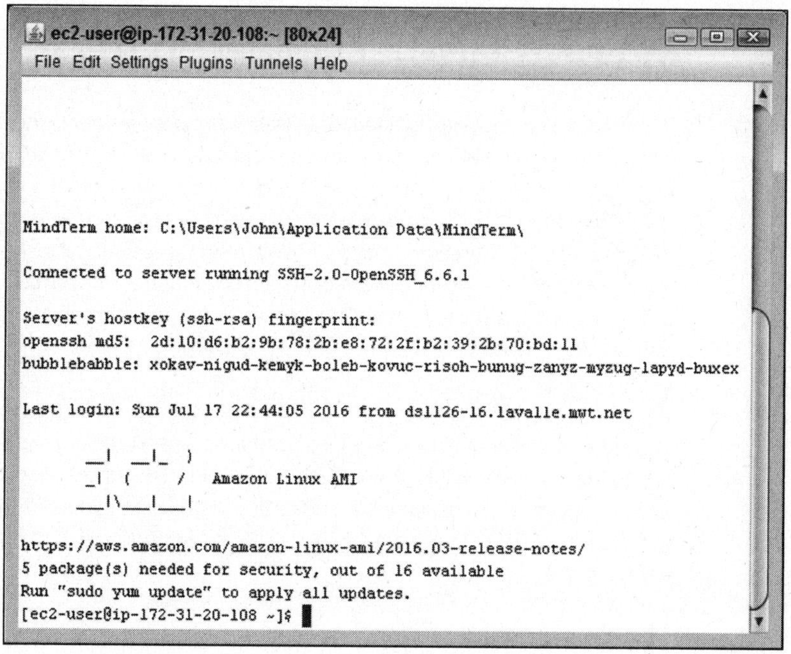

```
ec2-user@ip-172-31-20-108:~ [80x24]
File  Edit  Settings  Plugins  Tunnels  Help




MindTerm home: C:\Users\John\Application Data\MindTerm\

Connected to server running SSH-2.0-OpenSSH_6.6.1

Server's hostkey (ssh-rsa) fingerprint:
openssh md5:   2d:10:d6:b2:9b:78:2b:e8:72:2f:b2:39:2b:70:bd:11
bubblebabble: xokav-nigud-kemyk-boleb-kovuc-risoh-bunug-zanyz-myzug-lapyd-buxex

Last login: Sun Jul 17 22:44:05 2016 from dsl126-16.lavalle.mwt.net

      __|  __|_  )
      _|  (     /   Amazon Linux AMI
     ___|\___|___|

https://aws.amazon.com/amazon-linux-ami/2016.03-release-notes/
5 package(s) needed for security, out of 16 available
Run "sudo yum update" to apply all updates.
[ec2-user@ip-172-31-20-108 ~]$ █
```

FIGURE 8-7:
MindTerm
provides access
to your EC2
instance.

1. **Type** sudo yum update **in the terminal window and press Enter.**

   You see messages telling you that EC2 is installing any needed updates. If no
   updates exist, you see a No Packages Marked for Update message.

TIP

   The sudo (superuser do) command (http://www.computerhope.com/unix/
   sudo.htm) makes you a *superuser*, someone who has rights to do anything on
   the computer. The yum (Yellowdog Updater Modified) command is the primary
   method for getting, installing, updating, deleting, and querying the operating
   system features. You can learn more about it at http://www.computerhope.
   com/unix/yum.htm.

2. **If EC2 performed any updates, type** sudo reboot **and press Enter.**

   EC2 displays a message telling you that it has started the *reboot,* a process that
   stops and then restarts the system. You must close the terminal window.

3. **Reconnect to the EC2 instance using the steps in the previous section of
   the chapter.**

   EC2 displays the normal terminal window. You generally don't see any
   messages telling about the success of the update.

Installing the NFS client

To work with EFS, you need the NFS client. The NFS client gives you access to specialized commands to perform tasks such as mounting a drive. You can optionally use the NFS client to interact with the EFS file system in other ways. To install the NFS client, type **sudo yum -y install nfs-utils** and press Enter. (The yum -y command-line switch tells yum to assume that the answer to all yes/no questions is yes.) If EC2 needs to install the NFS client, you see a series of installation messages. Otherwise, you see the following message in most cases:

```
Loaded plugins: priorities, update-motd,
    upgrade-helper
Package 1:nfs-utils-1.3.0-0.21.amzn1.x86_64 already
    installed and latest version
Nothing to do
```

The message tells you whether you need to perform any updates. In this case, the message tells you that you already have the latest version installed. When you need to perform an update, type **sudo yum -y update nfs-utils** and press Enter.

Performing the mounting process

The EFS file system is ready for use and your EC2 instance has the correct software installed, but you still need to connect the two. It's sort of like having a car and a tire to go with the car, but not having the tire on the car so that you can drive somewhere. Mounting, the same process you'd use with that tire, is the step that comes next. The following steps show how to mount your EFS file system so that you can access it from an EC2 instance.

1. **Type** sudo mkdir efs **and press Enter.**

   This step creates a directory named efs using the mkdir (make directory) command (go to http://www.computerhope.com/unix/umkdir.htm for details on using the mkdir command). You can use other directory names, but using efs makes sense for this first foray into working with EFS. The next step involves a complicated-looking command. In fact, unless you're a Linux expert, you may have an incredibly hard time trying to decipher it. Fortunately, Amazon hides a truly useful bit of information from view, and the next step tells how to find it.

2. **Select the file system you want to use in the Elastic File System Management Console. Click the EC2 Mount Instructions link that appears in the File System Access section of the page.**

   You see the mount instructions, shown in Figure 8-8. Pay particular attention to the highlighted text. This is the command you need to type to mount your EFS file system in the EC2 instance. The command you see will likely differ from the one shown in Figure 8-8 because Amazon customizes the content of this dialog box to match your system.

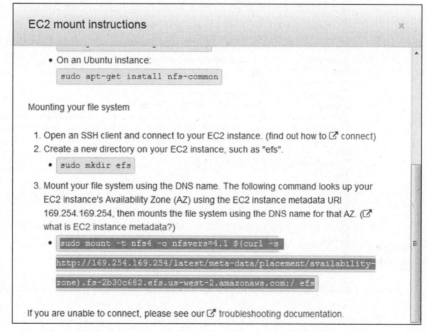

FIGURE 8-8: Amazon provides you with the long command you need to type when you know where to look.

3. **Highlight the command and paste it into your system's clipboard.**

4. **Paste the command into MindTerm by clicking the middle mouse button (unless you have changed the default paste key to something else).**

The command should look something like this:

```
sudo mount -t nfs4 -o nfsvers=4.1 $(curl -s
    http://169.254.169.254/latest/meta-data/placement/
    availability-zone).fs-2b30c682.efs.us-west-2.amazonaws.
    com:/ efs
```

5. **Press Enter.**

EC2 mounts the EFS file system. Of course, you have no way of knowing that the EFS file system is actually mounted.

6. **Type** cat /proc/mounts **and press Enter.**

You see a listing of all the mounted drives for your EC2 instance. Note that the EFS file system is the last entry in the list, as shown in Figure 8-9. The entry tells you all about the EFS file system, such as the mounting point location at /home/ec2-user/efs.

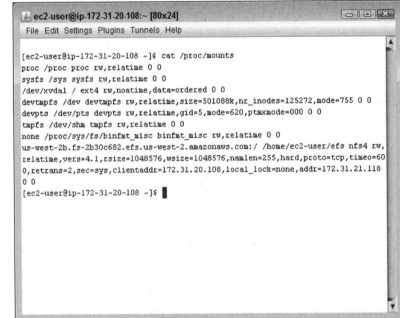

FIGURE 8-9: EFS is mounted and ready for use.

USING THE NFSSTAT COMMAND

The NFS statistics command (nfsstat) gives you all kinds of useful information about your EFS file system (which relies on NFS, as described in the "Understanding the connection to Network File System version 4 (NFSv4)" section, earlier in this chapter). When you use nfsstat alone, you see the usage statistics for your EFS configuration, such as the number of reads, writes, commits, and opens (among many other statistics).

However, the most useful nfsstat outputs require that you use a command-line switch. For example, type **nfsstat –m** (with a single dash) and press Enter to see statistics about the currently mounted NFS file systems (which is EFS in this case). If you aren't getting enough information, use the –v command-line switch to put nfsstat into verbose mode. In fact, nfsstat is simply fun to play with because you can learn so much about EFS while using it. To see a listing of other nfsstat command-line switches, type **nfsstat --help** (with two dashes) and press Enter.

Listing EFS content

When you're working with EFS, it pays to know where the content appears on the EC2 instance. The example in this chapter tells you to create a directory named efs. The full path to this directory according to the cat /proc/mounts command is /home/ec2–user/efs. To work in that directory, you type **cd efs** and press Enter because you start in the /home/ec2–user/ directory. When you need to display your current directory (because it really is easy to get lost), type **pwd** and press Enter. The pwd (print working directory) command (go to http://www.computer hope.com/unix/upwd.htm for more details about this command) outputs the full path to the current directory.

To see the content of the EFS directory, you type **ls** and press Enter. The ls (list) command (see http://www.computerhope.com/unix/uls.htm for more details) tells EC2 to list the content of a directory. However, this command comes with a host of command-line switches to tell EC2 what to list and to define how to list it. You see the ls command used a number of additional times in this chapter and the rest of the book to determine what to do next to configure an AWS service.

Configuring EFS security

The security you set as part of configuring your EFS file system determines who can access the drive from the outside. It doesn't control the security of the file system itself — the security used to determine whether someone could read or write files, for example. To change the security of the EFS file system, you must use EC2 commands within SSH. Of course, the first problem is figuring out what *rights* (capability to perform tasks) you currently have. You can determine rights in several ways. The easiest method is to use the `ls` command. Type **ls -al** and press Enter to see the long listing format of all the entries, including the hidden directory entries. Figure 8-10 shows typical output from the `efs` directory that you create in the "Performing the mounting process" section, earlier in this chapter.

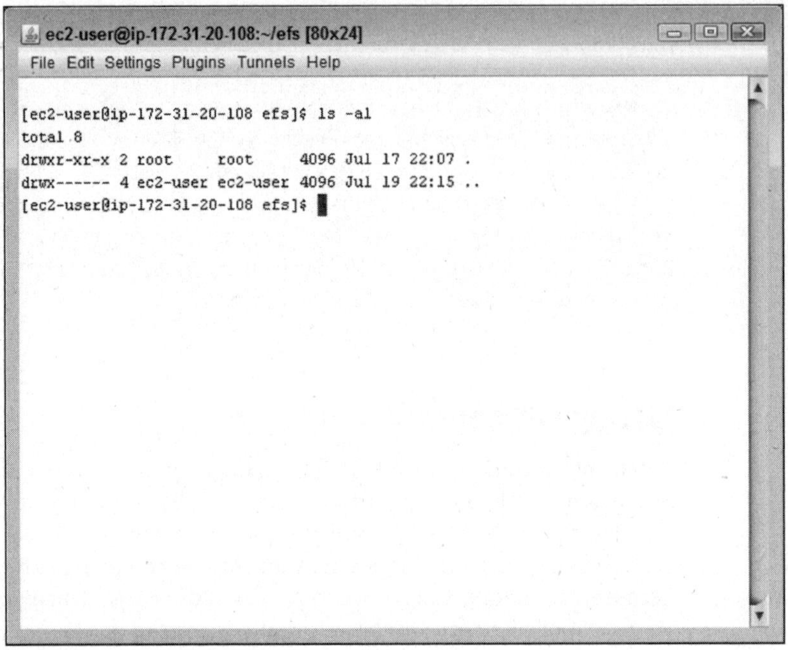

```
ec2-user@ip-172-31-20-108:~/efs [80x24]

File  Edit  Settings  Plugins  Tunnels  Help

[ec2-user@ip-172-31-20-108 efs]$ ls -al
total 8
drwxr-xr-x 2 root     root     4096 Jul 17 22:07 .
drwx------ 4 ec2-user ec2-user 4096 Jul 19 22:15 ..
[ec2-user@ip-172-31-20-108 efs]$
```

FIGURE 8-10:
Determine the current security settings for the `efs` directory.

The output might be puzzling unless you know the secret code for the `ls` command output. Moving from left to right, here is the meaning of all those letters:

>> **d:** This is a directory entry. The alternative is a file entry, which starts with a dash.

>> **rwx:** The owner has read, write, and execute permissions.

- **r:** read

- **w:** write

- **x:** execute

>> **r-x:** The group that owns the entry has read and execute permissions, but not write permissions.

>> **r-x:** Anyone else who accesses the directory has read and execute permissions as well.

- **2:** This entry has two links to it. In this case, the current directory and the parent directory are the only two links to this entry. The minimum number of links for a directory is 2 because every directory has a current directory and a parent directory entry.

- **root:** The owner's name is root.

- **root:** The owner's group name is root.

- **4096:** The entry consumes 4,096 bytes of disk space.

- **Jul 17 22:07:** The entry was created at this date and time.

- **.:** This is a special entry that defines the current directory. You can use a single period whenever you want to refer to the current directory in a command. The use of two periods (. .) signifies the parent directory.

Given that you have logged into EC2 as ec2-user in most cases, you have no rights to write any data to the efs directory. You can test this theory by using the touch command (using touch is explained at http://www.computerhope.com/unix/utouch.htm) to change the timestamp of a file that doesn't actually exist yet. (Touching the file creates an empty file entry.) Type **touch myfile.txt** and press Enter. You see an error message that tells you that the operating system denied permission to write the file, which is a requirement for touching it.

You have several options for correcting permission errors. The easiest way to fix the problem in this case is to use the chmod (change mode) command (go to http://www.computerhope.com/unix/uchmod.htm for details on using this command) to add the required right. In this case, you must give others the right to write data to the current directory as defined by the single period (.). The following steps lead you through this process:

1. **Type** sudo chmod o+w . **and press Enter.**

   Don't forget the period at the end of the command, or the command won't work. EC2 doesn't provide you with any output, so you need to validate the change you just made.

2. **Type** ls -al **and press Enter.**

   The output now shows drwxr-xrwx for the current directory (.).

3. **Type** touch myfile.txt **and press Enter.**

   No error message appears this time, but you don't know for certain that you created the file, either.

4. **Type** ls -al **and press Enter.**

   You see the output shown in Figure 8-11.

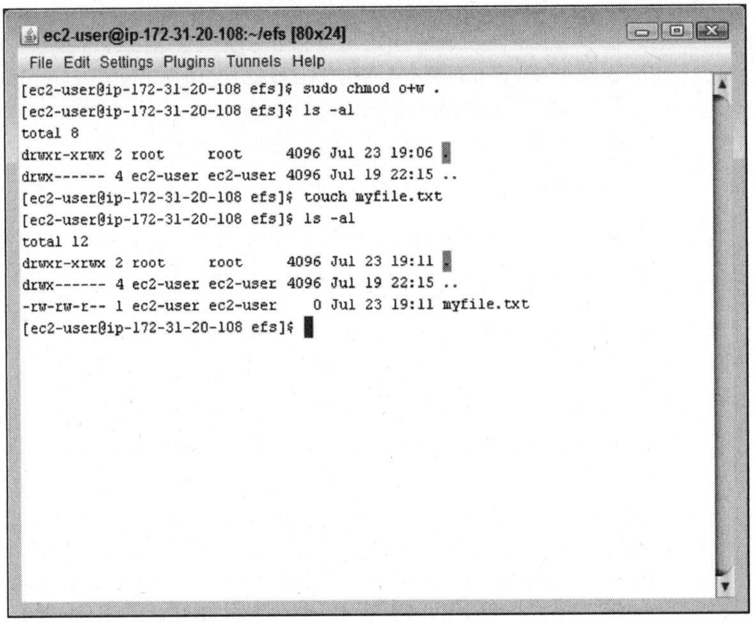

```
ec2-user@ip-172-31-20-108:~/efs [80x24]
File  Edit  Settings  Plugins  Tunnels  Help
[ec2-user@ip-172-31-20-108 efs]$ sudo chmod o+w .
[ec2-user@ip-172-31-20-108 efs]$ ls -al
total 8
drwxr-xrwx 2 root     root     4096 Jul 23 19:06
drwx------ 4 ec2-user ec2-user 4096 Jul 19 22:15 ..
[ec2-user@ip-172-31-20-108 efs]$ touch myfile.txt
[ec2-user@ip-172-31-20-108 efs]$ ls -al
total 12
drwxr-xrwx 2 root     root     4096 Jul 23 19:11
drwx------ 4 ec2-user ec2-user 4096 Jul 19 22:15 ..
-rw-rw-r-- 1 ec2-user ec2-user    0 Jul 23 19:11 myfile.txt
[ec2-user@ip-172-31-20-108 efs]$
```

FIGURE 8-11:
The new directory listing shows the file you just created.

The current directory entry now supports a green highlight, showing that you can perform tasks in it. Look carefully at the entries for the new file.

- This is a file type, so the security entries begin with a dash.

- No one has execute rights because this is a text file.

- The entry has only one link to it because it's a file, not a directory.

- The ec2-user owns the file, which makes sense given that ec2-user created it.

- The file size is 0, which also makes sense because you haven't given it any content.

You really don't need a superfluous file in your EFS file system, so deleting the test entry is important.

5. **Type** rm myfile.txt **and press Enter.**

   EC2 removes the file using the rm command (find details about this command at http://www.computerhope.com/unix/urm.htm). You can verify the removal using the ls -al command.

Unmounting and removing the file system

At some point, you may find that you want to unmount (dismount) your EFS file system. To perform this task, you type **sudo umount efs** and press Enter. As with mounting the file system, `efs` reflects the name of the folder you created for the file system. If you use a different name, you must replace `efs` with that name.

In most cases, you also want to remove the directory you created for EFS. To remove the directory, type **sudo rmdir efs** and press Enter.

At this point, you can remove the file system if desired by selecting the file system in the Elastic File System Management Console. Choose Actions➪ Delete File System. You see the Permanently Delete File System dialog box, shown in Figure 8-12. You must type the file system ID in the field immediately above the Delete File System button and then click Delete File System to make the change permanent.

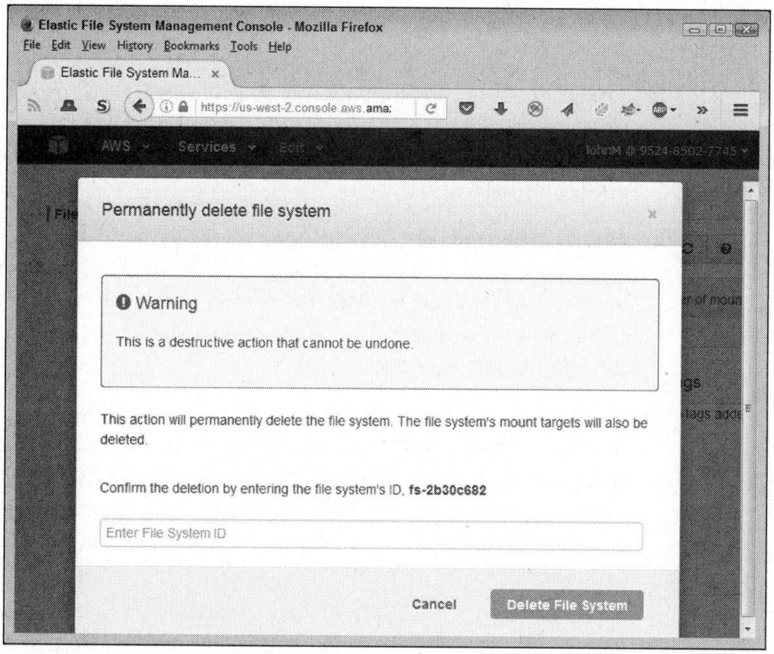

FIGURE 8-12:
Remove the EFS file system when you no longer need it.

Working with the Elasticsearch Service

The data your organization creates, manages, and monitors is the single most valuable resource that you own. Data defines your organization and helps you understand the direction your organization takes at various times during its evolution. Consequently, you need to have applications, such as the Amazon Elasticsearch Service, that can help you find what you need with as little effort as possible. The following sections help you discover more about the Amazon Elasticsearch Service so that you can use it to make working with your data substantially easier.

Understanding the Elasticsearch Service functionality

Organizations of all sizes need help in managing various kinds of data generated as part of application logging, application monitoring, user clicks in web applications, and the results of user text searches (among a growing number of data sources). Elasticsearch (the application, not the service) is an open source product that helps you perform a number of tasks:

>> **Searching:** Locating specific pieces of information is hard, and the larger the drive, the harder the task becomes. Entire companies are devoted to the seemingly simple matter of helping you find the particular piece of information you need. You know that the information exists; you just can't find it without help.

>> **Analyzing:** Data contains patterns, most of which aren't obvious without help. Until you see the pattern, you don't truly understand the data. Making sense of the data that appears on the hard drive is essential if you want to perform any useful tasks with it.

>> **Filtering:** Data storage objects today always have too much information. Anyone attempting to use the data gets buried beneath the mounds of useless data that doesn't affect the current target. Sifting through the data manually is often impossible, so you need help filtering the data to obtain just the information you need.

>> **Monitoring:** Looking without actually seeing is a problem encountered in many areas, not just data storage. However, because data storage serves so many data sources, the problem can become especially critical. Manually detecting particular data events, especially with a large setup, is impossible and there is no point in even attempting it. You need automation to make the task simpler.

Elasticsearch helps in these areas and many others. Here's the idea: You begin with a large data source, such as the logs generated when users perform tasks using you application, and you need to make sense of all the data the data source contains. When working with Elasticsearch, you mainly want to know about usage, which means performing analytics of various types. To make these analytics happen, Elasticsearch creates indexes that help it locate data quickly so that it answers requests for information in near real time. You can use this information to perform tasks such as identifying outages and errors, even when users don't directly report them (and even when the outage is so short that no one really notices that it occurred).

REMEMBER

Even though Elasticsearch is an open source product, it isn't necessarily a complete product. What Amazon is offering is a means to perform the required configuration details so that you can spend more time interacting with the data, rather than performing tasks such as creating data clusters and setting up redundancies to ensure that Elasticsearch works as intended. As with other services, you also gain access to the AWS security, scaling, and reliability features. Many of these added features rely on Amazon CloudWatch to perform the required monitoring (the same as used by other services). Therefore, the Amazon Elasticsearch Service is a value added proposition designed to make you more efficient. Fortunately, unlike your EFS setup, you won't spend a lot of time using SSH to set up Elasticsearch, it comes with full console support.

WARNING

As with many other Amazon services, Amazon doesn't charge you for configuring the Amazon Elasticsearch Service. However, you do pay for resources that Elasticsearch needs to perform its work. Therefore, you do pay for processing time and data storage access. You can find pricing information for this service at `https://aws.amazon.com/elasticsearch-service/pricing/`.

Creating the Elasticsearch domain

Before you can do anything with Elasticsearch, you must create a domain. The domain determines what Elasticsearch monitors. The following steps show you how to create a setup for the example EC2 system used in this book:

1. **Sign into AWS using your administrator account.**

2. **Navigate to the Elastic File System Management Console at** `https://console.aws.amazon.com/efs`.

You see a Welcome page that contains interesting information about the Amazon Elasticsearch Service and what it can do for you. However, you don't see the actual console at this point.

3. **Click Get Started.**

You see the Create Elasticsearch Domain page, shown in Figure 8-13. As shown in the figure, the first step is to give your domain a name.

4. **Type** my-domain **and click Next.**

Choose your domain name carefully. Amazon has some strict naming rules that it fully enforces.

You see a Configure Cluster page, where you must define the characteristics of the cluster you want to use. One of the most important settings for this example is the Instance Type, shown in Figure 8-14. To keep costs as low as possible (conceivably free), you must select one of the free instance types.

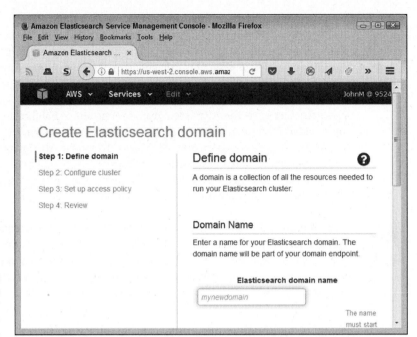

FIGURE 8-13:
Provide a name for your Elasticsearch domain.

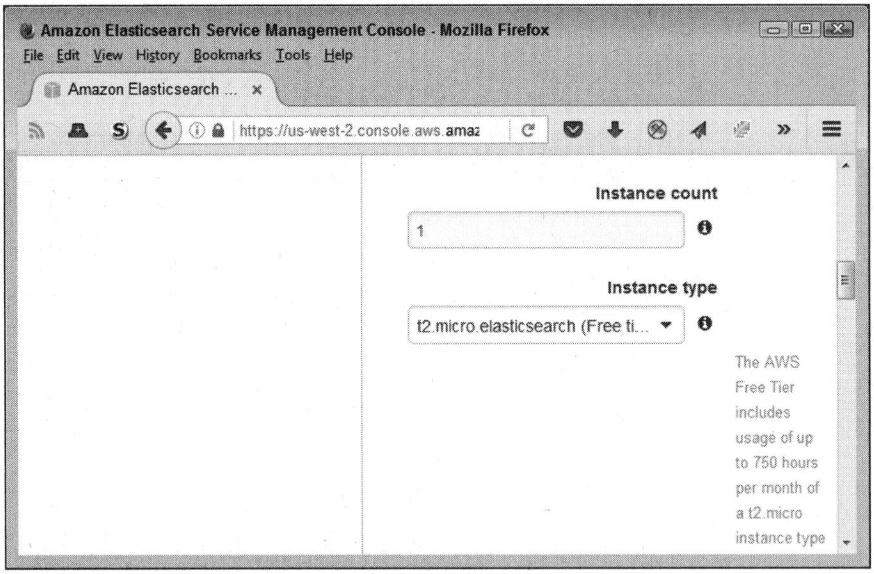

FIGURE 8-14:
Determine the cluster instance type, only some of which are free.

5. **Choose the t2.micro.elasticsearch option in the Instance Type field.**

6. **Scroll down to the Storage Configuration section of the page and choose EBS in the Storage Type field.**

Amazon automatically configures the other required settings, as shown in Figure 8-15. You must use EBS storage when working with the free instance types.

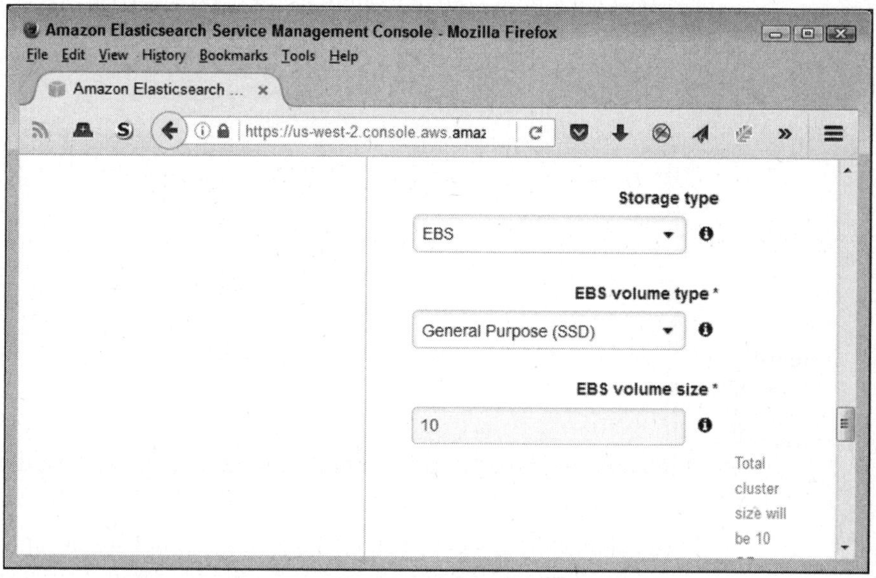

FIGURE 8-15: Specify the kind of storage to use for the cluster.

7. **Click Next.**

You see the Set Up Access Policy page, where you define who can access the Elasticsearch setup.

8. **Choose the Allow Open Access to the Domain option.**

Amazon automatically configures the access template for you, as shown in Figure 8-16.

WARNING

Normally Amazon doesn't recommend using the open access option because it creates a potential security hole. However, in this case, the open setup makes experimenting with Elasticsearch easier.

9. **Click Next.**

You see a Review page, where you can review all the configuration settings you made. Each section provides an Edit button so that you can change specific settings without having to change them all.

10. **Click Confirm and Create.**

AWS creates the Elasticsearch domain for you. The Domain Status field tells you about the progress AWS makes in completing your setup. The Loading indicator shows that AWS is still working on the Elasticsearch domain.

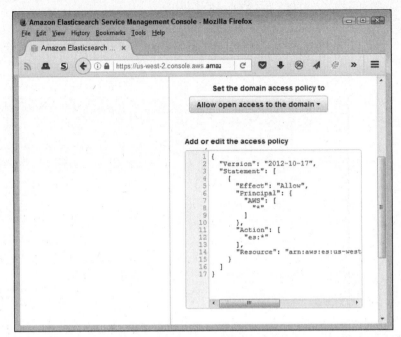

FIGURE 8-16:
Determine who can access the Elasticsearch data.

To complete this setup, you create a connection between the item you want to monitor using Elasticsearch and Amazon CloudTrail. For example, you can use Amazon CloudTrail to monitor log file output from your applications.

Deleting the Elasticsearch domain

Eventually, you may need to remove the Elasticsearch domain. Perhaps the application you use it with no longer exists. Use these steps to perform this task:

1. **Select the domain you want to remove in the Navigation Pane of the Elasticsearch Management Console.**

    AWS displays the selected domain page for you.

2. **Click the Delete Elasticsearch Domain link.**

    You see a Delete Domain dialog box that warns you about the permanent nature of a deletion.

3. **Click Delete.**

    AWS removes the domain for you.

Chapter **9**

Archiving Data Using Glacier

A*rchiving data,* the act of moving it from expensive high-speed storage to low-cost, low-speed storage, used to be an act akin to moving paper files from an office to the basement. Someone might use those files sometime, in some way, some day, but not today and possibly not ever. Today, however, archives take on added important because the methods available for analyzing data keep improving. Data that may not have held any new secrets yesterday may suddenly hold useful information today, so archiving is no longer the process of potentially putting data away forever — more a means of putting it away for now. Because data now moves between storage types more often, being able to access it simply and somewhat quickly has become more important. In addition, being able to find the data you need, even when it exists in an archive, has taken on new meaning with the various kinds of data analysis and manipulation available. This chapter is about Glacier, a new kind of archiving strategy that makes interacting with archived data easier, faster, and more flexible. The first section discusses the most important Glacier features so that you know how it differs from offerings in the past.

No matter what sort of archive product you use, having a good archiving strategy in place is important. After all, you don't want to archive data today only to take it back out tomorrow. Archives should help you use resources, including time, efficiently. In addition, you need to know that your archive will maintain your data in a usable condition, so having a strategy in place for periodic testing is important. After you have an archiving strategy in place, you need to consider how to get the data from its current location to the archive (migration) without incurring any data loss. Of course, you need to have the archive strategy in place before you consider any sort of migration. The next two sections of the chapter deal with these sorts of strategy issues.

Amazon provides a number of ways to use Glacier. The easiest method is as an object storage archive for S3, which is why this technique appears first in the chapter. You can also use the AWS Import/Export Service with Glacier to move data from anywhere to anywhere. For example, you can choose to archive data on a local hard drive to Glacier to ensure that the data remains safe, even in the event of a natural disaster. You can also integrate Glacier with third-party gateways so that you can make it part of any solution that you want to create. Because this third option, using a gateway, is dependent on the third-party software you use, this section of the chapter provides only an overview of the process.

Considering the Glacier Features

As previously mentioned, Glacier is a data-archiving product. It helps you produce long-term stores of data that you might use in the future (or might not). Archives are important for a lot of reasons, some of them quite practical, such as learning more about your business using data analysis tools, and some of them required by law, such as keeping track of what happened to those financial records from a number of years ago. Whatever your reason for creating an archive, Glacier can help you perform the task. The following sections tell you more about Glacier and help you explore precisely what using a data archival product means.

Archives versus backups

Some people confuse archives with backups. An *archive* is long-term storage for data that you're finished using. *Backup* is short-term replication of data that you're currently using. Even though an archive and a backup might seem to achieve the same purpose, they don't. An archive is permanent; a backup is temporary. Because of the significant differences between an archive and a backup, you shouldn't use Glacier as a backup replacement. The features that Glacier provides aren't well suited to those required of a backup. For example, restoring an archive takes longer than restoring a backup in most cases, so using an archive product to perform a backup will cost your organization a considerable amount of expense in time lost.

REMEMBER

The value of archive data remains more or less consistent no matter how long you store it. For example, the sales figures for a specific date remain the same no matter how long the data remains in archive. Likewise, the results of a patient's X-ray remain the same no matter when you want to review the results. On the other hand, the value of backup data decreases with time. The backup you made yesterday is the most valuable when it comes to restoring business functionality after a disaster occurs. The backup made the day before yesterday is less valuable because even after you recover the data, you must now consider the time required for manual entry of the data lost due to the backup's age. At some point, a backup loses value to the point at which it actually becomes easier not to employ it and to enter the data manually to reduce the potential for age-related errors.

Also, the kind of media used to make backups differs from the media typically used for archives. A backup costs more to make because you use higher-speed media to do it. A backup might appear on a lower-cost hard drive to ensure that you can access the data quickly. Archives typically rely on tape or other slow media that values price over speed. Because archives can become huge and backups tend to remain the same size as the current data (times the number of backups in a set), the cost per byte of archive storage quickly becomes an issue.

WARNING

Most people view data management in terms of CRUD (Create, Retrieve, Update, and Delete). However, archives aren't like other sorts of data management. When it comes to archives, you typically create the archive and retrieve from it. Because of the purpose of using archives, you never update the data. Instead, you create another version of the data and use a version number to identify it. A single file may appear in many different versions in the archive, but all the versions of that file must remain intact for the archive to achieve its purpose. Likewise, you never delete data from an archive, or the integrity of the archive becomes suspect. You can't trust the content of an archive when you can easily compromise the archive's data through deletions.

Defining long-term storage security issues

Long-term storage suffers from all the same security issues as short-term storage. For example, you must encrypt the data or someone can simply view it as needed. Hackers can use all the same sorts of attacks that are available with short-term storage as well. When deciding on a long-term storage strategy, you must begin with the same criteria that you use for short-term storage. However, these efforts aren't enough. When working with long-term storage, you must also consider these issues:

>> The encryption becomes outdated, making the data vulnerable tomorrow, even if it isn't vulnerable today.

>> The keys for decrypting the data become lost.

>> Everyone with knowledge of the data leaves the organization, making it possible to forget that the data even exists.

>> Data becomes unviable — storage technologies change, companies go out of business, applications used to read the data become unavailable, and so on.

Glacier helps overcome some of these issues. For example, Amazon will almost certainly update any required encryption for the data storage. Of course, you must still update the actual data encryption. Theoretically, the data will never become lost because Amazon will keep reminding you about it as part of your monthly statement. However, Glacier can't resolve issues such as lost keys, and Amazon won't care anymore about your data if it goes out of business. In short, despite what you might read in other sources, online storage doesn't fix every security issue or address every long-term storage need. You still need to have a good security strategy in place.

Comparing Glacier to localized alternatives

Glacier does resolve some of the issues that come with localized storage. For example, a fire in your building won't cause the archives to burn; they remain safe in the cloud. Amazon provides guarantees that it stores your data in redundant locations using the latest best-practice strategies. The risk of losing your archives is considerably smaller when using Glacier. However, never buy into the idea that nothing can go wrong. The risk is small (perhaps even infinitesimal) but is most definitely still present, and you need to consider potential loss as part of your archive strategy.

Because Glacier automatically scales to meet your needs, you no longer need to consider issues such as buying new storage or getting rid of old storage. Of course, you pay a premium price for the storage, but you must consider the trade-offs in personnel, equipment, and overall organizational efficiency. According to a number of sources, your data likely still appears on tape backup when archived. The difference is that you aren't maintaining the tape; Amazon is.

REMEMBER

When you review the pros and cons of cloud backup (and potentially archive as well) online, you read statistics about reliability, security, and availability. Articles often consider cost and efficiencies. However, what the decision really hinges on is trust. Given everything you know about Amazon's storage strategy, and considering the requirements for storing the data (such as HIPAA compliance), the issue is one of determining whether you trust Amazon to do the job. When working with a localized storage solution, the success or failure of that solution lies in your hands. Moving to the cloud means that you're placing trust in someone else to do the job as well as or better than you do it.

Creating a Glacier vault

You use a custom Glacier vault with any applications you create. To access the vault, you create application code that relies on the AWS API. However, you can manage Glacier vaults using the Glacier Management Console. The following steps show how to create a new vault:

1. **Sign into AWS using your administrator account.**

2. **Navigate to the Glacier Management Console at** https://console.aws. amazon.com/glacier/.

You see a Welcome page that contains interesting information about Glacier and what it can do for you. For example, you discover that Glacier can support vaults containing any object, define a data retrieval policy, or set event notifications. However, you don't see the actual console at this point.

3. **Click Get Started.**

You see the Create Vault page, shown in Figure 9-1. The first step is to give your vault a name. Amazon automatically selects a region for you in most cases. Using the default region is the best idea because doing so means that you won't incur cross-region charges.

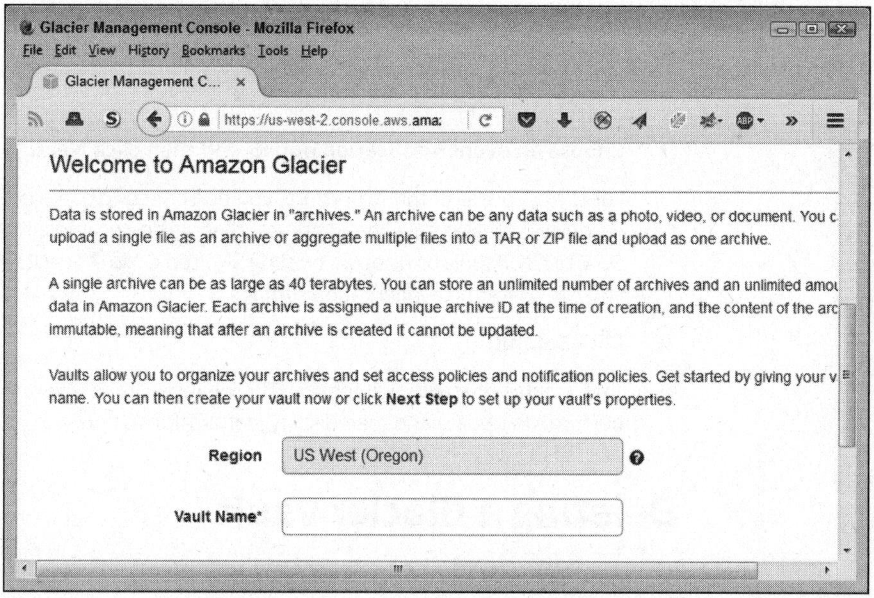

FIGURE 9-1: Create a vault to hold the archived data.

4. **Type a name for your vault and then click Next.**

   For the purposes of demonstration, this procedure uses the name ExampleVault. The next page, shown in Figure 9-2, asks you to set event notifications.

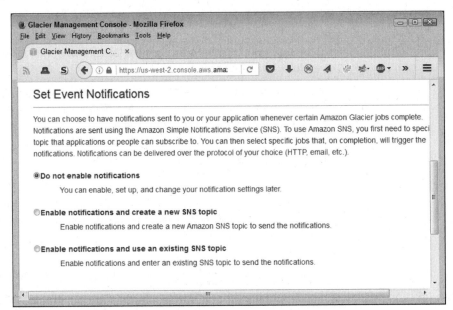

5. **Choose an event notification option and then click Next.**

   For the purposes of this procedure, you don't need to make use of notifications. However, you also have the option of creating a new Simple Notifications Service (SNS) topic or using an existing SNS topic. You see a Review page, where you can check the configuration settings.

6. **Click Submit.**

   AWS creates the new vault for you. The vault may take several minutes to perform an update and then display status information.

Deleting a Glacier vault

At some point, you need to remove Glacier vaults that you no longer need. To perform this task, select the vault you want to remove and then click Delete Vault.

AWS displays a Delete Vault dialog box that asks whether you're certain that you want to delete the value. Click Delete Vault to complete the task.

Defining a Migration Strategy

After you know how you want your archive to work and have policies in place for managing it, you need to consider how to move the data from its current location to the archive and back when you need the data again for some other task. The migration strategy you use depends on a number of factors, such as the amount of data you need to move and the current data location. In every case, you must follow a similar process to migrate the data:

1. Ensure data integrity and cleanliness before you migrate it.

2. Verify the connection to the target location.

3. Configure the data-transfer tools.

4. Send the data to the target location.

5. Ensure that the target data matches the source data.

6. Optionally, remove the data from the source site when the source isn't an archive.

The *data source* is always the current data location, even when that location is an archive. The *data target* is always the new data location, even when that location is a local hard drive. You need to keep the direction of data transfer in mind when performing archival tasks, because the kind of data source and data target do make a difference in the sorts of tools you use, the techniques you employ, the requirement for cleanup afterward, and the anticipated results of the migration.

REMEMBER

Fortunately, Amazon provides you with a number of tools that you can use to perform data migration, as described in Table 9-1. Each of these tools is free, but the data transfer comes at a price. As with many AWS services, you pay for the resources used to perform the task. However, when using some techniques, such as Direct Connect, you can also rely on third-party tools, some of which are free and some of which require that you buy the software, but then don't charge for resources used. How much a migration costs also depends on time invested (you need to pay your employees) and on other factors, such as data availability.

TABLE 9-1

TABLE 9-1   AWS Migration Tools

Tool	Description	Optimal Migration Type
Direct Connect	The customer creates a direct connection between the customer's data center and AWS.	Continual transmission of smaller pieces of information. This solution lets you work with both public and private data sources.
Kinesis Firehose	The customer defines a number of data sources and data targets. AWS manages the streaming of data from the sources to the targets automatically. The management technique used depends on the Kinesis Firehose definition. For example, you can combine Kinesis Firehose with the Amazon Elasticsearch Service (described in the "Working with the Elasticsearch Service" section of Chapter 8) to create a searchable data stream.	Streamed transmission of small to large-sized pieces of information. This solution lets you work with both public and private data sources.
Snowball	The customer creates a job using the AWS Import/Export Snowball Management Console. Amazon ships a physical appliance to the customer, and the customer installs it (and the required client software) on a host system. The transfer completes when the customer ships the appliance back to Amazon.	One-time transmission of huge amounts of data that won't transfer reliably or quickly using standard Internet connections. This service focuses specifically on your private data.
Storage Gateway	An appliance-based gateway creates a connection between the customer's data center and Amazon's data center. The appliance is a specialized piece of software rather than a physical device.	Intermittent or continuous transmission of moderate to large-sized pieces of information. This solution works best when you want to store all or part of your private data in the cloud.
Technology Partnerships	A wide assortment of third-party offerings builds on AWS services, freeing you from having to build custom solution.	Use determined by the kind of third-party offering and the manner in which you customize it.
Transfer Acceleration	The customer creates a direct connection between the customer's data center and AWS. In this case, the use of specialized software performs transfer-acceleration techniques, such as data compression, to help data move more quickly over slow networks.	Continual transmission of small to medium-sized pieces of information over long distances. This solution lets you work with both public and private data sources. Amazon guarantees that if the transfer isn't faster, you get Transfer Acceleration free (reducing your risk).

Using AWS S3 to Manage Cold Storage

Even though this section starts at the Glacier Management Console, what you're really doing is using Glacier to archive an S3 setup. In other words, you're connecting Glacier to an S3 bucket. However, the applications you create will likely continue to interact with the S3 bucket and not with Glacier. The following sections describe how to configure Glacier to interact with S3.

Defining the S3 Lifecycle rule

To connect S3 to a Glacier vault, you must create an S3 Lifecycle rule. This rule creates the connection between the two. You don't need to create a new vault in advance because S3 automatically creates a vault for you named GLACIER (all uppercase). The following steps tell you how to perform this task.

1. **Sign into AWS using your administrator account.**

2. **Navigate to the Glacier Management Console at** https://console.aws. amazon.com/s3/.

You see the S3 Management Console.

3. **Select the test bucket that you originally create in Chapter 2 and click Properties.**

You see a list of properties for the bucket.

4. **Open the Lifecycle entry by clicking its link.**

AWS tells you about life-cycle management.

5. **Click Add Rule.**

The Lifecycle Rules dialog box, shown in Figure 9-3, lets you create rules that define how S3 manages data you upload to it. The first step defines how to apply the rule. You can apply a rule to the entire bucket or just part of it by defining a specific location (such as a folder).

6. **Choose a rule target and supply any needed prefix information. Click Configure Rule.**

The example applies the rule to the entire bucket. S3 asks what action to perform on the storage object you selected, as shown in Figure 9-4.

7. **Select Archive to the Glacier Storage Class.**

AWS enables the Days After the Object's Creation Date field.

8. **Type a number of days in the Days After the Object's Creation Date field.**

The example uses a value of 90.

REMEMBER

Using Glacier won't always save you money, but Amazon often lets you know about the potential for this problem by displaying a warning message, as shown in Figure 9-5. You can delete the rule you're creating immediately after you create it (to see how the process works) to avoid additional costs.

S3 Management Console - Mozilla Firefox
File Edit View History Bookmarks Tools Help
S3 Management Console
https://console.aws.amazon.com/s3/
Lifecycle Rules
Step 1: Choose Rule Target
Step 2: Configure Rule
Step 3: Review and Name
Apply the Rule to:
Whole Bucket: johnm.test-bucket
A Prefix
e.g. MyFolder/ or MyFolder/MyObject
Cancel
Configure Rule >

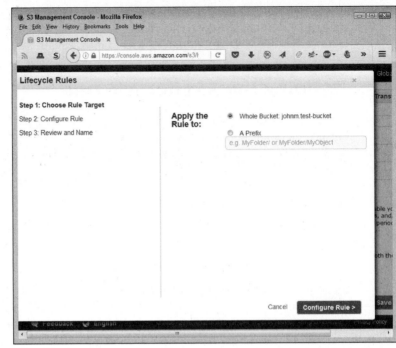

FIGURE 9-3: Specify how to apply a lifecycle rule.

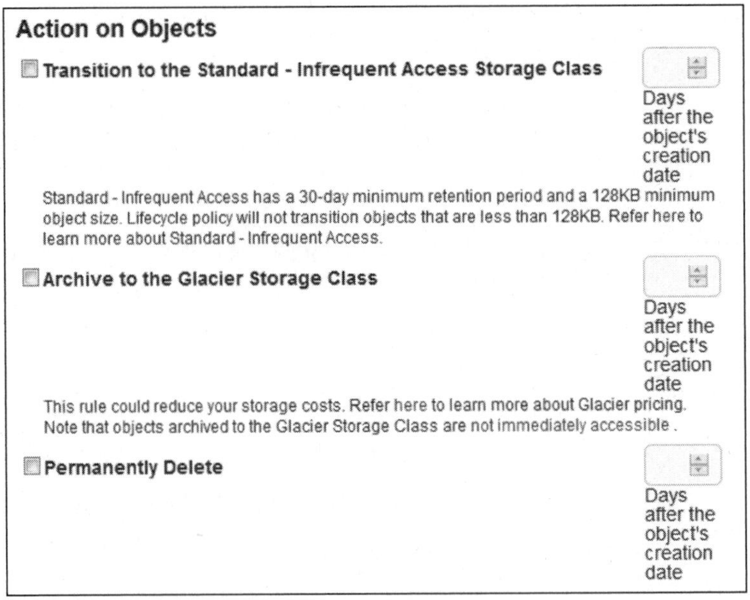

Action on Objects
Transition to the Standard - Infrequent Access Storage Class
Days after the object's creation date
Standard - Infrequent Access has a 30-day minimum retention period and a 128KB minimum object size. Lifecycle policy will not transition objects that are less than 128KB. Refer here to learn more about Standard - Infrequent Access.
Archive to the Glacier Storage Class
Days after the object's creation date
This rule could reduce your storage costs. Refer here to learn more about Glacier pricing. Note that objects archived to the Glacier Storage Class are not immediately accessible .
Permanently Delete
Days after the object's creation date

FIGURE 9-4: Determine what action to perform on the specified object.

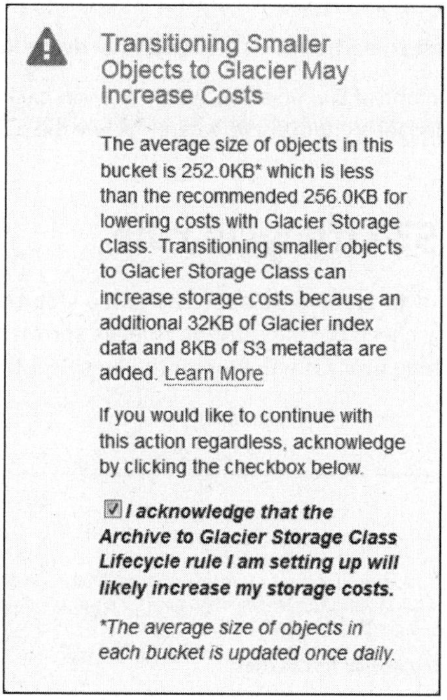

Transitioning Smaller Objects to Glacier May Increase Costs

The average size of objects in this bucket is 252.0KB* which is less than the recommended 256.0KB for lowering costs with Glacier Storage Class. Transitioning smaller objects to Glacier Storage Class can increase storage costs because an additional 32KB of Glacier index data and 8KB of S3 metadata are added. Learn More

If you would like to continue with this action regardless, acknowledge by clicking the checkbox below.

☑ *I acknowledge that the Archive to Glacier Storage Class Lifecycle rule I am setting up will likely increase my storage costs.*

*The average size of objects in each bucket is updated once daily.

FIGURE 9-5:
Amazon warns you when using Glacier may not save money.

9. **Agree to the warning message by selecting the check box; then click Review.**

   AWS presents the Review and Name page, shown in Figure 9-6. The rule name is optional, but it pays to provide one so that you can later remember what task the rule performs.

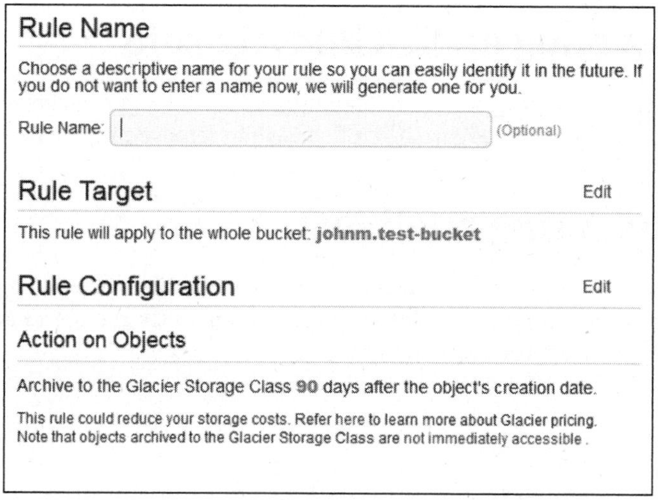

Rule Name

Choose a descriptive name for your rule so you can easily identify it in the future. If you do not want to enter a name now, we will generate one for you.

Rule Name: [|] (Optional)

Rule Target   Edit

This rule will apply to the whole bucket: **johnm.test-bucket**

Rule Configuration   Edit

Action on Objects

Archive to the Glacier Storage Class **90** days after the object's creation date.

This rule could reduce your storage costs. Refer here to learn more about Glacier pricing. Note that objects archived to the Glacier Storage Class are not immediately accessible.

FIGURE 9-6:
Provide a name for the rule you're creating.

10. Type a name for your rule; then click Create and Activate Rule.

The example uses a name of ExampleRule. AWS takes you back to the Lifecycle property of the S3 Management Console, where you see the rule you just created.

Disabling an S3 Lifecycle rule

You may not always want to archive files to Glacier. To stop the archival process temporarily, deselect the check box next to the rule, as shown in Figure 9-7, and then click Save. The archive process will stop until you select the rule's check box and click Save again.

Deleting an S3 Lifecycle rule

When you no longer need to maintain an S3 rule, you can click the circle with an X in it, as shown in Figure 9-7. Click Save to remove the rule permanently.

Restoring an object

At some point, you may need to restore an archived object. To perform this task, open the bucket that holds the object. Right-click the object and choose Initiate Restore from the context menu.

In some cases, you may find that you want to restore a number of objects at one time. To perform this task, select every object that you want to restore and then choose Actions ⇨ Initiate Restore.

REMEMBER

The restoration process doesn't happen immediately. When you choose Initiate Restore, you're actually creating a request. AWS receives the request and restores the object within three to five hours, in most cases.

As part of the restoration process, you must specify the number of days that you want the object to be available. The object's properties dialog box will tell you how much time you have left before AWS deletes the object from S3. During the time that you access the archived object, you pay storage costs for both the S3 and the Glacier copy.

Using the AWS Import/Export Snowball Service to Manage Objects

Your organization likely has a large backlog of data that you need to administer and keep safe. When your organization decides to move to the cloud, usually the administrator has to figure out how to get all the data to the cloud safely. In some cases, the job seems impossible because of the sheer mass of information to move, not to mention the security and other requirements for the move. A one-time data transfer tool such as Snowball (https://aws.amazon.com/importexport/) can make the job easier. What makes Snowball different is that you can perform a high-speed data transfer to the local device that Amazon supplies. Amazon sends you the device; you fill it with data using a special client and then mail the data back to Amazon. This route might seem ridiculous, but it can save time and effort. More important, you don't need to worry about the vagaries of transferring data over the Internet.

REMEMBER

The Snowball solution is meant for lots of data. When you review the Amazon information online, you see mentions of petabytes (PB) (where each PB is 1,000,000GB). This solution helps move huge amounts of data quickly, but it also requires more effort than some other methods that Amazon provides (see Table 9-1) and is more expensive. If you can define your data store as a number of GB or even TB, Snowball probably isn't the optimal way to move your data. Amazon's own documentation estimates that it would require 507 years to move 1PB of data using a 0.5 Mb/s data connection. Putting that into terms that actually reflect today's architecture (even I have a 30 Mb/s connection in my rural office), you're still looking at about 8.45 years. That's a long time to wait for a data transfer to finish.

USING OPEN SOURCE DATA TRANSFER SOFTWARE

Most of the third-party products you hear about require an investment. In fact, all of Amazon's solution partners require that you eventually buy the product you want to use to transfer data from one location to another. However, you can find open source data-transfer software that doesn't cost a penny to own. One such product is Tsunami UDP (`http://tsunami-udp.sourceforge.net/`). You can read a review and instructional article about it at `https://blogs.aws.amazon.com/bigdata/post/Tx33R88KHCWEOHT/Moving-Big-Data-into-the-Cloud-with-Tsunami-UDP`. Another product is rsync (`https://rsync.samba.org/`) (see the usage articles at `http://mybookworld.wikidot.com/rsync-backup-using-amazon-web-services` and `http://www.anthonychambers.co.uk/blog/rsync-to-aws-ec2-using-.pem-key/9`). In fact, you can find a number of these open source products online, and they do work relatively well, for the most part. The S3 Command Line Interface (CLI) (`http://docs.aws.amazon.com/cli/latest/reference/s3/index.html`) and Glacier CLI (`http://docs.aws.amazon.com/cli/latest/userguide/cli-using-glacier.html`) also offer methods for transferring data without resorting to an expensive add-on product. However, when using an open source product, you need to consider these issues:

- Most data transfer tools require knowledge of working at the command line (there are exceptions, such as the GUI-based Cloud 42, at `https://aws.amazon.com/code/Java/1995`, and Bucket Explorer, at `https://aws.amazon.com/customerapps/941`).

- The tool you select will likely focus on a specific need.

- Amazon doesn't provide any guarantees or support with these tools, which can mean a significant loss of time when you encounter problems.

- Most of these tools require that you write a script to provide any sort of automation, adding coding requirements back into the management picture.

Of course, you might wonder why you even have to install a special client to use Snowball. Amazon wants to ensure that any data transfer you make is secure, so part of the job is to ensure that the data is encrypted in a form that works with Amazon's infrastructure. One of the more interesting features of the Snowball device is that it contains an integrated shipping label, so you don't even have to worry about creating one. The integrated shipping label also tends to reduce the potential for lost devices. The device also includes monitoring software that tracks the device en route. Consequently, you know immediately when someone tampers with the device or the plane carrying it crashes.

WARNING

The one issue that isn't clear about using Snowball is precisely what Amazon does to erase the drive after transferring the data to your S3 drive. Modern data-recovery techniques make it quite hard to guarantee that every trace of your data is gone when Amazon ships the device to another location. As with any data-transfer technology, you lose the capability to guarantee data security the moment the data leaves your organization. When working with extremely sensitive data, you must ensure that it's legally acceptable to even use a device such as Snowball to transfer the data.

Relying on Third-Party Gateways

You likely can't create a complete solution using just AWS services because these services often don't provide the connectivity that most businesses require. What you need is a *gateway*, which is a connection between your business infrastructure and the cloud infrastructure that AWS provides. Most of the methods in this book rely on you to manipulate the service in question manually so that you can see how the service works in detail. Understanding the service is an essential first step in making it work properly. However, at some point you need to automate the connectivity between your organization and AWS because manual methods simply won't work. A gateway provides such automation. You have several options for automating connectivity using a gateway:

>> **Write an application using one or more of the AWS Application Programming Interfaces (APIs).** This solution requires developer support and probably isn't a good solution for most businesses because it places you back in the position of having to support a lot of code, which is something the cloud is supposed to alleviate.

>> **Use one of the AWS gateway solutions such as AWS Storage Gateway** (https://aws.amazon.com/storagegateway/)**.** This solution may not provide all the functionality you need in the way you need it. Most of these solutions can work for a smaller business, but would require modification and augmentation to work with larger businesses.

>> **Rely on a third-party solution.** Amazon is smart enough to know that it can't provide everything you need. As with other technology providers (such as Microsoft), it openly encourages third-party providers to create custom solutions that could meet your needs with just a few tweaks. The main problem with this solution is that now you're adding another layer to the solution, which necessarily makes the entire solution less reliable because it has more failure points.

This book doesn't provide you with programming strategies. However, the following sections do discuss the second and third solutions to the problem of automating connectivity between your organization and the Amazon storage services.

Understanding gateways

A *gateway* is a piece of network infrastructure that usually consists of a combination of hardware and software and used to create a connection between two disparate networks. The underlying technology lets you move data between locations by marshaling the data through the various protocols that make up the two networks. In most cases, especially when working with a product such as AWS Storage Gateway, the two networks aren't collocated. The location of the two networks is immaterial because the connectivity occurs over the Internet. All that is required is that both networks provide a connection to the Internet and have the required software installed to negotiate terms of the communication. Even though you might get the feeling that magic is somehow involved with creating the connection, the connectivity actually occurs using well-established standards-based technologies. In short, the AWS Storage Gateway is specialized software that is familiar with the AWS protocols and helps your organization make the required connections to the underlying services.

REMEMBER

When working with AWS Storage Gateway, you must install an AWS Storage Gateway Appliance that sits between your network and Amazon's network. The term *appliance* is a misnomer in this case because it's not a physical entity. Rather, the AWS Storage Gateway Appliance is a piece of software that resides within a Virtual Machine (VM) that you install on your host server. The appliance provides access to a number of storage types that you can read about at https://aws.amazon. com/storagegateway/details/. The quick take on these storage types is that they include primary storage, backup, and archives. The current gateway software works with S3, EBS, and Glacier. Amazon hasn't added support for EFS. The main reason to use the AWS Storage Gateway Appliance is to make the AWS cloud storage look like local storage to your applications so that you can run your applications using cloud storage without making any code changes.

The gateway provides connectivity — it doesn't determine how the storage works or how you interact with it. For example, the gateway works the same whether you use volume caching (meaning that some data resides on local drives to provide faster access) or volume storage (all the data resides in the cloud to provide better scalability). However, the gateway does do things like ensure that it encrypts the data before sending it between networks. Likewise, the use of snapshots to make recovering from a local drive failure easy is a function of the appliance's management support, rather than part of the gateway.

Working with full-featured, third-party solutions

Archiving isn't your only concern when working with storage solutions. A well-rounded configuration requires that you also address needs such as standard backup and alternative storage solutions. Amazon presents a list of storage-partner solutions at `https://aws.amazon.com/backup-recovery/partner-solutions/`. It breaks these storage solutions into the following groups:

>> **Backup:** Data backups ensure that a business can recover after a major incident, but a backup serves as a solution for only as long as the backup remains viable. The third-party solutions that you can access from Amazon all rely on S3 to perform backups.

>> **Primary storage:** The method through which you interact with data determines your choice of third-party vendor in this case. Vendors can provide you with solutions for file, block, object, and streamed data storage. Because of the way in which these various data storage methods work, you could find that a vendor provides support through S3, S3 – IA, Glacier, EFS, or any of the other Amazon-supplied services.

>> **Archive:** A data archive, the topic of this chapter, is an essential part of any data storage approach today. Modern businesses require archives to function properly and to provide proof of compliance to various laws (among other things). Of course, the emphasis on data analysis today also makes a speedy archive essential.

>> **Business Continuity and Disaster Recovery (BCDR):** At one time, business executives and technology experts worked in isolation. Business executives created plans to ensure that a business could continue to function after a major event, such as a natural disaster. Technology experts worked on plans to ensure that data remained useful after the occurrence of the same sorts of major events, but did so separately from their business counterparts. The result was that the business and technology plans often didn't work together, which meant that the business failed to continue working and possibly went out of business. BCDR solutions help integrate both business and technology needs to ensure that businesses really can continue to function and have the data required to do so. AWS provides support for both the Recovery Time Objective (RTO) and Recovery Point Objective (RPO). You can read more about how AWS makes this happen by downloading the white paper found at `https://aws.amazon.com/blogs/aws/new-whitepaper-use-aws-for-disaster-recovery/`.

>> **File transfer:** Getting data to and from your drives when interacting with the various Amazon storage services can prove difficult without help. Yes, you can install your own gateway or rely on open source solutions to help, but most of

these solutions aren't seamless and could result in downtime. The vendors that support file transfers through AWS ensure both that the data transfers occur quickly and include data encryption, bandwidth control, API automation, and transfer statistics.

You want to access the various solution providers from the Amazon page because you get practical information about each vendor in about the same format, making comparisons a little easier. Clicking a vendor displays a dialog box that contains links for obtaining any of a number of purchasing aids:

>> Case study/customer success stories

>> Contact information

>> Customer references

>> Customer video

>> Free trial/test drive

>> Meeting request

>> Product demo (simulation)

>> Purchasing information

>> Specification sheet

>> Tour (real-world scenario using actual product feeds)

Not every product provides all these aids. However, you should have enough information to start performing product evaluations.

REMEMBER

You have many issues to consider when creating a full-featured storage configuration for your business. Of course, cost appears at the top of the list for many people. The solution must also prove to be reliable, fast, and secure. However, many people make the mistake of creating a *Frankenstein solution,* one made of disparate parts that only sort of work together some of the time (see http://agreementexpress. com/2016/06/13/integrating-systems/ and http://ecommerce.shopatron.com/ blog/challenges-frankenstein-retail-technology as examples). Unfortunately, given the partners that Amazon has put together, creating a Frankenstein solution is extremely easy unless you choose vendors carefully and are willing to allow some flexibility in some areas (such as cost) to ensure that the resulting solution will actually work well.

4
Performing Basic Database Management

- » **Using the AWS Management Console to manage RDS**

- » **Initializing a database server**

- » **Including database support in an application**

- » **Adding load balancing and scaling to a database application**

Chapter **10**

Getting Basic DBMS Using RDS

relational database relies on tables to organize data, with rows holding individual records and columns holding individual data items. The tables focus on specific topics, such as employee names and dates of birth. They relate to other tables, which is what gives relational databases their names. For example, a single employee can have multiple telephone numbers, so the telephone numbers would appear in a separate table related to the employee table using a common element, such as the employee ID. If you aren't familiar with relational databases, you can find more about them at http://www.tutorialspoint.com/sql/sql-rdbms-concepts.htm and https://www.webucator.com/tutorial/learn-sql/relational-database-basics.cfm. The point is that the Amazon Relational Database Service (RDS) provides you with access to a relational database that you can use to store data that lends itself to organized storage techniques. Most business data, such as sales to individual customers, falls into this category. The first section of this chapter helps you understand RDS from the Amazon Web Service (AWS) perspective.

After you get an idea of how RDS works in AWS, you want to begin working with the RDS Management Console, which is the topic of the second section of the chapter. Relational databases can become quite complex, so the overview provided in this chapter focuses on the most common and easiest-to-use features. AWS can help you create a relational database of nearly any complexity to manage your business needs.

The third section of the chapter looks at the steps for creating a simple relational database using RDS. Of course, the real-world relational databases that you create are likely more complex and contain a great deal more information. This section of the chapter helps you get a feel for how you can perform significantly more complex tasks with RDS.

Creating the database doesn't fill it with data, manage the data in any way, or make the data accessible to the end user. To make databases useful, you must connect them to an application of some type (where an application could provide services to users, machines, or a combination of both). The application may not even include a user interface in the common sense of the word, but could simply be an API accessed by yet other applications. The point is that you need software to make your database useful, which is the topic of the fourth section.

Finally, you need to consider the requirement to make the database scale well. A database with a single user isn't particularly useful. Most databases support the needs of multiple users and some thousands (or possibly millions) of users. As the number of users increases, the need to balance the load among multiple servers and the requirement to provide scaling so that the database continues to deliver data at an acceptable rate both increase as well.

Considering the Relational Database Service (RDS) Features

The main purpose of a relational database is to organize and manage consistent pieces of data using tables that relate to each other through key fields. For example, an employee table may have a relation to a telephone number table connected through the employee ID. Because an employee can have multiple telephone numbers, each single entry in the employee table can have multiple connections to the telephone number table. Although this is a gross simplification of Relational Database Management System (RDBMS), it serves a purpose for this chapter.

To perform management tasks correctly, you must have a reliable Database Management System (DBMS) built upon a specific engine. The database engine you choose determines the characteristics and flexibility of the management environment. In addition, the database engine can also affect how well the RDBMS scales when you increase load, data size, or other factors. Also important is to have the means to create a copy of your database using both *replication* (the copying of individual data elements) or *cloning* (the copying of the entire database). The following sections describe how RDS helps you achieve all these goals.

Choosing a database engine

AWS RDS supports a number of database engines. Of course, supporting a single RDBMS might at first seem to do the trick because they all essentially do the same thing. However, you must consider a number of factors when choosing a database engine. These factors include

>> The RDBMS currently used for most of your existing projects

>> Security concerns that may override other needs for data storage

>> Data storage size or type requirements

>> Management requirements

>> Interoperability needs, especially when working with other organizations

>> Coding needs, such as the capability to execute scripts in specific ways

>> Automation needs, such as the capability to execute scripts in response to events or at a specific time

Given that the number of RDBMS engines available today is huge, RDS is unlikely to ever support them all. As of this writing, RDS supports six database engines, each of which has characteristics in its favor, as explained in the following list:

>> **Amazon Aurora:** This product is essentially a MySQL clone. If you like MySQL, you probably like Amazon Aurora as well. However, according to a number of sites, Amazon has managed to make Aurora faster, more scalable, and inclusive of a number of interesting additional features. Of course, you pay a higher price for Amazon Aurora as well, so if you don't need the extra features, then using MySQL is probably a better choice. The articles at http://2ndwatch.com/blog/deeper-look-aws-aurora/ and http://izoratti.blogspot.com/2014/11/it-does-not-matter-if-aurora-performs.html provide a more detailed comparison of Amazon Aurora to MySQL.

>> **MariaDB:** This is another MySQL clone, but it also has a significant number of additional features that you can read about at https://mariadb.com/kb/en/mariadb/mariadb-vs-mysql-features/. You need to consider a few major differences when choosing this product. For one thing, MariaDB is pure open source, which means that it uses a single license that is easier to manage. However, because of the licensing, enterprise customers will deal

with equivalent open source implementations in MariaDB (such as thread pool), instead of the original MySQL implementations, which could result in compatibility issues. MariaDB is also currently locked at the MySQL 5.5 level, so you may not have access to the latest MySQL features needed to make your application work.

» **MySQL:** This product isn't quite as old as some of the other RDBMS offerings that Amazon supports, but it does serve as the standard to which other products are judged. The problem with being the leader is that everyone takes pot shots at you and tries to unsettle your customers, which is precisely what is happening to MySQL. You can read about some of the pros and cons of choosing MySQL at http://www.myhostsupport.com/index.php?/News/NewsItem/View/58 and https://www.smartfile.com/blog/the-pros-and-cons-of-mysql/. The fact of the matter is that MySQL sets the standard, so it likely provides the most stable and reliable platform that you can choose when these issues are the main concern.

» **Oracle:** This product has been around for years, so it has a long history of providing great support and significant flexibility. What sets Oracle apart from a few other products, such as MySQL and SQL Server, is that Linux administrators and developers tend to prefer it. As with MySQL, Oracle is a standard setter that everyone likes to compare with other products, even when those comparisons aren't a good match. Unlike other products in this list, it's essential to view Oracle Cloud as a separate product from the enterprise setup — the two products aren't completely compatible and have differing feature sets. You can find some pros and cons of using Oracle Cloud at http://www.socialerp.com/oracle-private-cloud.php.

» **PostgreSQL:** This is a combination product in that most people view it as an open source version of Oracle but also go to great lengths to compare it with MySQL. Developers like PostgreSQL because it provides a significant number of features that MySQL tends not to support. In addition, the transition for developers from Oracle or SQL Server is relatively easy because PostgreSQL tends to follow their lead. However, MySQL tends to provide better ease of use and is somewhat faster than PostgreSQL. You can find some interesting pros and cons about this product at http://www.anchor.com.au/hosting/dedicated/mysql_vs_postgres and https://www.digitalocean.com/community/tutorials/sqlite-vs-mysql-vs-postgresql-a-comparison-of-relational-database-management-systems.

» **SQL Server:** This product provides essential RDBMS functionality with a considerable number of add-ons. The important thing to remember about SQL Server is that Microsoft created it for Windows, and everything about this product reflects that beginning. In general, administrators find that working with SQL Server is relatively easy unless they need to use a broad range of those add-ons. Developers like SQL Server because it integrates well with the Microsoft language products. You can read pros and cons about this product at `http://www.infoworld.com/article/3013601/application-development/new-features-in-sql-server-2016.html`, `http://www.theregister.co.uk/2013/05/28/sql_server_2012_second_look/`, and `http://www.sqlserverf1.com/pros-and-cons-of-running-sql-server-on-premise-vs-azure-cloud/`.

REMEMBER

Even with this short overview of the various choices, you can see the need to research your RDS choice completely before committing to a particular option. In some cases, you may need to configure a dummy setup and perform tests to see which option will work best for your particular application. After you begin to fill the RDBMS with real-world data, moving to another database engine is usually an expensive, error-prone, and time-consuming task. The smart administrator takes additional time to make a good choice at the outset, rather than discover that a particular choice is a mistake after the application moves into the development (or, worse yet, production) stage.

Understanding the need to scale efficiently

The capability of your application to scale depends on its access to resources. AWS provides consistent access to its resources by using autoscaling, which is a combination of automation and scaling. Monitors generate events that tell services when an application requires additional resources, such as servers, to maintain a constant level of output so that the user doesn't see any difference between a light and a heavy load. Even though the real-world performance of autoscaling may not provide precisely this level of consistency (see the "Problems with autoscaling" sidebar in Chapter 4 for details), the automation does work well enough so that most users won't complain from an AWS perspective.

REMEMBER

A problem with RDS, or any other database service for that matter, is that resources include data. No matter what you do, throwing additional resources at data management issues will only go so far. At some point, the sheer weight of the data becomes an encumbrance. Searching through several million records to find the one record you need is going to take time, no matter how many servers you allow and how much memory you provide. With this time factor in mind, you need to consider these issues when working with AWS to create an application that scales well when large amounts of data are involved:

> **Use the right RDBMS.** Amazon makes a number of database managers available, as described in the previous section of this chapter, "Choosing a database engine." Even though your first inclination is to use the database engine that you use most commonly in your organization now, speed considerations may trump consistency in this case. If you want your application to scale well, you may need to choose an RDBMS that provides optimal speed in a cloud environment.

>> **Organize the data using best practices.** This book doesn't address DBMS-specific concerns, such as the use of normalization. The use of best practices provides you with a good starting point to ensure that your application scales well. A best practice comes into play when experimentation shows that it provides good results in general.

>> **Experiment to find good RDBMS optimizations.** Knowledge resources usually focus on the general case because no one can possibly know about your specific needs. However, trade-offs occur when you use various general organizational and optimization techniques, and you need to consider the price of each trade-off when compared to application speed and the application's capability to scale well under load. In some cases, relying on a best practice that works well in general may not produce the desired result in your specific case.

>> **Play with AWS to determine whether additional resources will help.** AWS may really be able to help you overcome some speed and scaling issues by allowing you access to resources that you wouldn't normally have. The AWS documentation provides some clues as to when allocating additional resources (and spending more to do it) will yield a desired result. Unfortunately, the only way to verify that using additional AWS resources will provide acceptable gain for the price paid is to experiment and monitor the results of testing carefully.

Defining data replication

Data replication is often associated with data availability. When a failure occurs, RDS uses the replica instead so that users don't see much, if any, reduction in application speed. Amazon recommends that you place your replica in a different availability zone from your main database to ensure that the replica also addresses regional issues, such as a natural disaster. When a failure occurs because of a tornado or other natural disaster in one area, the replica in a region that has good conditions can take over until RDS makes repairs to the main database. Amazon relies on SQL Server Mirroring to provide data replication when you choose SQL Server as your RDBMS. You can also choose to use for replication Multi-AZ (`http://docs.aws.amazon.com/AmazonRDS/latest/UserGuide/Concepts.MultiAZ.html`) when using any of these RDBMSs:

>> MariaDB

>> MySQL

>> Oracle

>> PostgreSQL

Another use of data replication is as a means to help data scale better when working with large datasets or a large number of users. A *Read Replica* has a copy of the data in the main database, but you can't change it. Applications connect to the Read Replica version of the data, rather than the main copy, to reduce the load on the main database when performing read-only tasks such as queries and data analysis. This feature is available only to MySQL, MariaDB, and PostgreSQL RDBMS users. The main advantage is that your application gains a considerable scaling feature. The main disadvantage is that Read Replica updates occur asynchronously, which means that the read-only data may contain old information at times. You can read more about this feature at `http://docs.aws.amazon.com/AmazonRDS/latest/UserGuide/USER_ReadRepl.html`.

Cloning your database

Replication is data-based copying of data. You ask AWS to create a copy of your data, but not necessarily the entire database. Cloning focuses on copying the entire database, including the data. AWS supports cloning by using *database snapshots,* a sort of picture of the database at a specific instant in time. Database snapshots get used in multiple scenarios:

» **Backup:** Restoring a snapshot helps a failed RDS instance recover to a known state.

» **Testing:** Placing a snapshot on a test system provides real-world data that a developer or other party uses to test applications or processes.

» **Cloning:** Copying a snapshot from one RDS instance to another creates a clone of the source RDS instance.

Creating the snapshot means telling AWS where to copy the database and providing credentials for encrypted databases. You can create a database snapshot in a number of ways:

» Manually by using the RDS Management Console

» Automatically by scheduling the snapshot using the RDS Management Console

» Programmatically by using the RDS API

When you use automation to create the snapshot, AWS automatically deletes the snapshot at the end of its retention period, when you disable automated database snapshots for an RDS instance, or when you delete an RDS instance. You can keep manually generated database snapshots as long as needed.

WARNING

Copying a database snapshot from one region to another incurs data transfer charges in addition to any charges that you incur creating the snapshot or using other service features. You should consider the cost of performing this task in advance because the charges can quickly mount for a large database (see `http://aws.amazon.com/rds/pricing/` for pricing details). In addition, Amazon places limitations on copying database snapshots from certain sources. For example, you can't copy a database snapshot to or from the AWS GovCloud (US) region (see `http://docs.aws.amazon.com/AmazonRDS/latest/UserGuide/USER_Copy Snapshot.html` for details).

Accessing the RDS Management Console

As with every other part of AWS, you use a special management console to work with RDS. The RDS Management Console enables you to choose an RDBMS, create a database, add tables and other objects to the database, and make the database accessible to an application. You also use the RDS Management Console to per-form administrative tasks, such as to configure security. Use the following steps to access the RDS Management Console:

1. Sign into AWS using your administrator account.

2. Navigate to the RDS Management Console at `https://console.aws.amazon.com/rds`.

You see a Welcome page that contains interesting information about RDS and what it can do for you, as shown in Figure 10-1. However, you don't see the actual console at this point. Notice the Navigation pane at the left. You can click the left-pointing arrow to hide it as needed. Many of the RDS Dashboard options are the same as those used by EC2, which is no surprise, given that you use EC2 to support the database.

3. Click Get Started Now.

You see the Select Engine page, shown in Figure 10-2. Notice that you can select a major vendor and then a specific version of that vendor's product. For example, the screenshot shows three versions of SQL Server (there are others available).

The examples in this chapter rely on MySQL because you can also download a free local copy from `https://www.mysql.com/downloads/`. The MySQL Community Edition is free, and you can obtain trial versions of the other editions. Most vendors do provide a free version of their product for testing and learning purposes. In addition, MySQL works on most of the platforms that readers of this book will use.

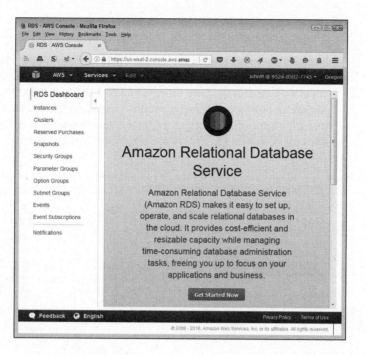

FIGURE 10-1:
Getting started with the Amazon Relational Database Service (RDS).

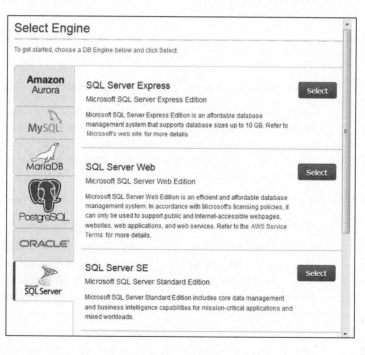

FIGURE 10-2:
Choose a vendor and then a specific vendor product.

4. **Click Select next to the MySQL Community Edition entry.**

   The wizard asks how you plan to use MySQL, as shown in Figure 10-3. You only see this step when working with certain DBMS. For example, you don't see it when working with SQL Server Express Edition. Notice that you must use MySQL for development and test work, as well as for the RDS Free Usage Tier. (Amazon Aurora doesn't offer a free usage tier.) Because this installation is for example purposes, you want to use MySQL, not Amazon Aurora.

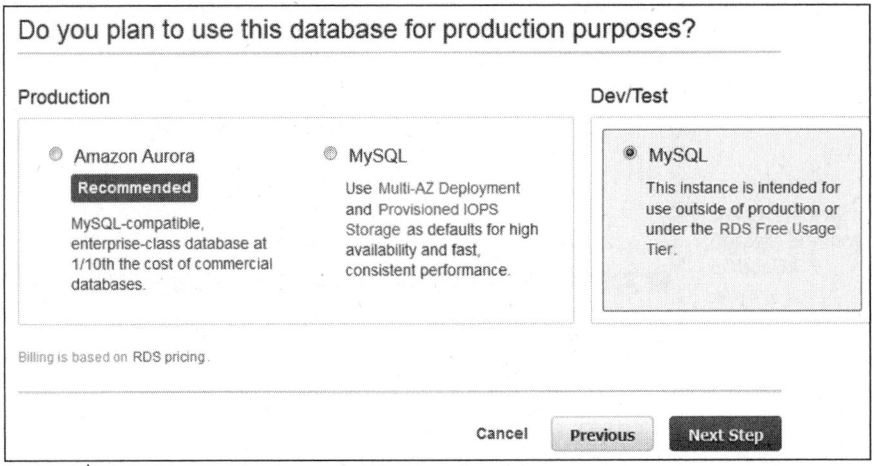

Do you plan to use this database for production purposes?

Production		Dev/Test
○ Amazon Aurora **Recommended** MySQL-compatible, enterprise-class database at 1/10th the cost of commercial databases.	○ MySQL Use Multi-AZ Deployment and Provisioned IOPS Storage as defaults for high availability and fast, consistent performance.	● MySQL This instance is intended for use outside of production or under the RDS Free Usage Tier.

Billing is based on RDS pricing.

Cancel   Previous   Next Step

FIGURE 10-3: Define how you plan to use the DBMS.

---

5. **Select the MySQL entry in the Dev/Test group and then click Next Step.**

   You see the Specify DB Details page, shown in Figure 10-4. Notice that the Navigation page specifies that this DBMS is free-tier eligible. The right pane contains all the details about the DBMS instance. You can specify that you want to see only free-tier-eligible options, which is always a good idea to reduce potential settings errors.

6. **Select the Only Show Options that are Eligible for RDS Free Tier.**

7. **Choose db.t2.micro in the DB Instance Class field.**

   To retain free-tier compatibility, you must choose this particular class. It pays to review the free tier requirements found at `https://aws.amazon.com/rds/free/`. This informational page provides details about free-tier usage, such as the instance type, the kinds of database product you can choose, memory requirements, and so on.

WARNING

Because the free-tier requirements can change at any time, you must review the free-tier materials before making choices about the database you want to work with. You may need to modify the selections used in this chapter to ensure that you maintain free-tier support and don't incur any expenses.

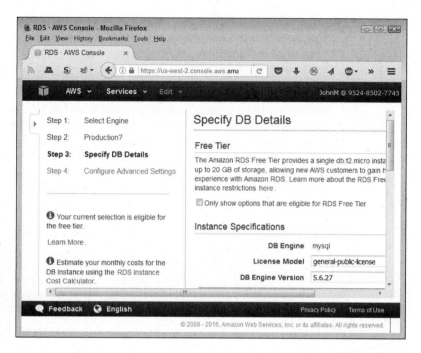

Step 1:   Select Engine
Step 2:   Production?
Step 3:   Specify DB Details
Step 4:   Configure Advanced Settings

ⓘ Your current selection is eligible for
the free tier.

Learn More.

ⓘ Estimate your monthly costs for the
DB Instance using the RDS Instance
Cost Calculator.

Specify DB Details

Free Tier

The Amazon RDS Free Tier provides a single db.t2.micro insta
up to 20 GB of storage, allowing new AWS customers to gain h
experience with Amazon RDS. Learn more about the RDS Fre
instance restrictions here.

☐ Only show options that are eligible for RDS Free Tier

Instance Specifications

DB Engine	mysql
License Model	general-public-license
DB Engine Version	5.6.27

Feedback   🌐 English   Privacy Policy   Terms of Use

© 2008 - 2016, Amazon Web Services, Inc. or its affiliates. All rights reserved.

FIGURE 10-4:
Specify the details
used to create
the database
instance.

8. **Choose General Purpose (SSD) in the Storage Type field and type** 20 **in the Allocated Storage field.**

When working with MySQL Community Edition, you must allocate at least 5GB of storage. However, the free tier allows you to allocate up to 20GB, which is the maximum amount that the MySQL Community Edition can use. To get the maximum performance from your experimental setup, you want to allocate as much memory as you can.

TIP

Depending on the DBMS you choose, the wizard may warn you that choosing less than 100GB of storage can cause your application to run slowly when working with high throughput loads. This warning isn't a concern when creating an experimental setup, such as the one defined for this chapter. However, you do need to keep the storage recommendations in mind when creating a production setup.

9. **Type** MyDatabase **in the DB Instance Identifier field.**

The instance identifier provides the means for uniquely identifying the database for access purposes. Usually you choose a name that is descriptive of the database's purpose and is easy for everyone to remember.

10. **Type a username in the Master Username field.**

The master user is the administrator who manages the database and will receive full access to it. A specific person should have the responsibility, rather than assign it to a group (where responsibility for issues can shift between people).

11. **Type a password in the Master Password field, repeat it in the Confirm Password field, and then click Next Step.**

You see the Configure Advanced Settings page, shown in Figure 10-5. This page lets you choose the VPC security group used to identify incoming requests (before they arrive at the DBMS); the authentication directory used to authenticate database users who rely on Windows Authentication; the networking options used to access the DBMS (such as the port number); the backup plan; the monitoring plan; and the maintenance plan. You do need to set the VPC security group to ensure that you can access the database. However, the remaining defaults will work for the examples in this chapter.

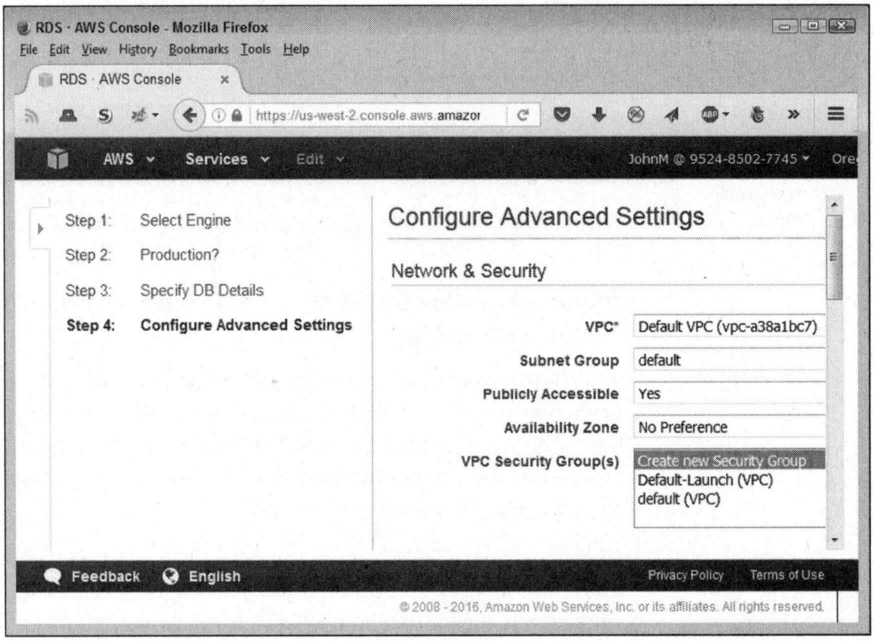

FIGURE 10-5:
Define the connectivity, backup, monitoring, and maintenance details.

12. **Choose the Default-Launch security group created as part of defining the EC2 setup.**

Depending on the DBMS you choose, you may find other database options that you can set. For example, MySQL lets you provide the name of an initial database. It pays to go through the settings carefully to ensure that you make maximum use of wizard functionality.

13. **Type FirstDatabase in the Database Name field and then click Launch DB Instance.**

AWS starts the instance creation process.

14. **Click View Your DB Instances.**

You see the RDS Management Console, as shown in Figure 10-6.

RDS · AWS Console - Mozilla Firefox
File   Edit   View   History   Bookmarks   Tools   Help

RDS · AWS Console

https://us-west-2.console.aws.ama:

AWS ▾   Services ▾   Edit ▾   JohnM @ 9524-8502-7745 ▾

Launch DB Instance   Show Monitoring ▾   Instance Actions ▾

Filter: All Instances ▾   Search DB Instances...

Viewing 1 of 1 DB Instances

		Engine ▾	DB Instance ▾	Status ▾	CPU	Current Activity	Maintenance ▾	Class ▾
	▶	MySQL	mydatabase	creating			None	db.t2.micro

Feedback   English   Privacy Policy   Terms of Use

© 2008 - 2016, Amazon Web Services, Inc. or its affiliates. All rights reserved.

REMEMBER

The database creation process can take several minutes to complete. The Status field (refer to Figure 10-6) tells you the status of the database. As long as the Status field continues to say "Creating," you must wait to perform any additional tasks. However, you can download and install any products required to access the database (if you haven't done so already).

Creating a Database Server

Creating a cloud-based database server works much like creating a local server except that you're performing all the tasks remotely on someone else's system. The change in venue means that you may find that some processes take longer to complete, that you may not have quite the same flexibility as you have when working locally, or that some features work differently. However, the overall workflow is the same. The following sections demonstrate how to work with a Microsoft SQL Server setup, but the techniques used with other RDBMSs are similar.

Installing a database access product

To use your new database, you need an application that can access it. For example, when working with SQL Server Express, you use the SQL Server Management Studio (`https://msdn.microsoft.com/library/mt238290.aspx`). Likewise, when you want to work with MySQL, you use the MySQL Workbench (`http://dev.mysql.com/downloads/workbench/`). No matter which DBMS you choose, you use an application outside of the RDS Management Console to manage it. You use the RDS Management Console only to control how the DBMS works with AWS. Because this chapter relies on MySQL as the DBMS, you need to download and install a copy of MySQL Workbench before proceeding with any of the other activities.

Accessing the instance

The database instance you created earlier will eventually become available. This means that you can interact with it. However, to interact with the database instance, you need to know its endpoint, which is essentially an address where applications can find it. When you select an instance in the RDS Management Console, a detailed view of that instance becomes visible and you can see the endpoint information, as shown in Figure 10-7.

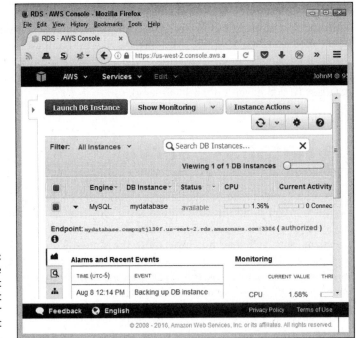

FIGURE 10-7:
Find the instance endpoint so that you can access it from your management application.

In this case, the endpoint is `mydatabase.cempzgtjl38f.us-west-2.rds.amazonaws.com:3306`, which includes the instance name, a randomized set of letters and number, the instance location, and the port used to access the instance. Every endpoint is unique. If the endpoints weren't unique, you'd experience confusion trying to access them.

When setting up a new connection like the one shown in Figure 10-8, you need to supply the entire endpoint, except for the port, as the hostname. In this case, that means supplying `mydatabase.cempzgtjl38f.us-west-2.rds.amazonaws.com` as the hostname. You must also supply the port, which is 3306. Even though Figure 10-8 doesn't show them, you must also provide your username and password to access the instance.

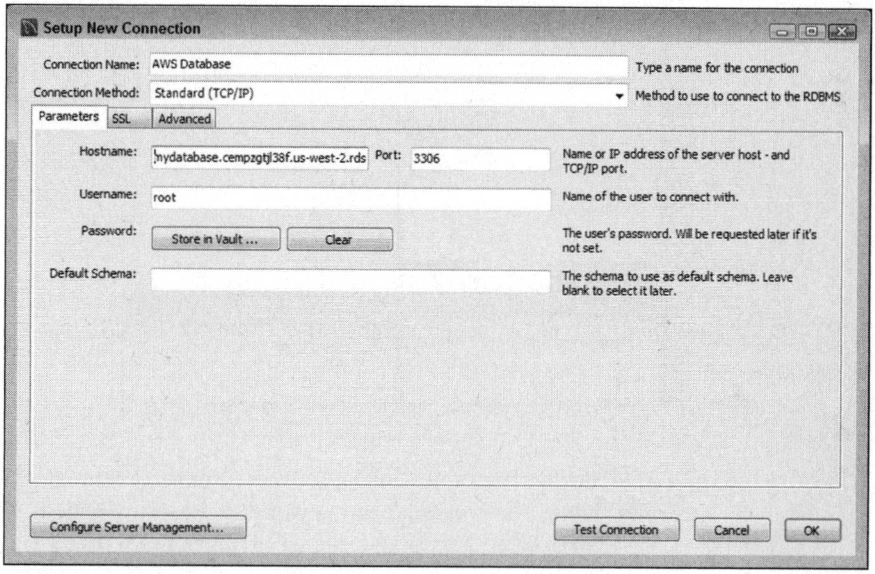

FIGURE 10-8:
Create a connection using the instance endpoint information from the RDS Management Console.

TIP

As shown in Figure 10-8, the MySQL Workbench provides a Test Connection button that you can use to determine whether the connection information will work. Most database management products provide such a button, and testing your connection before you move to the next step is a great idea. Otherwise, you can't be sure whether an error occurs because of a problem with the database or the connection to the database.

Adding tables

You work with your AWS database as you would any other database that you can access using the management tool of your choice. Everything works the same; you simply perform tasks in the cloud rather than on your local network or on your machine. Figure 10-9 shows a typical example using MySQL Workbench. Notice that FirstDatabase appears in the Navigator pane, just as you'd expect, after making the connection to the RDS database.

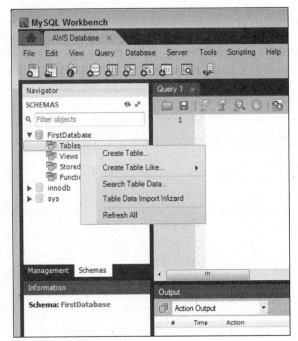

FIGURE 10-9:
Putting the database in the cloud doesn't change how your tools work.

Right-clicking the Tables entry produces a context menu in which you can choose Create Table. The creation process works as it normally does. The only difference you might note is that some tasks will require more time to complete because of the latency of the connection. Remember that you're accessing the database through a number of additional layers and that your connection speed also acts as a determining factor.

Working with other features

You must make a significant separation between the database instance and the database itself. An administrator may address the needs of the database instance, such as by ensuring that the database is backed up or by resetting the instance when it crashes using the RDS Management Console. On the other hand, a Database Administrator (DBA) is likely to interact with the actual database using a completely different tool (as demonstrated in this chapter). Because of the nature of cloud-based databases, you must consider how various administrators access tools and who can access them. The following sections detail the use of various RDS Management Console tools.

Monitoring the database instance

When working with RDS, an administrator works with the database at two levels. The first level is monitoring. The detailed view always provides you with some metrics about the database. You see a log of alarms and recent events. In addition, you see the current CPU, memory, and storage use. However, these indicators are in real time, and you often need historical data to make a determination about a particular course of action.

To perform monitoring tasks, you select the database and then choose one of the monitoring options from the Show Monitoring menu of the RDS Management Console. For example, Figure 10-10 shows the multigraph view of the server data. In this case, the graph shows the addition of a couple of connects to the database and the effect of adding a table and performing some other tasks. You'd need to look carefully at the CPU Utilization graph to detect any activity at all. Fortunately, you can click any of the graphs to expand it and get a better look. When you finish performing a monitoring task, click Hide Monitoring to see the detailed view again.

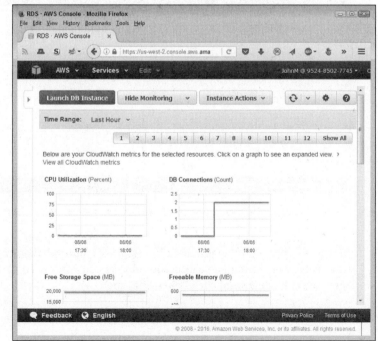

FIGURE 10-10: Monitoring provides much-needed historical data.

Rebooting after a crash

The Instance Actions menu lets you interact with the database instance at an administrator level. For example, when an instance does crash, you can restore it by choosing Instance Actions ⇨ Reboot.

Creating and deleting a snapshot

You may choose to create a read-only static view of the database (a snapshot) for archival reasons. In this case, you choose Instance Actions ⇨ Take Snapshot. The RDS Management Console displays the Take DB Snapshot page, shown in Figure 10-11. The note about the InnoDB storage engine doesn't apply to the MySQL Community Edition because RDS supports only the InnoDB storage engine in this case. To create the snapshot, type a name in the Snapshot Name field and then click Take Snapshot. After you create the snapshot, it appears in the RDS Management Console as another snapshot (choose Snapshots in the Navigation pane) that someone can access as needed.

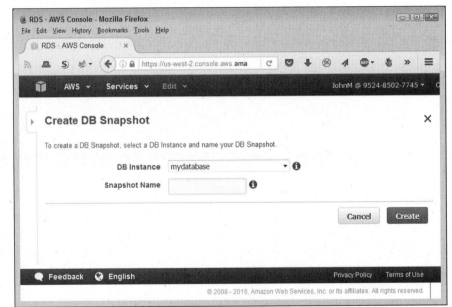

FIGURE 10-11: Create a snapshot to use as a read-only source of information.

Of course, you don't want to keep snapshots around that you're not using. Otherwise, you accumulate charges for objects you don't need. To remove a snapshot, select its entry and click Delete Snapshot.

Restoring a snapshot

The main reason to have a snapshot is for use as a backup. To restore a snapshot, select its entry in the snapshot list and then click Restore Snapshot. You see the Restore DB Instance page, shown in Figure 10-12. This page works much the same as the details page that you interacted when creating the initial database. However, the new database instance will contain everything found in the snapshot. It will have its own endpoint as well. Of course, you want to give the database a different instance name than the current database until you verify the snapshot's content.

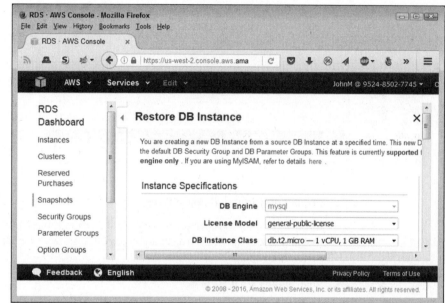

FIGURE 10-12:
Specify the details of the restored snapshot to a database instance.

Verification is an important part of the process of working with any database in any situation, but especially so in the cloud. After you verify that the restored snapshot database instance contains the data you need, you can exchange it with the original database that needs repair by following these steps:

1. **Select the original database.**

   You see the details for that database.

2. **Choose Instance Actions ⇨ Modify.**

   You see the Modify DB Instance page, shown in Figure 10-13. This page contains all the settings you used to create the database instance initially. You can modify any of the settings as needed.

3. **Change the DB Instance Identifier field content to something new.**

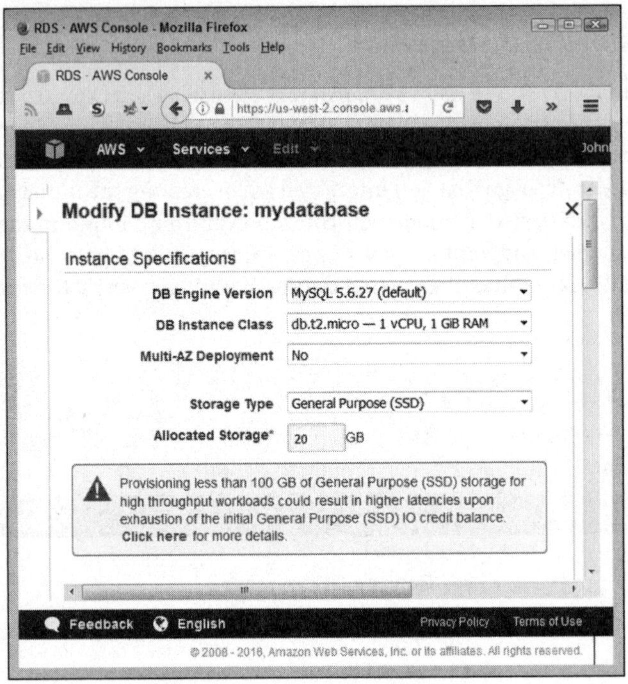

FIGURE 10-13:
Change database
instance settings
as needed to
accomplish
specific tasks.

The figure shows a browser window titled "RDS · AWS Console - Mozilla Firefox" displaying the Modify DB Instance page:

Modify DB Instance: mydatabase

Instance Specifications

DB Engine Version	MySQL 5.6.27 (default)
DB Instance Class	db.t2.micro — 1 vCPU, 1 GiB RAM
Multi-AZ Deployment	No
Storage Type	General Purpose (SSD)
Allocated Storage*	20 GB

⚠ Provisioning less than 100 GB of General Purpose (SSD) storage for high throughput workloads could result in higher latencies upon exhaustion of the initial General Purpose (SSD) IO credit balance. Click here for more details.

4. **Check Apply Immediately and then click Continue.**

   If you don't apply the change immediately, it won't take place until the next maintenance cycle. You see a summary page that shows the modifications that you want to apply.

5. **Click Modify DB Instance.**

   AWS applies the changes you requested.

   You must wait until AWS reboots the instance (you see Rebooting in the Status field) before the changes become permanent. When the Status field reads Available, you can move on to Step 6.

6. **Perform Steps 1 through 5 for the restored snapshot database instance, except give this instance the name of the original database.**

   You have now swapped the two databases and are using the restored snapshot database instance as your current database instance for applications.

Performing other modifications

The Modify DB Instance page, shown in Figure 10-13 (available by choosing Actions ⇨ Modify), also gives you access to a wealth of other database instance settings. For example, you can choose when backups occur and the level of monitoring provided. You can also change the database instance security settings.

Anything you defined as part of the original creation process is available for modification in the Modify DB Instance page.

Adding Database Support to an Application

After you have a database server created and configured, you can use an application to access it. The data doesn't serve any purpose until you provide access to it. The purpose of the application in this case is to provide Create Read Update and Delete (CRUD) support for the data. Users are interested in data and what it represents; the application used to perform the task is secondary. In fact, common practice today is to provide multiple applications to perform database tasks because user needs differ so widely because of usage environments, device, and personal preference. The sources of these database applications can also vary. A database vendor could provide a generic application, corporate developers could provide something specific, and a third party might provide a feature-rich version of the application.

When working with cloud data, accessing the data requires an endpoint, just as it does for your local network or drive. As shown in the "Accessing the instance" section, earlier in this chapter, nothing really changes from a procedural perspective, except that you must now provide a different endpoint than normal. From a developer perspective, the endpoint that RDS provides for a database instance is nothing more than a URL, which means that you can use the same techniques that you use for any online data. This consideration also applies to any administrator tools used for private data. Administrators must consider the following issues as part of the application migration:

>> Verify that a connection works before attempting to use it to perform tasks on the data.

>> Assume that the connection will go down at some point, so make sure to verify that the connection is still present before each task.

>> Assume that someone will hack your data, no matter what security precautions you take, because the data is now available in a public venue (so have a recovery plan in place).

>> Ensure that security measures work as anticipated so that every user group can access the data within the boundaries set by company policy.

>> Define security policies for working with data in a public venue that address social hacking issues.

>> Consider legal and privacy requirements before moving the data.

>> Develop a plan for dealing with sensitive data that inadvertently makes it to your hosted database, rather than staying on the local network or on a specific machine.

These precautions are in addition to the precautions you normally take when connecting an application to a database. The actual coding that you use may not change much (except for the addition of checks to address online access requirements), but the focus of how the application makes connections and performs required tasks does need to change. Otherwise, your organization might make front-page news after getting hacked and losing a lot of data to someone in another country.

Configuring Load Balancing and Scaling

The precise levels of load balancing and scaling that you receive with a particular RDBMS instance depends on how you configure the instance and which RDBMS you choose to use. It also depends partly on the application support you provide, how many users are accessing the database (and from where they access it), and many other factors too numerous to discuss in a single chapter of a book (or possibly in a whole shelf of books). With this in mind, the following sections discuss load balancing and scaling issues in a generic way that works with all the RDBMS that AWS supports. These discussions help you get started with both load balancing and scaling, but you may need to augment the information for your particular RDBMS to obtain a full solution to specific management needs.

Defining the purpose of load balancing

When your application gets large enough, you need multiple servers to handle the load. Of course, you don't want to configure each application instance to use a specific server; rather, you want to send the request to a general location and have it go to the server with the least load at any given time. The purpose of a load-balancing server is to

>> Act as a centralized request handler

>> Monitor the servers used to handle requests

>> Route responses to clients from the various servers

>> Determine the need for additional servers to handle increasing loads

Not all load-balancing scenarios perform all these activities, but most of them do. The point is that you use a single request point to allow access to multiple servers in order to hide the fact that a single server can't handle the load for the number of requests that users make. Using this approach enables you to scale your application across multiple servers in a transparent manner.

REMEMBER

When you're working with AWS, load balancing always occurs across multiple EC2 instances. Even though Amazon makes a point of telling you about the fault-tolerance features added through load balancing, the main focus is on the additional processing power that load balancing provides. However, if an EC2 instance does freeze or become otherwise unusable, you can substitute another EC2 instance without any problem. The application user will never see the difference.

Working with Elastic Load Balancing

When you first configure your EC2 instances, you won't have any Elastic Load Balancers configured — so you must create one. The Elastic Load Balancer must appear in the same region as the EC2 instances that it serves. The following steps help you create an Elastic Load Balancer:

1. **Sign into AWS using your administrator account.**

2. **Navigate to the EC2 Management Console at** https://console.aws. amazon.com/ec2.

   You see the EC2 Management Console.

3. **Verify that you have the correct region selected by choosing it in the region drop-down list at the top of the EC2 Management Console.**

4. **Select Load Balancing/Load Balancers in the Navigation pane.**

   You see the Load Balancer page, shown in Figure 10-14. Notice that the message specifies that you don't have any load balancers configured for the selected region; it doesn't say that you lack access to any load balancers.

5. **Click Create Load Balancer.**

   The wizard prompts you for a load balancer name, as shown in Figure 10-15. In addition, notice that you can add protocols for accessing the load balancer. You use the same protocols that your EC2 instances normally require. Remember that users will send requests to the load balancer instead of the EC2 instance. The load balancer will then send the request to the EC2 instance best able to handle it.

REMEMBER

   If you don't provide any secure ports for your load balancer, the wizard will ask you to reconsider during the security setup step. Whether you use a secure port depends on how you're using your EC2 instances. If you don't need a secure connection for your EC2 instances, you aren't likely to need a secure connection for the load balancer.

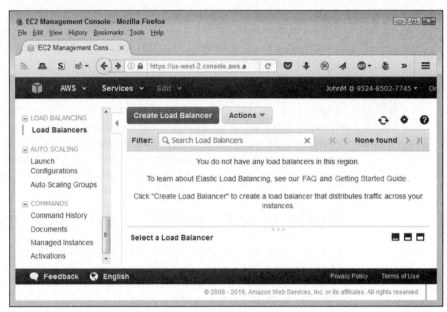

FIGURE 10-14:
The Load Balancer page tells you about any load balancers you have configured.

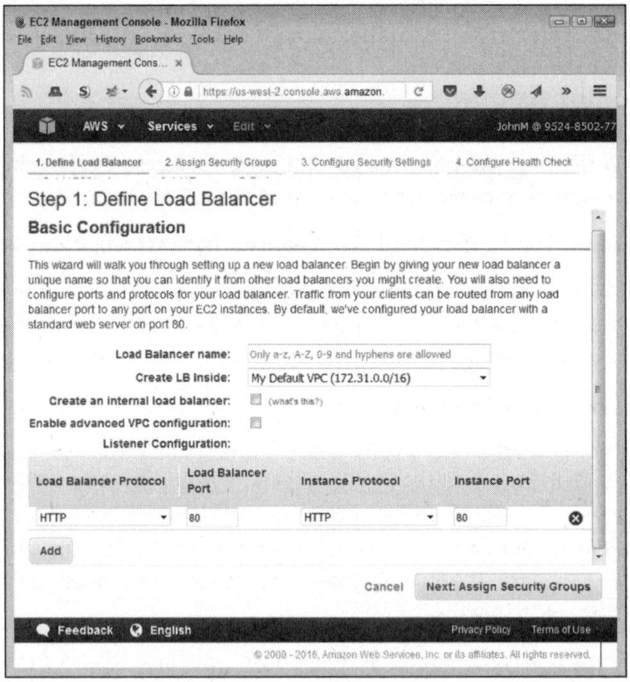

FIGURE 10-15:
Define the basic load balancer settings.

6. **Type** MyLoadBalancer **in the Load Balancer Name field.**

7. **Select the Default-Launch security group and then click Next: Configure Security Settings.**

You see a message regarding the load balancer's security. If you did select one of the secure options, the same screen asks you to provide an SSL certificate or allow AWS to generate an SSL certificate for you.

8. **Click Next: Configure Health Check.**

You see the Step 4: Configure Health Check page, shown in Figure 10-17. This step is especially important because it ensures that the Elastic Load Balancer sends requests to only EC2 instances that are able to respond. Using this approach adds a level of reliability to your setup. The default options normally work quite well, but you can choose to change them if desired.

9. **Click Next: Add EC2 Instances.**

The wizard presents you with a list of running instances. You likely have only one such instance running now if you worked through the examples in the book. Normally, you choose as many instances as you can to help support load balancing.

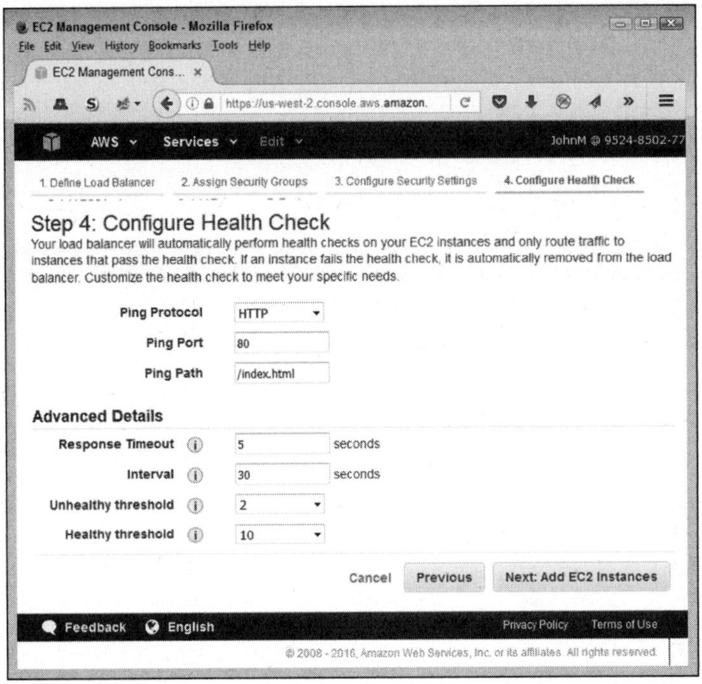

FIGURE 10-17:
Define the
method and
timing used to
verify EC2
instance health.

10. **Select each of the EC2 instances you want to use and then click Next: Add Tags.**

    The tags provide information that you can use for various organizational needs. You don't need to define any unless you use them as part of an application-programming requirement or some other need.

11. **Click Review and Create.**

    The wizard presents you with a screen showing the selections you made. Make sure to check the information carefully.

12. **Click Create.**

    AWS starts the Elastic Load Balancer for you and shows you the Load Balancer page, shown in Figure 10-14.

Defining the purpose of scaling

Load balancing generally refers to server farms, groups of servers connected through a central request point. Scaling refers to the capability to control all resources used to handle application request loads in an automated manner. When the load increases, the scaling functionality automatically increases the required resources. Likewise, a decrease on load makes the scaling functionality reduce the number of resources in use. The resources appear as part of a pool so that other applications can rely on the resources as needed. When you're working with Amazon, the resources may seem limitless, but they do truly have an end. Even so, it's unlikely that most applications will ever scratch the surface of the resources that Amazon makes available, so scaling doesn't become a problem.

REMEMBER

AWS makes a distinct difference between load balancing and scaling. The Elastic Load Balancing service is completely separate from the Auto Scaling service, even though you can coordinate the efforts of the two services to provide a robust end-user experience. Both services also deal with EC2 instances, but in different ways, so the outcomes can be different. The important difference for this book is that scaling provides a means of automatically adjusting available resources to meet specific application demands.

You can adjust the functionality and performance of Auto Scaling in a number of ways. The following methods are those that you most commonly use when working with Auto Scaling to provide database services to an application:

>> **Configuration:** The method that you use to configure Auto Scaling determines how the service reacts to EC2 events. For example, Auto Scaling automatically detects unhealthy EC2 instances and replaces them with healthy instances.

>> **Scheduling:** When you know in advance that your application will have a heavy load placed on it, you can create a schedule to ramp up the number of EC2 instances. This proactive approach may cost slightly more to use, but it always results in better application speed as long as you schedule the increased capacity at the right time.

>> **Amazon CloudWatch events:** You can create Amazon CloudWatch events that automatically react to and handle application-scaling events. This reactive approach provides adjustments as needed, but you may see a delay between the time when the event occurs and the additional resources arrive. Generally, using Amazon CloudWatch does provide faster response times than humans can provide.

>> **Elastic Load Balancing monitoring:** Combining Auto Scaling with Elastic Load Balancing helps you maintain a balanced server load, which uses resources more efficiently. You use a single set of servers to interact with a number of Auto Scaling groups to ensure that each group receives the resources it needs, but at a lower cost than when you manage each Auto Scaling group individually.

Working with the Auto Scaling feature

In Chapters 4 and 5, you read about autoscaling, a built-in feature that automatically adjusts how your setup reacts to loads. This chapter discusses Auto Scaling, the service you use to make your RDS setup autoscale within limits that you specify. When you see the term *autoscaling,* think of the generic use of a feature (not necessarily a service) to make applications, services, and other AWS features add and remove resources as needed to make applications scale better and provide a consistent user experience. When you see *Auto Scaling,* think about the service that you specifically use to make autoscaling feasible with certain AWS services. The Auto Scaling feature enables your EC2 instances to handle loads without a lot of human intervention. The following sections tell you how to use Auto Scaling to make your AWS services provide autoscaling functionality.

Applying Auto Scaling

You have several options for applying Auto Scaling to your EC2 instance, but the easiest method is to select one or more EC2 instances in the Instances page and then choose Actions ⇨ Instance Settings ⇨ Attach to Auto Scaling Group. You see the Attach to Auto Scaling Group dialog box, shown in Figure 10-18.

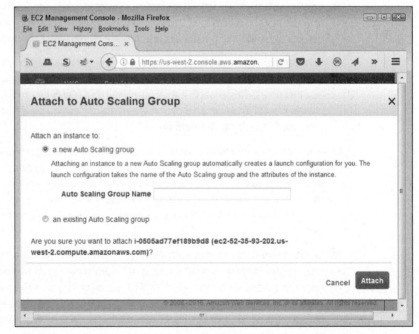

FIGURE 10-18: Create a new Auto Scaling Group or use an existing one.

Type a name for the group in the Auto Scaling Group Name field and then click Attach. AWS then automatically creates an Auto Scaling group for you that uses precisely the same settings as the selected EC2 instances.

Removing Auto Scaling

Unfortunately, you can't remove an EC2 instance from an Auto Scaling Group in the Instances page. Use the following steps to remove an EC2 instance from an Auto Scaling Group.

1. **Choose Auto Scaling\Auto Scaling Groups in the Navigation pane.**

    You see the Auto Scaling Group page. You may need to click an Auto Scaling Groups link to see the list of groups.

2. **Select the Auto Scaling Group for the EC2 instance.**

3. **Select the Instances tab of that group.**

    You see a listing of EC2 instances attached to that group, as shown in Figure 10-19.

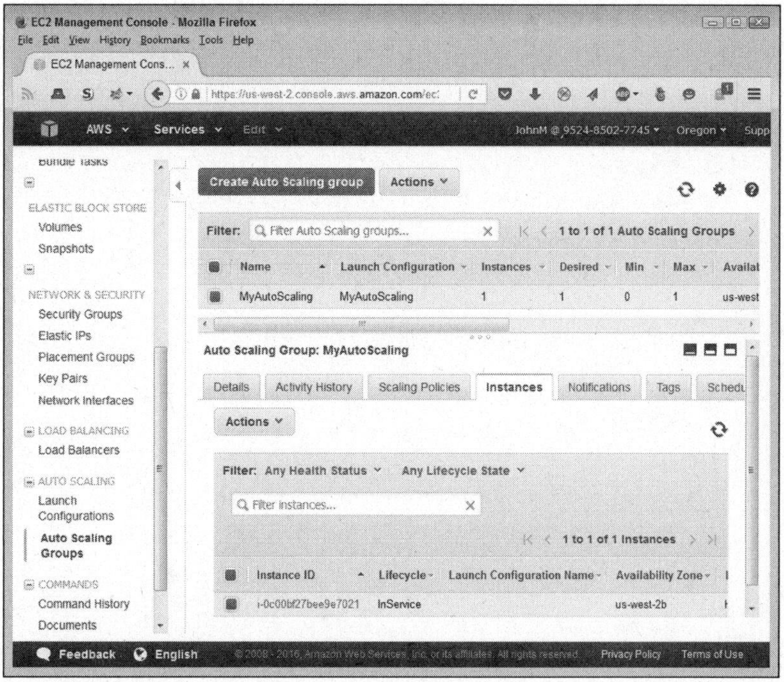

FIGURE 10-19: Locate the EC2 instance that you want to remove.

4. **Select the EC2 instance that you want to remove and then choose Actions ⇨ Detach in the Instances Panel.**

    Make sure that you choose the lower of the two Actions buttons. You see a Detach Instance dialog box.

5. **Click Detach Instance.**

   AWS removes the EC2 instance from the Auto Scaling Group.

WARNING

Simply deleting the Auto Scaling Group terminates the attached EC2 instance. After an EC2 instance is terminated, you can't recover it and must re-create the instance from scratch. The best way to avoid this problem is to provide your EC2 instance with termination protection by choosing Instance Settings ⇨ Change Termination Protection in the Instances page for the selected EC2 instance. You see a dialog box in which you confirm that you want to enable termination protection.

» Managing data movement between homogenous databases

» Managing data movement between heterogeneous databases

Chapter **11**

Moving Data Using Database Migration Service

Moving data between databases is an essential administration task. You can find all sorts of reasons to move data. Some of the most common reasons are

» Changing the database vendor

» Creating a common platform for all elements of an organization

» Upgrading to obtain an improved feature set

» Changing platforms (such as moving from a corporate server to the cloud)

Many other reasons exist for moving data, but the essential goal is to make data available to end users. If you consider all the kinds of data movement for a moment, you find that user needs trump everything else. Even data analysis boils down to serving a user need in some respect, such as the creation of *recommender systems* to help improve sales or productivity by predicting other choices that the user might want to have from a complex list of choices. The first section of this chapter helps you understand how the Amazon Web Services (AWS) Database

Migration Service (DMS) improves your capability to move data quickly, efficiently, and, most important, without errors. This last requirement is hard to meet in many cases because different databases have different structures, type support, features, and all sorts of other issues that make movement nearly impossible without some kind of mistake.

Database movement occurs in two scenarios: homogenous moves between installations of the same *Database Management System (DBMS) product* (the software that performs the actual management of the data you send to it for storage) and heterogeneous moves among different DBMS products. Homogenous moves are easiest because you don't need to consider issues such as differences in database features nearly as often (except, possibly, when performing an upgrade move). The chapter covers homogenous moves first for this reason. However, the chapter does discuss both homogenous and heterogeneous moves.

REMEMBER

This service is free, but the compute time, data transfer time, and storage resources above a certain amount aren't. The charges for these items are quite small, however. According to Amazon's documentation, you can migrate a 1TB database for as little as $3. A list of prices appears at `https://aws.amazon.com/dms/pricing/`. Pricing varies by EC2 instance type (with the t2.micro instance used in the "Creating an instance" section of Chapter 4 costing the least). Data transfer charges don't exist when you transfer information into a database, but you are charged when you transfer data out. Storage prices vary, but you get a certain amount of storage free (50GB in the case of the setup described in this chapter). The setups in this chapter won't cost you any money to perform. Actually completing a migration will cost you money, but not much. You need to decide how far you want to go in performing the exercises in this chapter. Actually performing the migration will cost you something but also provide experience in completing the tasks described.

Considering the Database Migration Service Features

It's important to know what to expect from the DMS before you begin using it in an actual project. For example, the main page at `https://aws.amazon.com/dms/` advertises zero downtime. However, when you read the associated text, you discover that some downtime is actually involved in migrating the database, which makes sense because you can't migrate a database containing open records (even with continuous replication between the source and target). The fact is that you experience some downtime in migrating any database, so you have to be careful about taking any claims to the contrary at face value. Likewise, the merits of a claim that a service is easy to use depends on the skills of the person performing the migration. An expert DBA will almost certainly find the DMS easy to use, but a less experienced administrator may encounter difficulties. With these caveats in mind, the following sections provide some clarification in what you can expect from the DMS in terms of features you can use to make your job easier.

Choosing a target database

You already have a source database in place on your local network. If you're happy with that database and simply want to move it to the cloud, you can perform a homogenous migration. A homogenous migration is the simplest type, in most cases, as long as you follow a few basic rules:

- » Ensure that the source and target database are the same version, have the same updates installed, and use the same extensions.

- » Configure the target database to match the source database if at all possible (understanding that the configuration may not provide optimal speed, reliability, and security in a cloud environment).

- » Define the same characteristics for the target database as are found in the source database, such as ensuring that both databases support the same security.

- » Perform testing during each phase of the move to ensure that the source and target databases really do perform the same way.

WARNING

Don't make the error of thinking that moving Microsoft SQL Server to Amazon Aurora is a homogenous data move. Anytime that you must *marshal* the data (make the source database data match the type, format, and context of the destination database data) or rely on a product such as the AWS Data Migration Service to move the data, you are performing a heterogeneous data move (despite what the vendor might say). Even if the two DBMSs are compatible, that means that they aren't precisely the same, which means that you can encounter issues related to heterogeneous moves. Treating a move that involves two different products, even when those products are compatible, as a heterogeneous move is the smart way to view the process. Otherwise, you're opening yourself to potential unexpected delays.

Chapter 10 mentions a number of the DBMSs that AWS supports. In some cases, you may decide to move data from a source database that works well in a networked environment to a target database that works well in the cloud environment.

The advantage of performing a heterogeneous move (one in which the source and target aren't the same) is that you can experience gains in speed, reliability, and security. In addition, the target database may include features that your current source database lacks.

The disadvantage is that you must perform some level of marshaling (modifying the data of the source database to match the target database) to ensure that your move is successful. Modifying data usually results in some level of *content* (the actual value of the data) or *context* (the data's value when associated with other data) loss. In addition, you may find yourself rewriting scripts that perform well on the source database but may not work at all with the target database.

REMEMBER

A decision to move to a new target database may come with some surprises as well (mostly of the bad sort). For example, you can move data from your Microsoft SQL Server database to the Amazon Aurora, MySQL, PostgreSQL, or MariaDB DBMS. Each of these target databases has advantages and disadvantages that you must consider before making the move. For example, Amazon provides statistics to show that Amazon Aurora performs faster than most of its competitors, but it also locks you into using AWS with no clear migration strategy to other cloud-vendor products. In addition, Amazon Aurora contains features that may not allow you to move your scripts with ease, making recoding an issue.

You also need to research the realities of some moves. For example, some people may feel that moving to MySQL has advantages in providing a larger platform support base than Microsoft SQL Server. However, Microsoft is now working on a Linux version of Microsoft SQL Server that may make platform independence less of an issue (see the *InfoWorld* article at `http://www.infoworld.com/article/3041450/sql/8-no-bull-reasons-why-sql-server-on-linux-is-huge-for-microsoft.html` for details). The point is that choosing a target for your cloud-based DBMS will require time and an understanding of your organization's specific needs when making the move.

Reducing downtime

No matter what a vendor tries to tell you, you will have some downtime when migrating data of any kind from any source to any target. The amount of time varies, but some sort of downtime is guaranteed, so you must plan for it. The following list provides some common sources of downtime during a migration:

>> Performing the data transfer often means having all records locked, which means that users can't make changes (although they can still potentially use the data for read-only purposes).

>> Data marshaling problems usually incur a time penalty as administrators, DBAs, developers, and DevOps all work together to discover solutions that will work.

- » Changing applications to use a new data source always incurs a time penalty. The changeover could result in major downtime when the change doesn't work as expected.

- » Unexpected scripting issues can mean everything from data errors to reports that won't work as expected. Repairs are usually time consuming at best.

- » Modifications that work well in the lab suddenly don't work in the production environment because the lab setup didn't account for some real-world difference.

- » Users who somehow don't get a required update end up using outdated data sources or applications that don't work well with the new data source.

- » Schema conversions can work well enough to transfer the data, but they can change its content or context just enough to cause problems with the way in which applications interact with the data. Consequently, full application testing when performing a heterogeneous move of any sort is a requirement that some organizations skip (and end up spending more time remediating than if they had done the proper testing in the first place).

- » Differences in the cloud environment add potential latency or other timing issues not experienced in the local network configuration.

TIP

An essential part of keeping downtime to a minimum, despite these many sources of problems, is to be sure to use real-world data for testing in a lab environment that duplicates your production environment as closely as possible. This means that you need to address even the small issues, such as ensuring that the lab systems rely on the same hardware and use the same configuration as your production environment. You also need to perform real-world testing that relies on users who will actually use the application when it becomes part of the production environment. If you don't perform real-world testing under the strictest possible conditions, the amount of downtime you experience will increase exponentially. Not only does an optimistic lab setup produce unrealistic expectations, but it also creates a domino effect in which changes, procedures, and policies that would work with proper testing don't work because they aren't properly tested and verified in the lab.

You must also use as many tools as you can to make the move simpler. The "Understanding the AWS Schema Conversion Tool" section, later in this chapter, discusses the use of this tool to make moves between heterogeneous databases easier. However, a great many other tools are on the market, so you may find one that works better for your particular situation.

Consolidating data

Organizations can end up with data in a number of different DBMSs because of mergers and inefficiencies within the organization itself. A workgroup database may eventually see use at the organization level, so some of these DBMS scenarios also occur as a result of growth. Whatever the source of the multitude of DBMSs, consolidating the data into a single DBMS (and sometimes a single database) can result in significant improvement in organizational efficiency. However, when planning the consolidation, view it as multiple homogenous or heterogeneous moves rather than a single big move. Each move will require special considerations, so each move is unique. All you're really doing is moving multiple sources to the same target.

REMEMBER

A potential issue with data consolidation occurs when multiple source databases have similar data. When you consolidate the data, not only do you have to consider marshaling the data from the source schema to the destination schema, but you must also consider the effects of combining the data into a coherent whole. This means considering what to do with missing, errant, outdated, or conflicting data. One database can quite possibly have data that doesn't match a similar entry in another database. Consequently, test runs that combine the data and then look for potential data issues are an essential part of making a consolidation work.

Replicating data

One of the ways in which you can use the AWS DMS is to replicate data. Data replication to a cloud source has a number of uses, which include:

» Providing continuous backup

» Acting as a data archive

» Performing the role of the main data storage while the local database acts as a cache

» Creating an online data source for users who rely on mobile applications

» Developing a shareable data source for partners

When used in this way, the AWS DMS sits between the source database and one or more target databases. You can use a local, networked, or cloud database as the source. Normally, the target resides in the cloud. Theoretically, you can create a heterogeneous replication, but homogenous replications are far more reliable because you don't need to worry about constantly marshaling the data between differing source and target DBMS.

Moving Data between Homogenous Databases

Moving data between homogenous databases (those of precisely the same type) is the easiest kind of move because you have a lot less to worry about than when performing a heterogeneous move (described in the "Moving Data between Heterogeneous Databases" section, later in this chapter). For example, because both databases are the same, you don't need to consider the need to *marshal* (convert from one type to another) data between data types. In addition, the databases will have access to similar features, and you don't necessarily need to consider issues such as database storage limitations.

REMEMBER

The definition for *homogenous* can differ based on what you expect in the way of functionality. For the purposes of this book, a homogenous data move refers to moving data between copies of precisely the same DBMS. A move between copies of SQL Server 2016 is homogenous, but moving between SQL Server and Oracle isn't, even though both DBMSs support relational functionality. Even a move between SQL Server 2016 and SQL Server 2014 could present problems because the two versions have differing functionality.

Trying a homogenous move before you attempt a heterogeneous move is important because the homogenous move presents an opportunity to separate database issues from movement issues. The following sections help you focus on the mechanics of a move that doesn't involve any database issues. You can use these sections to build your knowledge of how moves are supposed to work and to ensure that you fully understand how moves work within AWS.

Obtaining access to a source and target database

The example in this section uses the RDS database defined in Chapter 10 as a source. It relies on a second database created using the same procedure in the "Accessing the RDS Management Console" section of Chapter 10 to act as a target. The name of the target database is MyTarget.

REMEMBER

The target database won't be immediately available when you first create it. You must wait until the Status field of the Instances page of the RDS Management Console shows an Available indicator before you can access the database. If you try to test the database connection before then, the connection will fail.

Defining the move

Unlike many of the other tasks that you perform with AWS, performing a data migration is a task, rather than an object creation. As a result, you create one or more tasks that define what you want AWS DMS to do, rather than configure a virtual server (as with EC2) or a new database (as with RDS). The following steps are an overview of the series of steps that you might take in creating a migration task:

1. **Sign into AWS using your administrator account.**

2. **Navigate to the DMS Management Console at** `https://console.aws.amazon.com/dms`**.**

   You see a Welcome page that contains interesting information about DMS and what it can do for you, as shown in Figure 11-1. Notice that the Navigation pane contains options for creating new tasks and configuring endpoints. This console also lets you define replication instances. In the lower-right corner, you find information about the AWS Schema Conversion Tool, an application that you download to your local system rather than use online.

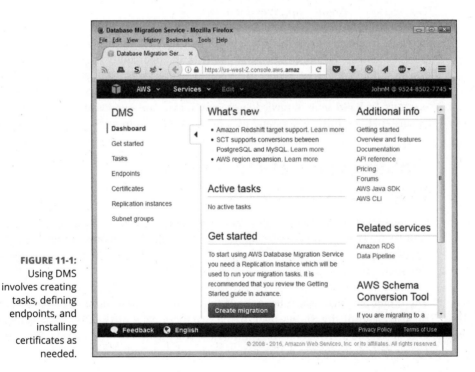

FIGURE 11-1:
Using DMS involves creating tasks, defining endpoints, and installing certificates as needed.

Moving the data

To move data, you must create a migration task. The following steps describe how to create a task that will migrate data from the source test database to the target test database:

1. **Click Create Migration.**

   A Welcome page appears that tells you about the process for migrating a database, as shown in Figure 11-2. This page also specifies the steps you need to perform in the Navigation pane and provides a link for downloading the AWS Schema Conversion Tool.

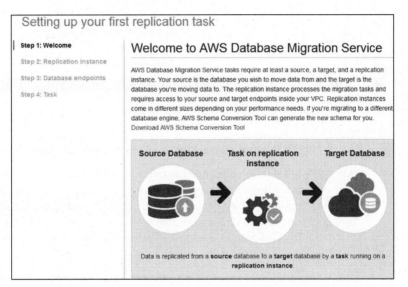

2. **Click Next.**

   The wizard displays the Create Replication Instance page, shown in Figure 11-3. This page helps you define all the requirements for performing the migration task.

3. **Type** MoveMySQLData **in the Name field.**

   Be sure to name your task something descriptive. You may end up using the replication task more than once, and trying to remember what the task is for is hard if you don't use a descriptive name.

4. **(Optional) Type a detailed description of the task's purpose in the Description field.**

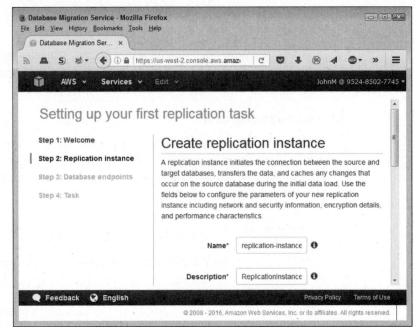

FIGURE 11-3:
Define the requirements for the migration (replication) task.

5. **Choose the dms.t2.micro option from the Instance Class field.**

   The move relies on your EC2 instance. To get free-tier EC2 support, you need to use the dms.t2.micro option. However, consider the cost of using the service. All incoming data is free. You can also transfer data between Amazon RDS and Amazon EC2 Instances in the same Availability Zone free. Any other transfers will cost the amount described at https://aws.amazon.com/dms/pricing/.

6. **Click the down arrow next to the Advanced heading.**

   You see the advanced options for transferring the data.

7. **Type 30 (or less) in the Allocated Storage GB field.**

   Remember that you get only 30GB of free EBS storage per month (see https://aws.amazon.com/free/), so experimenting with a larger storage amount will add to your costs.

8. **Choose Default-Launch in the VPC Security Group(s) field.**

   Using this security group ensures that you have access to the migration as needed.

9. **Click Next.**

You see the Connect Source and Target Database Endpoints page, shown in Figure 11-4. In creating a connection between servers, you need to provide

- An identifier for the connection

- The engine type used for the connection

- The location of the database, such as the RDS endpoint without the port information

- The port to use for the connection

- Any SSL mode requirement

- The username and password

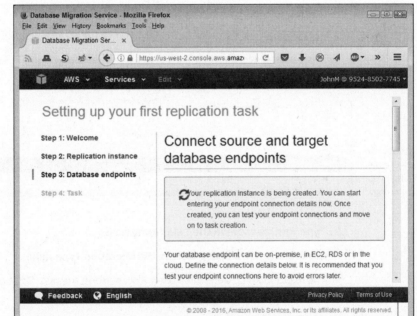

FIGURE 11-4:
Configure the source and target database specifications for the migration.

10. **Fill out the individual fields for the source and target database.**

11. **Click Run Test under each of the test databases to ensure that you can connect to them.**

The Run Test button doesn't become available until after AWS completes an initial configuration and you completely fill in the required blanks. You want to test each connection individually to ensure that it actually works before proceeding.

12. Click Next.

You see the Create Task page, shown in Figure 11-5. The fields on this page configure the task so that you can use it. You use the settings to determine how AWS performs the task, what sorts of data that AWS moves from one database to another, and precisely which tables AWS moves.

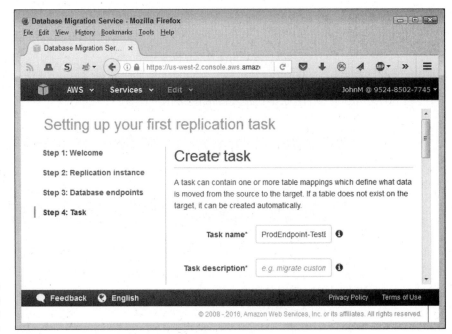

FIGURE 11-5:
Configure the
task so that you
can run it.

13. Type TestDataMove in the Task Name field.

14. Choose Migrate Existing Data in the Migration Type field.

The migration type determines how AWS perform the task. You have the following options when setting this field:

- **Migrate Existing Data:** Copies all the data from the source database to the target database.

- **Migrate Existing Data and Replicate Ongoing Changes:** Performs the initial data copy and then monitors the source database for changes. When AWS detects changes, it copies just the changes to the target database (saving resources and maintaining speed).

- **Replication Data Changes Only:** Assumes that the source and target databases are already in sync. AWS monitors the source database and copies only the changes to the target.

15. **Select the Start Task on Create check box.**

This option specifies that you want the migration to start immediately. If you deselect this check box, you need to start the task manually.

16. **Click Create Task.**

After a few moments, you see the Tasks page of the DMS Management Console, as shown in Figure 11-6. The task's Status field contains Creating until the creation process is complete.

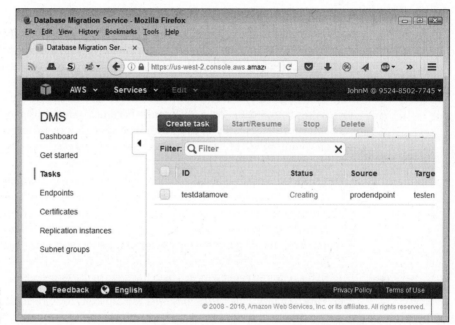

FIGURE 11-6:
Verify the task status.

Moving Data between Heterogeneous Databases

DBMSs come in many different forms because people expect them to perform a wide variety of tasks. The relational DBMS serves the interests of businesses because it provides organized data storage that ensures data integrity and moderately fast response times. However, the relational database often doesn't work well for data that isn't easy to organize, such as large quantities of text, which means that you must use a text-based DBMS instead. The popular NoSQL DBMSs provide a nontabular approach to working with big data and real-time applications that aren't easy to model using relational strategies. In short, the need for multiple DBMS types is well established and reasonable because each serves a different role. However, moving data between DBMS of different types can become quite difficult. The following sections can't provide you with a detailed description of every move of this type (which would require an entire book), but they do give you an overview of the AWS perspective of heterogeneous data moves.

Considering the essential database differences

This book can't discuss the particulars of every DBMS out there. Even if providing such a discussion were possible, considering the wealth of available DBMSs, the resulting text would be immense. Fortunately, you don't need to know the particulars of every DBMS; all you really need to think about are the types of differences you might encounter so that you're better prepared to deal with them. The following list presents essential database differences by type and in order of increasing complexity. As a difference becomes more complex to handle, the probability of successfully dealing with it becomes lower. In some cases, you must rely on compromises of various sorts to achieve success.

>> **Features:** Whenever a vendor introduces a new version of a DBMS product, the new version contains new features. Fortunately, many of these products provide methods for saving data in a previous version format, making the transition between versions easy. This same concept holds for working with products (the data target) that can import specific versions of another product's data (the data source). Exporting the data from the source DBMS in the required version makes data transfers to the target easier.

>> **Functionality:** One DBMS may offer the capability to store graphics directly in the database, while another can store only links to graphic data. The transition may entail exporting the graphic to another location and then providing that location as input to the new DBMS as a link.

>> **Platform:** Some platform differences can prove quite interesting to solve. For example, one platform may store paths and filenames in a manner in which case doesn't matter, while another stores this same information in a case-sensitive way. The data exchange may require the use of some level of automation to ensure consistency of path and filename case.

>> **Data types:** Most data type issues are relatively easy to fix because software commonly provides methods to marshal (change) one data type to another. However, you truly can't convert a Binary Large Object (BLOB) type text field into a fixed-length text field of the sort used by relational databases, so you must create a custom conversion routine of some sort. In short, data type conversions can become tricky because you can change the context, meaning,

or structure of the data in a manner that makes accurate analysis later nearly impossible.

>> **Automation:** Adding automation, such as code stored in data fields, to a DBMS significantly increases the complexity of moving data from one DBMS to another. In many cases, you must choose to leave the automation behind when making the data move or representing it in some other way.

>> **Data organization:** Dealing with DBMSs of different types, such as moving data from a NoSQL database to a relational database, can involve some level of data loss because the organization of the data between the two DBMSs is so different. Any conversion will result in data loss in this case. In addition, you may have to calculate some values, replace missing values, and perform other sorts of conversions to successfully move the data from one DBMS to another of a completely different organizational type.

>> **Storage methodology:** The reason that storage methodology can incur so many issues is because the mechanics of working with the data are now different. Having different storage technologies in play means that you must now consider all sorts of issues that you don't ordinarily need to consider, such as whether the data requires encryption in the target database to ensure that the storage meets any legal requirements. Given that cloud storage is inherently different from storage on a local drive, you always encounter this particular difference when moving your data to AWS, and you really need to think about all that a change in storage methodology entails.

Understanding the AWS Schema Conversion Tool

The AWS Schema Conversion Tool makes marshaling data from a source database to a target database relatively easy. To follow this example, you must create a target PostgreSQL example database using the same technique you use in Chapter 10. This odd requirement exists because the AWS Schema Conversion Tool supports specific source and target database combinations, as described at `http://docs.aws.amazon.com/SchemaConversionTool/latest/userguide/Welcome.html`. Fortunately, a free-tier version of PostgreSQL is available for development use, just as one is for MySQL. Name your target database MyTarget2. The following sections help you get started with the AWS Schema Conversion Tool.

Getting, installing, and configuring the AWS Schema Conversion Tool

You download this product to your system and install it. Amazon provides versions of this tool for Windows, Mac OS X, Fedora Linux (Redhat Package Manager, RPM), and Ubuntu Linux (Debian). Even though the following steps show the Windows version of the product, versions for other platforms work in the same way.

1. **Obtain and install a copy of the AWS Schema Conversion Tool for your platform.**

   You can find a list of the platforms at the bottom of the page at https://aws. amazon.com/dms/.

2. **Start the application.**

   You see a Create New Database Migration Project dialog box, similar to the one shown in Figure 11-7. (The screen will vary in appearance according to the platform you use, but the content will remain the same.)

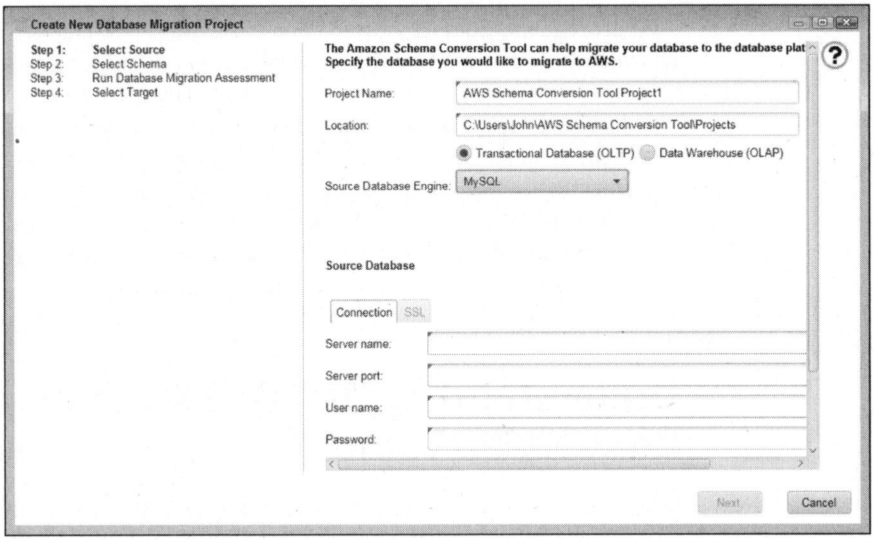

FIGURE 11-7: Create a new project.

3. **Choose MySQL in the Source Database Engine field.**

   The appearance of the dialog box will change to reflect the needs of the particular database engine you use.

4. **Type the endpoint information associated with your copy of MyDatabase without the port.**

5. **Type the port information for your copy of MyDatabase.**

6. **Provide the username and password for your copy of MyDatabase.**

7. Provide the location of a MySQL driver.

Amazon isn't very clear about where to obtain the driver. If you already have MySQL installed on your system, theoretically you also have the driver. However, if you installed only MySQL Workbench to interact with the cloud-based version of your MySQL database, you won't have the driver installed. You can obtain a copy of the driver needed for this example from `http://www.mysql.com/downloads/connector/j/`. If you need drivers for other DBMSs, check out the list at `http://www.sql-workbench.net/manual/jdbc-setup.html`.

8. Click Test Connection.

You see a success message if the connection is successful.

9. Click Next.

The wizard shows you a list of tables and asks which one you'd like to analyze, as shown in Figure 11-8.

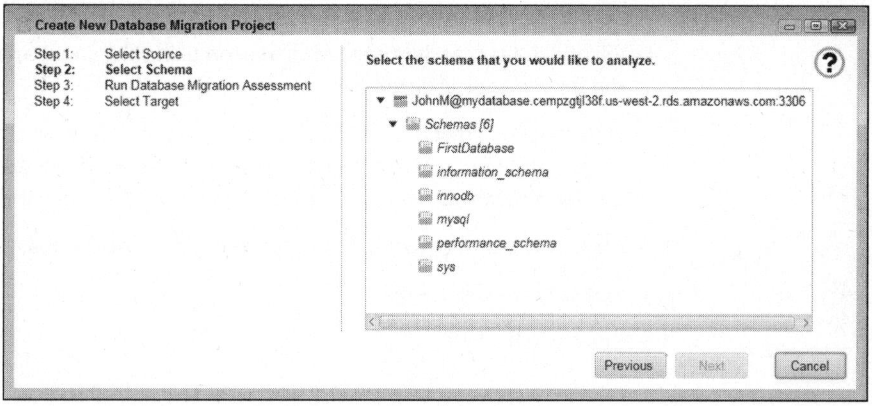

FIGURE 11-8: Choose a table to migrate.

10. Select the FirstDatabase entry and click Next.

You see a database migration report that tells you about the issues that you might encounter in migrating the database. The example database contains a single table with a couple of fields as a sample. It won't have any migration issues.

11. Click Next.

You see a target database dialog box like the one shown in Figure 11-9. Notice that this dialog box asks for the same information as the source dialog box does, including the location of the PostgreSQL driver. You can download this driver from `http://jdbc.postgresql.org/`.

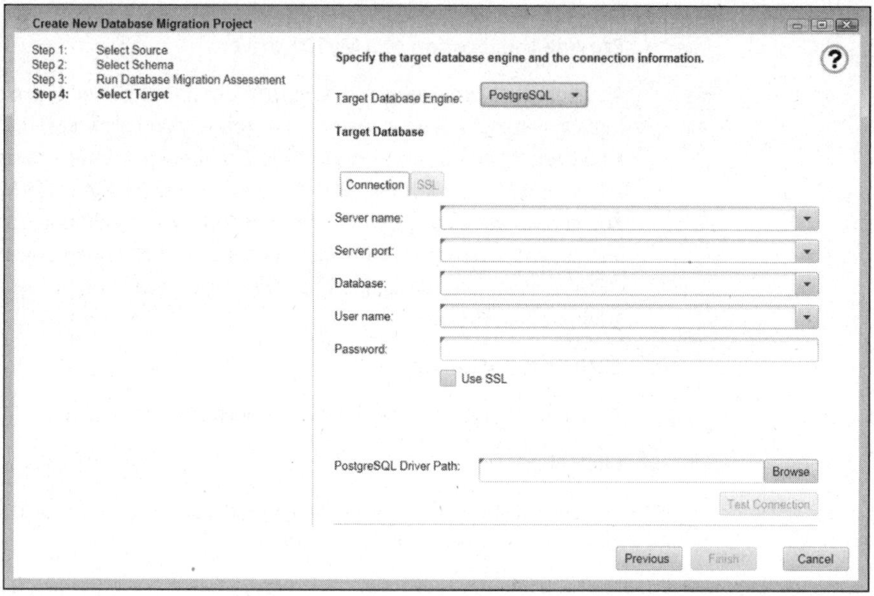

FIGURE 11-9:
Provide the connection information for the target database.

12. **Fill out the target database information using the same approach as you did for the source database.**

Note that PostgreSQL uses 5432 as its default port. Make sure to enter the correct port number when filling out the form. The example assumes that you created a database named FirstDatabase as part of creating the database.

13. **Click Test Connect to verify the connection to the database.**

You see a success message.

14. **Click Finish.**

You see an initial display like the one shown in Figure 11-10. At this point, you can perform any required conversions.

Performing the schema conversion

This chapter doesn't give you detailed usage information for every aspect of the AWS Schema Conversion Tool. However, the following steps offer a quick overview of how a schema conversion might proceed.

1. **Drill down into the source table and select a table for conversion.**

The source database Properties tab fills with information about the selected object, as shown in Figure 11-11.

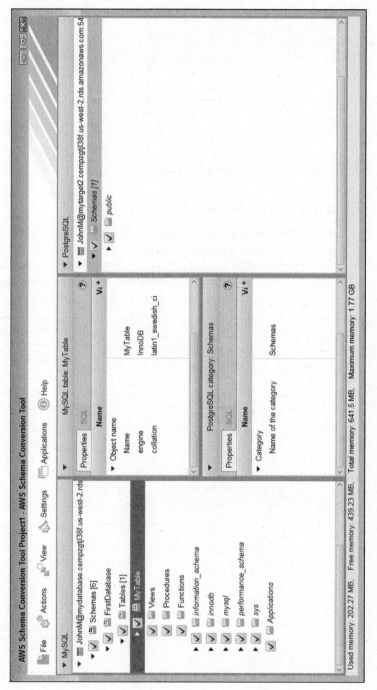

FIGURE 11-10: The initial display shows the two databases you want to work with.

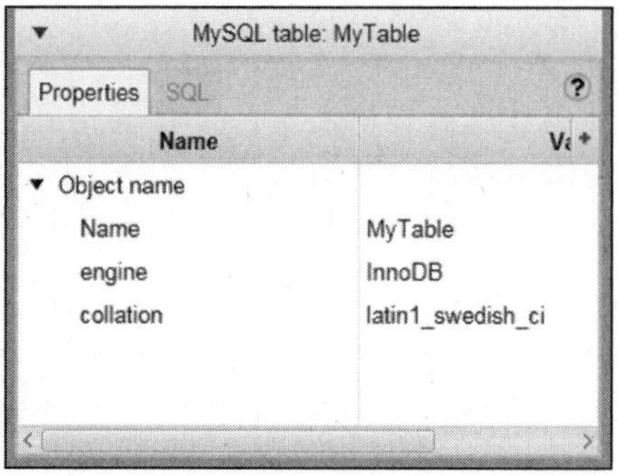

FIGURE 11-11:
The Properties
tab tells you
about the
selected object.

2. **Choose Actions ⇨ Convert Schema.**

After creating the required SQL statement, the AWS Schema Conversion Tool
sends the schema to the target database, as shown in Figure 11-12. However,
the changes aren't permanent at this point. The tool simply created a recommended change that you could modify if desired to obtain better results.

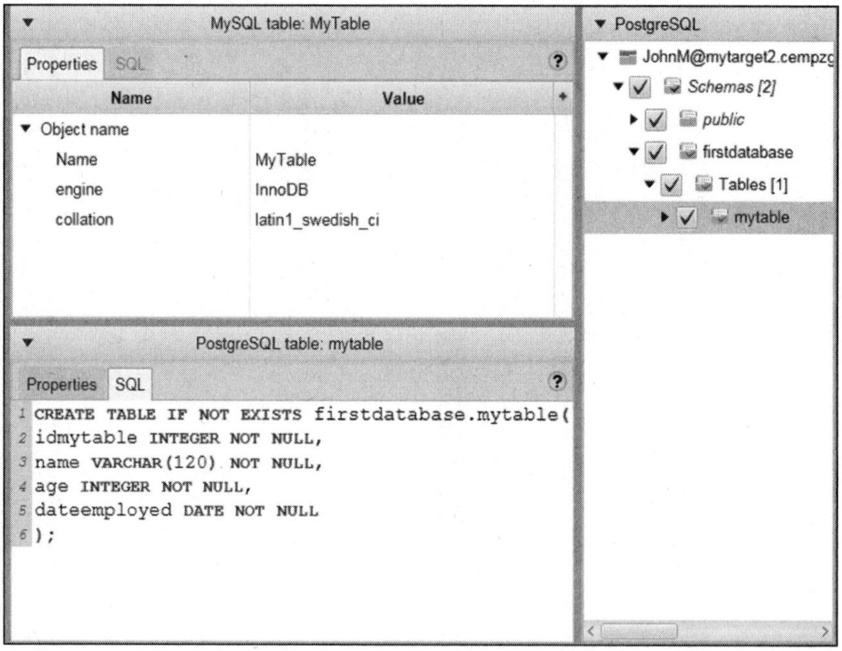

FIGURE 11-12:
Converting the
schema changes
the target
database.

3. **Select the FirstDatabase entry in the target database (right pane) and choose Actions ⇨ Apply to Database.**

You see a dialog box asking whether you're sure that you want to apply the changes.

4. **Click Yes.**

The AWS Schema Conversion Tool sends the resulting changes to the database. You see a new table added to the database containing the AWS modification information. In addition, you can drill down into the table and see the structure that you created, as shown in Figure 11-13.

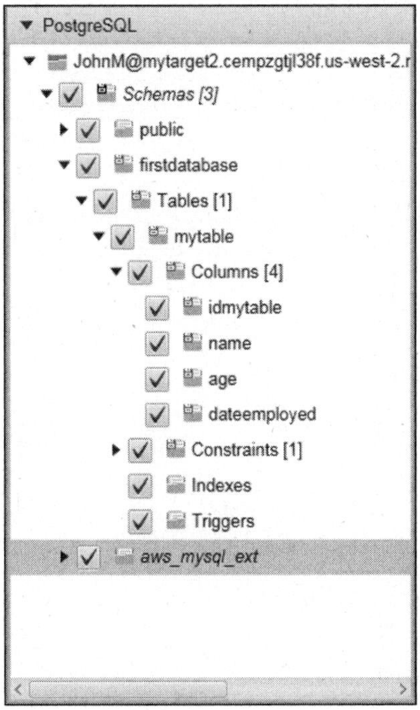

FIGURE 11-13:
The completed conversion shows the schema configured on the target database.

Chapter 12

Gaining NoSQL Access Using DynamoDB

The Structured Query Language (SQL) associated with relational databases (those that use tables of related data) makes up the bulk of Database Management System (DBMS) applications today. Using Relational DBMS (RDBMS) strategies makes sense for most kinds of data because information such as accounting, customer records, inventory, and a vast array of other business information naturally lends itself to the tabular form, in which columns describe the individual data elements and rows contain the individual records.

REMEMBER

However, some data, such as that used by big data or real-time applications, is harder to model using an RDBMS. Consequently, NoSQL or non-SQL databases become more attractive because they use other means to model data that doesn't naturally lend itself to tables. Because business, science, and other entities rely heavily on these nontraditional data sources today, NoSQL is more popular. DynamoDB is Amazon's answer to the need for a NoSQL database for various kinds of data analysis. This chapter begins by helping you understand DynamoDB so that you can better use it to address your specific NoSQL needs.

Before you can do anything with DynamoDB, you need to set up and configure a copy on AWS. That's where you'll use it for the most part, after you get past the early experimentation stage, and it's where the production version of any applications your organization develops will appear. The next section of this chapter looks at the process for using DynamoDB online.

The remainder of the chapter focuses on a test database that you create locally. You develop a simple database using a local copy of DynamoDB, perform some essential tasks with it, and then upload it to your online copy of DynamoDB. You usually follow this same path when working with DynamoDB in a real-world project.

Considering the DynamoDB Features

DynamoDB provides access to all the common NoSQL features, which means that you don't need to worry about issues like creating a schema or maintaining tables. You use a NoSQL database in a free-form manner when compared to a SQL database, and NoSQL gives you the capability to work with large data with greater ease than a SQL database allows. The following sections provide you with a better idea of just what DynamoDB provides and why NoSQL databases are important to businesses.

Getting a quick overview of NoSQL

The main reason to use NoSQL is to address the needs of modern applications. At one time, developers created applications that resided on just one or two platforms. An application development team might work on an application upgrade for months and use a limited number of data types to perform data manipulation. Today, the application environment is completely different, making the use of RDBMS hard for modern applications. NoSQL addresses these needs in a number of ways:

» Developers no longer limit themselves to a set number of data types. Modern applications use data types that are structured, semistructured, unstructured, and polymorphic (a data type used with a single interface that can actually work with objects of different underlying types).

» Short development cycles make using an RDBMS hard, requiring a formal change process to update the schema and migrate the data to the new setup. A NoSQL database is flexible enough to allow ad hoc changes that are more in line with today's development cycle.

» Many applications today appear as services, rather than being installed on a particular system. The use of a Service Oriented Architecture (SOA) means that the application must be available 24 hours a day and that a user can access the same application using any sort of device. NoSQL databases can scale to meet the demands of such an application because they don't have all the underlying architecture of an RDBMS to weigh them down.

» The use of cloud computing means that data must appear in a form that works with multiple online services, even when the developers don't know the needs of those services at the time that a development cycle begins. Because NoSQL doesn't rely on formal schemas and access methodologies, it's easier to create an environment where any service, anywhere, can access the data as needed.

» NoSQL supports the concept of *auto-sharding,* which lets you store data across multiple servers. When working with an RDBMS, the data normally appears on a single server to ensure that the DBMS can perform required maintenance tasks. The use of multiple servers makes NoSQL scale better and function more reliably as well, because you don't have just one failure point. DynamoDB extends the concept of auto-sharding by making cross-region replication possible (see the article at `http://docs.aws.amazon.com/amazondynamodb/latest/developerguide/Streams.CrossRegionRepl.html` for more details).

» Modern languages, such as R, provide data analysis features that rely on the flexible nature of unstructured data to perform its tasks. Because modern business makes decisions based on all sorts of analysis, it also needs modern languages that can perform the required analysis.

Most NoSQL databases provide several methods of organizing data. DynamoDB doesn't support all the various types. What you get is a key-value pair setup, in which a key provides a unique reference to the data stored in the value. The key and the value are both data, but the key must provide unique data so that the database can locate a particular piece of information. A value can contain anything from a simple integer to a document to a complex description of a particular process. NoSQL doesn't place any sort of limit on what the value can contain, which makes it an extremely agile method of storing data.

TECHNICAL STUFF

NoSQL databases typically support a number of other organizational types that DynamoDB doesn't currently support natively. For example, you can't create a graph store that shows interactions of networks of data, such as those found in social media. Examples of NoSQL databases that do provide this support are Neo4J (`https://neo4j.com/`) and Giraph (`http://giraph.apache.org/`). Fortunately, AWS recently added integration with Titan (`http://titan.thinkaurelius.com/`), a distributed graph database, to provide a level of this functionality.

DynamoDB also doesn't support documents such as those found in MongoDB (`https://www.mongodb.com/`). A document is a complex structure that can contain key-value pairs, key-array pairs (an array can contain a series of like values), and even other documents. Documents are a superset of the key-value pairs that DynamoDB does support.

Finally, DynamoDB doesn't support the specialized wide-column data stores found in products such as Cassandra (http://cassandra.apache.org/) and HBase (https://hbase.apache.org/). These kinds of data stores find use in large dataset analysis. Using this kind of data store enables databases, such as Cassandra and HBase, to group data in columns, rather than in rows, which is how most databases work.

Differentiating between NoSQL and relational databases

Previous sections of the chapter may lead you to believe that RDBMS development is archaic because it lacks support for modern agile development methods. However, RDBMS and NoSQL databases actually fulfill needs in two different niches, so a business often needs access to both kinds of data storage. Of course, that's why AWS includes both (see Chapters 10 and 11 for more information about how AWS handles RDBMS requirements).

REMEMBER

Even though NoSQL provides some significant advantages, you need to consider how an RDBMS can help your organization as well. The main consideration in favor of NoSQL is whether the data is unstable or especially complex. In this case, NoSQL presents the best strategy for storing the data because it provides the best flexibility options.

However, an RDBMS offers some special features as well. For example, an RDBMS offers consistency because of the schema that seems to hold it back in other areas. The schema ensures that the data in the database actually meets the criteria you set for it, which means that you're less likely to receive incomplete, missing, errant, or otherwise unusable data from the data source. The consistency offered by an RDBMS is a huge advantage because it means that developers spend less time coding around potential data problems — they can focus on the actual data processing, presentation, and modification.

An RDBMS usually relies on normalization to keep the data size small. When working with a NoSQL database, you can see a lot of repeated data, which consumes more resources. Of course, computer resources are relatively inexpensive today, but given that you're working in a cloud environment, the charges for inefficiencies can add up quickly. The thing to remember about having too much repeated data is that it also tends to slow down parsing, which means that a properly normalized RDBMS database can often find and manipulate data faster than its NoSQL counterpart can.

NoSQL and RDBMS databases offer different forms of reliability as well. Although a NoSQL database scales well and can provide superior speed by spreading itself over multiple servers, the RDBMS offers superior reliability of the intrinsic data. You can depend on the data in an RDBMS being of a certain type with specific characteristics. In addition, you get all the data or none of the data, rather than bits and pieces of the data, as is possible with a NoSQL database.

Because an RDBMS provides the data in a certain form, it can also provide more in the way of built-in query and analysis capabilities. Some of the major RDBMSs provide a substantial array of query and analysis capabilities so that developers don't spend a lot of time reinventing the wheel, and so that administrators can actually figure out what data is available without also getting a degree in development. When the form of the data is right (the lack of a wealth of large objects), an RDBMS can also present results faster because the organization makes parsing the information easier. DynamoDB partially offsets the enhanced query capabilities of an RDBMS by providing a secondary index capability (read more at http://docs.aws.amazon. com/amazondynamodb/latest/developerguide/SecondaryIndexes.html).

TECHNICAL STUFF

As with many data issues, no one single database solution works well in every case. Both RDBMS and NoSQL databases have definite places in an organization. In fact, that's why some vendors offer both solutions and some are working on methods to integrate the two. Interoperability between RDBMS and NoSQL databases is becoming more common with the development of APIs for products such as MongoDB by IBM (see the series of articles that begins at http://www.ibm. com/developerworks/data/library/techarticle/dm-1306nosqlforjson1/ for details). IBM is creating a data representation, query language, and wire protocol to make DB2 and MongoDB interactions relatively seamless.

Defining typical uses for DynamoDB

Most of the use cases for DynamoDB found at https://aws.amazon.com/ dynamodb/ revolve around unstructured, changeable data. One of the more interesting uses of DynamoDB is to provide language support for Duolingo (https:// www.duolingo.com/nojs/splash), a product that helps people learn another language by using a gamelike paradigm. Making learning fun generally makes it easier as well, and learning another language can be a complex task that requires as much fun as one can give it.

Obtaining a continuous stream of data is important in some cases, especially in monitoring roles. For example, BMW uses DynamoDB to collect sensor data from its cars. The use of streams in DynamoDB (see http://docs.aws.amazon.com/ amazondynamodb/latest/developerguide/Streams.html for more information) makes this kind of application practical. Dropcam (https://nest.com/camera/ meet-nest-cam/), a company that offers property monitoring, is another example of using streaming to provide real-time updates for an application.

DynamoDB actually provides a wide range of impressive features, which you can read about at https://aws.amazon.com/dynamodb/details/. The problem is finding use cases for these new features, such as ElasticMap Reduce integration, in real-world applications today. The lack of use cases is hardly surprising because most of this technology is so incredibly new. The important takeaway here is that DynamoDB has a place alongside RDS for more organizations, and you need to find the mix that works best for your needs.

Creating a Basic DynamoDB Setup

You have a number of ways to work with DynamoDB, many of which apply more to DevOps, DBAs, or developers than they do to administrators. For example, you can go with the local option described in the upcoming "Working with DynamoDB locally" sidebar. This option appeals mostly to developers because it lets a developer play with DynamoDB in a manner that combines it with languages that work well with NoSQL databases, such as Python. If you're truly interested in development as well as administrative tasks, you can find some helpful details in the sidebar.

WORKING WITH DYNAMODB LOCALLY

In contrast to many of the other AWS services, you can actually get a local copy of DynamoDB that you can work with offline. Using DynamoDB offline, on your local machine, means that you can try various tasks out without incurring costs or worrying about potential connectivity issues. In addition, you can use DynamoDB in a test environment, where you are using a copy of your data to mimic real-world situations. Unfortunately, the process for creating a local copy is relatively complex and error prone, so I chose not to cover in the book (but may eventually cover it in my blog at http://blog.johnmuellerbooks.com).

You can see the process for creating a local copy of DynamoDB at http://docs.aws.amazon.com/amazondynamodb/latest/developerguide/DynamoDBLocal.html. When you finish this initial installation, you have a command-line–driven interface that you can use, but it still doesn't show you much. To get a functional setup that really does help you understand DynamoDB a bit better, you need to install other products, such as Python 2.7. You can see an example of the series of steps needed at http://docs.aws.amazon.com/amazondynamodb/latest/developerguide/TicTacToe.Phase1.html. This tutorial covers the processes needed to build a tic-tac-toe game using DynamoDB, Python, and a few other bits and pieces.

Before you can do anything with DynamoDB, you must create an instance of it, just as you do for RDS. The following procedure helps you get started with DynamoDB so that you can perform some interesting tasks with it:

1. **Sign into AWS using your administrator account.**

2. **Navigate to the DynamoDB Management Console at** https://console. aws.amazon.com/dynamodb.

    You see a Welcome page that contains interesting information about DynamoDB and what it can do for you. However, you don't see the actual console at this point. Notice the Getting Started Guide link, which you can use to obtain access to tutorials and introductory videos.

3. **Click Create Table.**

    You see the Create DynamoDB Table page, shown in Figure 12-1. Amazon assumes that most people have worked with an RDBMS database, so the instructions for working with RDS are fewer and less detailed. Notice the level of detail provided for DynamoDB. The wizard explains each part of the table creation process carefully to reduce the likelihood that you will make mistakes.

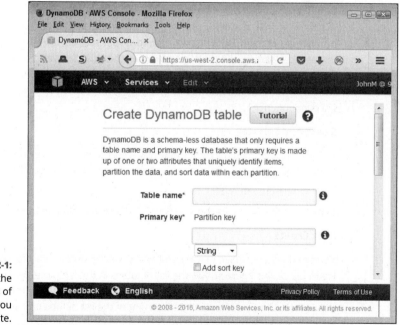

FIGURE 12-1:
Start defining the characteristics of the table you want to create.

4. **Type TestDB in the Table Name field.**

    Pick a descriptive name for your table. In this case, you need to remember that your entire database could consist of a single, large table.

5. **Type EmployeeID in the Primary Key field and choose Number for its type.**

When working with a NoSQL database, you must define a unique value as the key in the key-value pair. An employee ID is likely to provide a unique value across all employees. Duplicated keys will cause problems because you can't uniquely identify a particular piece of data after the key is duplicated.

A key must also provide a simple value. When working with DynamoDB, you have a choice of making the key a number, string, or binary value. You can't use a Boolean value because you would have only a choice between true and false. Likewise, other data types won't work because they are either too complex or don't offer enough choices.

TIP

Notice the Add Sort Key check box. Selecting this option lets you add a secondary method of locating data. Using a sort key lets you locate data using more than just the primary key. For example, in addition to the employee ID, you might also want to add a sort key based on employee name. People know names; they tend not to know IDs. However, a name isn't necessarily unique: Two people can have the same name, so using a name as your primary key is a bad idea.

Not shown in Figure 12-1 is the option to Use Default Settings. The default settings create a NoSQL table that lacks a secondary index, allows a specific provisioned capacity, and sets alarms for occasions when applications exceed the provisioned capacity. A provisioned capacity essentially determines the number of reads and writes that you expect per second. Given that this is a test setup, a setting of 5 reads and 5 writes should work well. You can read more about provisioned capacity at http://docs.aws.amazon.com/amazondynamodb/latest/developerguide/HowItWorks.Provisioned Throughput.html.

6. **Select Add Sort Key.**

You see another field added for entering a sort field, as shown in Figure 12-2. Notice that this second field is connected to the first, so the two fields are essentially used together.

7. **Type EmployeeName in the sort key field and set its type to String.**

8. **Click Create.**

You see the Tables page of the DynamoDB Management Console, shown in Figure 12-3. This figure shows the list of tables in the left pane and the details for the selected table in the right pane. Each of the tabs tells you something about the table. The More link on the right of the list of tabs tells you that more tabs are available for you to access.

Not shown in Figure 12-2 is the Navigation pane. Click the right-pointing arrow to show the Navigation pane, where you can choose other DynamoDB views (Dashboard and Reserved Capacity).

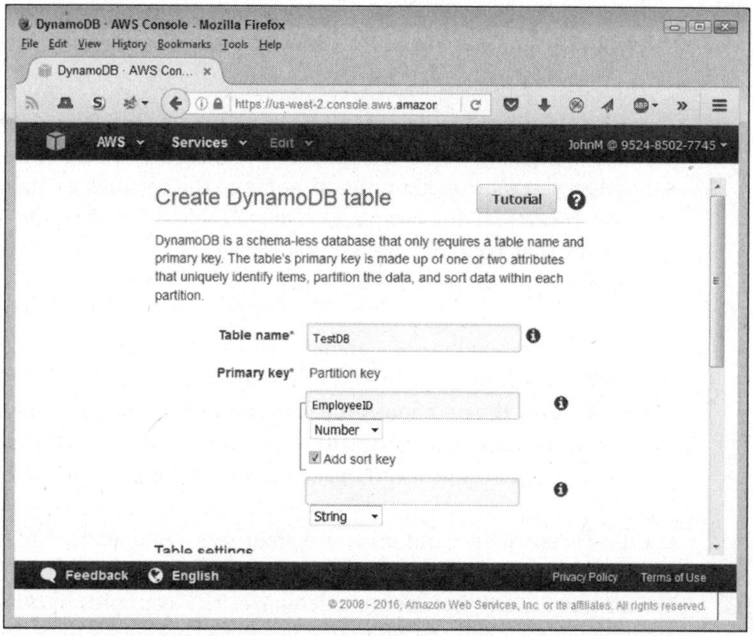

FIGURE 12-2:
Choose a sort key
that people will
understand well.

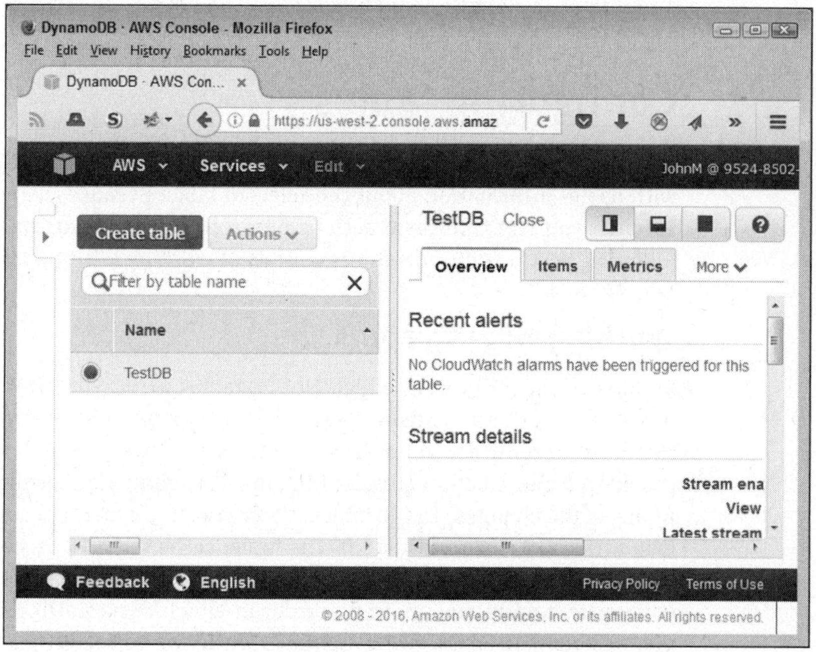

FIGURE 12-3:
The table you
created appears
in the Tables
page.

Developing a Basic Database

The act of creating a table doesn't necessarily mean that your database is ready for use. For one thing, even though you have the beginnings of a database, it lacks data. Also, you may need to modify some of the settings to make the database suit your needs better. For example, you may decide to include additional alarms based on metrics that you see, or to increase the capacity as the test phase progresses and more people work with the data.

Normally, you populate a database by importing data into it. The DynamoDB interface also allows you to enter data manually, which works quite well for test purposes. After the data looks the way you want it to look, you can export the data to see how the data you want to import should look. Exporting the data also allows you to move it to other locations or perform a backup outside of AWS.

REMEMBER

Databases normally contain more than one table, even NoSQL databases. Yes, creating a simple test database using a single table is possible, but multiple tables appear more often than not in a database. The examples in this chapter do rely on a single table — the one you create in the previous section. You use this table in the sections that follow to explore the techniques that DynamoDB provides for interacting with tables and the data they contain.

Configuring tables

The right pane in Figure 12-3 contains a series of tabs. Each of these tabs gives you with useful information about the selected table. Because the information is table specific, you can't perform actions on groups of tables using the interface. The following sections discuss the essentials of working with tables.

Working with streams

Because of the manner in which NoSQL tables work, you often need to synchronize copies of the same data. A table in one region might receive changes that you also need to replicate in another region. In fact, you might find other reasons to provide a *log* of changes (think of the log as a detailed procedure you could use to replicate the changes) to the tables you create. A *stream* is a record of table changes (the actual data used to modify the table, rather than a procedure detailing the tasks performed, as provided by a log). Each change appears only once in the log you create, and it appears in the order in which DynamoDB received the change. The ordered list enables anyone reading the log to reconstruct table changes in another location. AWS retains this log for 24 hours, so it doesn't need to be read immediately.

The Overview tab contains Manage Stream button you click to set up a stream for your table, as shown in Figure 12-4. This feature isn't enabled by default, but you can configure it to allow the storage of specific change information. You have the following options when creating the change log:

FIGURE 12-4:
Use the Stream option to create a log of table changes.

» **Keys Only:** Just the key portion of the key-value pair appears in the log. This option has the advantage of providing just a summary of the changes and makes the log smaller and easier to read. If the receiving party wants to do something with the change, the new value can be read from the table.

» **New Image:** Both the new key and value of the key-value pair appear in the log. The log contains the information as it appears after the modification. This is the right option to use for replication, in that you want to copy both the new key and value to another table.

» **Old Image:** Both the old key and the value of the key-value pair appear in the log. This log entry shows how the table entry appeared before someone modified it.

» **New and Old Images:** The entire new and old key-value pairs appear in the log. You can use this kind of entry for verification purposes. However, realize that this approach uses the most space. The log will be much larger than the actual table because you're storing two entries for absolutely every change made to the table.

Viewing metrics

The Metrics tab contains a series of graphs, which you can expand by clicking the graphs. Metrics help you understand how well your table is working and enable you to change settings before a particular issue becomes critical. Many of the metrics tables include multiple entries. For example, in the Read Capacity metric, shown in Figure 12-5, the red line shows the provisioned read capacity and the blue line shows how much of that capacity your application consumes. When the blue line starts to approach the red line, you need to consider modifying the read capacity of the table to avoid throttled read requests, which appear in the metric to the right of the Read Capacity metric.

TestDB   Close

| Overview | Items | **Metrics** | Alarms | Capacity | Indexes | Triggers | More ∨ |

View all CloudWatch metrics ☐   Time Range Last Hour   ▼   ↻

Capacity: table

Read capacity (Units/Second - 1 min avg) ⓘ   **Throttled read requests** (Count)

■ Provisioned ■ Consumed   ■ Get ■ Scan ■ Query ■ Batch get

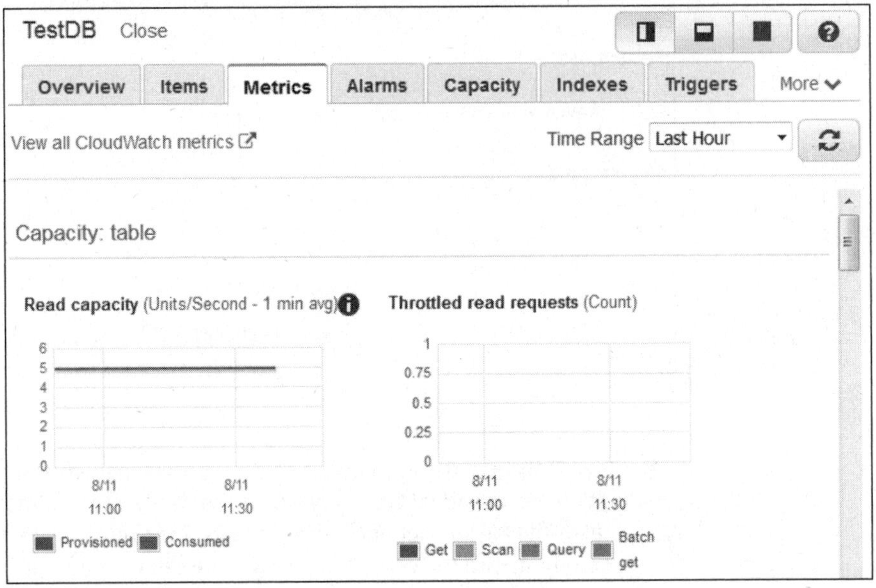

FIGURE 12-5: Metrics help you manage your table.

TIP

The *i* shown in the circle next to a metric graph tells you that you can get additional information about that graph. Hover your mouse over the *i* to see a pop-up containing helpful information. For example, the pop-up for the Read Capacity graph tells you that small surges in reads may not appear in the graph because the graph uses averaged data. The Throttled Read Requests graph is actually a better indicator of when small surges become a problem.

Checking alarms

The Alarms tab, shown in Figure 12-6, contains the alarms that you set to monitor your table. No one can view the status of a table continuously, so alarms enable you to discover potentially problematic conditions before they cause an application crash or too many user delays. The default table setup includes two alarms: one for read capacity and another for write capacity.

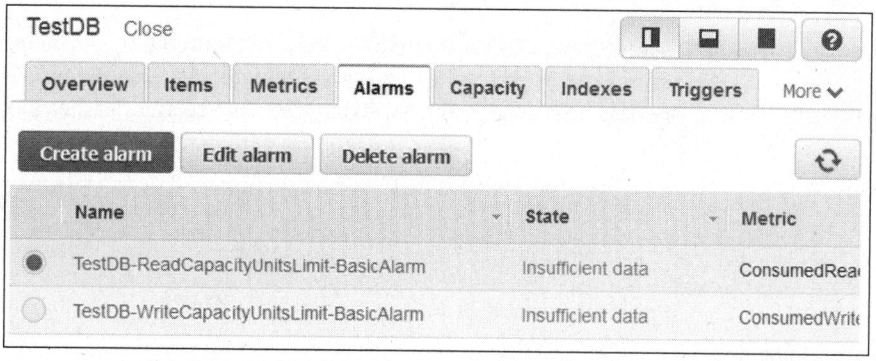

FIGURE 12-6:
Use alarms to monitor table performance when you aren't physically viewing it.

The options on the Alarms tab let you create, delete, and edit alarms. When you click one of these options, you see a dialog box similar to the one shown in Figure 12-7, in which you configure the alarm. Sending a Simple Notification Service (SNS) message lets you get a remote warning of impending problems.

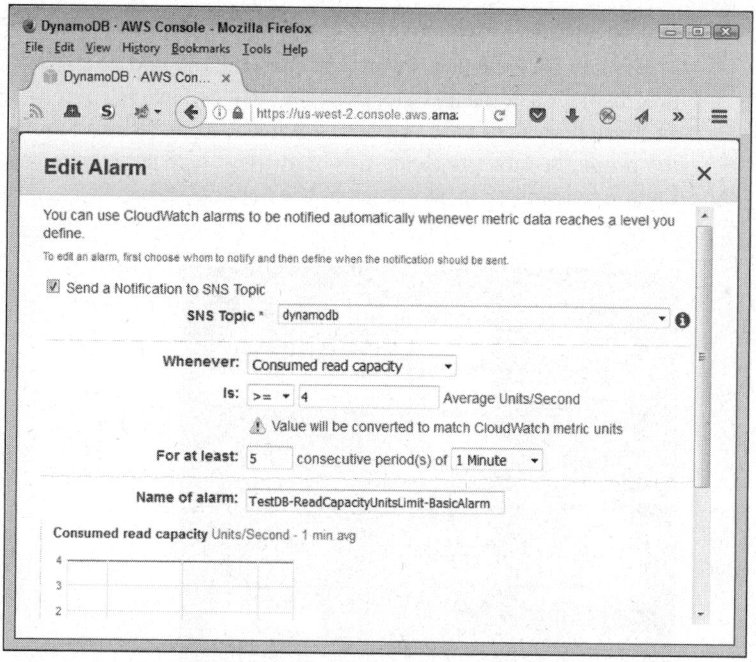

FIGURE 12-7:
Create new alarms or edit existing alarms as needed to keep tables working smoothly.

Modifying capacity

When you initially create a table, you get 5 units each of read and write capacity. As your application usage grows, you might find that these values are too small (or possibly too large). Every unit of capacity costs money, so tuning the capacity is important. The Capacity tab, shown in Figure 12-8, lets you modify the read and write capacity values for any table. You should base the amounts you use on the metrics discussed in the "Viewing metrics" section, earlier in this chapter.

FIGURE 12-8:
Manage the
read and write
capacity to
ensure that the
application works
as anticipated but
costs remain low.

The tab shows an anticipated cost for the current usage level. Changing the read or write capacity will also modify the amount you pay. The Capacity Calculator link displays a Capacity Calculator that you can use to compute the amount of read and write capacity that you actually need, as shown in Figure 12-9. Simply type the amounts into the fields to obtain new read and write capacity values. Click Update to transfer these values to the Capacity tab.

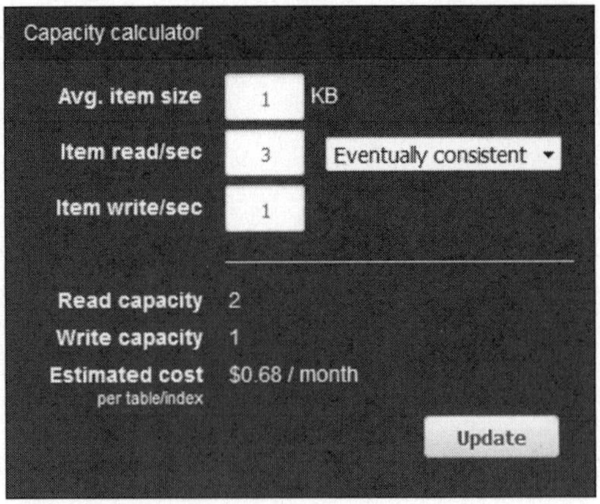

FIGURE 12-9:
The Capacity
Calculator
reduces the
work required
to compute
capacity values.

Creating a secondary index

Secondary indexes make finding specific data in your table easier. Perhaps you need to find information based on something other than the primary key.

For example, you could find employees based on name or ID using the primary key for the example table. However, you might also need to find employees based on their employment date at some point. To create a secondary index, click Create Index in the Indexes tab. You see a Create Index dialog box like the one shown in Figure 12-10. (This dialog box contains sample values that you can use for experimentation purposes in the "Performing Queries" section, later in this chapter.)

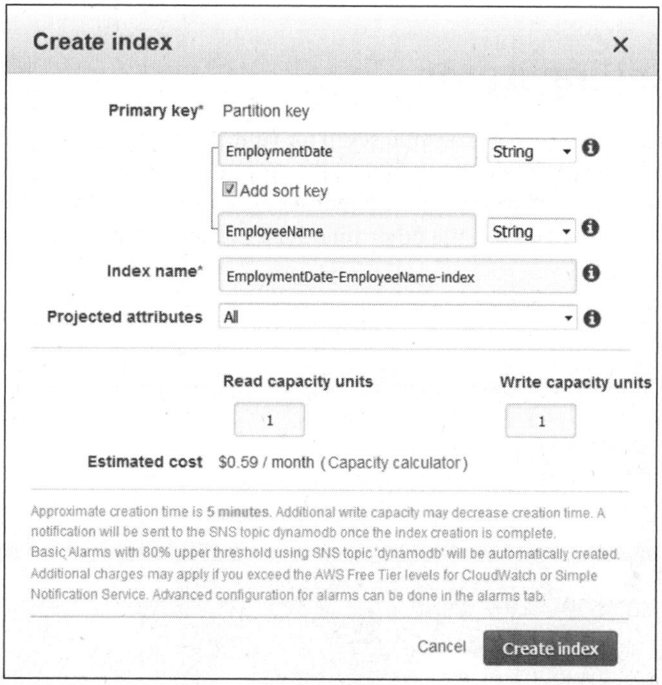

FIGURE 12-10:
Use secondary indexes to help look for data not found in the primary key.

A secondary index incurs an additional cost. You must allocate read and write capacity units that reflect the amount of usage that you expect the secondary index to receive. As with the table's capacity values, you can click the Capacity Calculator link to display the Capacity Calculator (shown in Figure 12-9) to provide an estimate of the number of units you need.

After you create a new index, you see it listed in the Indexes tab, as shown in Figure 12-11. The Status field tells you the current index condition. There is no option for editing indexes. If you find that the index you created doesn't work as anticipated, you need to delete the old index and create a new one.

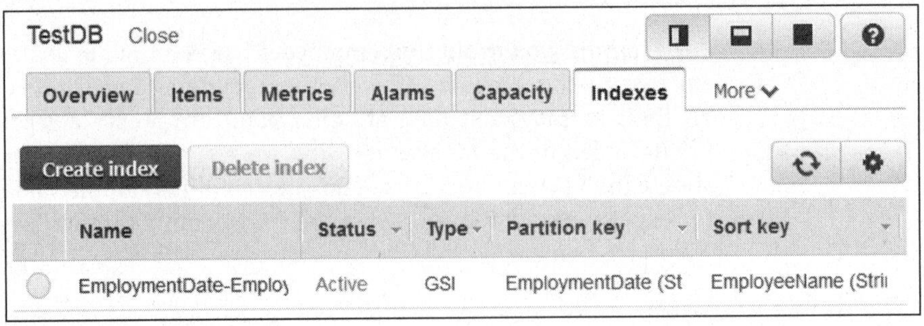

FIGURE 12-11:
The Indexes
tab provides a list
of indexes for
your table.

Name	Status	Type	Partition key	Sort key
○ EmploymentDate-Employ	Active	GSI	EmploymentDate (St	EmployeeName (Stri

Adding items

After you obtain the desired setup for your table, you want to add some items to it. The Items tab, shown in Figure 12-12, can look a little daunting at first because you can use it in several different ways. This section focuses on the Create Item button, but you use the other functions as the chapter progresses.

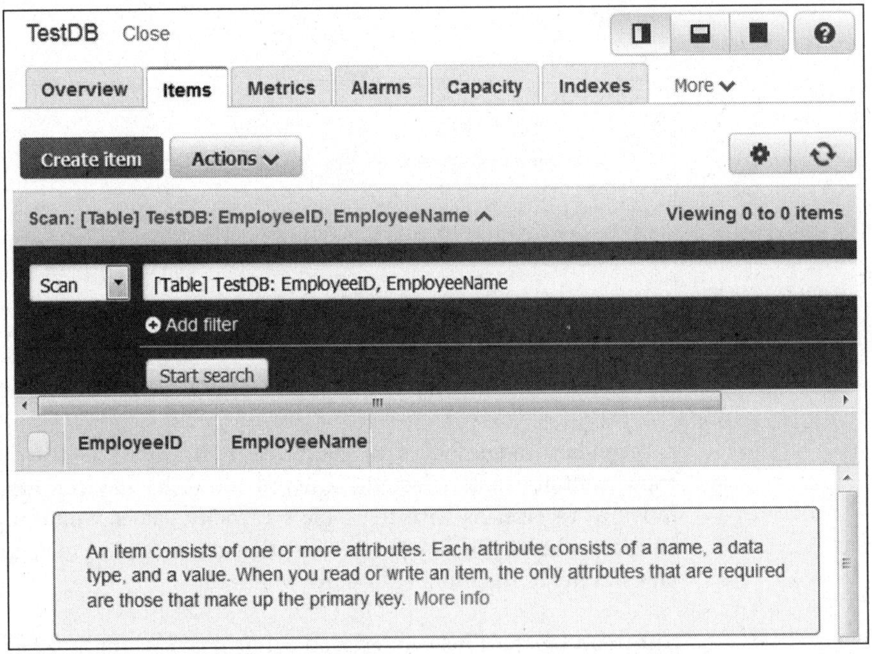

FIGURE 12-12:
The Items tab
combines a
number of tasks
into a single area.

The following sections describe how to add items to your table manually. You can also add items in bulk by importing them. Another option is to copy a table (exporting data from one table and importing it into another) or to use a stream to obtain data from another table (see the "Working with streams" section, earlier in this chapter, for details).

Defining the data types

When you create an item, you initially see all the fields that you've defined in various ways, but that isn't the end of the process. You can add more fields as needed to provide a complete record. Index and key fields, those that you define using the various methods found in this chapter, have a limited number of acceptable data types: String, Binary, and Number. However, other fields can use these data types:

>> **String:** A series of characters that can include letters, numbers, punctuation marks, and special characters.

>> **Binary:** A series of 0s and 1s presented as Base64-encoded binary data. DynamoDB treats every value in the string as an individual, byte-coded value but stores the entire string as a single value in the table.

>> **Number:** Any number that you could expect to find in other programming languages. You specify a number as a string but don't care whether the number is an integer or floating-point value. DynamoDB treats the strings you provide as numbers for math calculations.

>> **StringSet:** A group of strings that work together as an array of values. Every value in the array must appear as a string. The array can have as many strings as needed to complete the information. For example, you can create a StringSet called Address. Each entry can be another line in an individual's address, which means that some entries may have just one entry, while others may have two or three entries in the array.

>> **NumberSet:** A group of numeric strings that work together as an array of numeric values. Every value in the array must appear as a number, but not necessarily all as integers or floating-point values. DynamoDB treats the strings you provide as numbers for math calculations.

>> **BinarySet:** A group of binary values that work together as an array of values. Every value in the array must appear as a binary value.

>> **Map:** A complex data grouping that contains entries of any data type, including other maps. The entries appear as attribute-value pairs. You provide the name of an attribute, and then provide a value that contains any of the data types described in this section. You can access each member of the map using its attribute name.

>> **List:** A group of data of any supported DynamoDB type. A list works similarly to a set, but with elements that can be of any type. A list can even contain maps. The difference between a list and a map is that you don't name the individual entries. Consequently, you access members of a list using an *index* (a numeric value that indicates the item's position in the list, starting with 0 for the first item).

>> **Boolean:** A value of either true or false that indicates the truth value of the attribute.

>> **Null:** A blank spot that is always set to true. You use a Null attribute to represent missing data. Other records in the table contain this data, but the data is missing for this particular record.

Creating an item

To create a new item for your table, click Create Item in the Items tab. You see a dialog box like the one shown in Figure 12-13. This dialog automatically presents three attributes (fields). These fields are present because they represent required entries to support a primary key, sort key, or a secondary index.

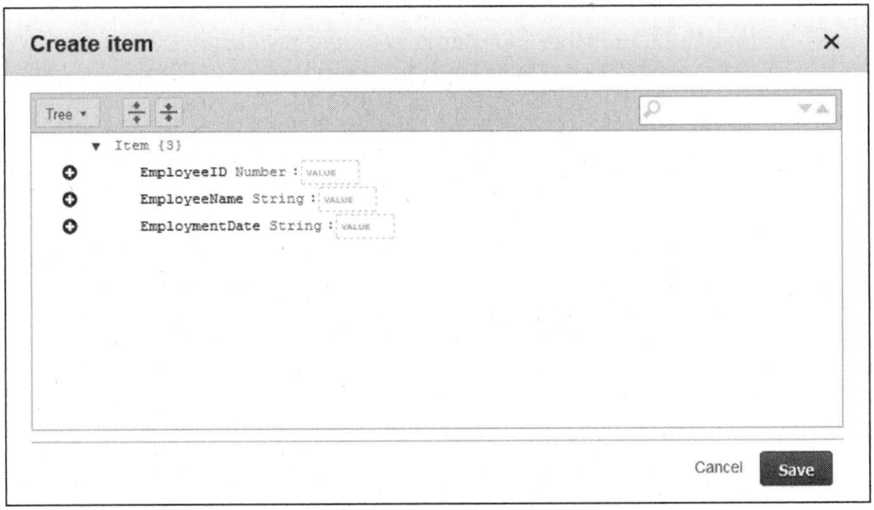

Create item ✕

Tree ▾

▾ Item {3}
- EmployeeID Number : VALUE
- EmployeeName String : VALUE
- EmploymentDate String : VALUE

Cancel   Save

FIGURE 12-13: Creating a new item automatically adds the required attributes for that item.

WARNING

The items you see when you first create an item are mandatory if you want the item to work as it should with other table items. However, you can remove the items if desired, which can lead to missing essential data in the table. DynamoDB does check for missing or duplicate key values, so you can't accidentally enter two items with the same key.

When you finish filling out the essential attributes, you can save the item (if desired) by clicking Save. DynamoDB checks the item for errors and saves it to your table. You have the option of adding other attributes, as covered in the next section.

Adding and removing attributes

Table items have key fields, sort fields, and secondary sort indexes that provide essential information to both the viewer and DynamoDB. These entries let you perform tasks such as sorting the data and looking for specific information. However, there are also informational fields that simply contain data. You don't normally sort on these attributes or use them for queries, but you can use them to obtain supplementary information. To add one of these items, you click the plus (+) sign next to an existing item and choose an action from the context menu, shown in Figure 12-14.

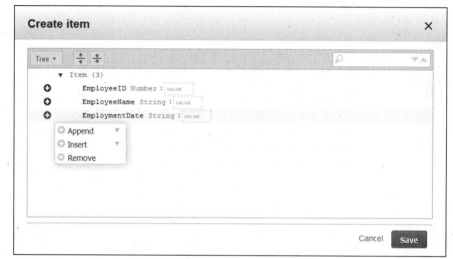

FIGURE 12-14: Choose an action to add or remove attributes from an item.

Appending an attribute means adding it after the current attribute. Likewise, inserting an attribute means adding it before the current attribute. You can also use the menu to remove an attribute that you don't want. Use this feature with care, because you can remove attributes that you really need.

After you decide to append or insert a new attribute, you choose an attribute type that appears from the drop-down list. The "Defining the data types" section, earlier in this chapter, describes all the types. Click a type and you see a new attribute added in the correct position. Begin defining the new attribute by giving it a name. When working with a simple item, you type the value immediately after the name, as shown in Figure 12-15. If you type an incorrect value, such as when providing a string for a Boolean attribute, DynamoDB lets you know about the problem immediately.

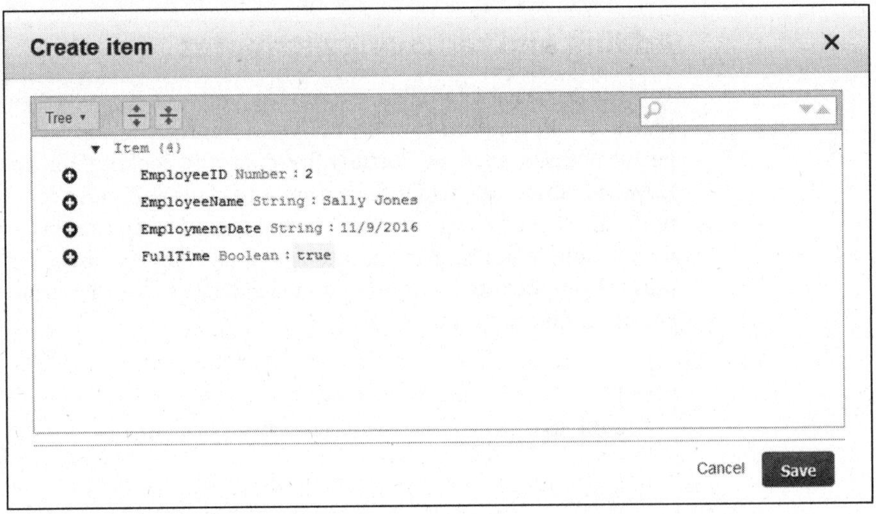

FIGURE 12-15:
Attributes
appear as
attribute-value
pairs.

Adding complex attributes take a little more time and thought. Figure 12-16 shows a map entry. Note how the attribute-value pairs appear indented. If this map had contained other complex types, such as a set, list, or map, the new data would appear indented at another level to the right. The map automatically keeps track of the number of map entries for you.

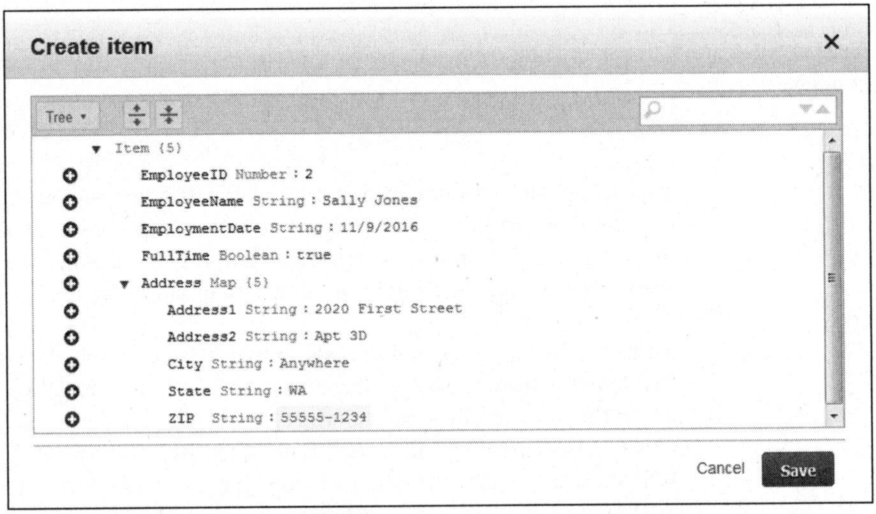

FIGURE 12-16:
Complex data
appears as
indented entries.

It isn't apparent from the figure, but you use a slightly different technique to work with attributes in this case. When you want to add a new attribute, one that's at the same level as the map, you actually click the plus sign (+) next to the map entry, which is Address in Figure 12-16. However, if you want to add a new entry to the map, you must click the + next to one of the map entries, such as Address1.

Modifying items

Several methods are available for modifying items. If you want to modify all or most of the entries in the item, select the item's entry in the list and choose Actions ⇨ Edit. You see a dialog box, similar to the one shown in Figure 12-16, in which you can edit the information as needed. (If the information appears with just the complex data shown, click the Expand All Fields button at the top of the dialog box.)

To modify just one or two attributes of an item, hover your mouse over that item's entry in the Items tab. Attributes that you can change appear with a pencil next to them when you have the mouse in the correct position. Click the pencil icon, and you can enter new information for the selected attribute.

Copying items

You may have two items with almost the same information, or you might want to use one of the items as a template for creating other items. You don't need to perform this task manually. Select the item you want to copy and choose Actions ⇨ Duplicate in the Items tab. You see a Copy Item dialog box that looks similar to the dialog box shown in Figure 12-16. Change the attributes that you need to change (especially the primary key, sort key, and secondary indexes) and click Save to create the new item. This approach is far faster than duplicating everything manually each time you want to create a new item, especially when you have complex data entries to work with.

Deleting items

To remove one or more items from the table, select each item that you want to remove and then choose Actions ⇨ Delete. DynamoDB displays a Delete Items dialog box, which asks whether you're sure about removing the data. Click Delete to complete the task.

Deleting a table

At some point, you may not want your table any longer. To remove the table from DynamoDB, select the name of the table you want to remove and then choose

Actions ⇨ Delete Table in the Tables page. DynamoDB displays a Delete Table dialog box that asks whether you're sure you want to delete the table. Click Delete to complete the action.

As part of the table deletion process, you can also delete all the alarms associated with the table. DynamoDB selects the Delete All CloudWatch Alarms for This Table entry in the Delete Table dialog box by default. If you decide that you want to keep the alarms, you can always deselect the check box to maintain them.

Performing Queries

Finding data that you need can become problematic. A few records, or even a few hundred records, might not prove to be much of a problem. However, hundreds of thousands of records would be a nightmare to search individually, so you need to have some method of finding the data quickly. This assistance comes in the form of a query. DynamoDB actually supports two query types:

>> **Scan:** Uses a filtering approach to find entries that match your criteria

>> **Query:** Looks for specific attribute entries

The examples in this section employ two test entries in the TestDB table. The essential entries are the EmployeeID, EmployeeName, and EmploymentDate attributes, shown here:

EmployeeID	EmployeeName	EmploymentDate
1	George Smith	11/11/2016
2	Sally Jones	11/09/2016

The two methods of querying data have advantages and disadvantages, but what you use normally comes down to a matter of personal preference. The following sections describe both approaches.

Using a scan

Scans have the advantage of being a bit more free-form than queries. You filter data based on any field you want to use. To scan the data, you choose either a [Table] entry that contains the primary key and sort key, or an [Index] entry that sorts the data based on a secondary index that you create, as shown in Figure 12-17.

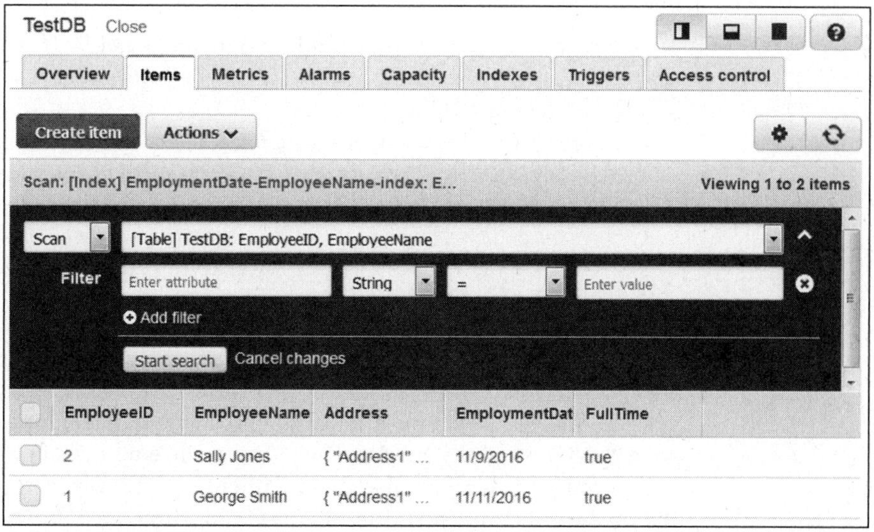

FIGURE 12-17:
Scans employ
filters to
locate data.

Using a scan means deciding on what kind of filtering to use to get a desired result. The following steps provide you with a template for a quick method of performing a scan (your steps will vary because you need to provide specific information to make the procedure work).

1. Choose Scan in the first field.

2. Select either a [Table] or [Index] entry in the second field.

The entry you choose determines the output's sort order. In addition, using the correct entry speeds the search because DynamoDB will have a quick method of finding the data.

3. Click Add Filter (if necessary) to add a new filter entry.

You can remove filters by clicking the X on the right side of the filter's entry.

4. Choose an attribute, such as in the first Filter field.

5. Select the attribute's type in the second Filter field.

6. Specify a logical relationship in the third Filter field.

This entry can be tricky, especially when working with strings. For example, if you want to find all the entries that begin with the name George, you choose the Begins With entry in this field. However, if you want to find all the employees hired after 11/08/2016, use the > entry instead.

7. Type a value for the fourth Filter field, such as George.

8. Click Start Search.

You see the entries that match your filter criteria. You can use as many filters as desired to whittle the data down to just those items you really want to see. Simply repeat Steps 3 through 8 to achieve the desired result.

Using a query

Queries are stricter and more precise than scans. When you perform a query, you look for specific values, as shown in Figure 12-18. Notice that the key value is precise. You can't look for a range of employment dates; instead, you must look for a specific employment date. In addition, the employment date is a mandatory entry; you can't perform the query without it. However, you can also choose an optional sort key and add filtering (as found with scans) as well.

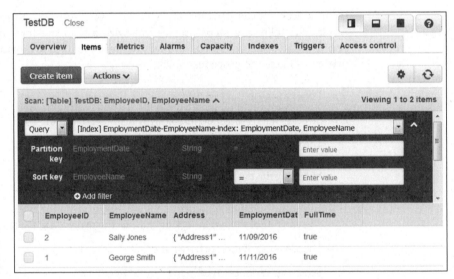

FIGURE 12-18:
Queries use specific values to find information.

In this way, using a query is more like asking a specific question. You can ask which employees, who were hired on 11/09/2016, have a name that begins with Sally. In this case, you see just one record. Scans can produce the same result by employing multiple filters. The advantage of a query is that it forces you to think in a particular way; also, because you use attributes that are indexed, using a query is faster.

5
Creating a User-Friendly Cloud Environment

Chapter **13**

Isolating Cloud Resources Using Virtual Private Cloud

U nderstanding the concept of a Virtual Private Cloud (VPC) can be daunting. Of course, you don't need to know the innermost details about how a VPC works to use one, but it helps to understand what it can do for you in order to understand how you can better use it effectively. The first section of this chapter examines what the Amazon VPC provides in the way of features. In addition, it helps you get past some of the hype to understand what it's really offering you in terms of useful functionality. You can try to define where you can use the Amazon VPC in your organization and where you might want to avoid it.

In many cases, an experimenter can ignore the VPC completely. In fact, a small business may not need to pay much attention to it, either. However, after your organization starts to get to a certain size, you can't really ignore the VPC any longer because you need to configure it to interact with your setup in the correct manner. This means performing some basic configuration tasks, as a minimum. This chapter doesn't get involved in low-level configuration details, which could actually require a whole book to talk about. Rather, you get an introduction to configuring the default VPC that you initially created as part of configuring EC2 in Chapter 4.

The default VPC can serve the needs of most individuals and small businesses. In fact, even a medium-sized business can probably use the default VPC without any problem. However, some situations exist, such as when you need to create custom subnets or obtain access to special VPC features, in which creating a custom VPC becomes important. This chapter gives you an overview of the process for creating a custom VPC. What you end up with is an idea of why, how, and when you use a custom VPC to meet specific business needs without delving into details that will cause your head to spin.

Considering the Virtual Private Cloud (VPC) Features

The idea behind a VPC is to create an environment in which a system separates the physical world from an execution environment. Essentially, VPC is a kind of virtual machine combined with a Virtual Private Network (VPN) and some additions that you probably won't find with similar setups. Even so, the concept of using VPC as a virtual machine is the same as any other virtual machine. You can read more about the benefits of using a virtual machine at `https://www.linux.com/learn/why-when-and-how-use-virtual-machine`. The connectivity provided by a VPC is akin to the same connectivity provided by any other VPN (read more at `https://community.jisc.ac.uk/library/advisory-services/overview-vpn-technology`).

When working with AWS, you never actually see or interact with the physical device running the code that makes the resources you create active. You don't know where the physical hardware resides or whether other VPCs are also using the same physical hardware as you are. In fact, you have no idea of whether the code used to create an EC2 instance even resides on just one physical machine. The virtual environment — this execution environment that doesn't exist in the physical world — lets you improve overall reliability and make recovering from crashes easier. In addition, the virtual nature of the environment fully separates the code that your organization executes from code that any other organization executes. This concept of total separation tends to make the environment more secure as well. The following sections describe what a VPC is in more detail and why you can benefit from one in making your organization Internet friendly.

Defining the VPC and the reason you need it

The Internet is the public cloud. Anyone can access the Internet at any time given the correct software. You don't even need a browser. Applications access the

Internet all the time without using one — a browser is simply a special kind of Internet access application. Despite the public nature of the Internet, it actually provides four levels or steps that you follow from being completely public to being nearly private:

1. The public, unrestricted Internet

2. Sites that limit access community data using logins and other means

3. Sites that provide access to individually identifiable data for pay or other considerations through a secure connection

4. A nearly private connection that is accessible only between consenting parties (and any hackers that may be listening)

The initial step that everyone takes is the public Internet. You do something to access the Internet; you may use your smart television or some alternative means, but you take this initial step every time you begin a session. What the Internet really provides is access to a much larger network in which anyone can find resources and use them to meet specific needs. For example, you might read the news stories on a site while someone else downloads precisely the same information and analyzes it in some manner. Seeing the data of the Internet is important because it helps you understand that the Internet isn't about games or information; rather, it's about connections to resources that mainly revolve around data.

To take the next step, you need to consider all the sites out there that limit your access to the data that the Internet provides. For example, when you want to read news stories on some sites, you must first log in to the site. The need to log in to the site represents a connectivity hurdle that you must overcome in order to gain access to the resource, which is data. Whether you read the data or analyze it, you must still log in. The site is still public. Anyone who has an account can access it.

A third step is public sites that host private data. For example, when you make a purchase at Amazon, you first log in to your account. The data is visible only to you, not anyone else with an account. All others with an account sees only their private data as well. However, the site itself is still public.

A VPC is the fourth step. In this case, you separate everything possible from everything else using a variety of software-oriented techniques, with a little machine-level hardware reinforcement. Keeping everything separated reduces security issues. After all, you don't want another organization (or a hacker) to know anything about what you're doing. Realize that you are potentially using the same physical hardware and definitely using the same cable as other people. The lack of capability to create a separate physical environment is the reason that hackers continue to create methods of overcoming security and gaining access to your resources anyway.

The reason you need a VPC is to ensure that your cloud computing is secure, or at least as secure as possible when it comes to allowing any connectivity to the outside world. In fact, without a VPC, you couldn't use the cloud for any sensitive data, even if you had no requirement for keeping the data secure legally or ethically. Without a VPC, every communication would be akin to creating a post on Facebook: Anyone could see it. VPCs are actually quite common because they're so incredibly useful. Here are some other vendors that make VPCs available as part of their offerings:

>> FortyCloud (http://fortycloud.com/)

>> HostVirtual (https://www.hostvirtual.com/)

>> HP Hybrid Cloud – HPE Helion (http://www8.hp.com/us/en/cloud/helion-overview.html)

>> Microsoft Azure (https://azure.microsoft.com/)

Other offerings exist, especially on the regional level. VPC certainly isn't unique to Amazon; it's becoming a common technology, and you need to ensure that the Amazon offering suits your needs. Of course, if you want to use a VPC with a product such as EC2, you really do need the Amazon offering because both are part of AWS.

Getting an overview of the connectivity options

How you make a connection to a VPC is important because different connection types have differing features and characteristics. Choosing the right connection option will yield significant gains in efficiency, reliability, and security. You might also see a small boost in speed. The following list describes the common VPC connectivity options:

>> **AWS Hardware VPN:** You generally use a hardware router and gateway to provide the Internet Protocol Security (IPSec) connection to your VPN. (You can find out more about IPSec at http://www.unixwiz.net/techtips/iguide-ipsec.html.) The AWS router connects to your customer gateway (and through it to your router) using a Virtual Private Gateway (VPG). You can discover more about this option at http://docs.aws.amazon.com/AmazonVPC/latest/UserGuide/VPC_VPN.html.

>> **AWS Direct Connect:** This high-end option relies on a dedicated connection between your network and AWS. The "Connecting directly to AWS with Direct Connect" sidebar, later in this chapter, provides additional information about using this connectivity option.

>> **AWS VPN CloudHub:** Sometimes you need to connect more than one customer network to a single AWS VPC. CloudHub works like having multiple AWS Hardware VPNs in many respects. You can find out more about this option at http://docs.aws.amazon.com/AmazonVPC/latest/UserGuide/VPN_CloudHub.html.

>> **Software VPN:** A software VPN offers a minimalistic approach to creating a connection between a VPC and your network. You rely on software to simulate the actions normally performed by hardware to create the connection. Of all the options, this one is the slowest because you rely on software to perform a task best done with hardware. However, small and even medium-sized businesses may find that it works without problem. The only issue is that AWS doesn't actually provide software VPN support, so you need to rely on one of the third parties listed in the AWS Marketplace (https://aws.amazon.com/marketplace/search/results/ref=brs_navgno_search_box?searchTerms=vpn) to provide the required functionality. (These third parties often provide a free trial of varying lengths, but then you must pay for continued use of the software.)

Discovering the typical use cases

Connectivity comes in many forms today, so you need to know the connectivity options that a particular solution offers. Choosing a particular kind of connectivity affects how you use your VPC. Here's an overview of the kinds of connectivity you can achieve using the AWS VPC:

>> **Public subnet:** Connect directly to the Internet from your EC2 or other supported service instance. Using a public subnet makes the information you present directly accessible from the Internet. This doesn't mean that anyone can access the information — you can still put security in place — but it does mean that anyone can gain access using a standard URL.

>> **Private subnet:** Connects EC2 or other supported service instances to the Internet using Network Address Translation (NAT). The IP address is now private, which means that the NAT controls access. You rely on a technique called port forwarding to assign a port to the virtual machine. Requests to the NAT using a specific port *access* (gain admission to) the virtual machine. However, the NAT provides an additional level of security.

>> **VPN:** Creates a connection to a data center using an encrypted IPsec hardware VPN connection. The resulting connection relies on the VPN to ensure both privacy and security.

>> **VPC:** Defines a connection between two VPCs, even VPCs owned by other vendors. When working with AWS, the connection relies on private IP addresses, so no single point of failure exists for the connection. You can read more at `http://docs.aws.amazon.com/AmazonVPC/latest/UserGuide/vpc-peering.html`.

>> **Direct service:** Creates a connection directly to an AWS service, such as S3, which allows you to interact with the content of that service, such as your S3 buckets, without having to rely on an Internet gateway or NAT. To use this approach, you need to create endpoints in the VPC to allow service access.

None of these usage options must be a stand-alone option. You can create any combination of connectivity types required by your setup. For example, creating both private and public subnets as needed is entirely possible. The point is that you use these connectivity options to make working with AWS easier.

CONNECTING DIRECTLY TO AWS WITH DIRECT CONNECT

WARNING

Throughout the book, you engage in some strange machinations at times to create a connection between your system and those supported by AWS. The problem is that you're on a local network and AWS is in the cloud — a fact that the connectivity issues remind you about on a constant basis. Yes, working with Internet connectivity has become more common, but for most organizations, a direct connection would be a lot better. Imagine how nice it would be to see a drive in a desktop application, such as Windows Explorer or Finder, and have it actually point to your S3 drive on AWS. You can't overestimate the value of the connectivity that a direct connection provides, especially from a user's perspective. The AWS solution to the problem is Direct Connect (`https://aws.amazon.com/directconnect/`). You use Direct Connect to create a special kind of virtual connection to AWS that has the appearance of a direct connection, even though it isn't.

It's important to realize that you can't create a precise replica of a direct connection with any setup. Short of running cables from your business to Amazon (which is impossible unless your business is close enough, plus Amazon may not even allow you to do it), direct connectivity must occur as a virtual connection over existing wires. However, Direct Connect relies on a dedicated connection, which means that you must pair up with an Amazon Partner (`https://aws.amazon.com/directconnect/partners/`) to get the job done. The dedicated connection is actually an 802.1q Virtual Local Area Network (VLAN) (`http://www.microhowto.info/tutorials/802.1q.html`). The process involves these four steps:

1. Define the connectivity location information.

2. Send a connection request to AWS using the Direct Connect Management Console at https://console.aws.amazon.com/directconnect after logging in to the Administrator account.

3. Obtain approval for the connection.

4. Establish the connection.

After you have Direct Connect set up, you need to perform some additional configuration tasks. You configure the virtual interfaces, which is the equivalent of telling Direct Connect how to make a direct connection appear to be in place. The level of seamlessness between your network and the AWS setup depends on getting the virtual interface configuration correct. Of course, nothing can quite match the speed, reliability, security, and convenience of a true physical direct connection, but using Direct Connect correctly can get you relatively close.

Direct Connect isn't currently part of the free tier of AWS. Amazon will charge you for the services rendered. Because a direct connection can prove to be so essential from a usage perspective and result in such a large increase in user productivity, the gains you get from using Direct Connect can overcome the costs involved in making the connection. You can find Direct Connect pricing information at https://aws.amazon.com/directconnect/pricing/.

Managing the Default VPC

The moment you create an instance of anything in AWS, you also create a default VPC. Actually, Amazon creates the default VPC for you, and you use it to launch instances of any service you want to use. The same VPC follows you around to any region you work in, so you don't need to create a new VPC if you decide to create instances of services in other regions as your business grows. Your default VPC includes these features:

>> A default subnet in each availability zone to support networking functionality

>> An Internet gateway enabling you to connect to your VPC

>> A route table that ensures that Internet traffic goes where it's supposed to go

>> The default security group used to keep your VPC secure

>> The default Access Control List (ACL) used to define which users and groups can access the resources controlled by the VPC

>> Dynamic Host Configuration Protocol support to provide IP addresses and other information associated with your VPC to requestors

Most businesses will never need anything more than the default VPC. However, many businesses will need to modify the default VPC so that it better meets their needs. Even though the following sections don't provide exhaustive coverage of anything you can do with your VPC, they provide enough information to get you started. By reviewing this content, you get a better idea of what is possible with your default VPC so that you don't create a custom VPC when you don't actually need one.

Creating an S3 endpoint

The direct connect option using an endpoint is quite attractive for less complex needs because it requires less effort and promises significantly reduced costs compared to other options. Currently, AWS supports endpoints only for the S3 service. However, Amazon promises to make endpoints available for other services in the near future.

REMEMBER

The most important feature of endpoints is that they offer a configuration-only option that you don't have to jump through hoops to use. An endpoint is actually a VPC component that provides the same redundancy and scaling that the VPC provides. The following steps help you create an S3 endpoint:

1. **Sign into AWS using your administrator account.**

2. **Navigate to the VPC Management Console at** https://console.aws.amazon.com/vpc.

   You see the VPC Dashboard page of the VPC Management Console, shown in Figure 13-1. Notice the Navigation pane on the left side of the screen. These entries represent the kinds of connection that you can create using the VPC, along with some configuration options. The Navigation pane also contains entries for configuring security and for creating some of the more complex connection types (such as customer gateways) discussed earlier in the chapter.

TIP

   AWS provides two main options for configuring an endpoint. Using the VPC Wizard creates a custom VPC for defining connectivity to a service. You use this option when you need to ensure that the communication remains private and doesn't interfere with your default VPC. However, this solution also adds to your costs because now you're running two VPCs (or possibly more).

FIGURE 13-1:
The Dashboard
page shows
the status of
your VPC.

Manually configuring the endpoint is more flexible. This is the option used for
the example in this chapter because it allows you to create an S3 connection to
your existing, default VPC. Both options will allow you to connect to S3 at some
point, but depending on your setup, one option may provide a better solution.
Generally, if you're in doubt as to which approach to use, try the manual configuration first. You can always delete the nonfunctional default VPC endpoint and
configure one using the wizard later.

3. **Click Endpoints in the Navigation pane.**

    You see the Endpoints page, which doesn't have anything in it now except a
    Create Endpoint button (or possibly two) and an Actions button.

4. **Click the Create Endpoint button.**

    AWS presents the Create Endpoint page, shown in Figure 13-2. This page lets
    you choose a VPC (you likely have only the default VPC) and a service (which is
    limited to S3 for now). You must also choose the level of access to provide.
    Normally you create a custom policy to ensure that only the people who want
    to have access to your S3 setup can do so. For the purposes of this example (to
    keep things simple), the steps use the Full Access option.

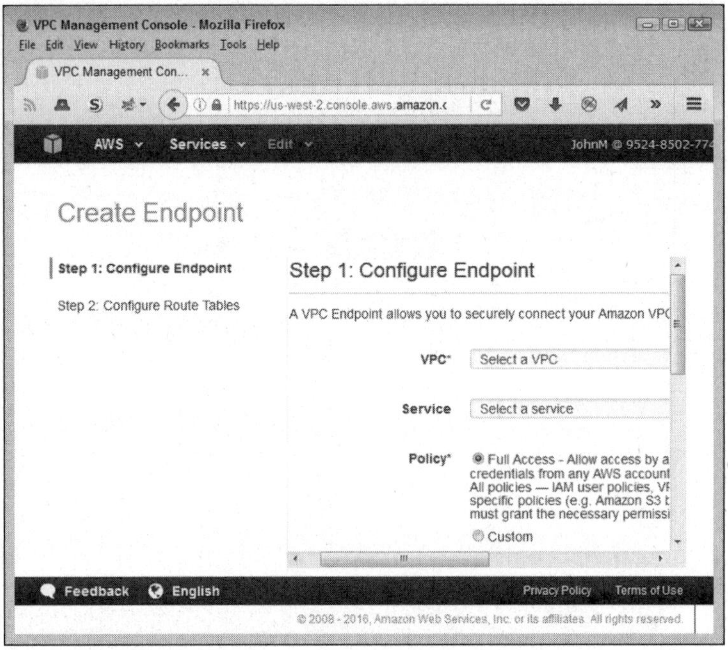

FIGURE 13-2:
Use the Create Endpoint page to configure your endpoint and associated route tables.

5. **Choose the default VPC entry in the VPC field.**

6. **Choose the S3 service entry that you want to use in the Service field.**

7. **Choose the Full Access option and then click Next Step.**

   You see the Step 2: Configure Route Tables page, shown in Figure 13-3. Notice that you aren't actually configuring anything. All you really need to do is select the only route table offered in the list. Unless you have created specialized route tables for your default VPC configuration, you don't need to provide anything more than a selection in this step.

8. **Select the route table that you want to use and then click Create Endpoint.**

   You see a Creation Status page, telling you that AWS has created the endpoint.

9. **Click the View Endpoints button.**

   You see a list of endpoints for the selected VPC similar to the list shown in Figure 13-4.

At this point, you have an endpoint, something to which you can connect. However, you don't have the means to connect to it. To create the required connection from your PC, you need an external connection to your VPC. After you have the connection to the VPC, you also have access to S3 through the endpoint.

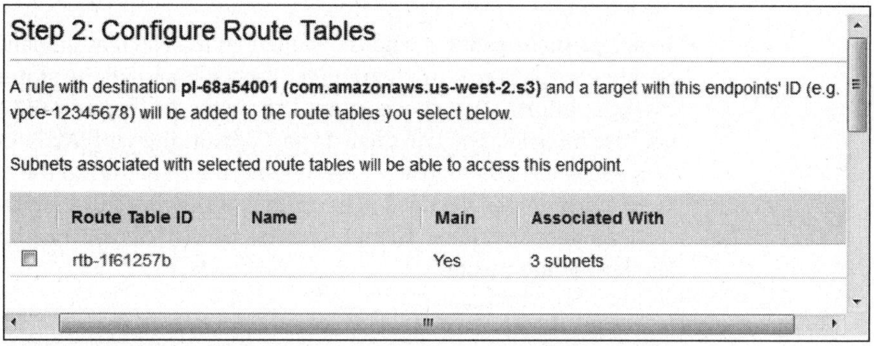

FIGURE 13-3:
Choose the route table that you want to use for the endpoint.

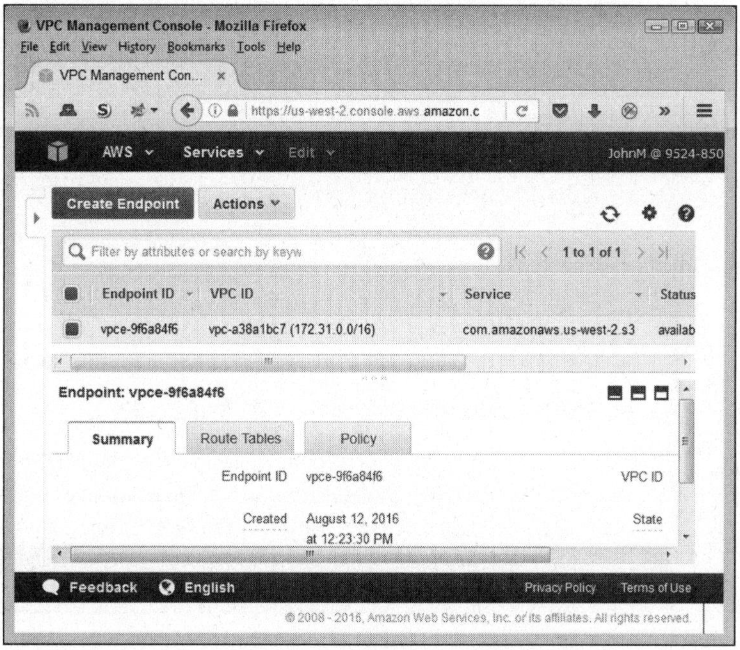

FIGURE 13-4:
The Endpoints page contains a listing of the endpoints defined for the current VPC.

Working with subnets

Generally, you begin with a number of subnets for your AWS setup, using one for each of the availability zones in your region. For example, when working in the us-west-2 region, you have three subnets: us-west-2a, us-west-2b, and us-west-2c. You want to avoid confusing the region with the availability zone. A *region* is a grouping of one or more availability zones. Each availability zone is a specific physical location within the region. When you're working with the command line and other AWS features, AWS might ask you to provide your region, not your availability zone (or vice versa). Using the wrong value can result in commands that don't work or that incorrectly configure features.

To access these subnets, choose Subnets in the Navigation pane. You see a listing of subnets, as shown in Figure 13-5. Each subnet lists its status along with other essential information that you need to access features in AWS. These three subnets are internal. You use them as part of working with AWS. Deleting these subnets will cause you to lose access to AWS functionality, so the best idea is to leave them alone unless you need to perform specific configuration tasks. The following sections describe some subnet-specific tasks that you can perform in the VPC Management Console.

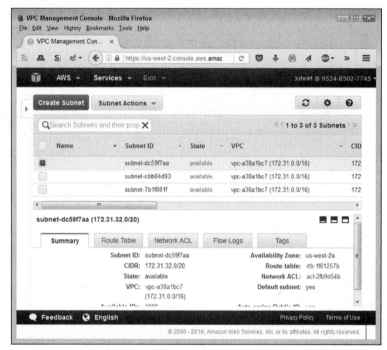

FIGURE 13-5:
Subnets provide connectivity between the AWS availability zones within a region.

Creating a new subnet

In some cases, you need to create new subnets to support specific VPC functionality. The best option is to allow the various wizards to create these subnets as needed for you, but sometimes you need to create them manually. In that case, you click Create Subnet to define a new subnet. The Create Subnet dialog box, shown in Figure 13-6, appears.

Type a descriptive name for the subnet in the Name Tag field. You also need to define a Classless Inter-Domain Routing (CIDR) entry in the CIDR Block field. The "Creating a New VPC" section, later in this chapter, describes how a CIDR works.

You can find a calculator for creating one at `http://www.ipaddressguide.com/cidr`. If a CIDR is outside the expected range, AWS displays an error message telling you what is wrong with the entry you typed. To create the subnet, click Yes, Create.

Create Subnet ✖

Use the CIDR format to specify your subnet's IP address block (e.g., 10.0.0.0/24). Note that block sizes must be between a /16 netmask and /28 netmask. Also, note that a subnet can be the same size as your VPC.

Name tag	
VPC	vpc-a38a1bc7 (172.31.0.0/16)
Availability Zone	No Preference
CIDR block	

Cancel   **Yes, Create**

Removing an existing subnet

At some point, you may also need to remove an existing subnet. To perform this task, select the subnet entry on the Subnets page and then choose Subnet Actions ⇨ Delete Subnet. AWS asks whether you're sure that you want to delete the subnet. Click Yes, Delete to complete the action.

Modifying the network ACLs

The Network ACL tab of a selected subnet on the Subnets page contains the Access Control List (ACL) associated with that subnet, as shown in Figure 13-7. The ACL controls the inbound and outbound rules for accessing that subnet. If you click Edit on that tab, you can choose a different Network ACL policy, but you can't change any of the rules. In general, you use the same policy for all the availability zones for a particular region. Consequently, the default configuration contains only one Network ACL to choose from.

The Network ACLs page (selected by choosing Network ACLs in the Navigation pane) controls the actual rules used to govern the subnet access, as shown in Figure 13-8. The default entry doesn't include a name, but you can give it one by clicking in the empty field associated with the Name column. The status information includes a listing of the number of subnets associated with the Network ACL. Only the initial Network ACL will contain Yes in the Default column.

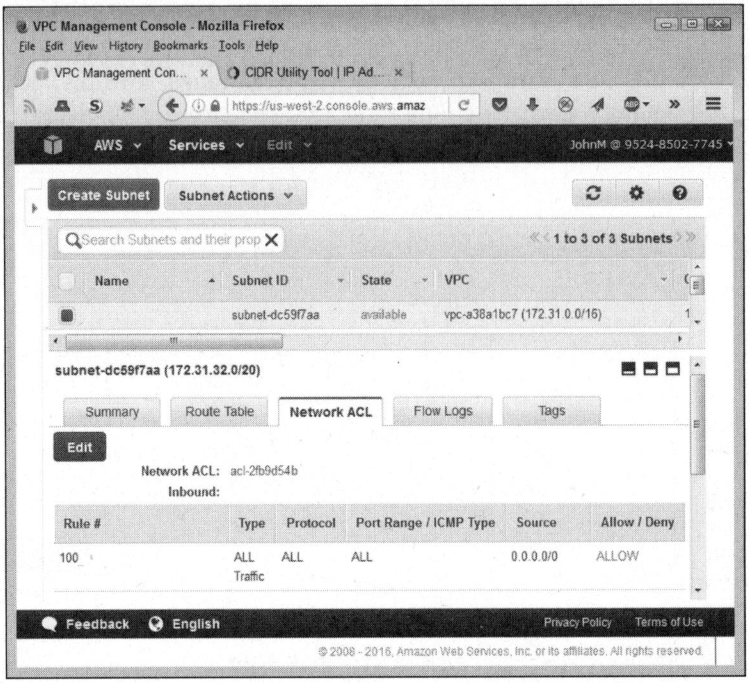

FIGURE 13-7:
Set the Network ACL policy that you want to use with the subnet.

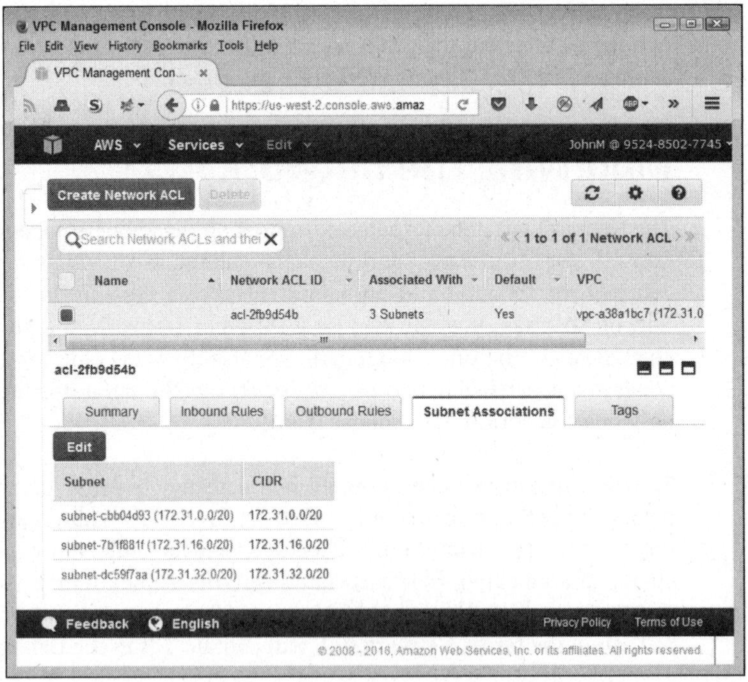

FIGURE 13-8:
The Network ACL listing contains basic information about the ACL.

Modifying a Network ACL

Network ACLs consist of a series of inbound and outbound rules. The inbound rules control access to the associated resources from outside sources, while the outbound rules control access to outside resources by inside sources. Both sets of rules play an important role in keeping your configuration safe. The inbound rules appear on the Inbound Rules tab of a select Network ACL, as shown in Figure 13-9. The Outbound Rules tab looks the same and works the same as the Inbound Rules tab.

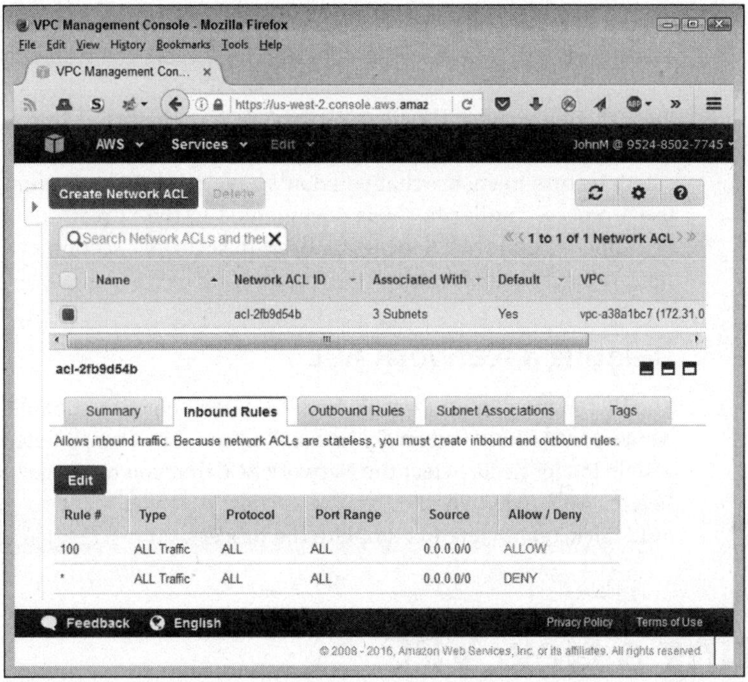

FIGURE 13-9: Control access to AWS resources by using a combination of inbound and outbound rules.

To change any of the rules, add new rules, or delete existing rules, click Edit. The display changes to show each of the existing rules with fields that you can modify. You can change the rule number, traffic type, protocol, port range, and the sources or destinations that are allowed access. To remove a rule, click the X at the end of its entry in the list of rules. Likewise, to add a rule, click Add Another Rule. The rule changes don't take effect until you click Save to save them.

Creating a Network ACL

To create a new Network ACL, click Create Network ACL. You see the Create Network ACL dialog box, shown in Figure 13-10.

FIGURE 13-10:
Define new
Network ACLs as
needed to create
specific rules for
certain resources.

Create Network ACL ✕

A network ACL is an optional layer of security that acts as a firewall for controlling traffic in and out of a subnet.

Name tag
VPC   vpc-a38a1bc7 (172.31.0.0/16)

Cancel   **Yes, Create**

Type a name for the new Network ACL in the Name Tag field. Choose a VPC to associate it with in the VPC field. Click Yes, Create to complete the process.

Even though you see the new Network ACL in the list at this point, you still need to configure it. The default settings don't allow any access in or out, which is a safety feature to ensure that you don't have rules that allow unwanted access. You use a process similar to those documented in the "Creating an instance" section of Chapter 4 and the "Setting application security" section of Chapter 5 to add or remove the required access.

Deleting a Network ACL

The VPC Management Console won't let you delete the default Network ACL or a Network ACL that's currently in use. You can, however, delete Network ACLs that you no longer need. Select the Network ACL that you no longer want and then click Delete. AWS asks whether you're certain that you want to delete the Network ACL. Click Yes, Delete to complete the process.

Creating a New VPC

You may decide to create a new VPC for any of a number of reasons. Perhaps you simply want to ensure that your private network remains completely separated from any public-facing applications that you install in AWS. The point is that you can create a custom VPC when needed to perform specific tasks. In most cases, you want the custom VPC in addition to the default VPC that AWS created for you when you started using AWS.

WARNING

As with most AWS objects, deleting your default VPC removes it entirely. There is no undo feature, so the default VPC is completely gone. It's essential to keep your default VPC in place until you no longer need it. The new VPC you create will definitely perform the tasks you assign to it, but keeping the old VPC around until you're certain that you no longer need it is always the best idea. Deleting a VPC also deletes all the subnets, security groups, ACLs, VPN attachments, gateways, route tables, network interfaces, and VPC peer connections associated with that VPC, along with any service instances attached to the VPC.

The "Managing the Default VPC" section, earlier in this chapter, tells you how to perform some essential VPC tasks. The following steps help you create a custom VPC that you can then configure as needed to perform the tasks you have in mind for it. When you get finished, you have an empty VPC that you can fill with anything you want.

1. **Sign into AWS using your administrator account.**

2. **Navigate to the VPC Management Console at** https://console.aws. amazon.com/vpc.

   You see the VPC Management Console, shown in Figure 13-11. The VPC Dashboard provides all the statistics for your default setup. The figure shows that this setup currently has one VPC containing all the usual default elements.

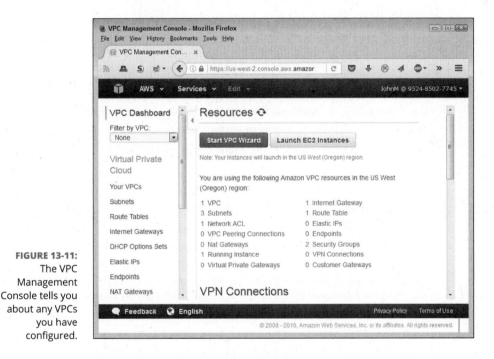

FIGURE 13-11:
The VPC
Management
Console tells you
about any VPCs
you have
configured.

3. **Click Start VPC Wizard.**

   You see the Select a VPC Configuration page, shown in Figure 13-12. Selecting the right VPC template saves configuration time later and ensures that you get the VPC you want with lower potential for mistakes. The basic templates shown offer the range of access options that most businesses need and can modify to address specific requirements.

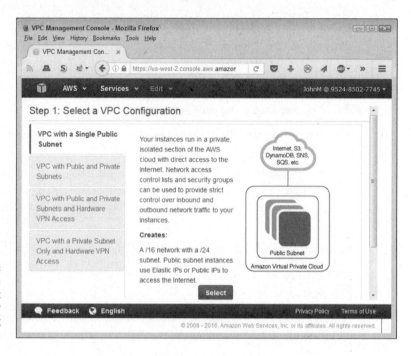

FIGURE 13-12:
Choose a template that bests suits your networking needs.

4. **Choose the VPC with a Single Public Subnet option and then click Select.**

   The wizard displays the Step 2: VPC with a Single Public Subnet page, shown in Figure 13-13. However, if you had selected one of the other options, you would see a similar page with configuration entries suited to that VPC template.

   A few of the entries might look quite mysterious. The Classless Inter-Domain Routing (CIDR) entry simply defines the number of IP addresses available to your VPC. You can read about it at http://whatismyipaddress.com/cidr. The handy CIDR calculator at http://www.ipaddressguide.com/cidr is also quite helpful. If you change the settings for the IP address range, the wizard automatically updates the number of available IP addresses for you.

   You must also decide whether you plan to use S3. If so, you need to add an endpoint to it so that people can access it. Given that the VPC has only one subnet, you have only one choice in selecting a subnet for S3.

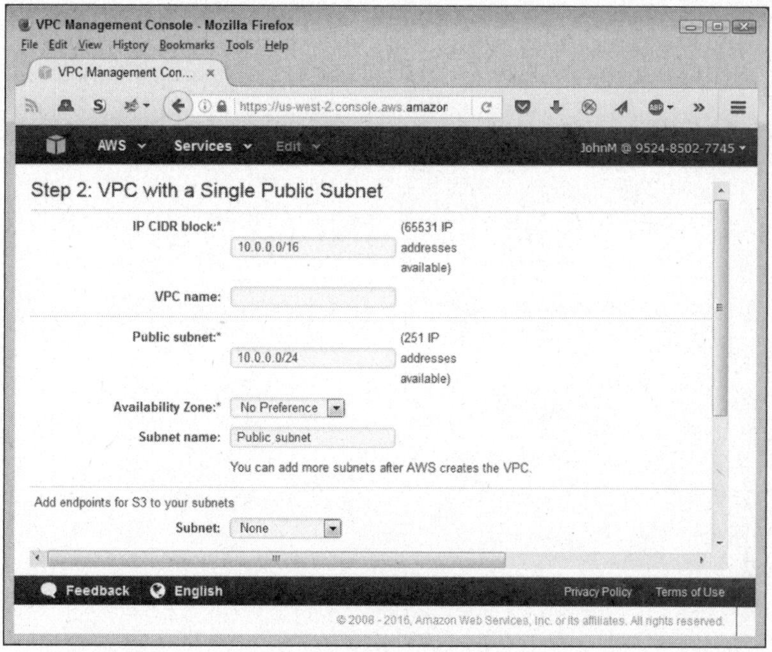

FIGURE 13-13:
Configure your
VPC as needed.

5. **Type** MyVPC **in the VPC name field.**

   Adding a name to your custom VPC makes it easier to identify.

6. **Select Public Subnet in the Subnet field.**

   The display changes to show the policy that will control access to S3. The default option provides full access to S3. However, you can create a custom security policy to provide controlled access to S3 as needed.

7. **Click Create VPC.**

   AWS creates the new VPC for you. You see a success message and additional instructions for launching an EC2 instance into the subnet.

The "Working with the Identity and Access Management (IAM) Console" section of Chapter 4 discusses many of the issues surrounding VPC security. After you create your custom VPC, you need to create security for it. The VPC Wizard doesn't perform this task for you. You also need to perform the other tasks described in Chapter 4, such as creating a key pair for your VPC. The best way to ensure that your custom VPC is accessible and will do what you need it to do at a basic level is to create an EC2 instance using the same techniques described in Chapter 4, and then work with it to begin performing various tasks.

Chapter **14**

Using the Infrastructure Software

mazon provides access to an amazing array of free software to use with your Amazon Web Services (AWS) setup. In fact, according to its site (https://aws.amazon.com/free/), Amazon offers access to about 700 pieces of software, a minimum of 300 of which are infrastructure applications. You use infrastructure software to support requirements such as workforce support, business transactions, and internal services and processes. This chapter reviews just three of the many offerings to give you a better idea of what you can find.

WARNING

As with everything else in AWS, you need to define the word *free*. In this case, you get to use the infrastructure software free during the 12-month free period of your AWS trial. To keep the software free, you must use it on a t2.micro instance. In addition, you can use it up to 750 hours per month. Also, realize that just the software is free. Any resources that the software uses, such as disk space, may incur a charge.

Creating a Linux Environment with CentOS

By default, the version of Linux you install when working with the free tier of AWS is Amazon Linux Amazon Machine Image (AMI) (https://aws.amazon.com/amazon-linux-ami/). This version of Linux is like Red Hat Enterprise Linux (RHEL)

Fedora (https://fedoraproject.org/wiki/Red_Hat_Enterprise_Linux), but is not precisely the same. It also has elements of the Community enterprise Operating System (CentOS) (https://www.centos.org/) included with it. Using this distribution is fine as long as you create AWS-only solutions.

TIP

To find your version of Linux, open a Secure Shell (SSH) terminal, such as MindTerm (click Connect after selecting an EC2 instance to work with). Type **cat /etc/*-release** and press Enter. You see a number of lines of information about the version of Linux you're using, including the version name and version number.

Unfortunately, no official distribution of Amazon Linux AMI exists outside of AWS, so using it in a multicloud environment (such as when you use AWS with Microsoft Azure) quickly adds to your costs and creates problems for administrators. (Read more at https://www.exratione.com/2014/08/do-not-use-amazon-linux/.) Chapter 17 discusses some of the multicloud tools that you can use with AWS, but none of them supports the native Linux version. Of course, using Amazon Linux AMI means that your developers will also have to rely on it during the development process to ensure that your apps will run as expected. With this issue in mind, you may need to install CentOS to power your AWS instances instead. The following sections discuss CentOS from an overview perspective and tell you how to get and install your CentOS distribution.

Considering the CentOS effort

CentOS is a Linux distribution that started as a reversion of RHEL. However, it uses only the freely available public resources from that distribution. It also relies on publicly available resources from other Linux distributions and some code that comes from the CentOS community. A number of management products support CentOS. You can install a copy on your local system for development, training, and other purposes. In addition, most cloud environments also support CentOS, making it a great choice for multicloud environments. The groups that build and maintain CentOS modules use the same structure as that used by the Apache Software Foundation (http://apache.org/). CentOS currently has three working groups:

>> **Core** (http://wiki.centos.org/SpecialInterestGroup/Core): Builds and releases the core CentOS Linux distribution.

>> **Xen4CentOS** (http://wiki.centos.org/Manuals/ReleaseNotes/Xen4-01): Creates the Xen 4 (http://wiki.xenproject.org/wiki/Xen_4.0_Release_Notes) distribution for CentOS. Xen 4 is a virtual machine manager (hypervisor) that lets you configure and support multiple operating systems on a single physical machine.

>> **CentOSDesign** (http://wiki.centos.org/ArtWork): Produces the artwork that makes working with CentOS easier.

Getting CentOS for your machine

If you plan to use CentOS for your own development needs or to provide an extension to a local environment, you need to obtain a copy for your system and install it. The best place to get CentOS for your machine is from `https://www.centos.org/download/`. Simply download the ISO version that best suits your needs and install it on your system. Using the DVD ISO option is the best choice if you want to boot your system and perform a clean install from a DVD.

Installing CentOS on AWS

Amazon offers you the choice of directly installing CentOS from the AWS Marketplace. As stated on the initial page at `https://aws.amazon.com/marketplace/seller-profile/ref=srh_res_product_vendor?id=16cb8b03-256e-4dde-8f34-1b0f377efe89`, the various offerings are free, but you pay for EC2 time when using this approach. Amazon makes you aware of the fees before you perform the installation. A better approach is to ensure you make use of your free-tier installation by using the following procedure:

1. **Sign into AWS using your administrator account.**

2. **Navigate to the EC2 Management Console at** `https://console.aws.amazon.com/ec2.`

   You see the initial dashboard display. If you already have an instance running, you see the view shown in Figure 14-1. Otherwise, you see a Welcome page.

3. **Click Launch Instance.**

   The EC2 Console displays the Step 1: Choose an Amazon Machine Image (AMI) page, shown in Figure 14-2. The default options, listed in the center of the page, are for Amazon-specific products. Note the AWS Marketplace option in the Navigation pane.

4. **Click AWS Marketplace.**

   You see a relatively long list of AWS Marketplace options.

5. **Type** CentOS **in the Search AWS Marketplace Products field and press Enter.**

   The page now displays the CentOS versions, as shown in Figure 14-3. The free options show that they're free-tier eligible.

6. **Click Select next to the CentOS version that you want to use.**

   The CentOS version you choose must match the version you have installed for development and other purposes. You also want to ensure that the versions match in each of the multicloud environments that you use to reduce portability and other issues. The example uses CentOS 7.

REMEMBER

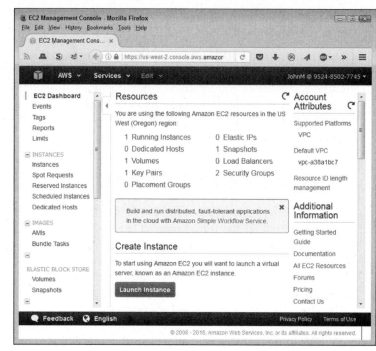

FIGURE 14-1:
The EC2 Dashboard shows the status of your EC2 configuration.

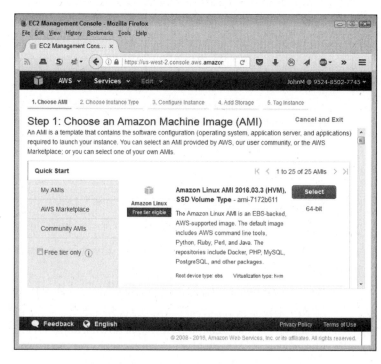

FIGURE 14-2:
Select a machine image option to use for your instance.

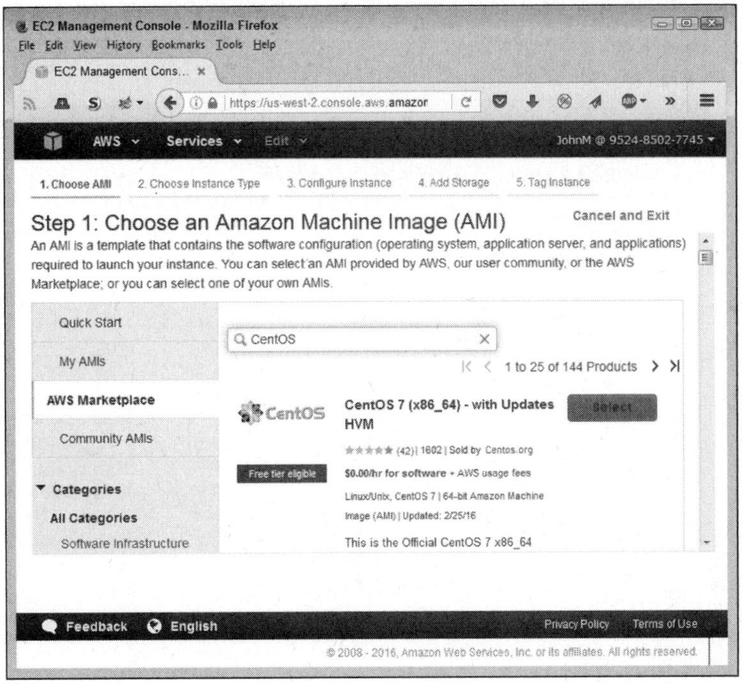

The EC2 Management Console screenshot shows:

EC2 Management Console - Mozilla Firefox

File Edit View History Bookmarks Tools Help

EC2 Management Cons... ×

https://us-west-2.console.aws.amazon

AWS ∨   Services ∨   Edit ∨   JohnM @ 9524-8502-7745 ∨

1. Choose AMI   2. Choose Instance Type   3. Configure Instance   4. Add Storage   5. Tag Instance

Step 1: Choose an Amazon Machine Image (AMI)   Cancel and Exit

An AMI is a template that contains the software configuration (operating system, application server, and applications) required to launch your instance. You can select an AMI provided by AWS, our user community, or the AWS Marketplace; or you can select one of your own AMIs.

Quick Start

My AMIs

AWS Marketplace

Community AMIs

▼ Categories

All Categories

Software Infrastructure

Q CentOS   ×

1 to 25 of 144 Products

CentOS 7 (x86_64) - with Updates HVM   Select
★★★★★ (42) | 1602 | Sold by Centos.org
Free tier eligible $0.00/hr for software + AWS usage fees
Linux/Unix, CentOS 7 | 64-bit Amazon Machine Image (AMI) | Updated: 2/25/16
This is the Official CentOS 7 x86_64

Feedback   English   Privacy Policy   Terms of Use

© 2008 - 2016, Amazon Web Services, Inc. or its affiliates. All rights reserved.

FIGURE 14-3:
Select a machine image option to use for your instance.

You see the price list, shown in Figure 14-4. The least expensive option for experimentation purposes is T2 Nano, which generally appears at the bottom of the list. Amazon requires that you agree to the pricing terms before you proceed. Keep in mind that using CentOS requires that you pay a certain amount per hour for your EC2 instance and an additional amount for EBS storage unless you qualify for one of the free-tier options.

7. **Click Continue.**

The wizard displays a list of instance types, as shown in Figure 14-5. If you qualify for a free-tier option, you see one or more of the instance types marked as being free-tier qualified, as shown in the figure. If you choose this option and don't go over the 750 hours allowed per month, you incur no charge for the EC2 resources used by the instance. Notice that the t2.micro instance type is free-tier eligible in this case.

8. **Select one of the instance types and then click Review and Launch.**

You also have the option of working through the various configuration screens described in Chapter 4. If this is your first instance, you need to generate a key pair for security purposes. Otherwise, Amazon uses your existing key pair. You can also configure a security group and all the other features that come with every other instance type. The CentOS instance is running at this point.

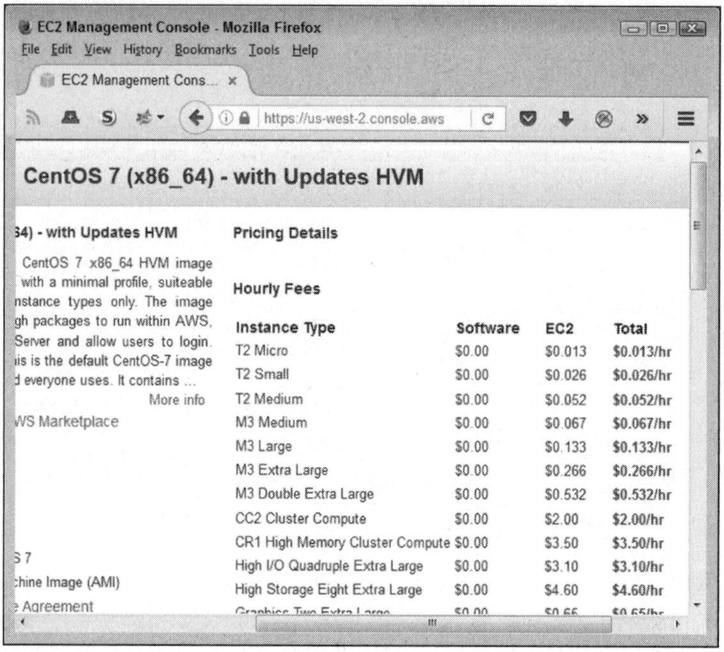

FIGURE 14-4:
Choose a pricing
model for your
instance.

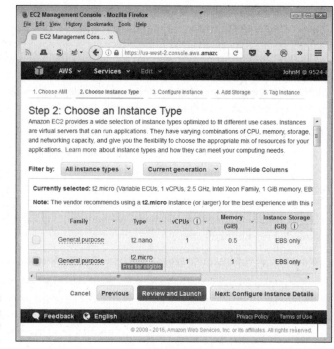

FIGURE 14-5:
Determine
which instance
type to use.

Building Websites Using LAMP Stack

A Linux, Apache, MySQL, and PHP (LAMP) stack is a configuration of four popular products for hosting websites. (Some implementations, such as the one from Turn-Key, feature three language products: PHP, Python, and Perl.) Nothing is magical about these four products, but they are used together often enough that some vendors have created turnkey solutions (ones in which you don't have to spend a lot of time performing the required configuration tasks yourself). The sections that follow look at the LAMP Stack product created by TurnKey Linux. You can find other LAMP stack solutions for use with AWS by reviewing the options in the AWS Marketplace. Just type **LAMP** in the Search AWS Marketplace field and press Enter.

REMEMBER

You can also create a LAMP stack using Amazon Linux AMI. However, the procedure is a bit on the tortuous side, and only the advanced administrator should attempt it. The tutorial at `http://docs.aws.amazon.com/AWSEC2/latest/UserGuide/install-LAMP.html` tells you how to perform this task. Compare the myriad steps needed to work with Amazon Linux AMI to the short process described in the sections that follow, and you quickly find that using a turnkey solution is much faster.

Considering the LAMP Stack features

The TurnKey LAMP Stack product (`https://www.turnkeylinux.org/lampstack`) is a basic web platform. You can find other products that include a combination of additional tools, such as the inclusion of WordPress. Choose this solution when you already have some content put together and have tools that you prefer to use for developing new content. The AWS Marketplace also includes offerings that have some content management tools, such as WordPress, included as part of the product, but many of these other offerings aren't free. TurnKey also offers a product version that uses PostgreSQL instead of MySQL, called LAPP Stack.

In addition to the operating system, web server, database management, and language product, LAMP Stack also comes with basic administration tools. For example, you get Adminer, a tool used to manage MySQL. The management tools are basic but usable. Be prepared to spend a lot of time working at the Command Line Interface (CLI) unless you get additional tools to install with LAMP Stack. (The "Using the Command Line Interface (CLI) to install packages" sidebar in Chapter 17 tells you how to install other packages as needed.)

Before you incur costs using this product on Amazon, you might choose to perform a local install instead. The LAMP Stack site provides links for installing a virtual machine on your current system or creating a new installation using an ISO file. You can also download the source code so that you can customize your installation to meet specific needs.

Getting and installing LAMP Stack

LAMP Stack includes an operating system, so you install it as you would any other EC2 Marketplace instance. Simply follow the procedure found in the "Installing CentOS on AWS" section, earlier in this chapter, but choose the LAMP Stack instance in place of the CentOS instance.

WARNING

However, when you get to the Step 2: Choose an Instance Type page, many of the options aren't available, as shown in Figure 14-6. Instead of the t2.micro instance that's available with other products, this one uses the t1.micro instance type, which provides reduced memory availability and significantly lower performance. The best you can say about the performance of this instance option is that it works for demonstration purposes but not much else. The vendor recommends using an m1.large or larger instance type.

FIGURE 14-6:
LAMP Stack offers a reduced number of instance type options.

In this case, you really do need to consider working with a local setup first to create test apps and other elements of the application you want to test. Then you can use an appropriate instance type for testing on AWS so that you can better see whether LAMP Stack provides what you need. Given that other LAMP and LAPP stack products will have similar needs and limits on AWS, you should count on using this setup as the standard for testing a basic website configuration.

TIP

Another installation point in this case is the Step 4: Add Storage page, shown in Figure 14-7. This configuration defaults to using the Magnetic storage option — the standard setting is to use General Purpose SSD (GP2). To ensure that you actually get free-tier support, you must move through the entire wizard rather than select Review and Launch as you might when performing another kind of EC2 instance setup.

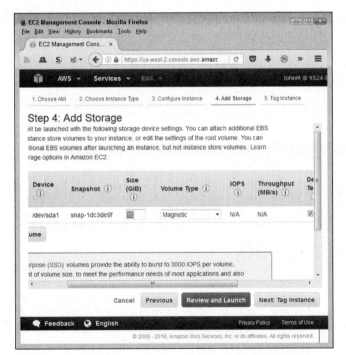

FIGURE 14-7: Make sure to configure the storage options appropriately to reflect free-tier usage.

The security group configuration, displayed on the Step 6: Configure Security Group page, is shown in Figure 14-8. The wizard automatically compensates for the free administration tools supplied with LAMP Stack and opens the appropriate ports. You still want to be sure that you limit access, as needed, to just those port ranges that you actually require and from the appropriate sources (usually your system). Given that you may need other tools, adding ports that these tools require is a good idea.

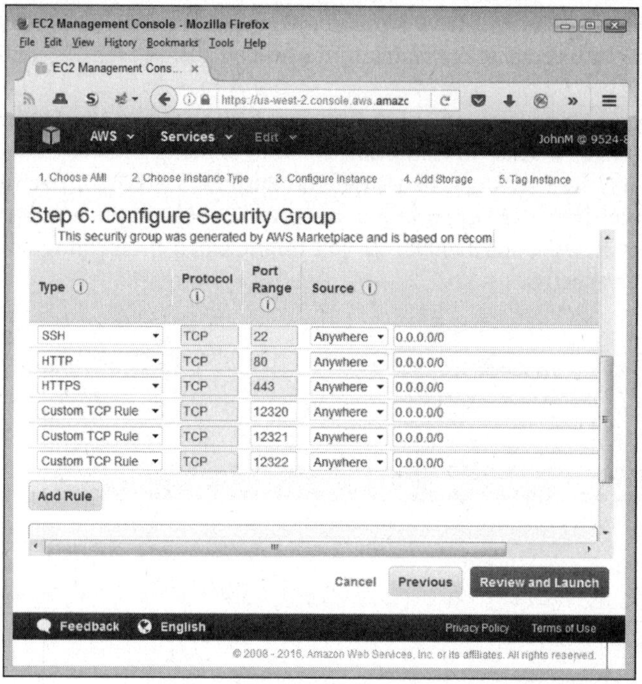

FIGURE 14-8:
The security settings automatically reflect the free tools supplied with LAMP Stack.

Supporting Web-Based Applications Using Couchbase

You may decide, for a number of reasons, that you don't want to use Amazon's NoSQL solution, DynamoDB (see Chapter 12 for details). Of course, you have many other options at your disposal. A key issue to consider when choosing a Database Management System (DBMS) is how the product actually works. Some products, such as Couchbase (http://www.couchbase.com/), focus heavily on speed. You always face trade-offs when choosing a product, and enhanced speed often comes at the expense of reduced security, features, or reliability (such as background features that constantly protect your data). The quick comparison chart at http://db-engines.com/en/system/Amazon+DynamoDB%3BCouchbase provides an overview of what you give up and what you gain when using Couchbase instead of

DynamoDB. The following sections give you additional details about working with Couchbase.

REMEMBER

This section contains only one of the many alternative solutions that AWS provides for database support. Getting the right database is essential if you want to be sure that your data remains safe while also providing users with the appropriate level of speed. To see other AWS options, type **Database** in the Search AWS Marketplace field and press Enter.

Considering the Couchbase features

The Couchbase website would have you believe that speed — lots of speed — is the main reason to get Couchbase. However, for an AWS developer or administrator, the main reason to get Couchbase may be compatibility. A recurring theme among AWS users is that the system tends to create lock-in problems, in which you find yourself stuck using an AWS solution that doesn't allow you to move your apps to another platform with any ease. Couchbase supports Linux, Windows, and OS X, so it can provide a significantly larger number of options when you want to support your app using multiple cloud platforms or determine that you want to use a combination of local and cloud support.

Also, Couchbase supports a significantly larger number of development languages. DynamoDB is missing C/C++ support, which is one of the more common enterprise languages. Couchbase provides this support along with these other languages:

>> .Net

>> Clojure

>> ColdFusion

>> Erlang

>> Go

>> Java

>> JavaScript (Node.js support)

>> Perl

>> PHP

>> Python

>> Ruby

>> Scala

>> Tcl

Getting and installing Couchbase

You install Couchbase by using the instructions found in the "Installing CentOS on AWS" section, earlier in this chapter, but you choose one of the Couchbase instances in place of the CentOS instance. In this case, you have a number of instance types to choose from, so you need to choose the instance type carefully. For example, to obtain full Couchbase support, you need either the Couchbase Server Community Edition or Couchbase Server & Couchbase Sync Gateway Community Edition instance. If you want to reduce the server load (to save money, for example) and don't require all the Couchbase features, you can use the Couchbase Sync Gateway Community Edition instance.

Couchbase requires that you select one of the three instance types mentioned in the previous paragraph to obtain the software for free. The other instance offerings have an hourly charge associated with them. Each of the instances has something different to offer, so you need to match them against your needs. For example, the Couchbase Sync Gateway Enterprise Edition (Gold) instance offers significantly greater scalability when compared to the other instance types, but you must pay an hourly fee for it.

WARNING

Because of the kind of product involved, you will always pay for the EC2 instance you create with Couchbase. The minimum configuration is an m3.medium instance type. This means that you have additional incentives to ensure that you have a good configuration put together locally before moving to the cloud. In addition, when adding storage, you must create both a Root volume and an Instance Store volume, as shown in Figure 14-9, which incurs additional storage costs. Scrimping on storage doesn't pay because databases typically need a lot of it to perform the required tasks.

As with LAMP Stack (refer to Figure 14-8), Couchbase comes with a number of management utilities that require you to open additional ports. Make sure that you check the ports and the sources that can access them to ensure that you don't accidentally open a security hole in your setup. The default settings allow access to the ports from any location, which just gives hackers another opportunity to crack your security and steal your data.

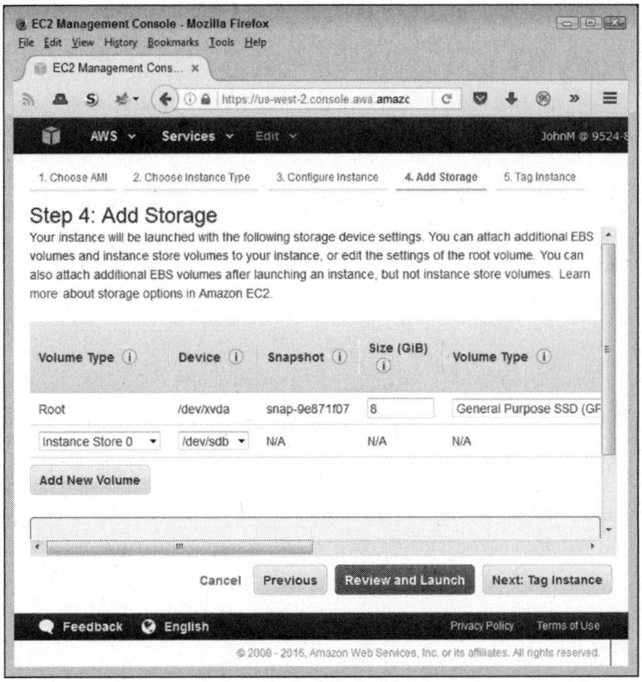

FIGURE 14-9:
Configure the storage options carefully to ensure you have enough space.

Chapter **15**

Supporting Users with Business Software

B usiness software, in contrast to the infrastructure software described in Chapter 14, provides users with resources needed to accomplish specific tasks. Some of these tasks directly affect data. However, business software also includes applications that increase productivity, measure productivity, and reduce costs through automation. Your business wouldn't run well without business software to make tasks manageable and, you hope, transparent to the end user. This chapter discusses just three of the more than 100 pieces of business software that you can view at `https://aws.amazon.com/free/`. These three selections should give you a better idea of what software is available so that you know what you can rely on Amazon to provide.

WARNING

The business software is indeed free, but with some important restrictions. When working with the Amazon highlighted products, you get to use the business software free during the 12-month free period of your AWS trial. To keep the software free, you must use it on a t2.micro instance. In addition, you can use it for up to 750 hours per month. Also, keep in mind that just the software is free. Any resources that the software uses, such as disk space, may incur a charge.

Managing Content Using WordPress

It may seem sometimes as if WordPress (`https://WordPress.com/`) is used everywhere that anyone creates either blog or website content. (If you haven't used WordPress, you can read a comprehensive review of it at `http://www.toptenreviews.com/business/internet/best-blog-services/wordpress-com-review/`.) Initially, WordPress focused on blogs, but everyone from web designers to common users found that it worked so well that many use it for website content as well. Today, you can get WordPress on nearly every hosted system, including AWS.

TIP

The best way to get started using WordPress is to create a free account on its site. You can experiment with the various WordPress features before moving on to a paid account to discover more about using WordPress. Because WordPress is so popular, it comes with literally hundreds of add-ons and free themes. Administrators can quickly become lost trying to figure out the best way to use WordPress for an organization, so starting slowly is the best option. The following sections offer some overview information about WordPress and tell how to install it on AWS.

Considering the WordPress features

A main attraction of using WordPress is that it lets you focus on content, rather than on how to get things done. All you really need to do to get started is to choose a theme, configure a few options, and then write your first blog post. The setup is extremely forgiving, so making a mistake or changing your mind isn't a problem. Using plug-ins (see `https://WordPress.org/plugins/` for details) and widgets (see `https://codex.WordPress.org/WordPress_Widgets` for details) enables you to create a customized feel for your WordPress blog or website.

The AWS Marketplace offers several vendors that support WordPress in a variety of ways. The biggest issue is determining whether you want to support a single site or more than one site. The multisite configurations require more EC2 instance horsepower, so starting with a single-site configuration for demonstration and experimentation purposes is a good idea.

REMEMBER

Some vendors don't provide Hardware Virtual Machine (HVM) support for WordPress installations. Using HVM makes your Amazon Machine Image (AMI) installation appear to be a physical system rather than a virtual system. You gain some additional functionality and speed when working with an AMI in this manner. The article at `https://docs.aws.amazon.com/AWSEC2/latest/UserGuide/virtualization_types.html` provides additional information about the EC2 virtualization types.

The vendor you choose also controls a host of other AWS issues. For example, when you choose a Bitnami (https://bitnami.com/) solution, you get a basic installation that can run on any of the EC2 instance types. On the other hand, choosing TurnKey (https://www.turnkeycloud.com/) means that you get features such as backup and migration, higher levels of security, and additional management options. The trade-off with TurnKey is that it doesn't work with any of the free-tier EC2 instance options. You must get one of the higher-end EC2 installations to ensure that the TurnKey setup runs well.

Getting and installing WordPress

The example in this section relies on the Bitnami single site solution. In addition, it assumes that you want to create a separate website instead of making the website your only EC2 instance. However, the following installation steps also work with other vendor solutions (such as TurnKey) that provide additional functionality. The "Getting and installing LAMP Stack" section of Chapter 14 discusses some of the additional considerations when working with a TurnKey product. Knowing that you need to make these additional decisions will help you get a good WordPress installation.

1. **Sign into AWS using your administrator account.**

2. **Navigate to the EC2 Management Console at** https://console.aws.amazon.com/ec2.

   You see an initial dashboard display like the one shown in Figure 15-1.

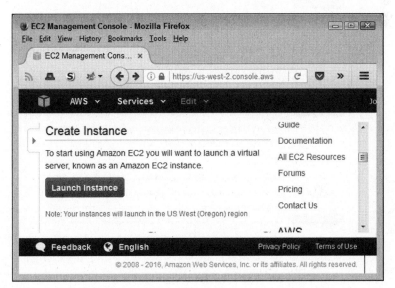

FIGURE 15-1:
Use the EC2 Dashboard to create a WordPress instance for your system.

3. Click Launch Instance.

The EC2 Console displays the Step 1: Choose an Amazon Machine Image (AMI) page.

4. Click AWS Marketplace in the Navigation pane.

You see a relatively long list of AWS Marketplace options.

5. Type Bitnami WordPress in the Search AWS Marketplace Products field and press Enter.

TIP

Entering a vendor name and a product name reduces the number of choices considerably. Otherwise, you might not find the option that you really want. In this case, you know that you want specific WordPress functionality.

You see the list of Bitnami options, shown in Figure 15-2. Even though the entries look similar, you must read the descriptions carefully. The first option provides HVM support, while the second doesn't. Both the first and second options are for single sites. The third option specifically states that it's designed for multisite use. All three options offer free software, but you might need to pay for EC2 and EBS resource usage. Of the three options, the second option, the one without HVM support, is the least likely to require you to pay extra, but it's also the slowest and least functional of the three options when you use the recommended setup.

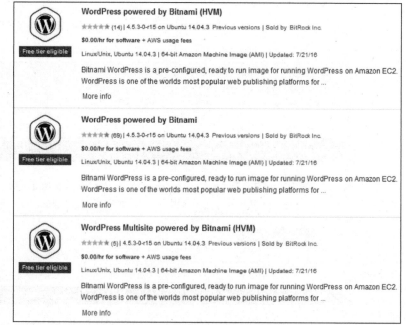

FIGURE 15-2: Select a machine image option to use for your instance.

WARNING

6. **Click the Select button next to the WordPress Powered by Bitnami option.**

   You see the price list, shown in Figure 15-3. The least expensive option for experimentation purposes is T1 Micro. This is also the option that you can use free as part of the free-tier evaluation period.

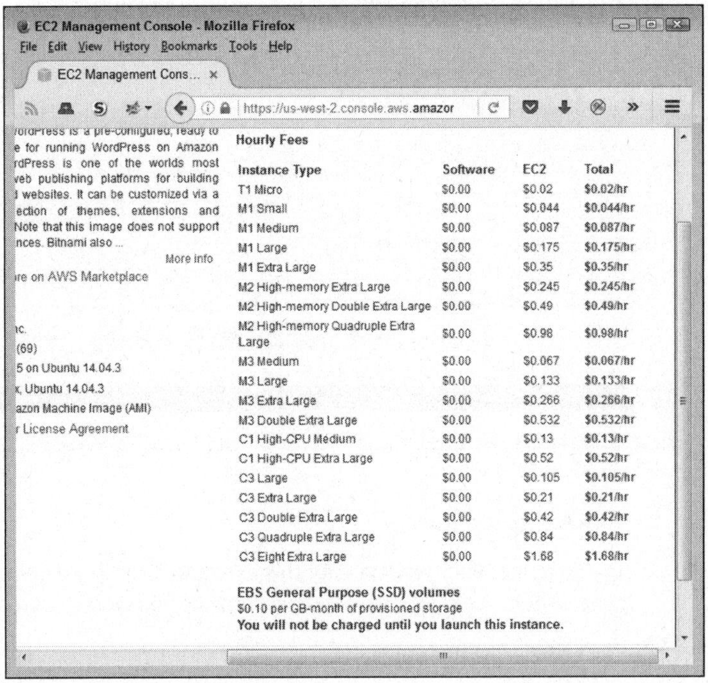

FIGURE 15-3:
View the pricing options for your WordPress setup.

Instance Type	Software	EC2	Total
T1 Micro	$0.00	$0.02	$0.02/hr
M1 Small	$0.00	$0.044	$0.044/hr
M1 Medium	$0.00	$0.087	$0.087/hr
M1 Large	$0.00	$0.175	$0.175/hr
M1 Extra Large	$0.00	$0.35	$0.35/hr
M2 High-memory Extra Large	$0.00	$0.245	$0.245/hr
M2 High-memory Double Extra Large	$0.00	$0.49	$0.49/hr
M2 High-memory Quadruple Extra Large	$0.00	$0.98	$0.98/hr
M3 Medium	$0.00	$0.067	$0.067/hr
M3 Large	$0.00	$0.133	$0.133/hr
M3 Extra Large	$0.00	$0.266	$0.266/hr
M3 Double Extra Large	$0.00	$0.532	$0.532/hr
C1 High-CPU Medium	$0.00	$0.13	$0.13/hr
C1 High-CPU Extra Large	$0.00	$0.52	$0.52/hr
C3 Large	$0.00	$0.105	$0.105/hr
C3 Extra Large	$0.00	$0.21	$0.21/hr
C3 Double Extra Large	$0.00	$0.42	$0.42/hr
C3 Quadruple Extra Large	$0.00	$0.84	$0.84/hr
C3 Eight Extra Large	$0.00	$1.68	$1.68/hr

Hourly Fees

EBS General Purpose (SSD) volumes
$0.10 per GB-month of provisioned storage
You will not be charged until you launch this instance.

7. **Click Continue.**

   The wizard displays a list of instance types, as shown in Figure 15-4. The wizard automatically selects the only free-tier instance option. The free tier provides plenty of power for experimentation, but you need an upgrade before moving on to a production setup. A production setup should also use the HVM option.

8. **Check the t1.micro instance and click Next: Configure Instance Details.**

   The default options on the Step 3: Configure Instance Details page normally work fine. However, you want to review them to ensure that you understand how Amazon is creating your website instance. For example, if you must maintain absolute separation between your corporate configuration and your public website, you may need to create a new VPC. VPC instances normally aren't Internet addressable by default. However, think about the fact that you're creating a public-facing website and may need the separation provided by another VPC. Even though this is an issue to consider for the future, the example relies on the default VPC used for the other examples in the book.

EC2 Management Console - Mozilla Firefox
File Edit View History Bookmarks Tools Help
EC2 Management Cons...
https://us-west-2.console.aws.amazon.
AWS Services Edit
JohnM @ 9524-8502-7745 Orego
1. Choose AMI
2. Choose Instance Type
3. Configure Instance
4. Add Storage
5. Tag Instance
Step 2: Choose an Instance Type
Amazon EC2 provides a wide selection of instance types optimized to fit different use cases. Instances are virtual servers that can run applications. They have varying combinations of CPU, memory, storage, and networking capacity, and give you the flexibility to choose the appropriate mix of resources for your applications. Learn more about instance types and how they can meet your computing needs.
Filter by:
All instance types
All generations
Show/Hide Columns
Currently selected: t1.micro (Variable ECUs, 1 vCPUs, 0.613 GiB memory, EBS only)
Note: The vendor recommends using a m1.small instance (or larger) for the best experience with this product.
Family
Type
vCPUs
Memory (GiB)
Instance Storage (GB)
EBS-Optimize Available
Micro instances
t1.micro
Free tier eligible
1
0.613
EBS only
-
Cancel
Previous
Review and Launch
Next: Configure Instance Details
Feedback
English
Privacy Policy
Terms of Use
© 2008 - 2016, Amazon Web Services, Inc. or its affiliates. All rights reserved.

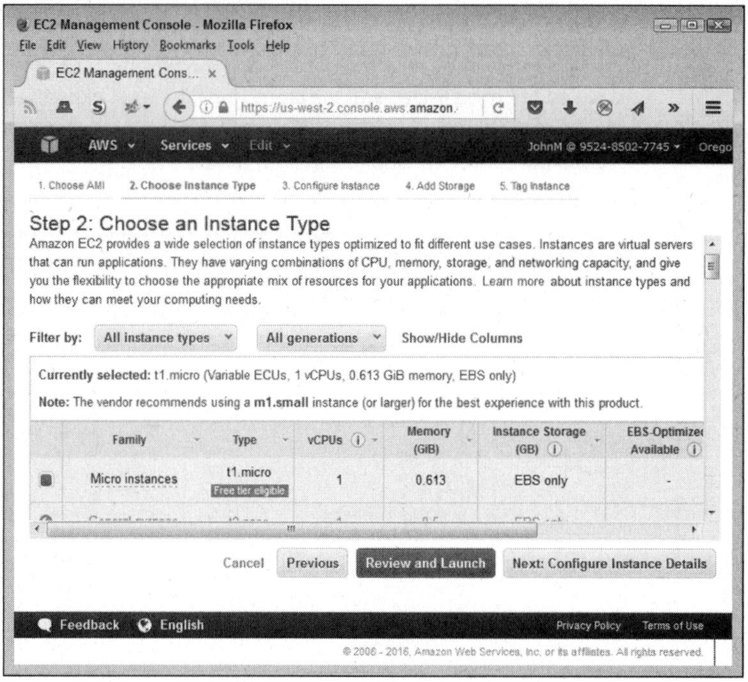

FIGURE 15-4: Specify the kind of instance you want to use.

9. Click Next: Add Storage.

The default options work fine for this example. The wizard defaults to using a general-purpose SSD drive, which will provide you with great response times.

10. Click Next: Tag Instance.

Unless you need additional identification information, you don't need to change anything on this page.

11. Click Next: Configure Security Group.

You see the security setup, shown in Figure 15-5. Notice that the default security for this publicly accessible website allows access from any source. Make sure that you lock security down when working with this configuration for experimentation purposes because you don't want just anyone accessing the site. Yes, there are still ways around the settings, but making the access limited by changing the source to My IP does help keep your website secure.

12. Click Review and Launch.

Amazon starts your new EC2 instance.

REMEMBER

Accessing your new instance works the same as when you work with Elastic Beanstalk. Chapter 5 discusses how to use the URL field to access your new site so that you can begin working with it. The `/wp-login.php` page provides access to your WordPress administration functionality.

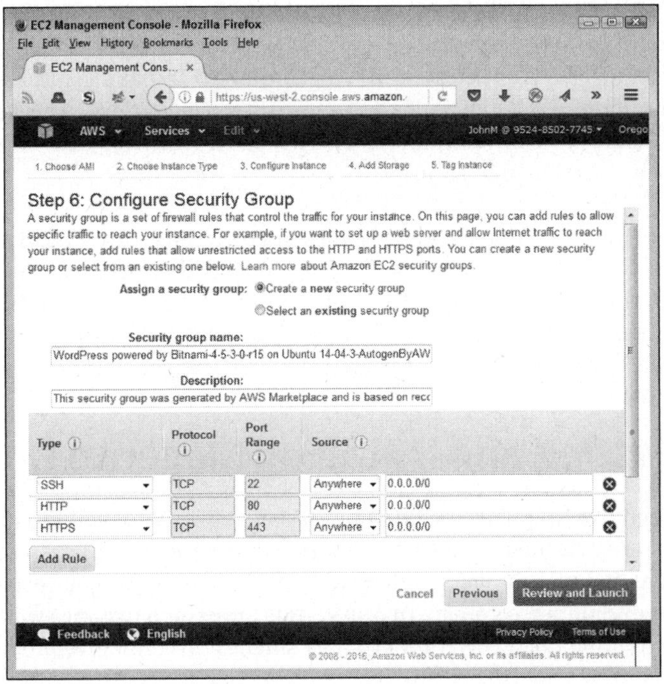

FIGURE 15-5:
Lock down your public-facing experimental website.

Supporting E-commerce Using Magento

To sell products online, you really need an e-commerce solution like Magento (`https://magento.com/`). Of course, because the field is so huge, many other products exist as well. Consider the following sections about Magento as a starting point — the tip of a much larger iceberg because a truly huge number of e-commerce solutions are available. To see how many are available just for AWS on the AWS Marketplace, type **ecommerce** (leaving out the hyphen gets better results) in the Search AWS Marketplace field. At the time of this writing, more than 130 solutions were available, and more are likely out there now. The following sections provide an overview of Magento.

Considering the Magento features

Magento actually comes in three flavors: digital commerce, order management, and industry solutions. The industry solutions are the most interesting in one respect: The other offerings are generic, but the industry solutions are quite specific. For example, there is a Magento for Fashion (`https://enterprise.magento.com/fashion/overview`). No matter how you view it, Magento is all about selling products of various sorts in specific venues. Getting the right product is important because you don't want to try to use a small business product in a B2B environment.

From an AWS perspective, you have two main options for running Magento: Bitnami and TurnKey. As with WordPress, the Bitnami solution is lower end and a bit more friendly when it comes to cost considerations. The TurnKey solution is oriented more toward higher-end customers who need a lot of additional support, such as backup and security.

Be sure to look at the various Magento offerings carefully. Two of the TurnKey solutions run on a 32-bit AMI, which means that they run slower than the other offerings. The offerings also run on different versions of Linux, and you have the option of choosing different versions of Magento. Make certain that you know which version of Magento you want before you get started.

Getting and installing Magento

When working with the Bitnami version of Magento, you can choose the t1.micro instance. As long as you have free-tier access and use only 750 hours of computing time in a month, you won't have to pay anything for your experimentation with the e-commerce system. Of course, this lower-end instance won't provide enough computing horsepower for even the smallest e-commerce production setup.

As with WordPress, you need to make sure that you have the instance details configured correctly. For example, you may want to run your copy of Magento on a separate VPC to keep hackers out of your corporate data. Remember that the VPC IP isn't publicly addressable by default, which is a great security feature for your private company data. However, if you make the VPC publicly addressable to provide access to your e-commerce setup (which is a given), you also open the doors to hackers.

Otherwise, you should have no surprises in configuring the Bitnami version of Magento — you just follow the same process described in the "Getting and installing WordPress" section, earlier in this chapter, and substitute *Magento* for *WordPress* when asked to search for the product you want to install. Make certain that you select Free Trial in the Navigation pane when searching for Magento or you may find yourself looking for a while. Magento is a popular package, but not all the packages have a free trial associated with them.

Interestingly enough, depending on the version of TurnKey Magento you choose, you can also get a t1.micro instance option for TurnKey. The presence of this option means that you can work with at least two different vendors when choosing these particular options to see which one provides better functionality and meets your needs better. Unlike Bitnami, the Magento version defaults to using a Magnetic volume type, as shown in Figure 15-6. Make sure to choose the General Purpose SSD (GP2) option instead to ensure that you retain free-tier pricing. In addition, using the GP2 option provides more speed, which means that you can see the product perform closer to the way it would in a real-world environment.

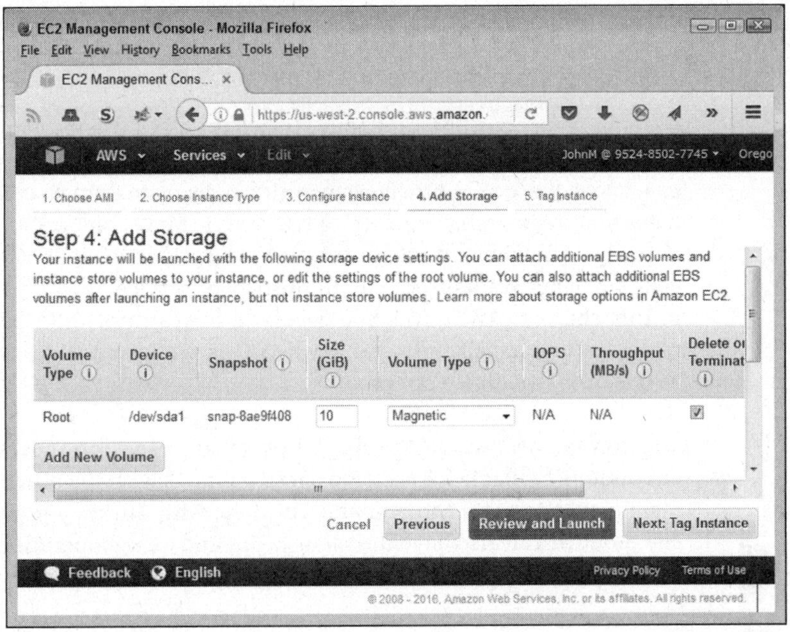

FIGURE 15-6:
Verify the storage settings to ensure that you get what you expect in the way of speed.

When comparing Bitnami to TurnKey security, note that TurnKey opens more ports, as shown in Figure 15-7. This is because TurnKey also provides additional utilities that require the port access. As with Bitnami, make sure to configure the ports as needed to ensure that your setup remains safe.

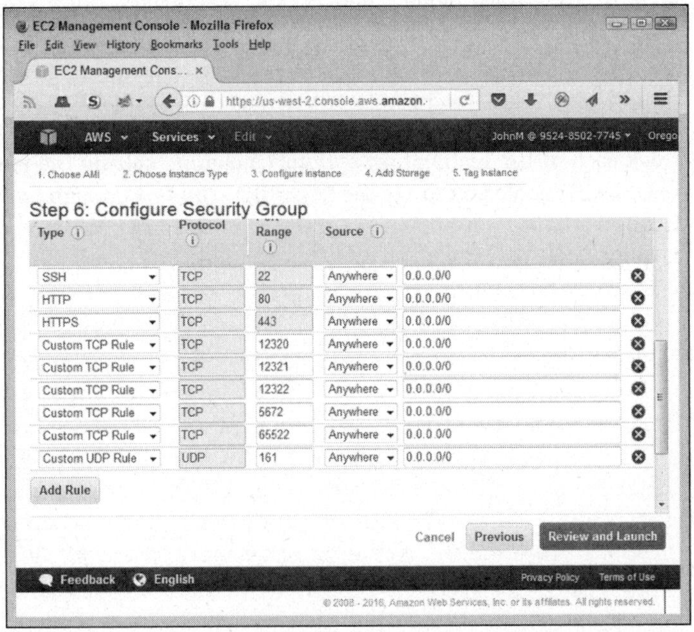

REMEMBER

FIGURE 15-7:
TurnKey opens more ports to support the additional utilities it provides.

Relating to Customers Using SugarCRM

Keeping your customers happy is what keeps them coming back to the e-commerce solution presented in the previous section. SugarCRM (https://www.sugarcrm.com/) provides an entire array of customer-pleasing options and helps you track each customer's preferences. More important, a Customer Relationship Management (CRM) solution helps you consider all the features that your customer wants from you in the way of service. As with the other products in this chapter, AWS gives you access to a wealth of CRM products because it really isn't a one-size-fits-all market. This section considers SugarCRM simply as one of the available options.

The previous sections of the chapter give you a basis for understanding the various options available for creating a test setup. As with the other products, the two main contenders are Bitnami and TurnKey, with TurnKey providing the higher-end product. You also have the same 32-bit and 64-bit operating system offerings that come with Magento (but apparently not with WordPress).

REMEMBER

There are even more vendors who want to sell you SugarCRM than the other products discussed in this chapter, but you need to look over the associated literature carefully. For example, you can get a copy of SugarCRM from Webuzo (http://www.webuzo.com/), but it'll cost you $0.01 per hour for the software (which, admittedly, isn't much). You can also find a number of combined solutions in this case. For example, SAIN3 (http://product.sain3.com/) will sell you a combination of SugarCRM, LAMP (see Chapter 14 for details), and Webmin (http://www.webmin.com/) for a modest hourly rate. (Rates vary, but all the options are less than a dollar as of this writing.)

All the free products also come with a free-tier-compatible EC2 instance, including TurnKey, which supports the t1.micro instance. Ensuring that you carefully track each of the installation options (including setting the storage volume type to G2) will enable you to see the SugarCRM run fast enough to determine whether it will work for your business. However, in this case, the low-end free tier really is quite slow.

6

The Part of Tens

Chapter **16**

Ten Ways to Deploy AWS Quickly

A mazon Web Services (AWS) started as a relatively small web service designed to make programmatic access of Amazon data easier. You could do all sorts of interesting things, such as search for products, upload your own product listings, perform sales tasks, and make purchases, but at the outset, everything focused on Amazon. Today AWS is a huge undertaking that focuses on your organization and its needs. You can move all or part of your organization's computing needs to the cloud using AWS. You can interact with other organizations as well. In fact, almost anything you can do with a homegrown solution, you can do with AWS.

Added to this functionality, AWS makes what you need available almost everywhere and on a variety of devices. To get full functionality, you must use the Command Line Interface (CLI) as demonstrated in some chapters of this book (see Chapter 8 for some interesting examples using the Elastic File Service, or EFS). Some advanced features also require programming, a topic not discussed in this book because this book is oriented toward the needs of the administrator.

Because AWS can do so much, getting up and running with AWS could take longer than you want, prove to be error prone in some cases, and create frustration. The point of this chapter is to provide you with ten methods you can use to reduce the learning-curve time, keep errors to a minimum, and minimize your frustration.

Starting Slowly

You get 12 months in which to try specific AWS services free (see Chapter 2 for details). If you start with one of the harder services, such as EFS, you risk spending a good amount of that time overcoming obstacles rather than getting useful work done — a recipe for frustration. Begin by using one of the simpler services, such as S3, instead. After that, move on to services with progressively greater learning requirements to discover how AWS works before you make any decisions about it. Even though every IT endeavor today seems to have a "due yesterday" date on it, trying to tackle something like AWS without enough ramp-up time can waste more time than it saves.

After you've gained enough experience with AWS, start working with small test sets of your organization's data and performing simple tasks on AWS with it. Look at AWS with a critical eye, because you need to determine whether some moves are even feasible (or prudent, if so). For most administrators, working in the cloud is an entirely different experience from what they're used to, so moving too quickly is potentially the worst possible way to get started.

REMEMBER

As you experiment with AWS, keep the various issues presented in this book in mind. For example, make sure to keep any hidden costs in mind. Some services are free, but the resources they use aren't. Setting the service up and working through configuration settings won't cost you a penny, but after you begin using the service to perform useful work, you need to start paying for the resources. The best way to keep costs low is to work through a setup-and-configuration plan first, and then actually begin working with data.

When working with developers, make sure that the developers install a local copy of the service (when available) and use it to create mockups for testing. Fully unit-test the application before you begin to work with it over the cloud so that you can keep cloud issues (such as network requirements and security configuration) separate from application issues (such as design issues and bugs). You have less control over your environment when working in the cloud, so taking small steps when creating custom cloud-based solutions is a must.

Researching AWS Interactivity with Third-Party Products

You likely have a number of third-party solutions already in place for your organization. For example, you probably have a favored Database Management System (DBMS) that you use. Although AWS provides a broad range of support for various products, it doesn't support every product out there. In fact, no single cloud vendor can support every possible combination of products and services. Consequently, you need to determine whether AWS provides support for all the products you use. Don't be tempted to move to other products in an effort to force AWS as a cloud-based solution for your organization. Even if you believe that doing so could result in better efficiencies and lower costs, making this strategy work is nearly impossible. Therefore, always ensure that AWS supports your products of choice before you begin doing anything with it.

WARNING

The problem with AWS is that, even when you find out that a service seems to provide the kind of support you need, it may not provide full support, or it may provide variant support that could create compatibility issues with yet other third-party products. For example, AWS does provide support for NFSv4, but as discussed in the "Understanding the connection to Network File System version 4 (NFSv4)" section of Chapter 8, you don't get full support for this feature. As a result, if a third-party product you use requires full support for NFSv4, AWS may not be the solution you need.

Third-party products also interact with each other. You may find that a current combination of third-party products works fine when you have them all installed on a local hard drive. However, a lack of configuration options or other support issues may cause the products to fail or work incorrectly when moved to the cloud. Be sure to keep cloud differences in mind as you work through the AWS issues. Applications, services, technologies, protocols, and any number of other elements of your current solution are apt to work differently in the cloud than they do on your local drive.

Developing a Plan for Sensitive Data

The various storage solutions discussed in this book (most of which you find in Chapters 7 through 12) also give you information about sensitive data. Just what constitutes sensitive data depends on your organization requirements. You may have legal or other requirements beyond those defined as best business practices to meet. Any plan you create for using AWS as your cloud solution must include a strategy for meeting these requirements.

WARNING

Many businesses fail to realize that no cloud solution will fulfill their legal requirements with regard to data safety. The cloud works only when you can maintain the proper (and legally required) data safety net. It's best to determine these requirements sooner than later in your AWS adventure because making changes to a data solution later is extremely expensive when it comes to time and resources. Unfortunately, Amazon can't advise you in this regard: Data safety is a requirement that you must address as part of your own cloud strategy planning.

Use Tools to Enhance Productivity

Tools enable you to focus more fully on getting a task done than on how to perform the task. Having the right tools in your toolbox can significantly reduce the time required to perform a task because you rely less on your memory to know how to perform the task and more on the capabilities of the tool. Fortunately, you have access to all sorts of tools when working with AWS, including the following:

>> **Built-in:** You have access to all the built-in tools (many of which you find demonstrated in this book in the form of the various consoles and wizards).

>> **Third party:** Vendors such as Scalr (http://www.scalr.com/), RightScale (http://www.rightscale.com/), Hybridfox (https://code.google.com/p/hybridfox/), CloudMGR (http://www.cloudmgr.com/), and Enstratius (http://www.enstratius.com/home) all offer strong management platforms for AWS.

>> **Developer:** Some developer tools can lend themselves to administrator use as well. The Amazon pages at https://aws.amazon.com/developertools and https://aws.amazon.com/tools/ offer some ideas on what Amazon makes available.

TIP

Be sure to look into various tool categories as you perform research for your AWS configuration. For example, some vendors make browser-specific extensions such as ElasticFox-EC2Tag (https://github.com/cookpad/elasticfox-ec2tag). You can use these tools to perform specific tasks that might otherwise require coding, the use of a special wizard, or a third-party add-on product. The article at `http://www.serverwatch.com/server-tutorials/8-trending-third-party-management-tools-for-amazon-web-services.html` provides a listing of some interesting browser extensions.

Choosing the Right Service

Amazon often offers multiple services that can answer a particular need. The issue is one of choosing the right service at the outset so that you don't waste time trying to set up and configure a service that Amazon didn't design to do the job. For example, Chapter 8 discusses the differences between Amazon storage options, and you can bet that Amazon will only increase these options as customers signal a need for them (in other words, because of the extreme level of monitoring that Amazon uses when you work with its services, you shouldn't be surprised to see that Amazon anticipates your future needs). Each of these storage options comes with myriad configuration options, so you can easily become lost just by trying to make a choice of which storage option to use, never mind the other services you might need to use.

TIP

The Amazon documentation often leaves you wondering about the various service options. Even watching the videos and interacting with the other kinds of information that Amazon makes available may not help you make a decision. The secret to the problem of which service to choose is to look at who else is using that service, define how they're using it, and consider what restrictions they put in place when using it. Other organizations have already paved the way to using many of the AWS services you need for your organization, so learning from the mistakes these other organizations have made is key in reducing the time it takes to create your own solution.

Ensuring That Your Plan Considers Loss of Control

Most administrators are used to having godlike control over the systems they manage. However, when working in the cloud, you need to consider the fact that the cloud provider now has the godlike control, and you have only a subset of the administration rights you used to have. The host determines what your rights are, when you can have them, and how you use them. This loss of control means that administrators may now find themselves in a position of having to ask permission to perform certain tasks or of requesting that the host perform the task for them.

One such example is Elastic Beanstalk (EB). When you configure EB, EB automatically creates an S3 bucket for you. You can view the contents of this bucket and interact with it in other ways. Removing your EB instance doesn't remove the S3 bucket. Unfortunately, you can't delete the bucket, either (see `https://forums.aws.amazon.com/thread.jspa?threadID=145366` as an example of this problem). To remove the bucket, you must ask Amazon to do it for you. In short, yes, the bucket is empty, and no, you're not paying for it anymore, but it's still there, and you may truly want to get rid of it.

Fortunately, Amazon documents most of the cases that require you to ask permission to do something or have someone at Amazon do it for you. The documentation normally contains an email address for contact and, theoretically, you can get the task done quite quickly — usually in less than a day. That's not the point, though. The issue is that you no longer have full control, so you need to know in advance when you need to obtain permission to perform certain tasks and create a plan for asking for these permissions as soon as you are able so that your deployment isn't held up while waiting for Amazon to respond.

Looking for All-in-One Solutions That Aren't

The documentation for AWS Identity and Access Management (IAM) leads you to believe that it can provide everything needed to ensure that your users can authenticate quickly and gain access to the applications and data needed to perform tasks. However, reality is different from theory in this case. Most organizations today must deal with mobile users. A user may want to access the same application from a smartphone, tablet, and PC. The user wants the data used with that application to appear on all three devices and may even use multiple devices simultaneously to work with the data. To provide a seamless mobile experience, you also need to work with Amazon Cognito (`https://aws.amazon.com/cognito/`).

Unfortunately, now you have another problem. This solution provides a number of methods for authenticating users. For example, you can rely on social identity providers such as Facebook, Twitter, or Amazon. The users might be happy about this situation, but Health Insurance Portability and Accountability Act (HIPAA) requirements may make this sort of authentication impossible (or, at least, ill advised). To ensure that you can get up and running quickly, be certain that you understand the following:

>> What level of support each service provides

>> Other services that you might need to obtain a full solution

>> Limits of each service that could impact your business

>> Potential service problems that could cause legal or other issues that you must work out before using AWS

Spending Free Time Where You Need It Most

An important part of the AWS ramp-up experience is to use the free-tier time wisely. The main service that you need to know about is EC2 because so many of the other services rely on it to perform essential tasks. The more you can learn about EC2 by playing around with it on Amazon's nickel, the faster you'll get your cloud-based strategy running. To gain a basic idea of how things will work with your cloud-based solution at the outset, focus your time on these services:

>> EC2 (computing)

>> S3, EBS, and EFS (storage solutions)

>> IAM and Cognito (security)

Getting these services down will help you develop a strategy for deploying your data faster. Working through data and security issues is a requirement. Trying to work with complicated services or to deploy applications before you have a good understanding of the basics will cause you to waste considerable time and effort. The need to work through these issues in a reasonably straightforward manner is the reason that this book takes the path that it does through the various services. Yes, you can take other paths, but be sure to build a great foundation for later efforts. Doing so will make you more efficient and help you understand when moving your current needs to the cloud is not a good idea.

Working with Templates

Amazon CloudFormation (`https://aws.amazon.com/cloudformation/`) enables you to automate some processes through templates. You won't really need this particular service when working with simple setups that involve just one or two EC2 instances. However, as you begin to add complexity to your setup, the need to use templates to manage application resource requirements becomes more important. In short, during your experimentation phase, you need to look at Amazon

CloudFormation to determine how it will help you manage tasks as you begin to move toward a production deployment. You can find a list of these templates at https://aws.amazon.com/cloudformation/aws-cloudformation-templates/.

This book also makes extensive use of automation to reduce the knowledge required to perform any given task. The various consoles and the templates provided by them will make your job considerably easier. Yes, you do gain control by using the CLI, but the advantage of using the console is that you don't have to remember a lot of arcane parameters and the precise syntax for issues commands that the CLI requires.

You also find automation mentioned in the documentation for each of the services. Amazon values automation because it reduces your workload, makes you less likely to experience errors, and increases your efficiency. The time to use the CLI is when you start moving toward batch processes and working with services such as Amazon Lambda to perform tasks (see Chapter 6 for a discussion of Lambda).

Discovering Implied Third-Party Use

Amazon also makes use of the cloud for its services. For example, you may not have caught the oddity in Chapter 8 of the Amazon ElasticSearch Service (see the "Working with the Elasticsearch Service" section of Chapter 8 for details). ElasticSearch (the name by itself) is actually an open source product that anyone can use (see https://www.elastic.co/products/elasticsearch for details). Amazon doesn't own it. However, Amazon's ElasticSearch Service is part of AWS. The use of similar terms for two different products might prove confusing, and it's important that you understand when Amazon fully supports a service as opposed to merely providing an interface to someone else's service.

The implication of using a third-party service within AWS is that you need to perform additional research about that third party. All the research that you performed to ensure that AWS would work as your cloud-based solution also applies to that third party. If you don't perform the required research at the outset, you might find later that using the third-party product (even though you access it through AWS) breaks a legal or other requirement that your organization must meet.

Chapter **17**

Ten Must-Have AWS Software Packages

This book presents you with a wealth of information on how to use Amazon Web Services to your advantage. In addition, it discusses some of the packages that you can interact with while working with AWS. All these packages are nice, but they aren't necessarily must-have packages — the sort that every administrator will want to put in a toolbox today.

This chapter takes a different view of AWS, one in which you discover those tools that can make your AWS experience significantly easier and a lot more fun. These software packages work with AWS in specific ways to ensure that you have a better AWS experience. Some of these packages ship as part of the operating system, and others are ones you add through an Internet connection (consult the individual descriptions for details). Even if you don't end up adding every package to your toolbox, you'll at least want to review each of the packages to see where it might fit in the future.

Using the Console Internet Tools

Even though AWS provides you with a wealth of Internet-specific tools, you sometimes need to perform tasks in a batch process or in a more convenient way. The Console Internet Tools group package that comes with your Linux setup contains the following packages (listed as either a default package or an optional package — see the upcoming "Using the Command Line Interface (CLI) to install packages" sidebar for more details):

Utility/Package	What It Does
Default Packages	
elinks	Provides a text-based browser for use in the SSH session. See http://elinks.or.cz/ for additional details.
Optional Packages	
fetchmail	Provides a text-based email program that can access POP3, IMAP, ODMR, and ETRN-based stores. See https://sourceforge.net/projects/fetchmail/ for additional details.
ftp	Provides a text-based File Transfer Protocol (FTP) application for sending and receiving files to and from an FTP server.
jwhois	Determines the owner and other information associated with a particular web domain. See https://directory.fsf.org/wiki/Jwhois for additional details.
lftp	Performs advanced batch processing of HTTP-specific commands, akin to the manner in which the bash shell works. You typically use this utility for scripted FTP uploads or other repetitive tasks. See https://lftp.yar.ru/ for additional details.
mutt	Provides a text-based email program that can access all the common data stores. This utility is a little more GUI-based and friendlier than fetchmail. See http://www.mutt.org/ for additional details.

USING THE COMMAND LINE INTERFACE (CLI) TO INSTALL PACKAGES

In most cases, you use the CLI to install packages. AWS does provide a number of distributions, but most people rely on Linux distributions. If you're working with the free tier, you most definitely have a Linux distribution. When working with a Linux distribution, you must decide between installing a single package or a group of packages. The command for installing a single package is

```
sudo yum install <package name>
```

In this case, the sudo (super user do) command allows you to perform almost any task conceivable with a Linux distribution. The yum (Yellowdog Updater, Modified) command is the method used to tell Linux to install, delete, query, or otherwise manage packages. In this case, you tell yum to install a new package, which you define by specifying a *<package name>*.

Of course, you need to know the package name in order to install it. The Amazon documentation tells you which packages to install to perform specific tasks. You can determine whether a particular package is available using the following command:

```
rpm -qa | grep '<package name>'
```

The rpm command performs the actual package search. You use the –qa switch to tell rpm to find all the packages. Outputting all the installed packages would provide too much information. So, you take the output of the rpm command and send it to the grep command using a pipe (|). The pipe is handy because it lets you combine commands. In this case, grep takes the whole list of installed packages and searches for packages that contain the text you provide. For example, if you want to find all the Python-related packages on your system, you type **rpm -qa | grep 'python'** and press Enter. As an alternative to using rpm, you can rely on the following yum command:

```
sudo yum search '<package name>'
```

The yum version returns more information because it includes all the available packages, not just those installed on your system. A package can contain more than one utility. To obtain a listing of utilities in a package, use the following command:

```
rpm -ql '<package name>'
```

(continued)

(continued)

Installing single packages works fine when you have only one or two packages to install. However, you may want to install a number of packages that appear as part of a group of packages. In this case, you can use the `groupinstall` version of the yum command.

```
sudo yum groupinstall "<group package name>"
```

A group package name normally appears in quotes because it's actually a string that tells Linux which group to use. For example, if you want yum to install all the performance tools, you specify the "Performance Tools" as a string. To obtain a list of available groups, type **sudo yum grouplist** and press Enter. Likewise, to learn the content of a particular group, type **sudo yum groupinfo "*<group package name>*"** and press Enter.

By default, yum installs only the mandatory packages for a group. If you want to install all the packages, you must modify the previous command to look like this:

```
sudo yum --setopt=group_package_types=mandatory,default,optional
groupinstall "<group package name>"
```

The `--setopt` command-line switch tells yum which package features to install. In this case, you tell yum to install the mandatory, default, and optional packages from the group package.

Changing Configuration Using Command Line Editors

When working with Linux, you sometimes need to modify configuration files at the command line. Trying to perform this task without an editor is nearly impossible. The Editors group package provided with your Linux setup includes a number of editors that you can use to perform configuration file editing tasks. The following minitable gives an overview of each editor (listed as either a default package or an optional package — see the "Using the Command Line Interface (CLI) to install packages" sidebar for more details):

Utility/Package	What It Does
Default Packages	
vim	Allows editing of text files using the Vi IMproved (VIM) editor. See http://www.vim.org/ for additional details.

Utility/Package	What It Does
Optional Packages	
ctags etags	Creates a tag file containing identifiers based on the content of code files for use with a text editor. The tags help the editor provide amplifying information when displaying the file onscreen. The etags utility is an Emacs-specific version that produces more information for this particular editor. See `http://ctags.sourceforge.net/` for additional details.
emacs	Displays an extensible, customizable, real-time text editor generally used to modify code files, hence the original name Editing Macros, or Emacs (but you can use it for any other text-editing purpose as well). See `https://emacswiki.org/` for additional details.
emacs-auctex	Provides support for tau-epsilon-chi (TeX) files in the Emacs editor. See `https://www.gnu.org/software/auctex/` for additional details.
emacs-gnuplot	Provides gnuplot support for the Emacs editor. See `https://mkmcc.github.io/software/gnuplot-mode.html` for additional details.

Checking System Performance

AWS provides you with a number of methods for monitoring AWS-specific services. However, you may have underlying system performance issues or non-AWS application issues to deal with, which means having tools that can work outside of AWS. The Performance Tools group package contains a number of Linux-specific tools for accomplishing this task as follows (listed as mandatory, default, or optional packages — see the "Using the Command Line Interface (CLI) to install packages" sidebar for more details):

Utility/Package	What It Does
Mandatory Packages	
blktrace	Performs block I/O tracing tasks to determine the time required to perform tasks such as data transfers. See `http://www.cse.unsw.edu.au/~aaronc/iosched/doc/blktrace.html` for additional details.
sysstat (includes: sar, sadf, mpstat, iostat, tapestat, pidstat, cifsiostat, and sa)	Provides access to a set of utilities to perform a series of specific, system-level checks. For example, the sar command collects, reports, and saves system activity information. See `http://sebastien.godard.pagesperso-orange.fr/` for additional details.

Utility/Package	What It Does
Default Packages	
dstat	Generates system resource statistics for CPU, disk, I/O, memory, and network activity. See `http://dag.wiee.rs/home-made/dstat/` for additional details.
iotop	Focuses on generating statistics for block read and block write requests for disks. See `http://linux.die.net/man/1/iotop` for additional information.
oprofile	Performs continuous, system-wide monitoring of resources and activity. See `http://oprofile.sourceforge.net/news/` for additional information.
Optional Packages	
oprofile-jit	Provides the capability of creating Executable and Linkable Format (ELF) files after an OProfile monitoring session. See `http://oprofile.sourceforge.net/doc/getting-jit-reports.html` for additional details.

TIP

Group packages that contain mandatory packages install those packages no matter how else you might install the group package. Mandatory packages give you the minimal functionality needed to use the group package.

Working at the System Level

All the AWS tools are relatively high-level tools designed to give you a good overview of what your system is doing. These tools normally provide what you need because they summarize information in a way that makes it easy to work with. However, sometimes it's helpful to have a low-level view of your system using the tools that come in the System Tools group package. The following list offers a brief overview (listed as either a default package or an optional package — see the "Using the Command Line Interface (CLI) to install packages" sidebar for more details).

Utility/Package	What It Does
Default Packages	
conman	Provides connectivity with other remote consoles. See `http://www.tutorialspoint.com/unix_commands/conman.htm` for additional information.
mgetty	Allows connectivity with modems. See `http://linuxcommand.org/man_pages/mgetty8.html` for additional information.

Utility/Package	What It Does
mkbootdisk	Creates a boot disk for starting the system. See `http://linuxcommand.org/man_pages/mkbootdisk8.html` for additional information.
net-snmp-libs	Contains the libraries used for Simple Network Management Protocol (SNMP)-related tasks.
nmap	Performs detailed network mapping tasks. See `https://nmap.org/` for additional information.
ntp	Synchronizes the clocks of the systems within a given network with a master time source (ultimately allowing synchronization with an Internet source, such as time.nist.gov). See `http://www.ntp.org/` for additional information.
openldap-clients	Contains the libraries used for the Lightweight Directory Access Protocol (LDAP)-related tasks.
quota	Manages disk quotas for both users and groups. See `http://www.tldp.org/HOWTO/Quota.html` for additional information.
rng-tools (includes: rngd and rngtest)	Performs testing and configuration of the random number-generation capabilities of a system. Because a virtual machine can't access the underlying hardware, this set of utilities isn't useful when working with AWS.
screen	Allows use of multiple shell windows when working with SSH. See `https://www.rackaid.com/blog/linux-screen-tutorial-and-how-to/` for additional information.
xdelta	Performs delta compression on C libraries to make them smaller. See `http://xdelta.org/` for additional information.
zisofs-tools (includes: mkzftree)	Contains the tools needed to work with compressed disks. See `http://freecode.com/projects/zisofs-tools` for additional information.
zsh	Provides access to a shell used for interactive and scripted command-line tasks. See `http://zsh.sourceforge.net/` for additional information.
Optional Packages	
adjtimex	Displays and sets the Linux kernel time variables. See `http://linuxcommand.org/man_pages/adjtimex8.html` for additional information.

Utility/Package	What It Does
amanda-client	Contains the tools required to implement the Advanced Maryland Automatic Network Disk Archiver (AMANDA). These tools are designed for use with Windows, so they won't work with your free-tier Linux installation. See http://www.amanda.org/ for additional information.
arptables_jf	Contains the tools required to work with the Address Resolution Protocol (ARP). See http://kb.linuxvirtualserver.org/wiki/Using_arptables_to_disable_ARP for additional information.
arpwatch	Tracks Ethernet and IP address pairings. See http://linuxcommand.org/man_pages/arpwatch8.html for additional information.
audit (includes: augenrules, aureport, ausearch, and autrace)	Contains the tools required to perform audits of processes. See https://linux-audit.com/tag/autrace/ and https://www.digitalocean.com/community/tutorials/how-to-use-the-linux-auditing-system-on-centos-7 for additional information.
avahi-tools	Contains the tools used to implement the Avahi zero-configuration networking system. See https://wiki.archlinux.org/index.php/avahi for additional information.
createrepo	Provides the means for working with RPM-metadata (repodata). See http://createrepo.baseurl.org/ for additional information.
gnutls-utils (includes: certtool, gnutls-cli, gnutls-cli-debug, gnutls-serv, and psktool)	Contains utilities for working with the GNU Transport Layer Security (TLS) features of AWS. See http://www.gnutls.org/ for additional information.
iptraf	Performs IP monitoring tasks. See http://linuxcommand.org/man_pages/iptraf8.html for additional information.
ktune	Performs kernel-tuning tasks. Because a virtual machine can't access the underlying operating system, this utility isn't useful when working with AWS.
lslk	Lists local locks on files. This utility is outdated. See http://linux.die.net/man/8/lslk for additional information.

Utility/Package	What It Does
lsscsi	Obtains information about Small Computer System Interface (SCSI) drives attached to the local system. Because a virtual machine can't access the underlying hardware, this utility isn't useful when working with AWS. See `http://sg.danny.cz/scsi/lsscsi.html` for additional information.
mc	Provides the means to manage files on disk using the Midnight Commander utility. See `https://www.midnight-commander.org/` for additional information.
mrtg	Tracks the activities of any routers attached to the system using the Mult-Router Traffic Grabber. See `http://oss.oetiker.ch/mrtg/` for additional information.
net-snmp-utils (includes: encode_keychange, snmpbulkget, snmpbulk-walk, snmpdelta, snmpdf, snmpget, snmpgetnext, snmpinform, snmpnetstat, snmpset, snmpstatus, snmptable, snmptest, snmptranslate, snmptrap, snmpusm, snmpvacm, and snmpwalk)	Contains a number of tools for performing SNMP-related tasks. See `http://net-snmp.sourceforge.net/` for additional information.
pinentry	Displays dialog boxes used to enter Personal Identification Numbers (PINs) and other security information. See `https://www.gnupg.org/related_software/pinentry/index.en.html` for additional details.
uuidd	Generates Universally Unique Identifiers (UUIDs) to ensure that apps and other system processes can recognize unique instances of any object. See `http://linux.die.net/man/8/uuidd` for additional information.
vlock	Locks a virtual console, enabling you to save your current session. See `http://linux.die.net/man/1/vlock` for additional information.
watchdog	Performs tests to ensure that the system hasn't frozen because of an errant process. See `http://linux.die.net/man/8/watchdog` for additional information.

Some of the utilities mentioned in this section, such as mkbootdisk, won't see any use while you work with AWS. You have no need to create an emergency boot disk (assuming that you can still find a system that has a floppy disk). It helps to know that these utilities exist, just in case someone gets curious and you end up with odd output from the system.

REMEMBER

Linux offers a wealth of other group packages not found in this chapter that you might find helpful. For example, you might find that you need the tau-epsilon-chi (TeX) editor support provided by Linux, which means installing the TeX Support group package. (TeX is a typesetting system originally created by Donald Knuth; you can read more about it at `https://www.tug.org/whatis.html`.)

Making Cloud Management Easier with CloudMGR

CloudMGR (`http://www.cloudmgr.com/`) is a cloud-management solution that enables you to interact with AWS using an alternative interface. The overall goal of CloudMGR is to reduce the confusion that many people feel when faced with the myriad AWS consoles and the sometimes buried options required to control the services. This particular product focuses on the needs of service providers, independent vendors, and enterprise users. AWS supports three levels of CloudMGR:

>> **CloudMGR Business:** The basic solution for automating business-related tasks in the cloud.

>> **CloudMGR for Autotask:** This solution works with Autotask (`https://www.cloudmgr.com/autotask`) to manage huge arrays of AWS servers in support of multiple clients.

>> **CloudMGR for cPanel Web Host Manager Complete Solution (WHMCS):** This solution integrates with cPanel (`https://www.cloudmgr.com/cpanel-whm`) to let you work with websites with greater ease.

TIP

This chapter contains only a small sampling of the packages available for AWS. In addition to the many discussions about AWS packages online, you can also search the Amazon Marketplace (`https://aws.amazon.com/marketplace/search/`) for a product that will meet your needs. Researching and testing the various products using a test setup and a real-world database (but not your production database) helps you sort out the vendor claims from the realities of using the packages in your specific environment.

Going Outside the Marketplace with Enstratius

Enstratius (http://www.enstratius.com/aws) is one of the more interesting cloud-management products, partly because it doesn't appear anywhere in the Amazon Marketplace. It points to the need to research more than the Amazon Marketplace if you want to find the best possible product for your needs.

This product works with both public and private clouds. It focuses on the EC2, ELB, RDS, SNS, and S3 services. One of this product's special features is its capability to connect various cloud solutions, which enables you to easily use AWS as just part of your overall cloud strategy.

TIP

In contrast to some of the other products described in this chapter, you can also choose how to install Enstratius. The vendor supports both Software-as-a-Service (SaaS) and on-premises installations. This means that you can control access better because you have local control over the product.

Managing and Scaling Your Apps Using Heroku

Heroku (https://www.heroku.com/) is a multipart product that works with developers as much as it does with DevOps and administrators. The product defines three phases of custom app management:

>> Deployment

>> Management

>> Scaling

Although an administrator can become involved in deployment, the scope of Heroku likely applies more to developers and DevOps in this case. Unlike many products out there, you can use Heroku with AWS, Google, and Azure (simultaneously, if necessary). It also works with both Linux and Windows. The supported Linux distributions are

>> CoreOS

>> Ubuntu

>> Red Hat Enterprise Linux (RHEL)

Developers, DevOps, and administrators can also use a variety of languages to support custom apps using Heroku. Even though administrators don't code as often or at the same depth as developers, the huge deployments that Heroku is designed to support will likely lead administrators to perform some coding tasks (for scripting, if nothing else). You can use these languages directly with Heroku:

>> Node

>> Ruby

>> Java

>> PHP

>> Python

>> Go

Except for the inclusion of C/C++, this list represents the most commonly used languages for business applications according to *InfoWorld* (http://www. infoworld.com/article/3103514/application-development/businesses-stick-with-java-python-and-c.html). The bottom line is that Heroku is one of the better choices for major enterprise custom app management. However, the complexity and size of this product makes it less suitable for a small-to-medium-sized business environment.

Performing Browser-Based Management Using Hybridfox

Hybridfox (https://github.com/CSSCorp/hybridfox) provides a simplified but limited management solution for a number of cloud environments: AWS, Eucalyptus, OpenStack, OpenNebula, and HP Cloud. The goal of this product is to allow you to use a single-browser environment, Firefox, to manage the supported cloud environments seamlessly. You can switch among cloud environments without using a different interface for each one.

However, the functionality that this add-on provides is limited. You can use it for quick tasks in an enterprise environment, but you're more likely to find it being used in smaller environments. Currently, you can use Hybridfox to perform these kinds of tasks:

- » Manage platform images

- » Start and stop instances

- » Manage instances

- » Manage Elastic IPs

- » Manage security groups

- » Manage Key-pairs

- » Manage Elastic Block Storage (EBS)

The management limits mean that you can't use this product to perform a number of tasks included in this book, such as working with Glacier or DynamoDB. Fortunately, you still get a substantial amount of flexibility in working with all the core, computational features of all the supported cloud environments. This is the kind of product that you might use to verify that your setup is still working when you're away from the office. Theoretically, you can use it to perform certain management tasks right from your smartphone.

Getting a Complete Management Package with RightScale

RightScale (http://www.rightscale.com/) provides administrators with an all-encompassing management package designed to meet particular needs. In other words, this is a custom management configuration and is more oriented to the needs of large enterprises with an even larger cloud presence. This solution helps you do everything from creating a cloud strategy to choosing the cloud environments best suited to meet your needs to deploying the selected solution. RightScale appears to provide full support for all the popular cloud environments, including AWS, Google, Azure, and SOFTLAYER. After you have a solution in place, you use RightScale to perform daily management tasks. RightScale even offers training to the members of your administration team.

WARNING

Everything comes with a price. When using a product such as RightScale, you also pay for all the services provided. In addition, you need to consider the costs associated with vendor lock-in (an inability to move to other solutions without starting from scratch). After helping you create a cloud solution, you become dependent on the RightScale products, which is fine as long as you do it knowing about the lock-in potential in advance.

Employing Policy-Based Management with Scalr

Scalr (http://www.scalr.com/) focuses on using policies for management tasks, and that focus is immediately evident when you visit its site. Unlike any other product discussed in this chapter, Scalr comes in hosted, enterprise, and community editions. This means that you can get Scalr at a size that works best for your organization and that you can choose access methodologies that work best with your method of performing management tasks. For example, downloading the community edition lets you work with your cloud setup using your PC. You gain the efficiencies and speed that the PC environment provides. In addition, using your local system for management means that you can potentially bypass some privacy and security issues that a cloud-based solution would present. Interestingly enough, the community edition is free (see the pricing guide at http://www.scalr.com/pricing.html), so you can try Scalr before you move on to one of the higher-priced versions.

You can use Scalr to manage the AWS, Azure, and OpenStack cloud environments using a special engine that works by interpreting directives you create. This method of management means that you need to learn how to perform scripting tasks using the Scalr approach, but it also means that you can work with multiple cloud environments without necessarily having to learn each cloud environment's API individually. As do several other products in this chapter, Scalr provides training, but you can download the case studies, white papers, webinars, blog posts, and videos without having to buy anything. Of course, you can also view the documentation (as with any of the other products) if you have a strong interest in learning more.

Index

Symbols and Numerics

IP address changes, 115
IP spoofing, 98
`iptraf` package, 358
Isilon, 177

J

Java, 100
Joyent, 17–18
`jwhois` package, 352

K

Key Management Service (KMS), 50
key pairs
  connecting to instances, 101
  generating, 94
  selecting, 98–99
Kinesis Firehose, 146–147, 158, 206
KMS (AWS Key Management Service), 50
Knuth, Donald, 360
`ktune` package, 358

L

Lambda. *See* AWS Lambda
`lftp` package, 352
Linux. *See also* Community enterprise Operating
    System
  Console Internet Tools group package, 352
  Editors group package, 354–355
  multicloud environments, 318
  Performance Tools group package, 355–356
  System Tools group package, 356–360
  versions, 317–318
Linux command tutorials, 186
LinuxCommand.org, 186
List data type, 287
load balancing (in Relational Database Service)
  Elastic Load Balancers, 241–244
  purpose of, 240–241
Logentries, 135
Logsene, 135–136
`lslk` package, 358
`lsscsi` package, 359

M

Magento
  general discussion, 337
  installing, 338–339
  solutions, 338
  versions of, 338
make directory (`mkdir`) command, 187
managed policies, defined, 79
Map data type, 287
MariaDB, 221–222
marshalling data, defined, 251
`mc` package, 359
`mgetty` package, 356
microservices, 11
Microsoft Azure, 17–18, 300
Microsoft SQL Server, 252
MindTerm, 318
`mkbootdisk` package, 357
`mkdir` (make directory) command, 187
MongoDB, 273, 275
MPLS (Multi-Protocol Label Switching), 32
`mrtg` package, 359
Mueller, John Paul, 162
Multi-AZ, 224
Multi-Protocol Label Switching (MPLS), 32
`mutt` package, 352
MySQL, 222, 226, 252
MySQL Workbench, 232–234

N

NAS (Network Attached Storage), 175
NAT (Network Address Translation), 301
Neo4J, 273
`net-snmp-libs` package, 357
`net-snmp-utils` package, 359
Network Access Control Lists (ACLs), 68
Network Address Translation (NAT), 301
Network Attached Storage (NAS), 175
Network File System version 4 (NFSv4)
  installing NFS client, 186
  lack of full support for, 175–176, 345
  `nfsstat` command, 189

About the Author

John Mueller is a freelance author and technical editor. He has writing in his blood, having produced 101 books and more than 600 articles to date. The topics range from networking to artificial intelligence and from database management to heads-down programming. Some of his current books include a book about machine learning, a couple of Python books, and a book about MATLAB. He has also written a Java e-learning kit, a book on HTML5 development with JavaScript, and another on CSS3. His technical editing skills have helped more than 63 authors refine the content of their manuscripts. John has provided technical editing services to both *Data Based Advisor* and *Coast Compute* magazines. John has had an interest in Amazon Web Services (AWS) since its inception. In fact, he wrote *Mining Amazon Web Services* (Sybex) back in 2004 based on that humble beginning. AWS has gone a long way since that time. Be sure to read John's blog at http://blog.johnmuellerbooks.com/.

When John isn't working at the computer, you can find him outside in the garden, cutting wood, or generally enjoying nature. John also likes making wine, baking cookies, and knitting. When not occupied with anything else, he makes glycerin soap and candles, which come in handy for gift baskets. You can reach John on the Internet at John@JohnMuellerBooks.com. John is also setting up a website at http://www.johnmuellerbooks.com/. Feel free to take a look and make suggestions on how he can improve it.

John's Dedication

Life is about change, about overcoming difficulties, about learning new things, and about living through uncomfortable experiences. This book is dedicated to the amazingly large group of people who have helped me through all the changes I've experienced as of late — some delightful, others quite challenging, but all necessary to make me the person I am today. I'm humbled to know that people care enough to help so much.

John's Acknowledgments

Thanks to my wife, Rebecca. Even though she is gone now, her spirit is in every book I write, in every word that appears on the page. She believed in me when no one else would.

Russ Mullen deserves thanks for his technical edit of this book. He greatly added to the accuracy and depth of the material you see here. Russ worked exceptionally hard helping with the research for this book by locating hard-to-find URLs and also offering a lot of suggestions. This was also an exceptionally difficult book from a testing perspective, and Russ was there to help me try various methods of achieving tasks to obtain specific goals.

Matt Wagner, my agent, deserves credit for helping me get the contract in the first place and taking care of all the details that most authors don't really consider. I always appreciate his assistance. It's good to know that someone wants to help.

A number of people read all or part of this book to help me refine the approach, test scripts, and generally provide input that all readers wish they could have. These unpaid volunteers helped in ways too numerous to mention here. I especially appreciate the efforts of Eva Beattie, Glenn A. Russell, Luca Massaron, and Ronald Davis, who provided general input, read the entire book, and selflessly devoted themselves to this project.

Finally, I would like to thank Katie Mohr, Susan Christophersen, and the rest of the editorial and production staff for their unparalleled support of this writing effort.

Publisher's Acknowledgments

Acquisitions Editor: Katie Mohr

Project Manager and Copy Editor:
Susan Christophersen

Technical Editor: Russ Mullen

Editorial Assistant: Serena Novosel

Sr. Editorial Assistant: Cherie Case

Production Editor: Vasanth Koilraj

Cover Image: © MF3d/iStockphoto

Apple & Mac

iPad For Dummies,
6th Edition
978-1-118-72306-7

iPhone For Dummies,
7th Edition
978-1-118-69083-3

Macs All-in-One
For Dummies, 4th Edition
978-1-118-82210-4

OS X Mavericks
For Dummies
978-1-118-69188-5

Blogging & Social Media

Facebook For Dummies,
5th Edition
978-1-118-63312-0

Social Media Engagement
For Dummies
978-1-118-53019-1

WordPress For Dummies,
6th Edition
978-1-118-79161-5

Business

Stock Investing
For Dummies, 4th Edition
978-1-118-37678-2

Investing For Dummies,
6th Edition
978-0-470-90545-6

Personal Finance
For Dummies, 7th Edition
978-1-118-11785-9

QuickBooks 2014
For Dummies
978-1-118-72005-9

Small Business Marketing
Kit For Dummies,
3rd Edition
978-1-118-31183-7

Careers

Job Interviews
For Dummies, 4th Edition
978-1-118-11290-8

Job Searching with Social
Media For Dummies,
2nd Edition
978-1-118-67856-5

Personal Branding
For Dummies
978-1-118-11792-7

Resumes For Dummies,
6th Edition
978-0-470-87361-8

Starting an Etsy Business
For Dummies, 2nd Edition
978-1-118-59024-9

Diet & Nutrition

Belly Fat Diet For Dummies
978-1-118-34585-6

Mediterranean Diet
For Dummies
978-1-118-71525-3

Nutrition For Dummies,
5th Edition
978-0-470-93231-5

Digital Photography

Digital SLR Photography
All-in-One For Dummies,
2nd Edition
978-1-118-59082-9

Digital SLR Video &
Filmmaking For Dummies
978-1-118-36598-4

Photoshop Elements 12
For Dummies
978-1-118-72714-0

Gardening

Herb Gardening
For Dummies, 2nd Edition
978-0-470-61778-6

Gardening with Free-Range
Chickens For Dummies
978-1-118-54754-0

Health

Boosting Your Immunity
For Dummies
978-1-118-40200-9

Diabetes For Dummies,
4th Edition
978-1-118-29447-5

Living Paleo For Dummies
978-1-118-29405-5

Big Data

Big Data For Dummies
978-1-118-50422-2

Data Visualization
For Dummies
978-1-118-50289-1

Hadoop For Dummies
978-1-118-60755-8

Language &
Foreign Language

500 Spanish Verbs
For Dummies
978-1-118-02382-2

English Grammar
For Dummies, 2nd Edition
978-0-470-54664-2

French All-in-One
For Dummies
978-1-118-22815-9

German Essentials
For Dummies
978-1-118-18422-6

Italian For Dummies,
2nd Edition
978-1-118-00465-4

Available in print and e-book formats.

Math & Science

Algebra I For Dummies,
2nd Edition
978-0-470-55964-2

Anatomy and Physiology
For Dummies, 2nd Edition
978-0-470-92326-9

Astronomy For Dummies,
3rd Edition
978-1-118-37697-3

Biology For Dummies,
2nd Edition
978-0-470-59875-7

Chemistry For Dummies,
2nd Edition
978-1-118-00730-3

1001 Algebra II Practice
Problems For Dummies
978-1-118-44662-1

Microsoft Office

Excel 2013 For Dummies
978-1-118-51012-4

Office 2013 All-in-One
For Dummies
978-1-118-51636-2

PowerPoint 2013
For Dummies
978-1-118-50253-2

Word 2013 For Dummies
978-1-118-49123-2

Music

Blues Harmonica
For Dummies
978-1-118-25269-7

Guitar For Dummies,
3rd Edition
978-1-118-11554-1

iPod & iTunes
For Dummies, 10th Edition
978-1-118-50864-0

Programming

Beginning Programming
with C For Dummies
978-1-118-73763-7

Excel VBA Programming
For Dummies, 3rd Edition
978-1-118-49037-2

Java For Dummies,
6th Edition
978-1-118-40780-6

Religion & Inspiration

The Bible For Dummies
978-0-7645-5296-0

Buddhism For Dummies,
2nd Edition
978-1-118-02379-2

Catholicism For Dummies,
2nd Edition
978-1-118-07778-8

Self-Help & Relationships

Beating Sugar Addiction
For Dummies
978-1-118-54645-1

Meditation For Dummies,
3rd Edition
978-1-118-29144-3

Seniors

Laptops For Seniors
For Dummies, 3rd Edition
978-1-118-71105-7

Computers For Seniors
For Dummies, 3rd Edition
978-1-118-11553-4

iPad For Seniors
For Dummies, 6th Edition
978-1-118-72826-0

Social Security
For Dummies
978-1-118-20573-0

Smartphones & Tablets

Android Phones
For Dummies, 2nd Edition
978-1-118-72030-1

Nexus Tablets
For Dummies
978-1-118-77243-0

Samsung Galaxy S 4
For Dummies
978-1-118-64222-1

Samsung Galaxy Tabs
For Dummies
978-1-118-77294-2

Test Prep

ACT For Dummies,
5th Edition
978-1-118-01259-8

ASVAB For Dummies,
3rd Edition
978-0-470-63760-9

GRE For Dummies,
7th Edition
978-0-470-88921-3

Officer Candidate Tests
For Dummies
978-0-470-59876-4

Physician's Assistant Exam
For Dummies
978-1-118-11556-5

Series 7 Exam For Dummies
978-0-470-09932-2

Windows 8

Windows 8.1 All-in-One
For Dummies
978-1-118-82087-2

Windows 8.1 For Dummies
978-1-118-82121-3

Windows 8.1 For Dummies
Book + DVD Bundle
978-1-118-82107-7

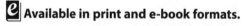 **Available in print and e-book formats.**

Available wherever books are sold. For more information or to order direct visit www.dummies.com

Take Dummies with you everywhere you go!

Whether you are excited about e-books, want more from the web, must have your mobile apps, or are swept up in social media, Dummies makes everything easier.

For Dummies is the global leader in the reference category and one of the most trusted and highly regarded brands in the world. No longer just focused on books, customers now have access to the For Dummies content they need in the format they want. Let us help you develop a solution that will fit your brand and help you connect with your customers.

Advertising & Sponsorships

Connect with an engaged audience on a powerful multimedia site, and position your message alongside expert how-to content.

Targeted ads • Video • Email marketing • Microsites • Sweepstakes sponsorship

21 Million Monthly Page Views & 13 Million Unique Visitors

Custom Publishing

Reach a global audience in any language by creating a solution that will differentiate you from competitors, amplify your message, and encourage customers to make a buying decision.

Apps • Books • eBooks • Video • Audio • Webinars

Brand Licensing & Content

Leverage the strength of the world's most popular reference brand to reach new audiences and channels of distribution.

For more information, visit www.Dummies.com/biz